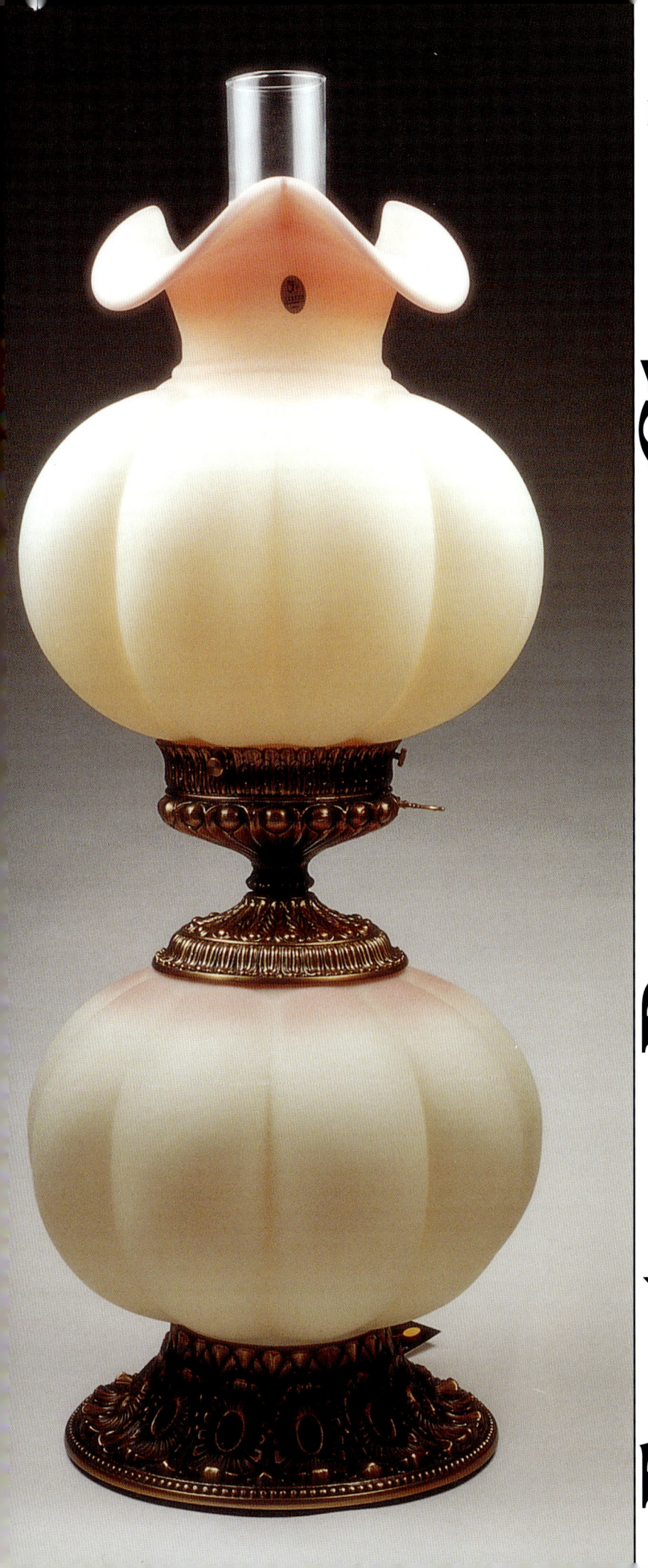

Fenton Burmese Glass

Debbie & Randy Coe

Schiffer Publishing Ltd
4880 Lower Valley Road, Atglen, PA 19310 USA

Dedication

Frank M. Fenton

has always been a true inspiration to us as we gather information to share with others. He is always there to listen to our requests and do the best he can to help out. Frank is a very thoughtful person who cares for his family, friends, collectors, and employees. His enthusiasm for sharing should be an encouragement to everyone to do more to assist others.

Bill Fenton

loved Burmese glass. He was there to witness the first piece coming off the lehr. He suggested the possibility of pressing Burmese. Most of all though, he was a great charming spokesman on the QVC shows for promoting Fenton glass. As he came into our homes with QVC, it was like we all grew to know him better. We think people who never even met him in life will forever remember him. He is dearly missed.

Charlie Goe

had talent that we greatly admire. His persistence on developing the Burmese glass, enabled all of us to have some beautiful glass to enjoy. We believe Burmese glass is available today because of this dedicated man.

Library of Congress Cataloging-in-Publication Data

Coe, Debbie.
Fenton Burmese glass / by Debbie & Randy Coe.
p. cm.
ISBN 0-7643-1968-X (Hardcover : lg. print)
1. Fenton Art Glass Company--Catalogs. 2. Burmese glass--Collectors and collecting--Catalogs. 3. Art glass--Massachusetts--New Bedford--History--20th century--Catalogs. I. Coe, Randy. II. Title.
NK5198.F4 A4 2004
748.2'09754'22--dc22
2003019663

Copyright © 2004 by Debbie and Randy Coe

All rights reserved. No part of this work may be reproduced or used in any form or by any means—graphic, electronic, or mechanical, including photocopying or information storage and retrieval systems—without written permission from the copyright holder.

"Schiffer," "Schiffer Publishing Ltd. & Design," and the "Design of pen and inkwell" are registered trademarks of Schiffer Publishing Ltd.

Designed by Bonnie M. Hensley
Cover design by Bruce Waters
Type set in Benguiat Bk BT/Zurich BT

ISBN: 0-7643-1968-X
Printed in China
1 2 3 4

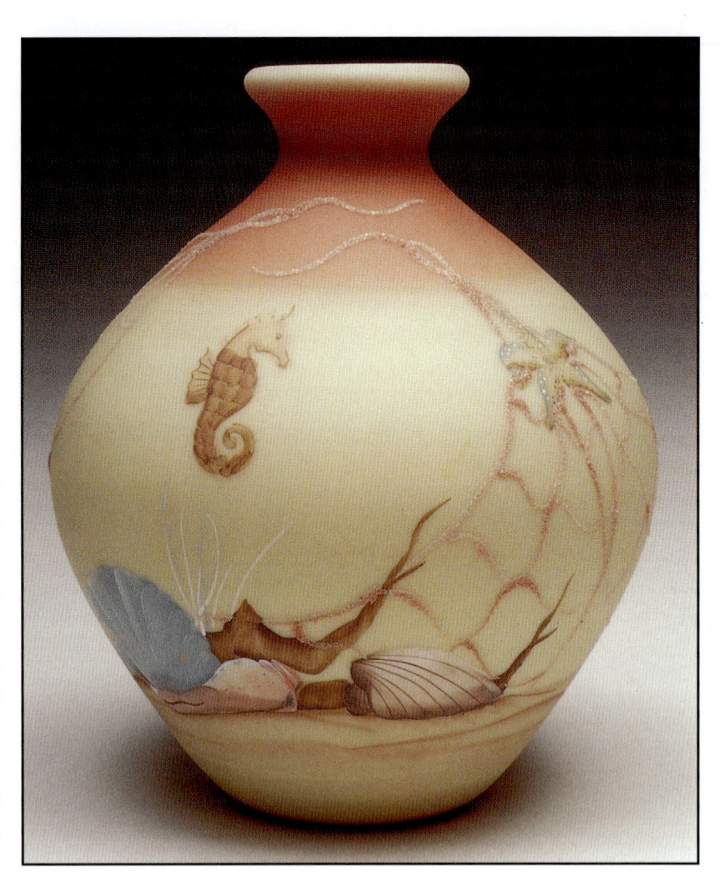

Published by Schiffer Publishing Ltd.
4880 Lower Valley Road
Atglen, PA 19310
Phone: (610) 593-1777; Fax: (610) 593-2002
E-mail: Schifferbk@aol.com
Please visit our web site catalog at **www.schifferbooks.com**
We are always looking for people to write books on new and related subjects. If you have an idea for a book, please contact us at the above address.

This book may be purchased from the publisher.
Include $3.95 for shipping. Please try your bookstore first.
You may write for a free catalog.

In Europe, Schiffer books are distributed by
Bushwood Books
6 Marksbury Ave. Kew Gardens
Surrey TW9 4JF England
Phone: 44 (0)20 8392-8585; Fax: 44 (0)20 8392-9876
E-mail: Bushwd@aol.com
Free postage in the UK. Europe: air mail at cost.
Please try your bookstore first.

Contents

Acknowledgments 4
Preface 6
    Measurements 6
    Value Guide 6
Mt. Washington Glass Company 7
Fenton Art Glass Company 9
    Charlie Goe 10
Family Members 13
Skilled Workers 15
Decorating Department 18
Channels of Distribution for Fenton Burmese Glass 22
The 1970s 24
The 1980s 54
The 1990s 95
The New Century 161
The Future 186
Blue Burmese 187
Lotus Mist 188
Other Companies 189
    Gibson Glass Company 189
    Crider Glass Company 191
    Confusing Burmese 191
Resources 191
Bibliography 191
Index 192

Acknowledgements

This has definitely been a project of caring and sharing. Everywhere we turned, everyone was so generous with their time and glass to photograph. We are so very appreciative of the collectors. Without beautiful glass to photograph, there wouldn't be much of a book. All of your contributions have enabled this book to exist. We have deep gratitude for all the collectors and dealers that lent us their support in this project. A comprehensive project such as this could not have happened without all the support we received. We can put together information, but it really takes beautiful glass to photograph to make the book come alive. All of you should be immensely proud of your contribution to assuring this book became a reality.

First, we would like to thank our children. Our family has picked up two fine son in laws in the last couple of years. Tara and her husband Jeff shared the many fine examples of Burmese cats. We really appreciate their support. They were a big help in taking care of the house and pets while we were gone photographing. When we started this project, Myra was engaged and finishing her last year of college at Oregon State University. Now she has graduated, finished her own book, married Stephen and started a new job with Target. Myra also helped with the care of the house and pets when she could be home. Myra and Stephen have shared the many different types of elephants and puppies. We value the input they gave us. We love all of them dearly!

Beverly Darling furnished us a nice piece, that we did not have, as we were wrapping up the project.

Robin and Jack Gadomski were only too glad to help with this project. Besides the day we spent at their house photographing, they have packed up things they got later and brought them up to us, on three different occasions! They are so terrific.

John Gager is an absolute wonder on all the QVC items he keeps meticulous records on for the Fenton Fanatics web site. He spends countless hours getting the information updated. The site is available to all to use as a research source. It was a real joy to finally see and get to photograph his Burmese collection. He was such a wealth of information. He is a very generous man we really admire.

Donna and Ron Miller, two long time friends, once again were only too happy to contribute to our newest book project. Donna and Ron publish the best Antique paper on the west coast called "Old Stuff". They recently acquired several Burmese items from the estate of a deceased PNWFA subscriber. After photographing all of the Burmese items, which they had originally purchased for resale, the glass kind of grew on them. Now they have a wonderful Burmese display on a shelf in their home that seems to have become a permanent fixture. The soft warm and delicate beauty of Burmese does speak for itself.

Jackie Shirley, besides being a great friend, was once again a tremendous help in tracking down information. In addition, when we got to the point of needing a fresh outlook on the book, she gladly spent the time with us going over all the information to see that it made sense. We really appreciate her input and the glass she allowed us to photograph.

Don and Gladys Snyder have a wonderful Burmese collection and were able to provide us with many of the hard to find lamps to photograph. They are an enthusiastic couple who has many different examples of Fenton glass that they shared with us on this project. We really enjoyed seeing their immense collections.

Marian Thornton owns two wonderful Fenton gift shops here in the Northwest. Collectors Showcase is located in Snohomish and Centralia, Washington. Marian let us have full access to her shop and we were able to photograph many examples of sample items. This sure made things easier for us. Centralia Square Antique Mall manager Pauline, moved things around giving us a place to photograph the glass from Collectors Showcase.

John Walk lives clear across the country from us, but that didn't stop him from helping us. He provided us with some much needed information and graciously offered to help where he could. It was so nice to be able to count on John for things at the last minute. He is a great asset to Fenton collectors for all of his sharing of information. John brings to life the old saying "If you want something done, ask a busy person".

Mary Walrath Jachim is a wonderful lady that I have known for years but have never met in person. I purchased her collection many years ago and have added the pieces she has come out with later. She is such an inspiration to talk with about the background of her collection. I called Mary and told her about the book and she was so thrilled to be asked to contribute information. She thought this was such a great project that would highlight her favorite type of glass. Her daughter, Joyce Colella, was also a big help in delivering the emails to her mom. Joyce also provided us with some photos we needed and correct information on the special limited editions she has done in addition to Mary's.

Everyone at the Fenton factory contributed in so many ways. Frank Fenton was there to answer all of our many questions. He was also gracious enough to proof all of our material. He is so generous with his time to help us gather information so that we could share with others. Frank also told us of Burmese pieces around the factory that should be included in this project. The multitude of stories Frank told us are so wonderful that we are sharing them with all of you.

Nancy and George Fenton also worked with Frank to go over all of material and check for accuracy. Nancy also talked to us about having Burmese back in the line for 2003 after many years absence. She also gave some insightful information on things to come.

Pam Dick was another person so generous with her time. She is an assistant to Frank and works in museum storage. Pam was a tireless help in figuring out all the decorators who created the designs on the glass. Many hours were spent pouring over records for us. We wanted to make sure that the decorators were properly credited with their work. Pam was a fantastic assistant in gathering lots of information for us to use.

Bob Hill offered us some information about the Fenton mould shop. He told us about the many steps and costs involved in developing a mould. His daughter, Amber, works in the gift shop and she was a tremendous help in continuing to find Burmese items that needed to be photographed. Amber constantly kept checking to see what might appear that we could use. While working in museum storage she found things that she thought should get photographed too.

Wayne King was great to talk to about the Burmese formula itself and all the many changes that have occurred. Wayne's contributions to the Fenton Burmese formula have not been recorded in a book until now.

Jennifer Maston in the Fenton museum was such a big help in tracking down all the special order information. Countless hours were involved in getting us the correct contacts.

Jon Saffell has created many of our favorite items in the short time he has been with Fenton. We dearly love all his new animals that have been made in Burmese. He was terrific to answer all of our questions about his designs.

Howard Seufer is now retired from Fenton but that didn't slow him down in helping. He graciously offered to photograph anything we needed. All the terrific shots at the factory we owe to him. He also dug out some information to share with us that we could put in the book.

The Pacific Northwest Fenton Association offered us great opportunities to photograph during their glass show and at their convention. This enabled us to have access to many pieces of glass. They are a great organization that specializes in researching information and offering opportunities to any collector.

Gerald Crail was great to be able to connect with and talk to about the special orders he did in the 1990s. Gerald provided some background information on why he selected the pieces he did and gave the count on how many were made.

Gary Levi of Levay Distributing Company was a real joy to get to talk to. Through the years, he has had Fenton make a variety of different types of glass for him in limited editions. The only time he had Burmese made was in the late 1970s. He gladly gave us the background of his pieces.

Suburban Photo in Beaverton, Oregon once again has provided us with great customer service. The staff is so friendly and absolutely terrific. They set such a fine example of what is great customer service. When was the last time you walked into a store and they knew you by name?

Nancy Schiffer, our editor was once again terrific to work with. We appreciate being able to contact her at any time to help with whatever comes up. She is such a great person to have to be able to turn to when we need input on ideas.

Preface

The desire to do this book came from our love of Burmese glass and desire to share what we had learned. It was fun to learn about the background and all the many people who contributed to its development. Up until this time, only a few Burmese pieces were covered in many different books. We wanted to prepare a comprehensive view of the many shapes and styles available in this beautiful glass. Even after collecting Burmese for years, we learned many facts while writing this book.

Please share with us any new discoveries of Burmese items not found here. There are countless pieces of sample and whimsy items among collections and the collective knowledge can grow only with the continuing input from readers.

We are always looking for old glass catalogs, reprints, and original advertising to obtain accurate information. If you have older glass catalogs, supplements, original advertising, special order brochures, or advertisements that you would like to share or sell, we are interested in obtaining them. Please let us know by writing us. Our addresses are listed on the front flap of the book.

Measurements

We have obtained the measurements of each piece of glass shown here. Like all handmade glass, you will find some variations in size among like pieces. For lamps we give the overall height, including the top of the chimney when applicable. We include the shade size as Fenton lists their shades. Student lamps are either 7" or 10" in diameter of the fritter that the shade fits into. On the 10" ball shades that are found on Gone with the Wind lamps, the size applies to the overall diameter of the shade.

Value Guide

All values given here are for glassware in **mint condition** only. Any type of damage, such as a chip or crack, will greatly diminish the value. Pieces that have been repaired should reflect a below-normal value, depending on their appearance. Burmese is one of the types of glass that cannot normally be repaired with satisfactory results.

Since Burmese is a heat sensitive glass, much of the value will be determined by the intensity of the salmon blush. Collectors like to see a real distinction between the yellow and salmon colors. If the glass has very little salmon blush, a lower price should be given. Differences in color between the blown and pressed pieces is apparent. Pressed pieces have less salmon blush than blown pieces.

We have canvassed both collectors and dealers to compile the values and obtain a true reflection of the current market. They include actual dealer sales, what collectors have paid, prices seen at shows, auction results, and published values in national publications. As with all types of collectible glass, there are some regional differences in supply and demand.

The collector ultimately needs to decide what he is willing pay for a specific item. This book is to be used only as guide when determining what an item is worth based on available information.

Neither the author or nor publisher assumes any responsibility for transactions that may occur because of this book.

Mt. Washington Glass Company

The Mt. Washington Glass Company was founded in 1837 by Deming Jarves, who also established the Boston and Sandwich Glass Company. This new company was located in South Boston and Deming had set up the company primarily for his son, George Jarves. At the time George had no interest in the glass business, but his father thought he eventually would. After a few years he finally came at his father's insistence to run the business, but his heart was not in it, and the factory closed in 1869.

William Libbey, who had received his training at Mt. Washington, bought the factory by the end of 1869. The new company kept its original name, Mt. Washington, but was moved to New Bedford, Massachusetts. Several investors joined Libbey and for a few years the company was successful. By 1872, William Libbey accepted a position at the New England Glass Company. There was a downturn in the economy and the factory closed again in 1873.

By the end of 1874, the economy had improved and the factory opened once again. This time the company was placed in the hands of Robert King, A. H. Seabury, Frederick Shirley, and Robert Tobey. After Seabury died in 1887, William Rotch became the company's president. Under his direction, Mt. Washington was finally able to attain monumental sales and the factory was expanded and updated.

Burmese Glass Is Born

Frederick Shirley was responsible for developing different glass formulas at Mt. Washington. His earliest art glass was Lava, in 1878, and Lusterless, in 1881. Following the success of Joseph Locke at New England Glass for developing the Amberina formula in 1883, Shirley thought a formula could be developed for an opaque version. He had been experimenting with a translucent white glass but thought if he could add color, the result would be more popular. He added different oxides and finally settled on the uranium oxide that changed white glass to lemon yellow. He was not yet quite satisfied and added a small amount of gold to the mix. This addition

Three-piece fairy Light, plain satin finish, 5.75" tall, 4.25" wide, Made for Clarke by Webb utilizing the Mt. Washington license, **$595**
The insert on this piece is clear glass and marked around the inside inner edge with "Mark-Cricklight-Clarke's-Trademark". Also in the center of these words is the embossed Fairy logo used by Clarke.

made the glass sensitive to heat by causing it to change colors when it was reheated in the glory hole. The glass that was touched by the heat turned a beautiful shade of pink. This new color formula was patented on December 15, 1885.

The new glass was an immediate success for Mt. Washington. Its delicate yellow color in combination with salmon pink blush caused quite a sensation in the glass world. Mould blown and freehand pieces were made both plain and decorated. Applied leaves and flowers also made the pieces more elegant. Shirley was immensely proud of his invention. He gave four vases to U. S. President Cleveland's new wife.

In order to protect his invention, the decision was made to also patent the formula in England. This patent was granted on June 16, 1886. Shirley felt so proud of his glass that he presented some pieces to England's monarch, Queen Victoria, and her daughter, Princess Beatrix. It is said that the queen gave this glass the name we know it by today. Upon first unwrapping the gift, she claimed it reminded her of a sunset in Burma. Thus the name Burmese was born. The queen was so thrilled with this new glass that she ordered a whole tea set to be made for her.

With Queen Victoria so admiring, Thomas Webb & Sons of England purchased a license from Frederick Shirley, in December of 1886, to make this glass at their factory in Stourbridge. The glass made in England became known as Queen's Burmese. The decorated pieces were known as Queen's Design.

At Mount Washington Glass Company, Frederick Shirley went on to design many more popular glass types. He developed his own type of Amberina in 1886 that was called Rose Amber. Peach Blow and Mother of Pearl also appeared that year and Crown Milano was introduced in 1893. Royal Flemish and Verona made their debut in 1894.

Mt. Washington Glass Company merged with Pairpoint Manufacturing Company in 1894 and became known as Pairpoint Glass Company. Burmese continued to be made until the late 1890s. By this time, tastes had changed and the era of elegant decorating was over. Many changes occurred at Pairpoint and a reorganization took place in 1900. The company was renamed Pairpoint Corporation and retained this name until 1938.

The Depression of the 1930s took a heavy toll on Pairpoint as huge losses were sustained. Robert Gunderson, a glass blower from the factory, took over the business and renamed the company as Gunderson Glass Works. This company became profitable and in 1952 was given another name, Gunderson-Pairpoint. During this time the Burmese glassmaking was revived. Its color was not quite the same as the earlier pieces and it was heavier. Unfortunately, this later version did not appeal to the public and soon it was discontinued. By 1956, the factory needed major repairs, but a decision was made to close it. A brand new facility was built in Sagamore, Massachusetts, in 1970. The new factory was named Pairpoint Crystal, and continues to operate today.

Three-piece fairy Light, hand painted "Queens Burmese", 5.4" tall, 3.2" wide, tight ribbon crimp & turned up, Made for Clarke by Webb utilizing the Mt. Washington license, **$895**
The insert on this piece is clear glass and marked around the inside inner edge with "Mark-Cricklight-Clarke's-Trademark". Also in the center of these words is the embossed Fairy logo used by Clarke.

Fenton Art Glass Company

Main entrance to the Fenton Art Glass Company.

The Fenton Art Glass Company was established in 1905, in Williamstown, West Virginia, with the meager savings of brothers Frank L. and John Fenton. Later, three other brothers, Charles, Robert, and James, would join the family company. John had plenty of ideas of his own and decided to leave and form his own company, Millersburg Glass.

In the early 20th century, there were hundreds of glass companies operating in the United States. Consolidation took place gradually, but Fenton remained independent. Fenton remained successful and found different ways to survive.

When founder Frank L. Fenton died in 1948, the company continued under the direction of his sons, Frank M. and Bill. They felt an obligation to their family and the town to work hard to make sure the company stayed in business to provide incomes for everyone.

Bill and Frank M. Fenton found new ways to expand sales in tune with the decorating tastes of the public. While they worked hard on new products, Frank M. and Bill never forgot what also worked well for their father.

Fenton has stayed successful by reaching back to the past. Many of the long-forgotten glass formulas have been revived at Fenton. The formulas were closely guarded secrets never shared with their competition. Fenton Glass has been fortunate through the years to have had some master chemists.

The first chemist at Fenton was Jacob Rosenthal. He was hired in 1906 and stayed at Fenton until he retired in 1929. His son, Paul, had come to work at Fenton in 1907 and his father trained him in the work at the glass factory. Paul worked alongside his father and learned the precious glass formulas. Upon Jacob's retirement in 1929, Paul took over as chemist and continued working with the glass formulas developed by his father. A chemist can get quite possessive of his formulas and never completely write them down. Special notebooks are kept with codes that only the chemist could understand. When Paul was approaching retirement in 1949, the Fentons asked him to write down the formulas. He refused, saying they belonged to him. Finally, with a substantial payment, Paul was convinced to write down more than 50 glass formulas that the Fenton company would keep.

Knowing that Paul would retire, it seems odd that no one had thought about training a replacement for him. For the next year, while a search continued for a chemist, Frank M. worked with a Lawrence Badgley to keep the glass batches mixed. Ike Willard, a senior student at the University of Pittsburgh, learned about the chemist position at Fenton and applied for it. Ike started working at Fenton Glass in July, 1950. His primary job was mixing glass batches, with a limited amount of time for research.

Frank M. Fenton had a long acquaintance with Charlie Goe when the company he worked for was going to transfer him to New Jersey. Charlie was instead hired to come to Fenton and immediately set to work, in 1960, on old glass formulas. This work fascinated Charlie and kept his interest in solving glass mysteries. He was persistent and developed many of the formulas Fenton uses today. His crowning achievement was unlocking the mystery of the Mt. Washington Burmese formula. He revealed his success in 1969, when a beautiful piece of Burmese emerged from the lehr. Unfortunately, the same day Charlie Goe died from a heart attack.

Charlie's death created a terrible void at the Fenton company for the next two years. Ike Willard only had time to mix glass. A new chemist, Subodh Gupta, was hired in 1971 to do the research Charlie Goe had begun. That same year Wayne King was hired to assist Ike Willard and Subodh Gupta. Then Ike Willard died in 1973, and Wayne King took over his job. Subodh Gupta suddenly left Fenton Glass in 1983, and Wayne King took over his job, too.

Wayne King has adjusted the Burmese formula over the years and worked on various other ones. As one wanders around a store today, and looks at the new decorating colors on fabric or paint, imagine what it would be like to develop a color in glass that would match them. Countless hours are spent experimenting with different chemicals to see which work together. Then imagine the formula working one day and not the next. It takes great dedication to be a glass chemist.

The Fenton Art Glass Company continues today when other companies have permanently closed. Family is one reason. The company is still family owned, with

Detail of a Fenton Art Glass Company tag.

fourth generation members now working together. Another reason is adaptability. The Fentons have brought out new products to suit their customers, not always staying with what has worked in the past.

Exposure is another reason Fenton Glass continues. Fenton has set up a fantastic marketing program that includes the QVC television home-shopping network. They have showed thousands of new people Fenton glassware. Three collector organizations also work hard to generate enthusiasm for Fenton glass. Fenton's unique glass types, such as Burmese, continue to attract collectors. Fenton cares about the quality of their glass and still has it all made in Williamstown, West Virginia, at their factory. Fenton is a genuine American Glass company that has employees whose parents and grandparents worked here. Their unique types of glass, such as Burmese, continues to attract many new collectors. No other company offers as much creativity in their glass as Fenton does. Fenton proudly states their glass is Made in America. They are definitely on the right coutrse to a bright future.

Charlie Goe

Have you ever wondered how a chance situation can forever make a difference in the path taken by a company? How can one

Charlie Goe, Fenton Art Glass chemist. *Photo courtesy of the Fenton Art Glass Company*

decision forever alter events? It was an unusual request by Frank M. Fenton that brought Charlie Goe to his acquaintance.

Charlie was the chemist who developed the formula for Fenton's Burmese and other Victorian types of glassware. Charlie was persistent in trying to figure the original Burmese formula. He was fascinated by the beauty of the Victorian glass and worked many long years in trying to perfect the right formula.

When we started working on this Burmese project, we asked Frank M. Fenton to give us some information about Charlie that had not been published before. Frank, always generous with his information, gave us this story.

Of course, Bill has a story that he has told many times on QVC about Charlie developing the Burmese and getting the final successful experiment made on the day that he died. I'd like to go back to when we first came in contact with Charlie Goe.

Back in the 1940s, I was director of the First United Methodist Church choir here in Williamstown. I remained the director for about thirty years. I needed a tenor; we didn't have a good one in our choir. So I went to the lady who directed the Marietta High School music program and the choirs at the high school and asked if she had anybody she could recommend who might sing in our choir. She recommended Charlie who was in high school at that time. His family went to the Baptist Church in Marietta. I contacted Charlie and asked if he would come and sing in our choir. We would pay him $5 a Sunday for each Sunday he was able to sing with us. He agreed, so we then had a good tenor. He continued to sing in the choir throughout the rest of his high school years and through all of four years at Marietta College. When he did his graduate work at Ohio University, he still lived at home in Marietta and we continued to pay him. He had a wonderful tenor voice. Everyone just loved listening to him.

After he graduated from college and got his master's degree from Ohio University in mathematics, he went to work for the American Cyanamid Company factory here in the local area. So he came to me and said I didn't need to pay him anymore. He would continue to sing in the choir but since he now had a job, he didn't need the money. So he continued to work at Cyanamid for a number of years, still singing in the choir. Finally he came to me and told me Cyanamid wanted to transfer him to New Jersey.

I thought, "Gosh, are we going to lose Charlie?" Ike Willard was our glassmaker at that time and Ike was kept quite busy just making production batches. He often didn't have time to do the kind of glass research and color research that we wanted to do. So we hired Charlie to do our color research and be our research chemist. He came to work on September 1, 1960. We also engaged Dr. Alexander Silverman, a noted glass technologist and Chairman of the Department of Chemistry at the University of Pittsburgh to come down two days a month to work with Charlie and Ike on experimental glass chemistry. Charlie loved the job and we loved Charlie. Charlie's dad had died of a heart attack at age 38, so when Charlie got to be 38, he began to worry about how much longer he might live. I think he was about 44 years old when he died. So he lived six years longer than his father did.

He and I sang in a madrigal group, traveling around the area giving concerts singing madrigals. I sang bass, Charlie tenor. He helped us develop the Vasa Murrhina treatments. He also worked on the Rosalene batch and many other experimental colors.

Finally, in October of 1969, Charlie excitedly went and found Bill Fenton. He truly believed that finally he had the right chemical combination to achieve the original-looking Burmese glass. He grabbed Bill and took him to the lehr to see the Burmese coming out. Charlie was right, the Burmese pieces were absolutely beautiful.

As was typical of Charlie, he went off to play his normal game of handball. He was so thrilled with his newest achievement. Unfortunately, in the dressing room after the game, Charlie fell over and died of a heart attack. As sad as everyone was, it was heartening to know that Charlie had finally succeeded in his goal to perfect Burmese glass.

This story should answer the question how a chance request can change so many lives. Charlie Goe certainly changed the course for the types of glass made and marketed by the Fenton Glass Company. Beautiful Burmese glass has been made available to many collectors. Charlie also changed the authors' lives by having this glass available from collectors to photograph for this book.

Like the original Mt. Washington Burmese glass, Fenton's Burmese contains uranium oxide and gold. This glass is heat sensitive and the original color resembles custard glass. Upon reheating, the yellow opaque glass takes on a salmon blush color. This color change is caused by the gold molecules combining and growing in size. The chemical content of the glass allows it to fluoresce under a black light, like Vaseline (uranium) glass or Topaz, as Fenton called this color. Custard glass will also glow. The new shaded glass proved to be one of Fenton's top accomplishments in reviving old formulas.

Many people through the years have been responsible for different stages of Burmese glass, since Charlie Goe perfected the formula.

STRIKING GLASSES - as told by Charlie Goe

Howard Seufer - "How do striking glasses work, Charlie?"

Charlie Goe- "To understand how they work, I'll give YOU an explanation, Seuf. This isn't what happens, but perhaps YOU will be able to understand it!"

'Pretend that the molten glass in the tank is full of flower seeds, equally spaced throughout the batch. This isn't true, but just pretend it's so.

'When the glass is formed into a shape and cooled it will be a certain color:
French Opalescent will be Crystal looking, and
Burmese will be Custard in color, for examples.
Those flower seeds that are near each other will come together forming clumps or groups of seeds. (Again, this isn't true, but pretend it's so.)

'If no further treatment, these glasses will stay crystal and custard in color. However, if the glasses are temporarily cooled after being formed (say ten to twenty seconds in a cooling breeze) AND THEN REHEATED, those clumps of seeds will grow into flowers (crystals), blocking all light except one color. In French Opalescent this is White. and in Burmese this will be Pink or Red.

'This is called STRIKING!

'IF the glass is reheated too long, the flowers (crystals) will get thinner and thinner, and the original color of the glass will appear.

'To get a pattern, such as coin spot or fern in a glass, the technique is to form the glass first into a mould that results in a RAISED spot or fern pattern on the outside. Then the shape is reheated, causing only the raised areas to turn to the striking color. The areas not raised will remain the original color.

'This treated shape is then blown into, usually, a smooth mould. The result is a vase, cannonball pitcher, etc. with a coin spot or fern pattern in the glass!

'Again, Seuf. This is a SIMPLE explanation that YOU MIGHT understand. This isn't how it happens, but it illustrates how the process works."

(He was right! I did understand!)
French Opalescent uses phosphate and fluoride for striking;
Burmese uses gold, Selenium Ruby uses selenium and cadmium.

note: Charlie Goe was the chemist of Research & development at Fenton Art Glass Company from 1960-69. He rediscovered the Burmese glass formula, among other accomplishments. He was highly intelligent and a good friend.

Glass Chemist Charles Goe

Hand-out from one of Howard Seufer's talks. *Reprinted with permission from Howard Seufer*

Family Members

Frank M. Fenton

Frank grew up among six sisters and one brother (Bill). A full household with eight children created many interesting moments. Frank spent many summers working at the factory where there were always new things to learn. During the 1930s, Frank worked a little while in the factory and then moved back to the office, learning how to figure the payroll. He attended his first wage conference in 1937 with his father. Frank became assistant general manager in 1942 and was only 32 at the time of his father's death in 1948. He was elected to be the company president, treasurer, and general manager. About six months later, Robert C. Fenton, Sr. passed away, and Bill then became also vice president and secretary. While his father, Frank L., had the ability to design glass, Frank M. had not been exposed to this end of the business. He had to develop his ideas from what he saw or adapt ideas from other pieces of glass. These were the same techniques that his father had used before him. Frank frequented antique shops and shows looking for ideas. He was responsible for the purchase of moulds from the Rubel, Paden City, Verlys, and U.S. Glass companies. Charlie Goe was hired by Frank to develop new glass formulas. The decorating department, with Louise Piper, had been set up by Frank. When Frank's wife, Elizabeth, fell ill in 1978, Frank stepped down as president so he could spend more time with her. After her death in 1980, he continued as chairman of the company's board of directors. He created the Fenton museum and later became the company historian. Frank has been an active speaker at many Fenton conventions sponsored by different organizations. Frank conveys his quest for knowledge. He is willing to answer any question on glass, whether it be about Fenton or glass from another company. Questions need answers and Frank always wants to make sure the answers are correct. Frank is at the factory every day to assist with whatever situations come up and to go through his large stack of mail. Frank works with the Special Orders Department to assist the collector organizations in having their special pieces made. It is a privilege to witness Frank's years of experience and knowledge.

Frank Fenton, past president and current historian.

Bill Fenton

Bill Fenton, the younger son of Frank L. Fenton, as a boy spent many summers working at the glass factory. After attending Marietta College in 1942, he entered the U.S. Army in 1943 and served until 1946. Then he worked full-time for the glass company. Bill started his career in the sales department and expected to work with his cousin, Robert C. Fenton, Jr. (Bob), who was the Sales Manager; but three weeks after Bill started working Bob had a heart attack and died. With some advice from his Uncle Bob, Robert C. Fenton Sr., who was 78 years old at the time, Bill had to learn the job the hard way. When Frank L. Fenton died in 1948, Bill and Frank M. were thrust with the responsibility of running the company. With the death of their Uncle Bob, also in 1948, Bill took his place as Vice-President, Secretary and Sales Manager. Bill changed the way Fenton handled sales by eliminating the jobbers. Bill was a natural salesman and excelled in this job. His enthusiasm spilled over whenever he talked about Fenton glass to retailers. Bill witnessed the first Fenton Burmese glass coming off the lehr with Charlie Goe when he perfected the formula.

Bill Fenton, past president & QVC spokesman. *Photo courtesy of the Fenton Art Glass Company*

After Frank M. retired as president in 1978, Bill took on that responsibility. In 1986, Bill turned the presidency over to Frank's son, George. One of Bill's most visible jobs was as spokesman for Fenton on the television programs with QVC, starting in 1989. A national audience got to know Bill and learn about Fenton's glass. Many of the special pieces made for QVC had Bill Fenton's signature on them. His excitement about the types of glass offered influenced many items selling out. Bill retired as QVC spokesman in January of 2002. Through the years he was also a valued promoter of the three national Fenton collector organizations. One of Bill's favorite types of glass was Burmese. Bill died in December 2002; we miss him dearly.

George Fenton

George was one of the four sons of Frank M. and Elizabeth Fenton. He grew up around the factory and

Left: Nancy Fenton, director of design; **Right**: George Fenton, president.

did odd jobs there. After graduation from college, he became employed full time at the factory in 1972. For awhile, he was Frank's assistant, doing mostly whatever his dad wanted, including helping with union relations and industrial engineering, becoming decorating supervisor, and finally manager of manufacturing. Being involved with several different jobs gave him first-hand knowledge of the factory. By 1985, George had moved into the position of Vice-President, and when uncle Bill stepped down as president in 1986, George assumed that job. George had an advantage over his father when he assumed the presidency; there were many family members he could turn to when a problem came up. In the late 1980s and 1990s, George encouraged the development of new colors and enhanced Fenton's decorating techniques. George feels the pride Fenton employees show in their products and that helps the company promote them more effectively. During the year, George remains visible to collectors by appearing at signing events and speaking at conventions.

Nancy Fenton

Nancy became acquainted with George Fenton at the age of 13 when her family moved next door to his family. They immediately began dating and were married after Nancy graduated from college. Nancy was doing marketing work through Ohio University when she was offered a job at Fenton. She researched what people were buying in the giftware market and this experience led her to a position in the sales department. She soon became new product development manager. As Director of Design, Nancy is constantly searching for new ideas and trends in the market place that can be used at Fenton. She is also involved with Fenton family signing events across the country, and likes to speak with collectors about what they would like in Fenton glass. The new Burmese line for 2003, Let's Bee Burmese, was Nancy's idea. She thought it was time to have one of their historical colors back in a line for the general catalog.

Nancy Fenton showing her husband, George, a hand painted Diamond Optic ewer.

Skilled Workers

Wayne King

Wayne King is Fenton's master chemist. He was hired in 1971 to assist Isaac Willard, supervisor of mixing, and Subodh Gupta, research and development. Later, Wayne became a lab technician. In 1973, after the death of Isaac Willard, Wayne became the supervisor of mixing and furnace. When Subodh Gupta left Fenton in 1983, Wayne moved into research and development. His job is to design new color formulas and work with old ones. He develops new colors to match the current decorating trends. Many factors affect each resulting color, such as the formula, melting temperature and time, burner condition, and the pot itself. This is especially true of Burmese glass, which Wayne calls a temperamental color that reacts with every type of change imaginable.

Wayne was responsible for developing the pressed Burmese formula in 1985. Wayne also experimented with the original Burmese formula to see if he could alter the color. By removing the uranium oxide and adding powder blue, also known as cobalt oxide, Wayne produced the blue Burmese color. In the mid-1990s, Wayne also worked to adjust the Burmese formula to meet new EPA requirements, adjusting how the uranium could be mixed and making the yellow a little creamier. Lotus Mist, the new green version of Burmese, was also created by Wayne. Being a glass chemist is a very complex job. Wayne has mastered it and enabled Fenton to come out with some wonderful new colors.

Wayne King, Fenton Art Glass Company chemist.

Jon Saffell

Jon Saffell, Fenton mould designer.

Jon Saffell joined Fostoria Glass's design department in 1957 and was later promoted to be design department manager and later to be the director of design. He was working at Fostoria when Fostoria was purchased by Lancaster Colony in 1986 and remained a consultant for them for another two years. In 1988 he started freelance work under the business name Design Prototypes. Jon was hired by Fenton in 1994 to be the product designer and sculptor. Finally Jon could design what he had always wanted, sculptured items. Jon has thrived at Fenton and attracted collectors to his type of work. Many of his new animals have been made in Burmese glass, including a stylized cat, mini-cat, small rooster, frog, butterfly, and new lop-eared bunny. Other of his items include the Santas, snowman fairy light, ballerina, and new style of praying kids. Two of his seven grandchildren were used as models for the "kids" pieces. Many of the Connoisseur mould shapes were his creations, too, such as those used for the Trout, Veil Tail, and Hummingbird vases as well as the Fenced Garden and Bluebird baskets. We hope to see his new elephant made in Burmese.

Bob Hill

Bob began working in the glass industry at Wheaton Glass from 1965 to 1967. He was hired by Fenton in 1967 to work at Armstrong Tank Work, a company then owned by Fenton. There he learned to make the fabricating forms used for concrete in making bridges, building roofs, and baseball stadiums. In 1969, Bob began his apprenticeship in the Fenton mould shop and worked all the different phases of making glass moulds. Twenty years later, on December 1, 1989, Bob was made supervisor of the mould shop, being in charge of having new moulds made and keeping current moulds in top form. After extensive use, the moulds get wear spots or develop some type of damage.

The time needed to make a new mould can take from two months to a year, depending on when the item is needed. The process takes from seven to eleven steps: the design, Jon Saffell's master, drawing, foundry work, a silicone cast, making a deckle master, milling the joints, duplicating, vise work, lathe work, and assembly. Depending on the piece, there could be eight people involved to complete these steps. Besides the time involved, the cost of the moulds ranges from $500 for a paperweight to $16,000 for a new animal. There is only one blown mold made. Animal figurines are made four moulds to the set. All the other types of press moulds are made in sets of two. Fenton's mould shop usually makes their own moulds, but occasionally Island Mould will get the contract. Maintenance of the moulds is important. If

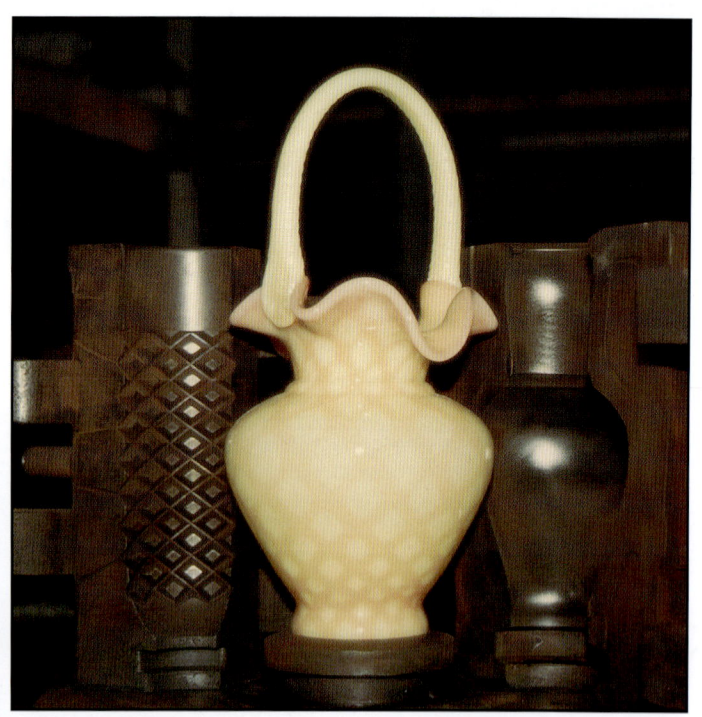

Detail of Basket #V51468, shown sitting in front of the cast iron moulds used in the production of this piece.

Bob Hill, Fenton mould shop foreman.

the presser and mould cleaning personnel take proper care of them, the moulds can last for years. Several of the Fenton moulds date from the 1920s and are still in good working order.

Members of Bob's family also work at Fenton: his wife, Pat, is a selector; daughter Amber works in the Fenton Gift Shop; and his son, Bob Jr., is a tour guide.

Pam Dick

Pam Dick began working for Fenton as a decorator in 1978. Since then she has had many responsibilities. Some of them include work in the hot metal department, the shipping area, and the finishing department. In 1985, while working as a tour guide for the Fenton Gift Shop, she was introduced to Fenton collectors. Since then Pam has been involved with the collector clubs and made many friends through them. Currently her responsibilities include keeping the company history and designs, and working with Frank M. Fenton in the museum storage area cataloging each piece and creating an inventory for special orders, QVC products, glass from other companies, and souvenirs from many glass clubs. Besides these, Pam is an assistant to Martha Wright, Fenton's marketing consultant. Pam also speaks at collector group gatherings.

Pam Dick, Fenton Art Glass Company, assistant to Frank M. Fenton.

Jennifer Maston

Jennifer came to work for Fenton in 1988 as the museum curator and she has a multitude of tasks. One is to maintain the museum and to keep track of where all the glass is located; some are photographed and others are borrowed for projects. She provides assistance and answers questions from collector. All reference books and videos are sold through the museum, which is divided into two sections: the Ohio Valley room and the Blue Ridge room (the Fenton Art Glass Company is located in the Ohio Valley beside the Blue Ridge Mountains). The original museum occupies the Ohio Valley room where glass made up to 1980 is housed. A display case holds Burmese glass, including Roses, Maple Leaf, and some Connoisseur items. The Blue Ridge room houses glass made from 1980 onward. There is a full display case in this room with more Burmese glass, many Diamond Optic pieces from QVC, and other newer items.

Jennifer Maston, Fenton Art Glass Company Museum curator.

Decorating Department

The decorating department was re-started in April of 1968 with the arrival of Louise Piper. Louise was hired to develop new designs and train half a dozen people to duplicate them. Today, there are over 70 men and women working here on different decorations. The original decorating department was in the basement of the factory, but later a special area was made available for the decorators that enabled people on a factory tour to watch the decorators work. The factory tours brought the public in to see how glass was really made, and the addition of the decorators enabled them to see all the steps, right to the sales shelf and check-out counter.

Louise Piper

Louise began her glass decorating career at Jeannette Shade and Novelty Company. Through Tony Rosena, a designer at Fenton, Louise was hired to set up a new Fenton decorating department in 1968. Her first design was Violets in the Snow. When the production of Burmese began in 1970, she designed the Rose and Scene patterns. Fenton's first Special Order for Burmese came from Frederick and Nelson and the design of Pink Butterflies was developed by Louise. Through the years, Louise Piper has developed countless decorations. Initially, none of her pieces were signed, but later she was signing the pieces she decorated for collectors in the gift shop. Louise retired from Fenton in 1989, at the age of 81. She dearly loved the work that kept her on the job long after when most people would have retired. Louise passed away in 1995.

Frances Burton

Frances started her decorating training at Fenton in 1973 under the watchful eye of Louise Piper. Louise was always concerned that her pupils learned the right techniques. Eventually, Frances moved on to train other new decorators. She became a designer and then head designer. In 1991 she took over the position of department supervisor. Frances received the Discovery award for her achevements. The Glass Messenger Burmese tulip vase, titled Morning Glo-

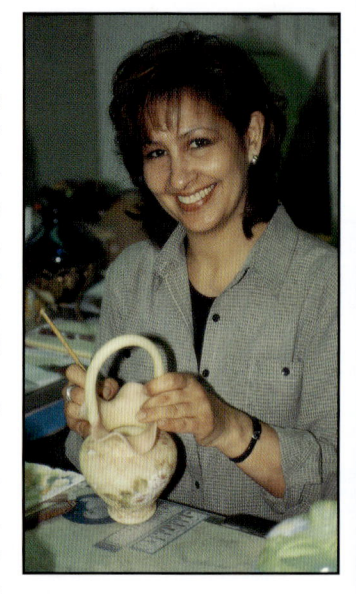

Louise Piper, Fenton head of decorating department and designer. *Photo courtesy of the Fenton Art Glass Com-*

Frances Burton, Fenton decoration designer, shown painting on 2003 TSV (today's special value) basket, that was a QVC piece.

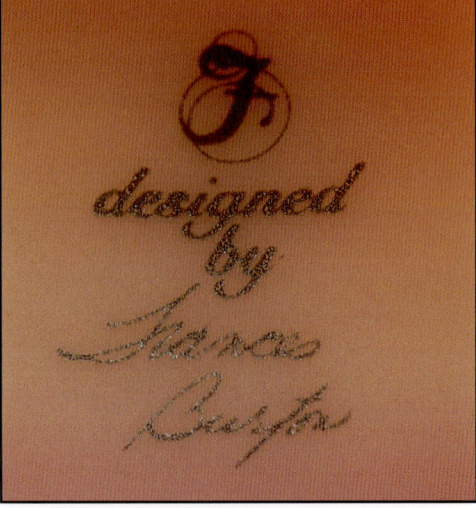

Detail of Louise Piper's signature.

Detail of Frances Burton's signature.

ries, received recognition from the National Association of Limited Edition Dealers (NALED) as a first runner-up in their competition. Frances updated a former design of Louise Piper, Scene, to be part of the 85th anniversary line. A Burmese pitcher in the 1996 Connoisseur Collection had a dragonfly and water lily that was designed by Frances. Her favorite pieces are the Sea of Dreams feather vase and the Daybreak pillar lamp, both done in 1995. Burmese is her favorite type of glass and she enjoys the chance to design on it. Frances felt privileged to have been selected by Bill Fenton to design the decoration on his Centennial vase, since she knew Burmese was a favorite of his.

Kim Barley

Kim began her work at Fenton in 1979 as a decorator. Through the years she has worked to train other decorators and has become a designer. Outdoor scenes involving water are frequently part of her designs.

Kim Barley, Fenton decoration designer, shown painting on 2002 Bill Fenton retirement pitcher, that was a QVC piece.

Detail of Kim Plauche's signature.

Like other of her colleagues, she has received the Discovery Award and others from the National Association of Limited Edition Dealers (NALED). The Papillon vase that featured an artistic butterfly was designed by Kim for the 1998 Connoisseur Collection. A realistic Blackberry Bouquet basket from the same year was also designed by Kim. Her favorite piece is Bill Fenton's retirement pitcher, from the January 2002 QVC show. Now that Bill is gone, Kim and the other decorators feel a great loss. Kim Plauche was married in October, 2002, and now will be painting under the name Kim Barley.

Robin Spindler

Robin Spindler's love of art and painting led her to work at Fenton in 1979 as a decorator. Though her name is Judith Kay, she goes by Robin but signs her pieces JK Spindler. In 1996, the Trout vase was based on her love for fishing and it is her favorite piece. Both of the Burmese pieces in the 1997 Connoisseur Collection, Fenced Garden, and Trillium, were Robin's designs. When her son, Scott, was ten years old, he picked a bouquet of trillium for her and among them she found one flower with four petals instead of the normal three. Robin pressed this special Trillium in a wildflower book and still cherishes it today. The Memories lamp from the 1999 Connoisseur Collection won a Discovery Award for Excellence in Design in the glass lighting division by the Society of Glass and Ceramic Decorators. She is grateful every day to have a job in which she can utilize her God-given abilities.

J.K. "Robin" Spindler, Fenton decoration designer, shown holding 2003 Showcase dealer exclusive vase.

Detail of J.K. "Robin" Spindler's signature.

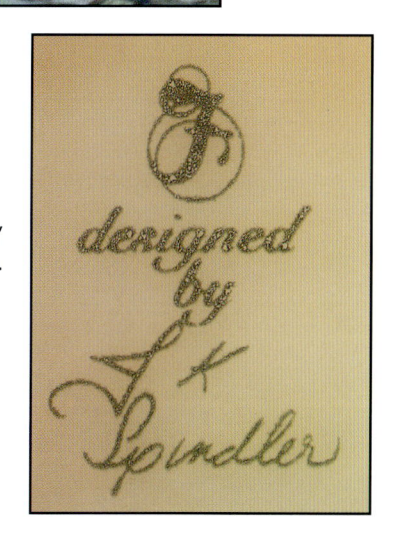

Stacy Williams

After graduating from the Columbus College of Art and Design in 1993, Stacy Williams began work decorating at Fenton. Seven years later she became a designer. Recently she has created the scenes on the Veil Tail vase and Song Sparrow lamp. While Stacy was growing up, she owned goldfish and loved to watch them swim around in the bowl and outside in the garden pond. The Veil Tale is her favorite piece.

Martha Reynolds

Martha Reynolds began working for Fenton in 1990 as one of the decorating designers. Through the years, Martha has been honored with many prestigious awards for her very expressive decorations, including the Vandenoever Award from the Society of Glass and Ceramic Decorators. The very elegant Queens Bird was Martha's creation for the 1996 Connoisseur Collection. In 2001, Martha retired from Fenton to start her own design company.

Stacy Williams, Fenton decoration designer, shown painting on 2003 Bill Fenton Memorial Vase.

Martha Reynolds, Fenton decoration designer. *Photo courtesy of the Fenton Art Glass Company.*

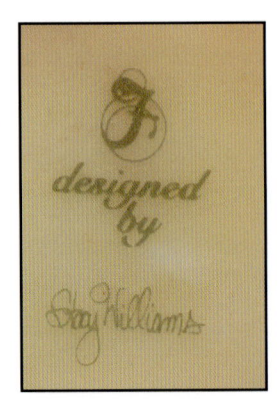

Detail of Stacy William's signature.

Detail of Martha Reynold's signature.

Decorating Department 21

Group photo of Fenton decorators, **Left-to-right**: Linda Everson, Jeanne Cutshaw, Pam Lauderman, and Dianna Barbour.

Group photo of Fenton decorators, **Left-to-right**: Donna Robinson, Debra Cutshaw, Sharon Hart, and Carol Griffiths.

Group photo of Fenton decorators, **Left-to-right**: Susan Bryan, Dane Frederick, and Alice Farley.

Channels of Distribution for Fenton Burmese Glass

Burmese glass was produced at Fenton for different types of categories and was distributed through the following ways.

General catalog: Each item listed this way was a regularly produced piece that was generally available for the entire year.

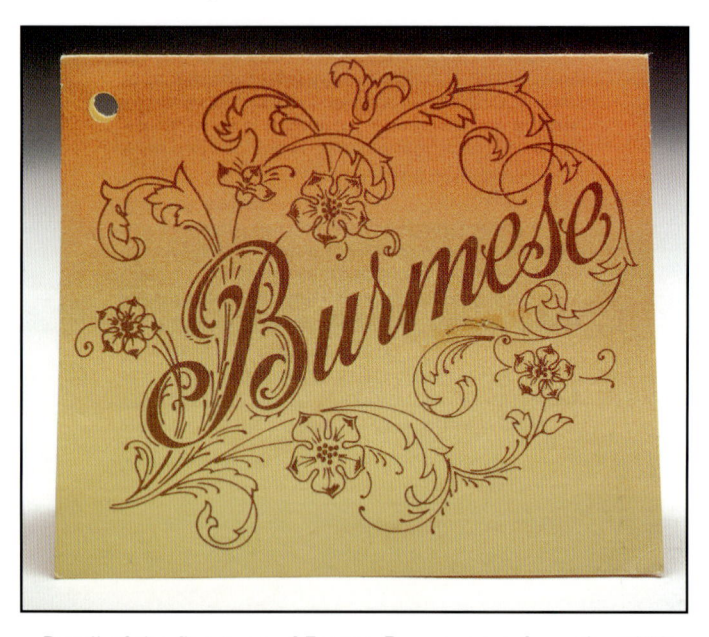

Detail of the first type of Fenton Burmese tag from the 1970s.

A Reproduction of One of the Rare Glass Treatments of the 19th Century Handmade in the Fine Fenton Tradition

Burmese was the name given this lovely glass treatment in 1885 by its creator Frederick Shirley, of the Mt. Washington Glass Company in New Bedford, Massachusetts.

Produced only for a very limited number of years, legend states that the name was provided by Queen Victoria who, upon receipt of a gift of this glass, was said to have exclaimed that the rich tones of blushing pink reminded her of a Burmese sunset.

Queen Victoria was so delighted with Burmese glass that she ordered several additional items which, in turn, influenced Thomas Webb & Sons, a famous English glassmaker, to purchase a license to produce the treatment in England. These pieces are known as Queen's Burmese. Both the original Burmese and Queen's Burmese are among the rarest and most prized pieces collected by glass connoisseurs.

Enamored with the soft translucent beauty of Burmese, Fenton Glass chemist Charles W. Goe experimented with innumerable formula variations over a period of many years until he found just the right formula to faithfully reproduce the delicate blushing loveliness of the original Burmese treatment.

Fenton is extraordinarily proud to offer once again to the American public Burmese Glass; one of the finest examples of America's wonderful heritage in hand glass craftsmanship.

Fenton
THE FENTON ART GLASS COMPANY
WILLIAMSTOWN, WEST VIRGINIA 26187

Detail of inside of the first type of Burmese tag.

Spring Supplement: These items were produced for a short period of time, usually from January until April or May. The items may also be a numbered limited edition or made just for this time frame.

Connoisseur: For the June supplement, there were special items, usually a type of art glass. This collection debuted in 1983 under the influence of Frank M. Fenton. The artists were given the opportunity to develop unique items of interest to collectors. New techniques were sometimes tried for this collection. These items were usually numbered and/or were made in limited editions.

Centennial Collection: This collection was begun in 2000 to celebrate the countdown to Fenton's 100th anniversary in 2005. Favorite types of glass chosen by various family members were highlighted. Each year, two family members select their favorite type of glass. Each piece made is signed by that person.

Showcase Dealer Exclusives: Certain Fenton retailers were given the status of being a Showcase Dealer by having a high sales volume. This program was begun in 1994 to reward Showcase Dealers. For them, an exclusive glass piece was made to encourage collectors to come into their stores.

Catalog Exclusive: In the early 1990s, a smaller version of the general catalog was made available. These catalogs have the store name printed on them and could be sent to their mail-order customers. In 1995, a new program was started for the retailers who used this catalog: limited edition pieces were featured that could be ordered only through the store listed on the catalog.

Glass Messenger Exclusive: With all the glass they were producing, Fenton began their own publication to highlight their glass, artists, decorators, family members, and special stories. *The Glass Messenger* made its debut in early 1996. Each subscriber to this quarterly newsletter was given a certificate for the opportunity to purchase an exclusive Fenton piece made of a unique type of glass. Lynn Fenton Erb was originally in charge of this publication and later responsibility for the *Glass Messenger* was transferred to Jim Measell, who is now its editor.

Showroom Exclusive: In each area of the United States, gift showrooms exist for retail shop owners to visit and see the merchandise first-hand. Special pieces were made by Fenton for shop owners who visited these showrooms.

Fenton Gift Shop: There is a gift shop at the Fenton glassworks that carries first quality merchandise, seconds, overruns, and short runs. Some of the pieces may have a slight blemish on them that deems them not perfect for the catalog; they may be put in the gift shop as a "second." Pieces made for the regular line may be left over after the decorating department is done, so the plain pieces are put in the gift shop for sale. Also, if glass is left in the melting pot unused, then a mould or two may be pulled to use up the molten glass. Each year for the annual February sale, special pieces are made. Likewise, in June of each year a tent sale is conducted to clean out overruns and the previous year's merchandise. As an additional attraction, special pieces are also made for this sale. In August, the Fenton Art Glass Collectors of America have a convention in Williamstown, West Virginia, and Fenton makes special edition pieces for the convention attendees. These items are put in a special glass room and a lottery is held to determine who goes into the room first. It is like a treasure hunt, and after each group leaves additional pieces are added for the next group.

The QVC television show: QVC stands for Quality, Value, and Convenience. This home shopping television network was conceived in 1986. Joe Segel, the QVC founder, formerly worked for the Franklin Mint in Media, Pennsylvania. He was responsible for vaulting the mint into their successful collectibles market. In the mid-1980s, Fenton was looking for ways to expose Fenton glass to a new consumer base. Shelley Fenton had previously worked with Whitney Smith, head of new products at the Franklin Mint. Whitney left the Franklin Mint to work with QVC obtaining new collectibles to sell on their programs. Because of her past association with Shelley, Whitney thought Fenton would be a good fit with QVC. Several discussions took place about the various types of Fenton glassware before it was decided to offer Fenton glass on QVC. The first item was the birthstone bear. In 1988, the items on QVC were from Fenton's general catalog. After a few shows, everyone agreed that to be really successful, the Fenton glass items sold this way should be made exclusively for QVC as special pieces for this program. Bill Fenton became the main spokesman for Fenton on these select shows. Generally there are six to eight Fenton programs a year with about a dozen different types of items per show.

Special Orders: In between producing glass for themselves, Fenton does make special pieces for individuals, companies, and collector groups. A wide range of items has been made through the years. When a special order is placed, Fenton generally requires the order to be a "turn," that is the amount of glass that can be made in four hours. A small mould will produce many items while a larger mould will result in fewer pieces.

Detail of the Fenton Burmese tag from the 1990s.

Detail of inside of the Burmese tag from the 1990s.

The 1970s

The introduction of Fenton's new Burmese line in 1970 brought rave reviews. The public apparently was ready for an entirely new type of glass. The first Burmese glass was developed only as a blown formula. Initially the shading was a deeper red color that at times shifted towards a purple hue. The first year there were six plain pieces and six decorated pieces available for sale.

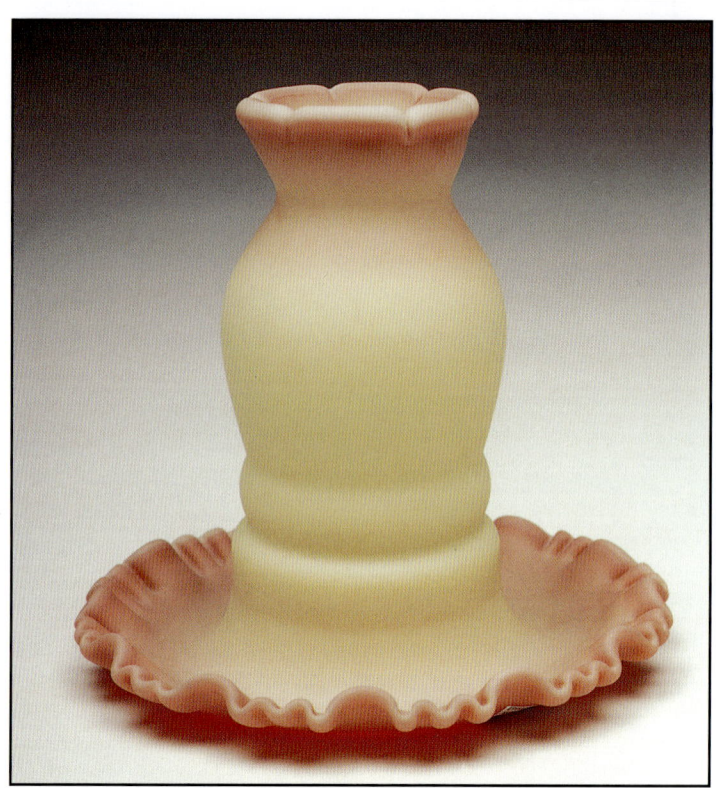

One piece fairy light #7392BR, plain satin finish, 5.75" tall, 6.5" wide (at base), tight single crimp, General Catalog 1970-1971, **$195**

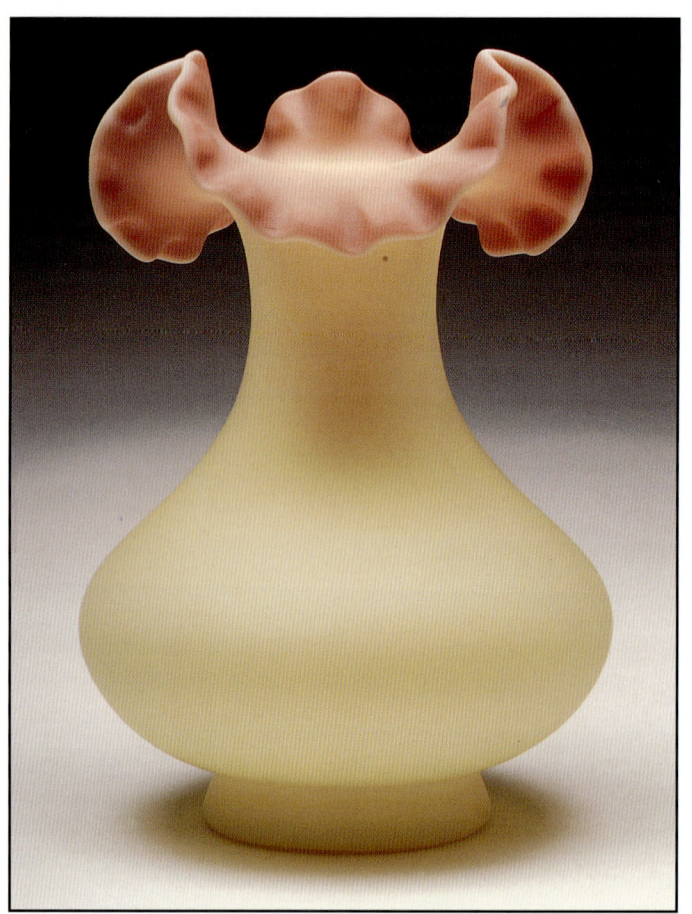

Vase #7252BR, plain satin finish, 7" tall, double crimp, General Catalog 1970-1971, **$65**

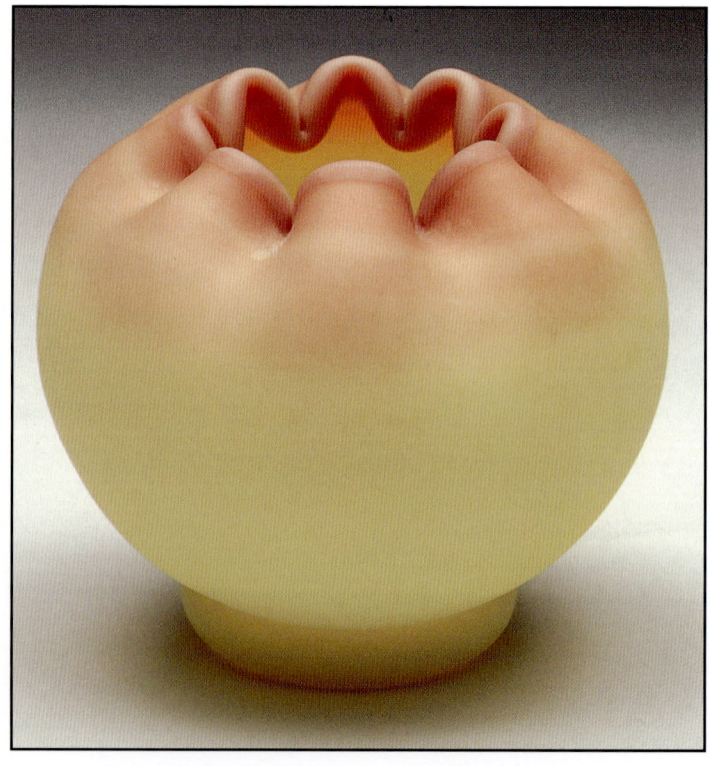

Rose bowl #7424BR, plain satin finish, 3.4" tall, 4" wide tight single crimp & cupped in, General Catalog 1970-1971, **$55**

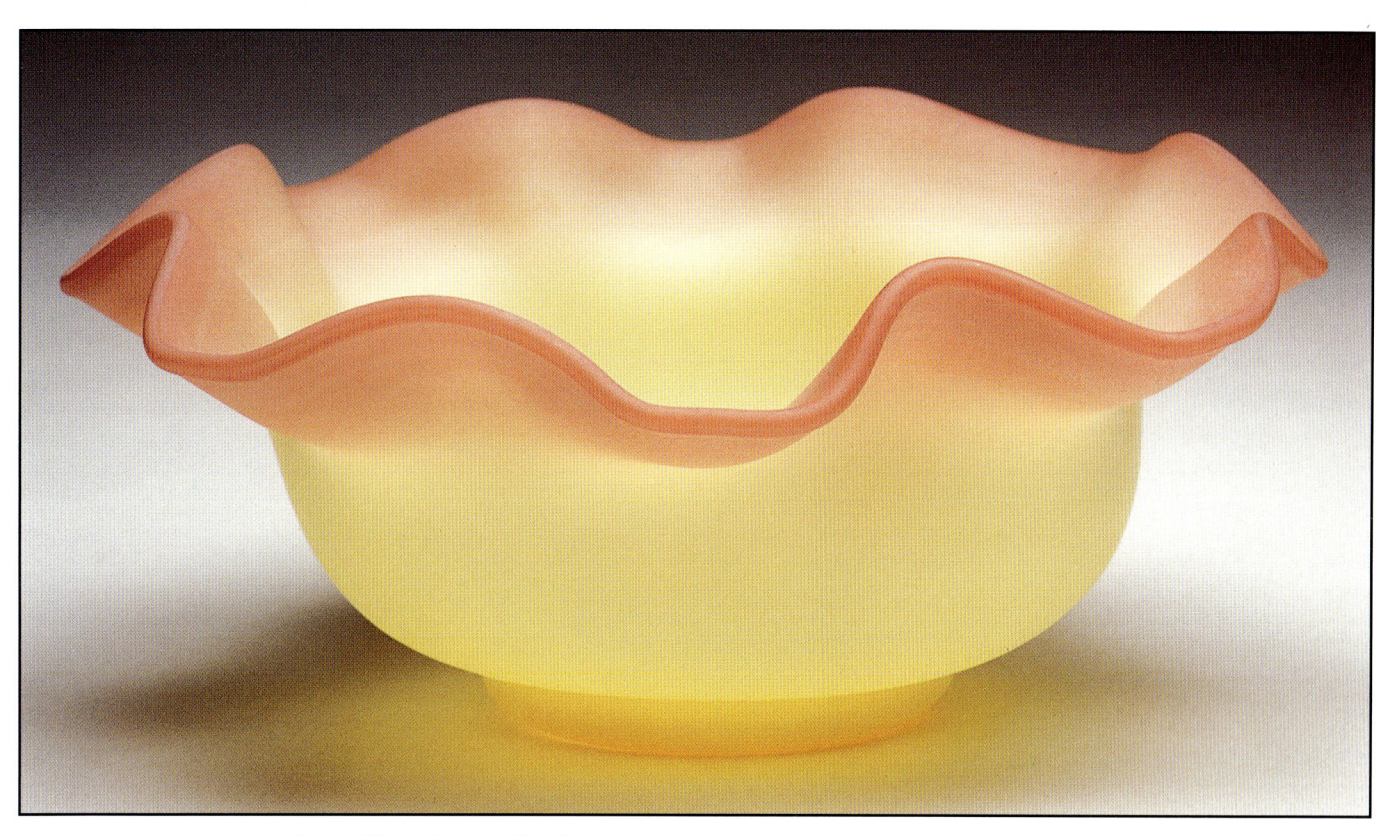

The 1970s   25

Bowl #7422BR, plain satin finish, 9" wide, single crimp, General Catalog 1970-1971, **$85**

Basket #7437BR, plain satin finish, 7" tall, 5" wide, single crimp, General Catalog 1970-1971, **$85**

Cream pitcher #7461BR, plain satin finish, 4.4" tall, 4.25" wide, General Catalog 1970-1971, **$45**

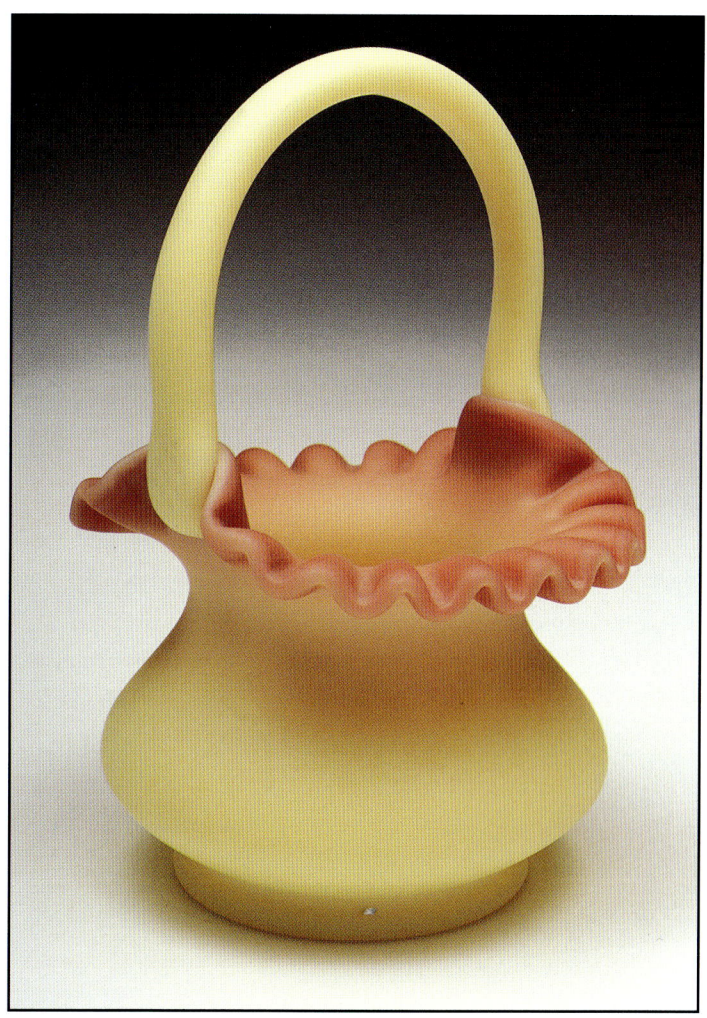

26   The 1970s

The decoration consisted of green and brown leaves that were known as Leaf Decorated, BD, but most collectors now refer to this as Maple Leaf. This was not really a hand-decorated design, but was actually a decal that was applied and fired to make it adhere permanently to the glass. At the time, the decorating department was being set up by Louise Piper who had not yet sufficiently trained her personnel to hand-decorate items. Since Louise had worked with decals at her previous employment at the Jeannette Shade and Novelty Glass Company, the decision was made to try a decal as decoration on some of the Burmese glass. The decals were difficult to apply, and this was the only time that a decal was used on Fenton glass. That summer turned out to be a hot one. Decorators working with the decals in the factory basement found themselves with perspiration dripping from their brows onto the glass. To make their work a little more comfortable, the decorators would go without their shoes. One day, a tour group was coming through and they were asked to put their shoes back on. The answer to this was, "This is West Virginia."

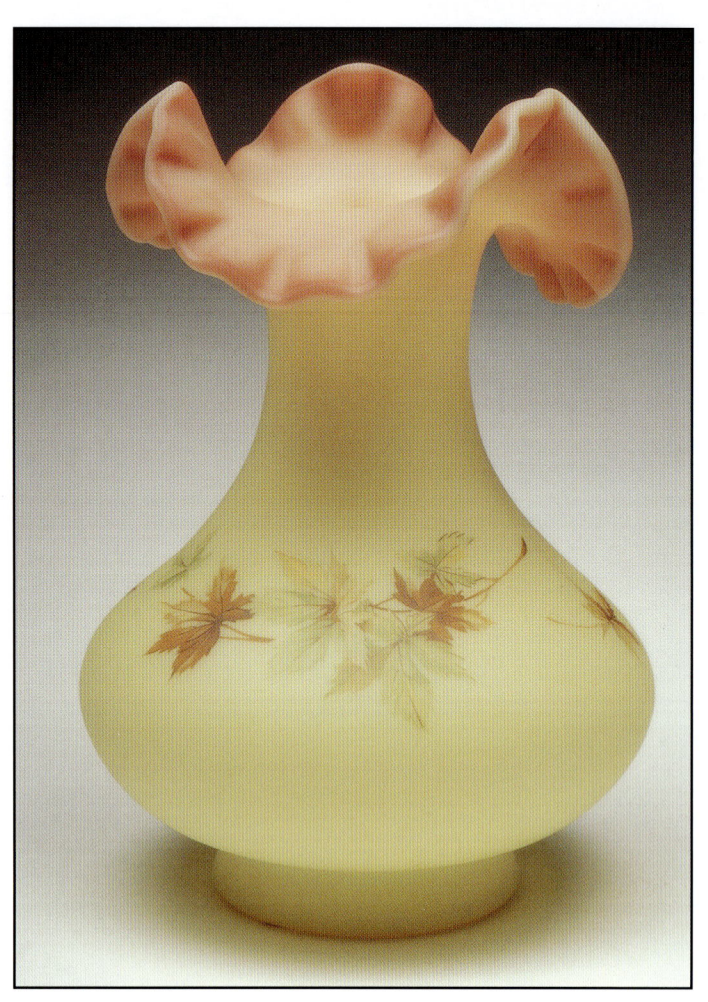

Vase #7252BD, decal "Maple Leaf" decoration, 7" tall, double crimp, General Catalog 1970-1971, **$85**

Detail of decal "Maple Leaf" decoration.

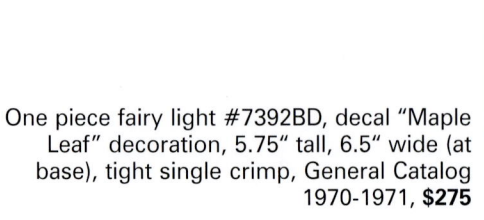

One piece fairy light #7392BD, decal "Maple Leaf" decoration, 5.75" tall, 6.5" wide (at base), tight single crimp, General Catalog 1970-1971, **$275**

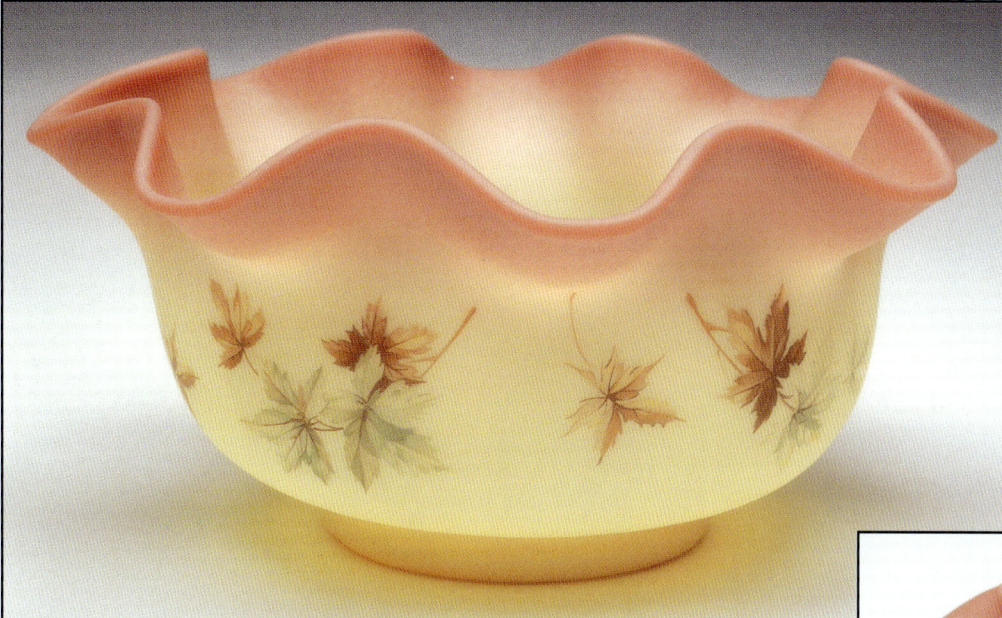

The 1970s   27

Bowl #7422BD, decal "Maple Leaf" decoration, 8.5" wide, single crimp, General Catalog 1970-1971, **$110**

Rose bowl #7424BD, decal "Maple Leaf" decoration, 3.25" tall, 4" wide, tight single crimp & cupped in, General Catalog 1970-1971, **$75**

Basket #7437BD, decal "Maple Leaf" decoration, 7.5" tall, 4.75" wide, single crimp, General Catalog 1970-1971, **$145**

Cream pitcher #7461BD, decal "Maple Leaf" decoration, 4.35" tall, 4.25" wide, General Catalog 1970-1972, **$75**

28   The 1970s

The Fenton gift shop featured gloss versions of the items that appeared in the catalog with a satin finish.

Vase #7252BE, plain gloss finish, 7" tall, double crimp, From Fenton Gift Shop 1970-1971, **$68**

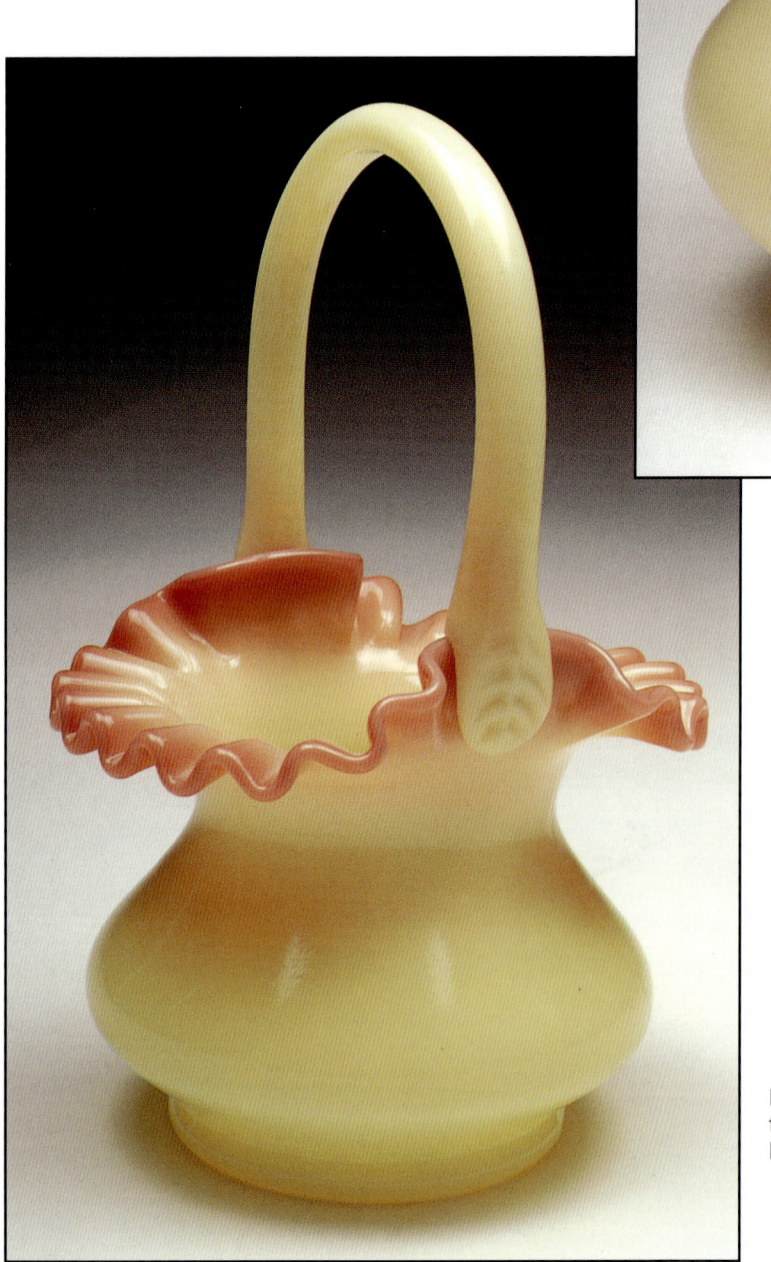

Basket #7437BE, plain gloss finish, 7.5" tall, 4.75" wide, single crimp, From Fenton Gift Shop 1970, **$95**

The 1970s   29

Detail of 1971 General Catalog, Burmese offering. (Reprinted with permission from the Fenton Art Glass Company)

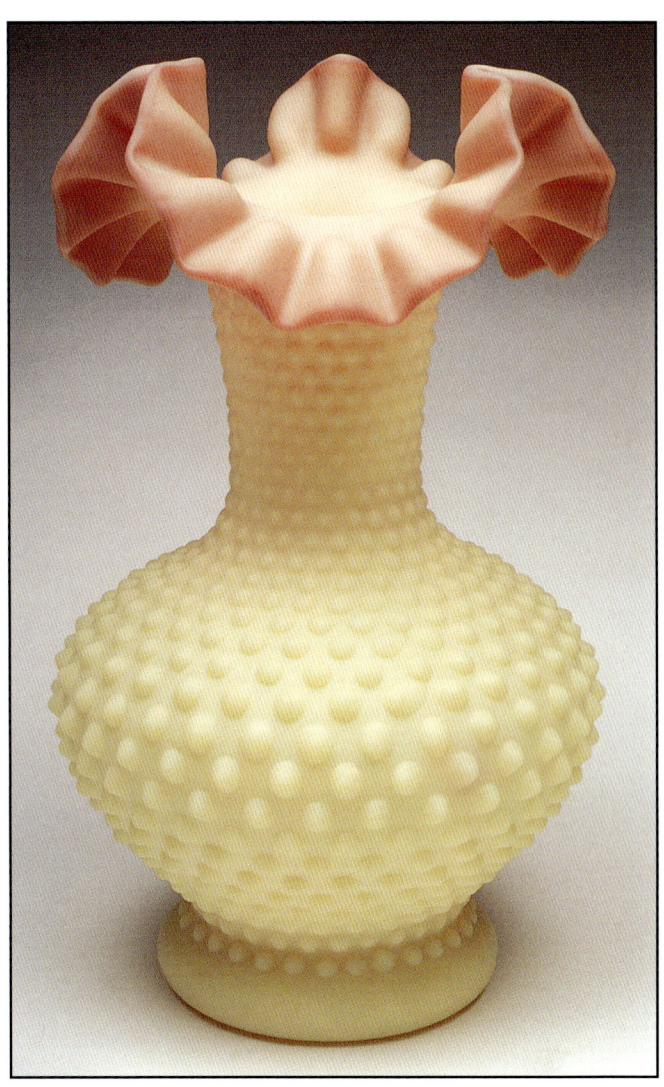

Vase #3752BR, embossed "Hobnail" pattern, plain satin finish, 10.5" tall, double crimp, General Catalog 1971, **$295**

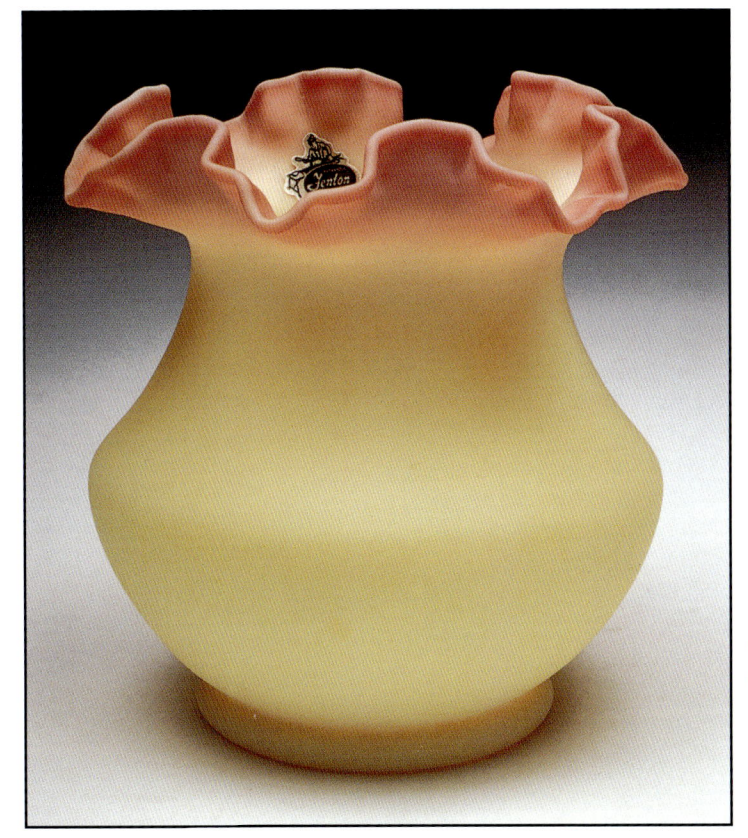

Vase #7253BE, plain satin finish, 7" tall, double crimp, General Catalog 1971, **$70**

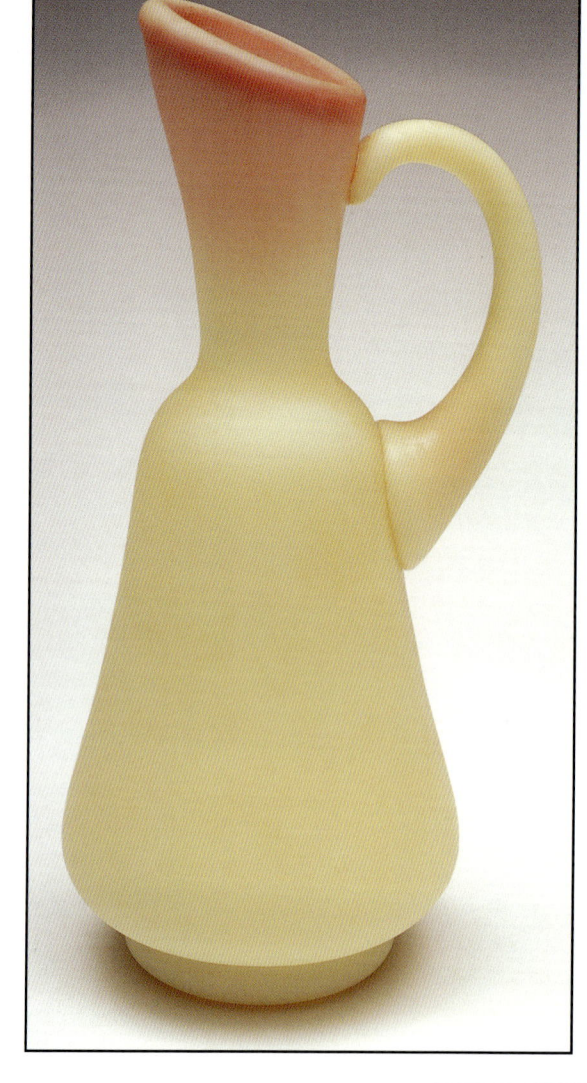

30 The 1970s

Pinch vase #7359BR, plain satin finish, 7.4" tall, single crimp, General Catalog 1971, **$48**

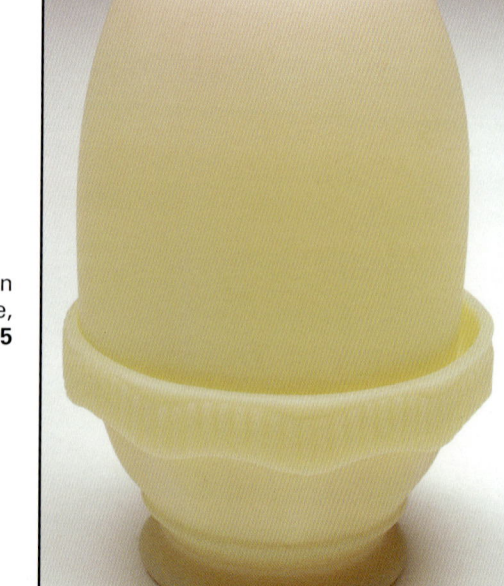

Cruet vase #7462BR, plain satin finish, 6.35" tall, General Catalog 1971, **$65**

Two piece fairy light #7492BR, plain satin finish, 4.75" tall, 3.15" wide, General Catalog 1971, **$85**

The 1970s   31

Ribbed vase #9055BR, plain satin finish, 4.75" tall, tight ribbon single crimp, General Catalog 1971, **$145**

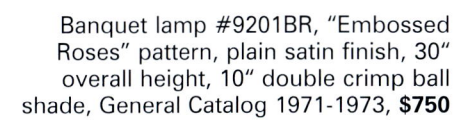

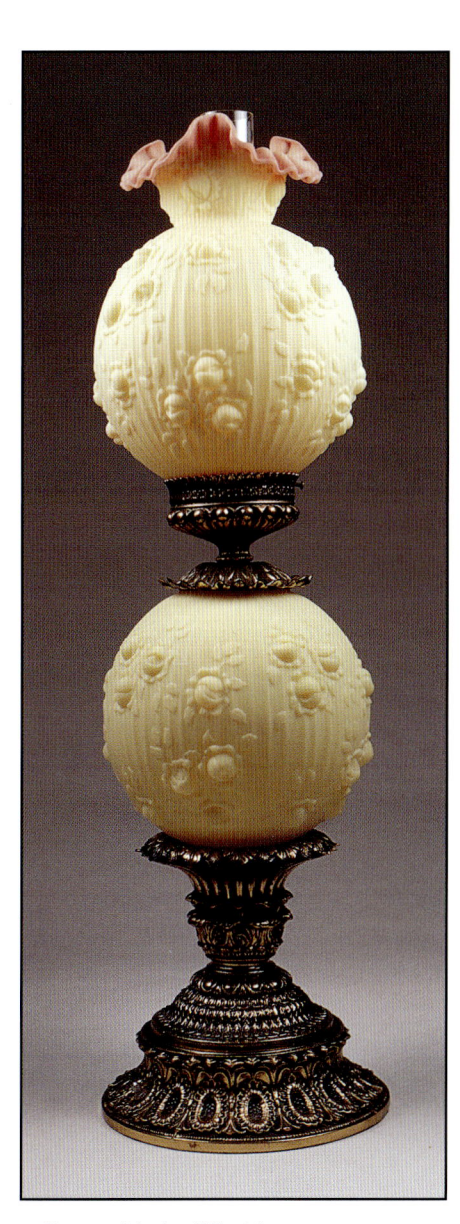

Banquet lamp #9201BR, "Embossed Roses" pattern, plain satin finish, 30" overall height, 10" double crimp ball shade, General Catalog 1971-1973, **$750**

Gone with the Wind Lamp #9202BR, "Embossed Roses" pattern, plain satin finish, 35" overall height, 10" double crimp ball shade, General Catalog 1971-1973, **$995**

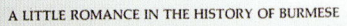

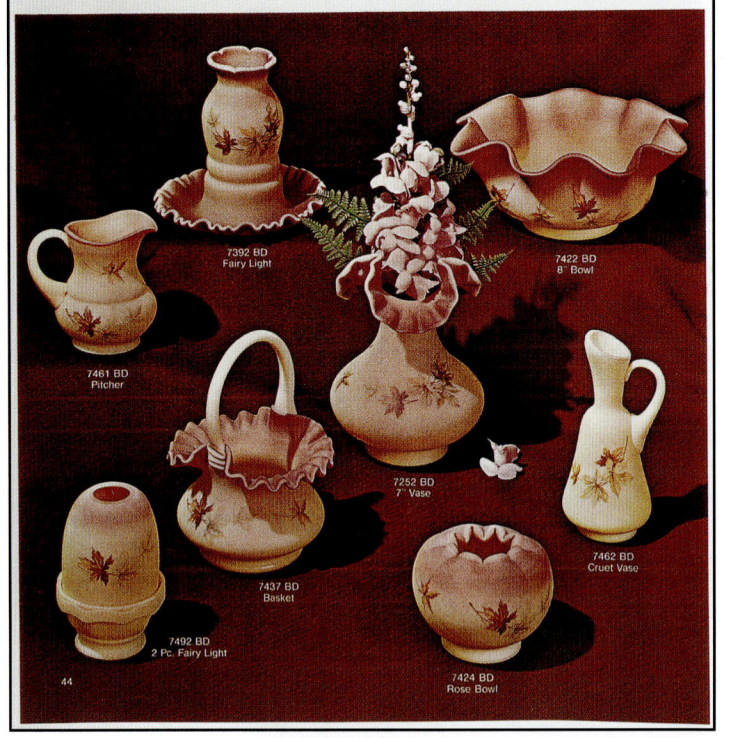

32   The 1970s

Detail of 1971 General Catalog "Maple Leaf" decoration on Burmese offering. (Reprinted with permission from the Fenton Art Glass Company)

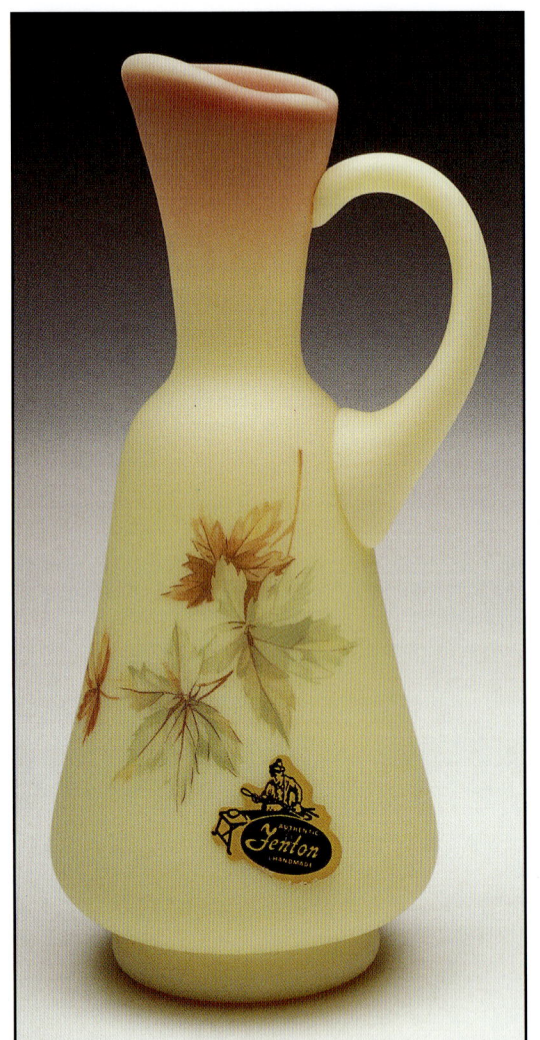

Cruet vase, 7462BD, decal "Maple Leaf" decoration, 6.35" tall, General Catalog 1971-1972, **$125**

Two piece fairy light #7492BD, decal "Maple Leaf" decoration, 4.75" tall, 3.15" wide, General Catalog 1971-1972, **$165**

The 1970s   33

Examples of three progressive stages of a two piece fairy light. **Left:** #7492BE, plain gloss finish, (**Note,** this one has not been cut apart. Two piece fairy lights come from the mould as one piece of glass & then are cut into); **Center:** #7492BR, plain satin finish; **Right:** #7492BD, decal "Maple Leaf" decoration.

Detail of hand painted "Rose" decoration.

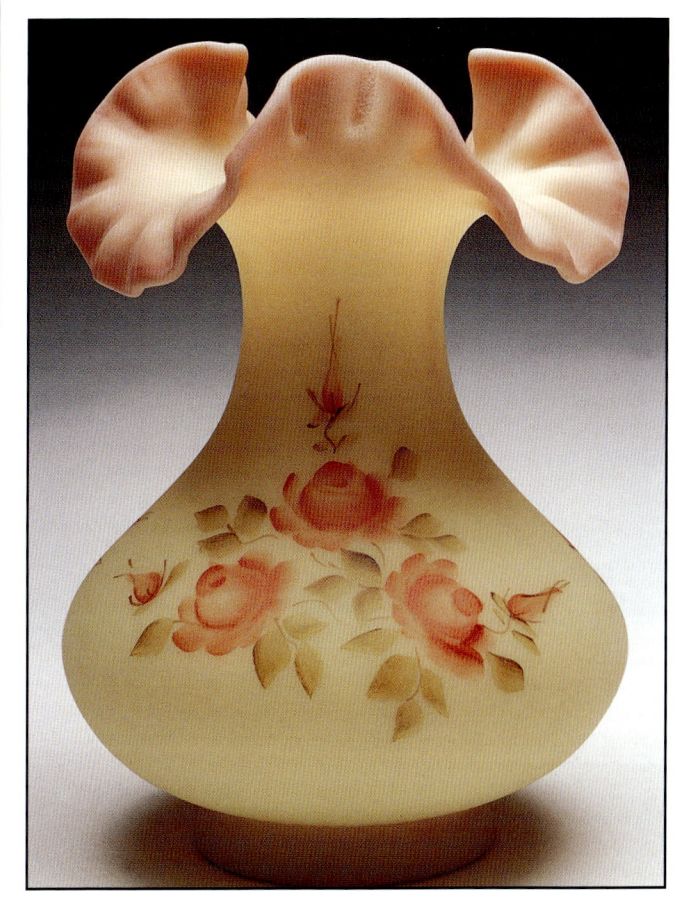

Vase #7252RB, hand painted "Rose" decoration, 7" tall, double crimp, Decorated by D. Kennedy, General Catalog 1971-1980, **$95**

34   The 1970s

Vase #7253RB, hand painted "Rose" decoration, 7" tall, double crimp, General Catalog 1971-1973, **$110**

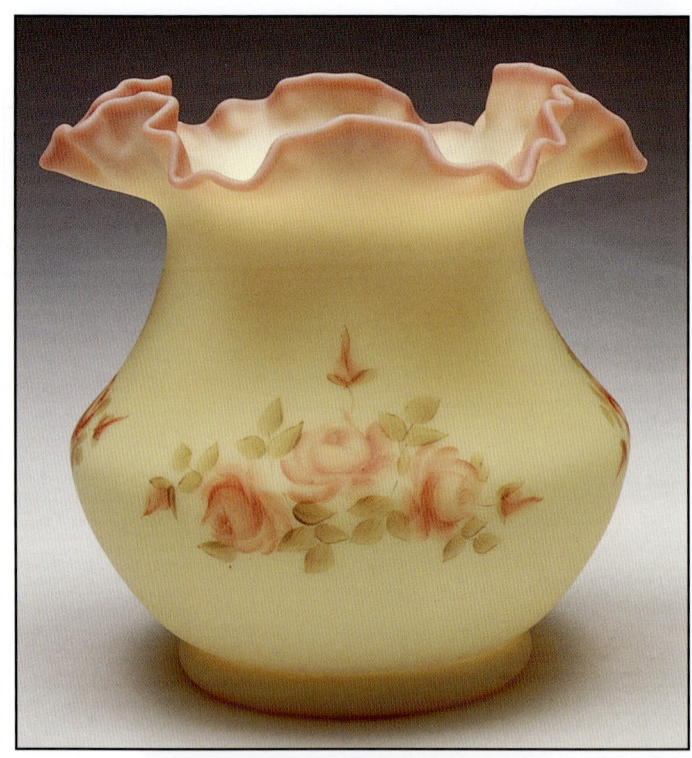

One piece fairy light #7392RB, hand painted "Rose" decoration, 5.75" tall, 6.5" wide (at base), General Catalog 1971, **$275**

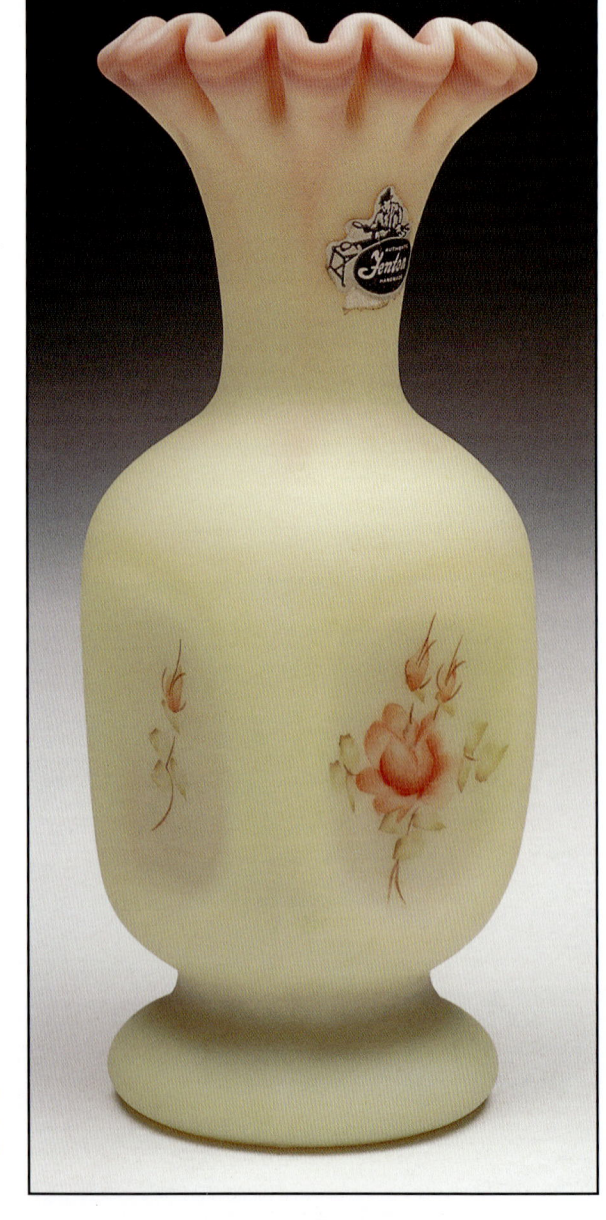

Pinch vase #7359RB, hand painted "Rose" decoration, 7.1" tall, tight single crimp, General Catalog 1971-1979, **$85**

The 1970s   35

Lamp #7405RB, hand painted "Rose" decoration, 33" overall height, cloth shade, General Catalog 1971, **$250**

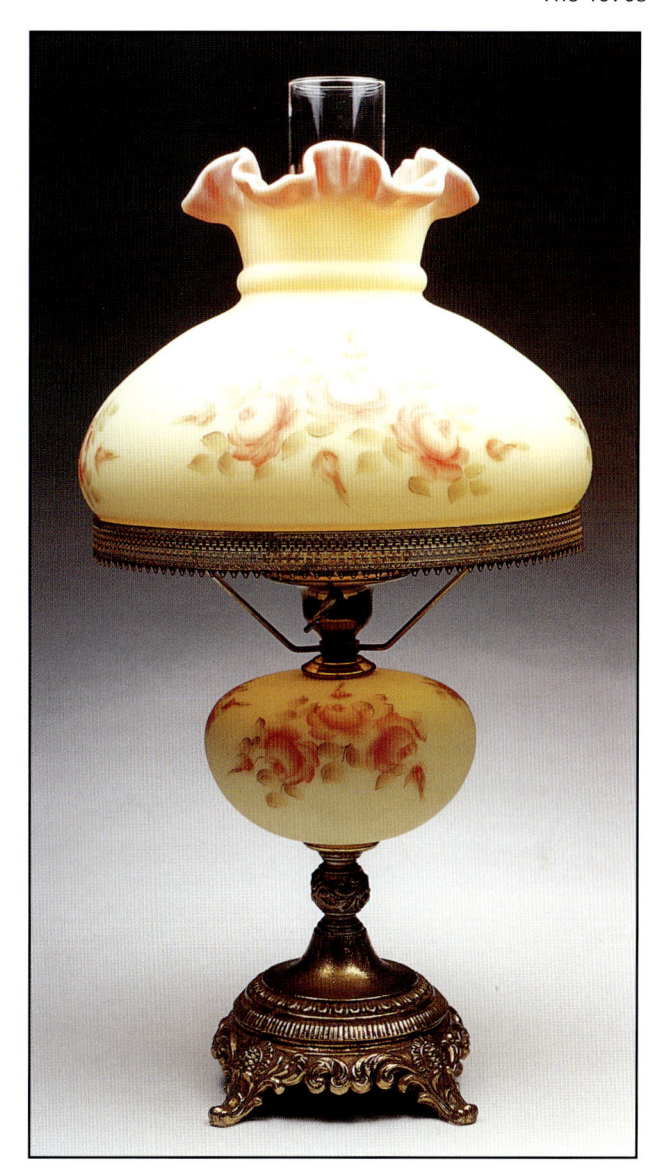

Student lamp #7410RB, hand painted "Rose" decoration, 20.5" overall height, 10" double crimp shade, General Catalog 1971-1979, **$495**

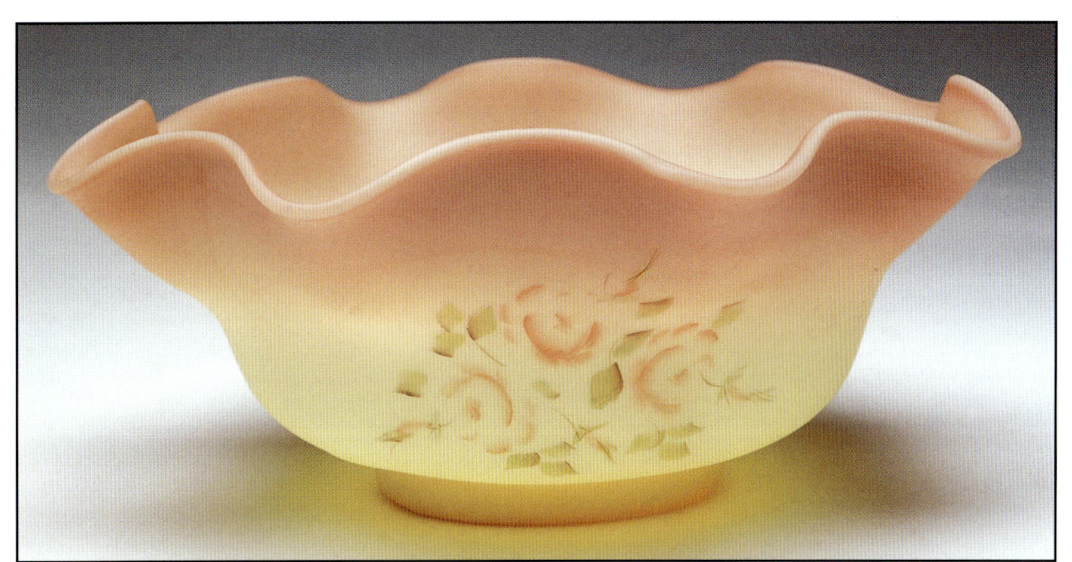

Bowl #7422RB, hand painted "Rose" decoration, 8" wide, single crimp, General Catalog 1971-1976, **$110**

Rose bowl #7424RB, hand painted "Rose" decoration, 3.5" tall, 4" wide, tight single crimp & cupped in, General Catalog 1971-1977, **$75**

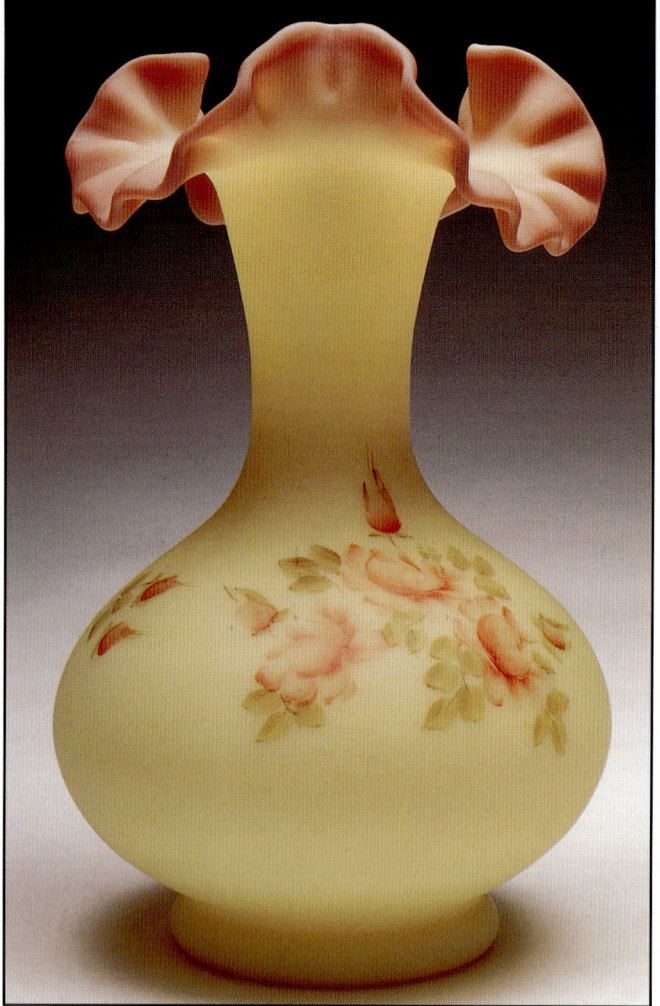

Vase #7459RB, hand painted "Rose" decoration, 8" tall, double crimp General Catalog 1971-1976, **$85**

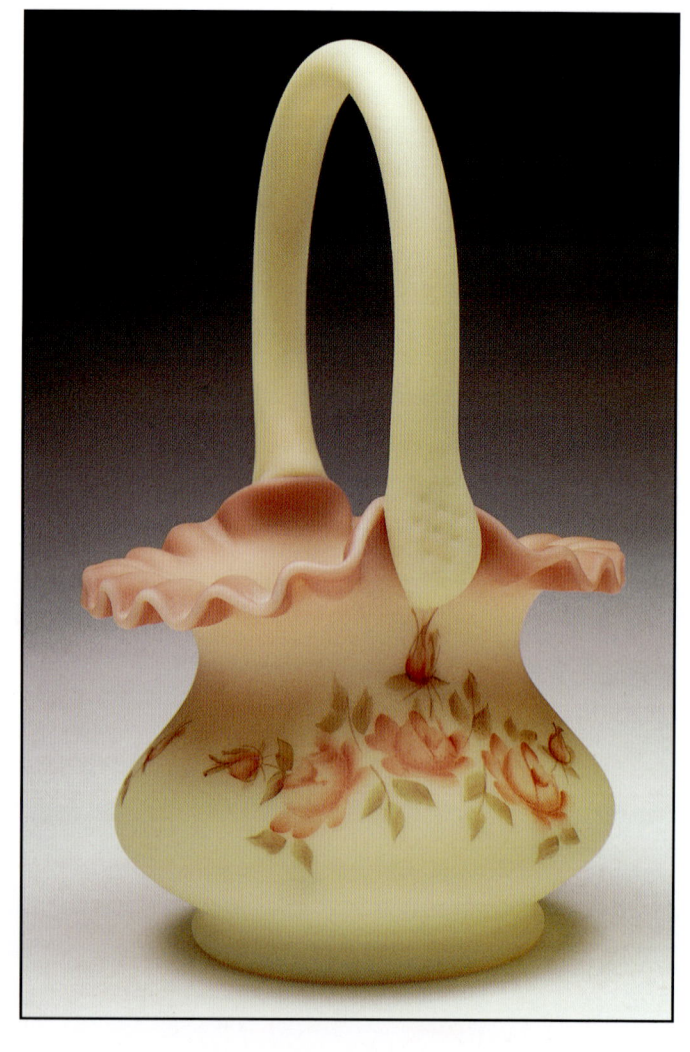

Basket #7437RB, hand painted "Rose" decoration, 7" tall, 4.85" wide, single crimp, General Catalog 1971-1979, **$135**

The 1970s 37

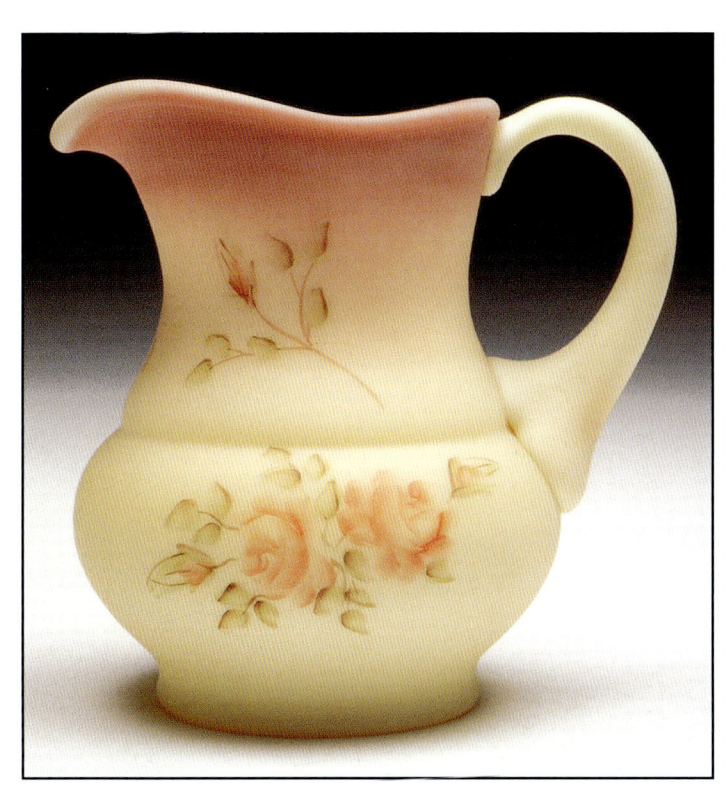

Cream pitcher, 7461RB, hand painted "Rose" decoration, 4.25" tall, 4.25" wide, General Catalog 1971-1976, **$75**

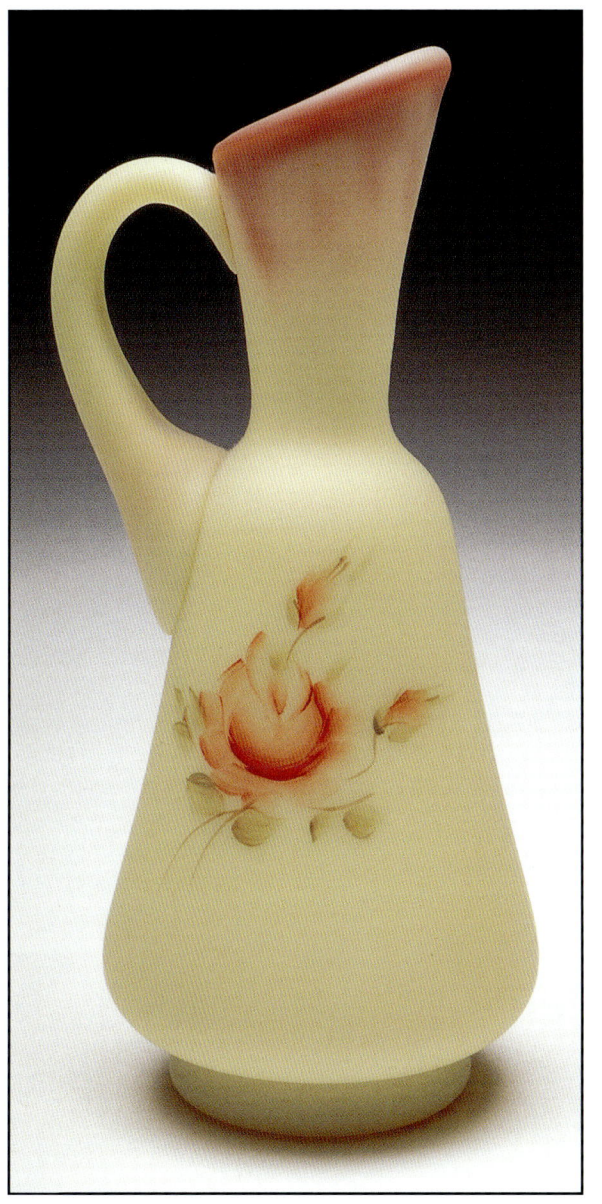

Two piece fairy light #7492RB, hand painted "Rose" decoration, 4.75" tall, 3.15" wide, General Catalog 1971-1977, **$165**

Cruet vase, 7462RB, hand painted "Rose" decoration, 6.35" tall, General Catalog 1971-1973, **$95**

1971

In 1971, eight more undecorated pieces were added along with two additions of Maple Leaf. New this year was the Rose Burmese decoration. Louise Piper, head of the decorating department, developed this design. There was a cluster of roses and rose buds among brown leaves. The decorating department was set up with several new decorators trained to apply hand-painted roses.

The gift shop had a few different decorated items than were used in the catalog. There were also several gloss items.

Vase #7253BE, plain gloss finish, 7" tall, double crimp, From Fenton Gift Shop 1971, **$75**

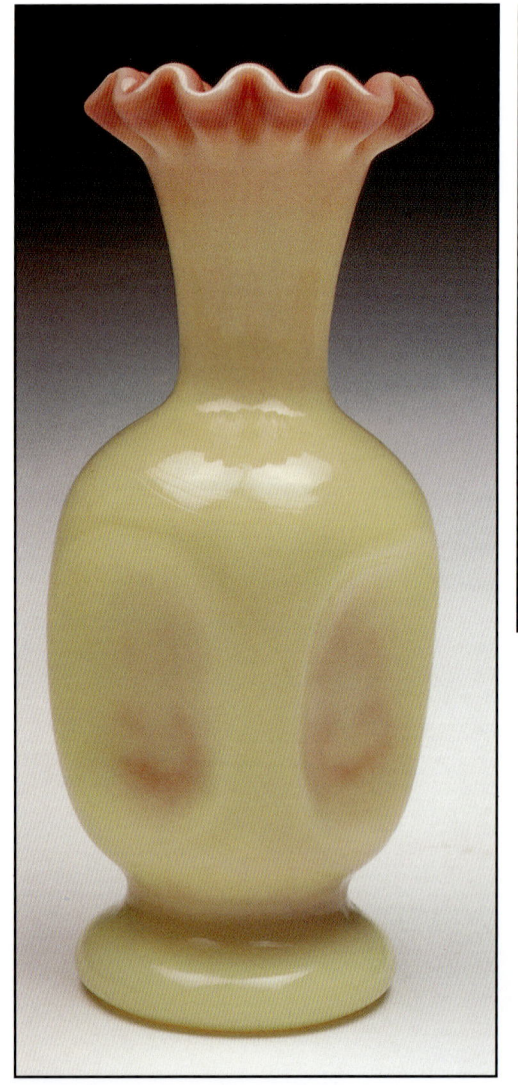

Bowl #7422RB, hand painted "Roses" decoration, 7.5", double crimp & pulled out, Sample from Fenton Gift Shop 1971, **$175**

Pinch vase #7359BE, plain gloss finish, 7.25" tall, tight single crimp, From Fenton Gift Shop 1971-1972, **$60**

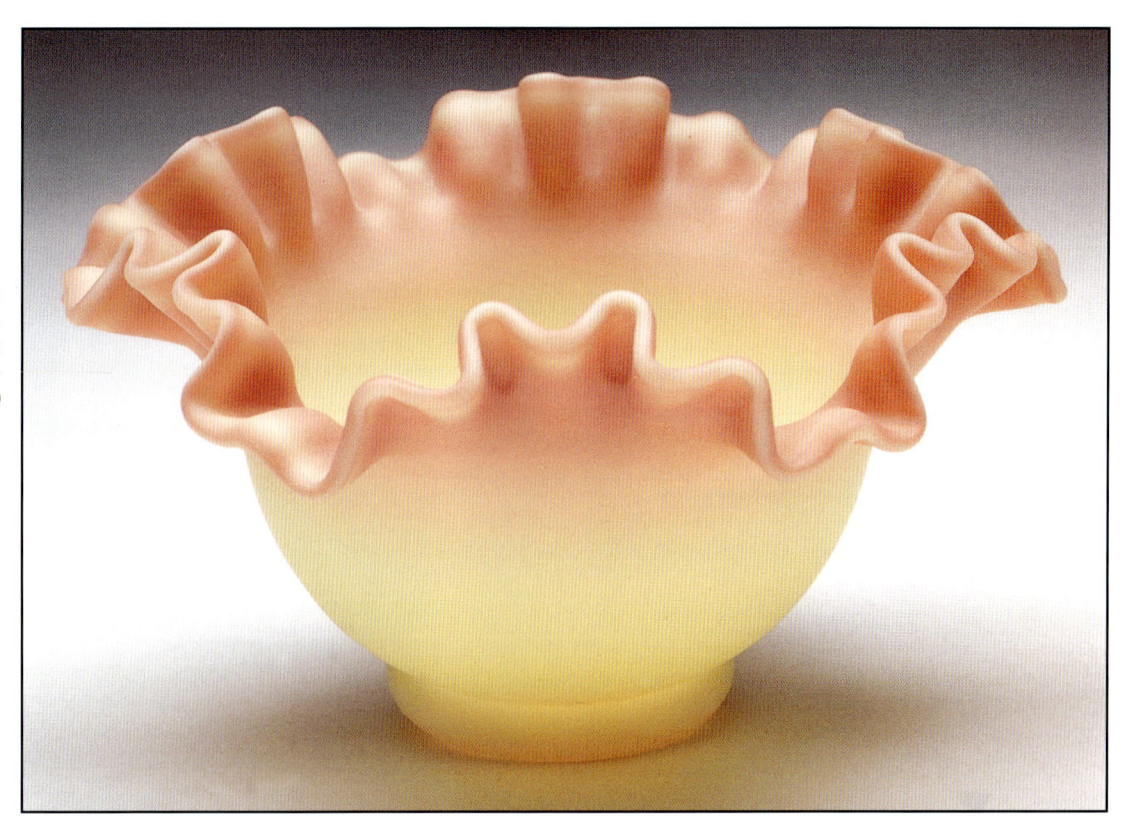

The 1970s 39

Bowl #7422BR, plain satin finish, 7.75", double crimp, From Fenton Gift Shop 1971-1972, **$60**

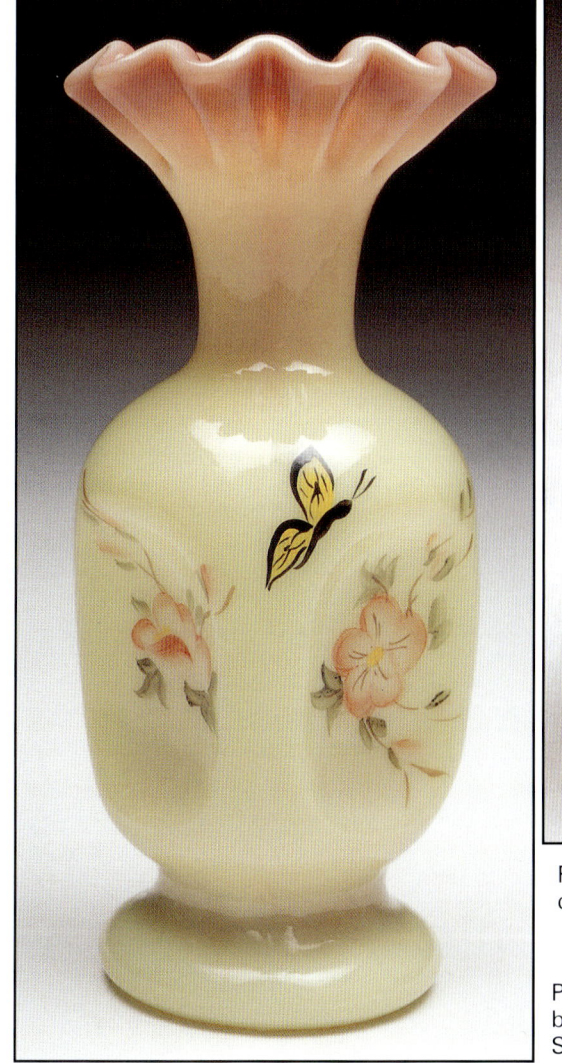

Rose bowl #7424BR, plain satin finish, 3.4" tall, 4" wide, tight ribbon crimp & cupped in, From Fenton Gift Shop 1971, **$95**

Pinch vase #7359, hand painted pink flowers & butterfly (yellow & black), gloss finish, 7" tall, tight single crimp, From Fenton Gift Shop 1971, **$95**

The 1970s

Two piece fairy light #7492BD, decal "Maple Leaf" decoration, 6" tall, 3.15" wide, made from the top part of the one piece fairy light being cut off & set on the bottom of the two piece fairy light, From Fenton Gift Shop 1971, **$195**

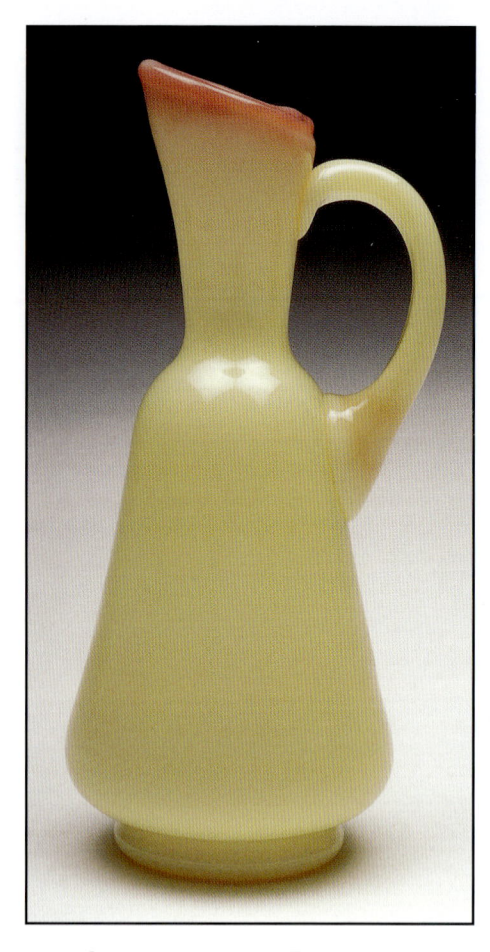

Cruet vase #7462BE, plain gloss finish, 6.35" tall, From Fenton Gift Shop 1971-1974, **$60**

Cruet vase #7462, hand painted orange frit flowers & purple butterfly, 6.35" tall, Decorated by E. Thomas, From Fenton Gift Shop 1971, **$95**

Two piece fairy light #7492BE, plain gloss finish, 5.5" tall, 3.15" wide, From Fenton Gift Shop 1971, **$195**
Note, this one has not been cut apart. The two piece fairy lights are made as one piece of glass and then cut into making the top & bottom.

1972

For 1972, there was only one new Burmese piece offered, the cruet that was painted with roses. The cruet was offered with a plain handle or with a reeded handle.

Cruet #7468RB, hand painted "Rose" decoration, 7.5" tall, General Catalog 1972-1977, **Left**: Plain handle, **$185**; **Right**: Reeded handle, **$195**

1973

The year 1973 saw the addition of three new pieces in the Rose decoration. That year there was a new pattern of decoration called Decorated Burmese in the catalog. This has come to be known as Tree Scene or Scene by collectors. Louise Piper also designed this pattern. The first piece offered was a student lamp.

Detail of 1973 General Catalog, hand painted "Rose" Burmese offering. (Reprinted with permission from the Fenton Art Glass Company)

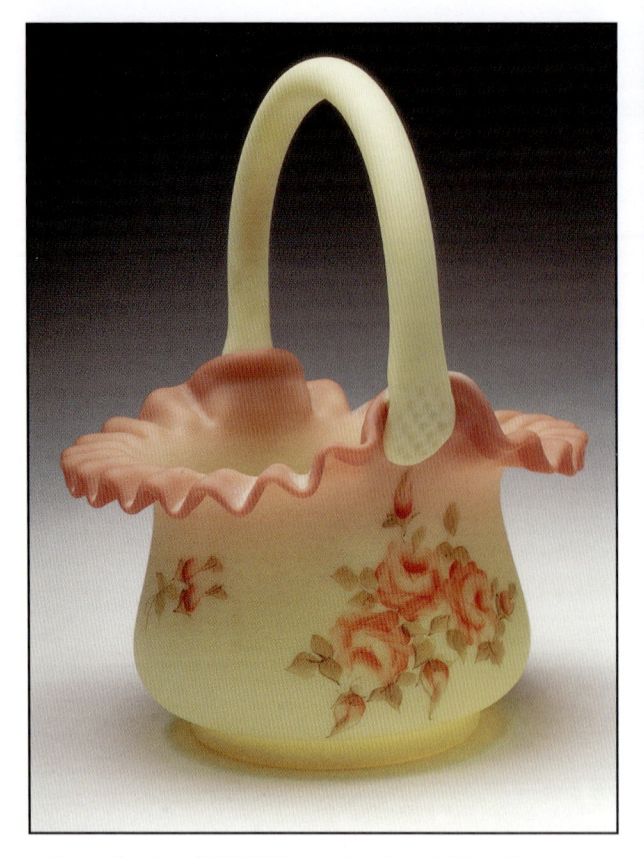

42   The 1970s

Deep basket #7238RB, hand painted "Rose" decoration, 7" tall, 7.35" wide, single crimp, General Catalog 1973-1976, **$275**

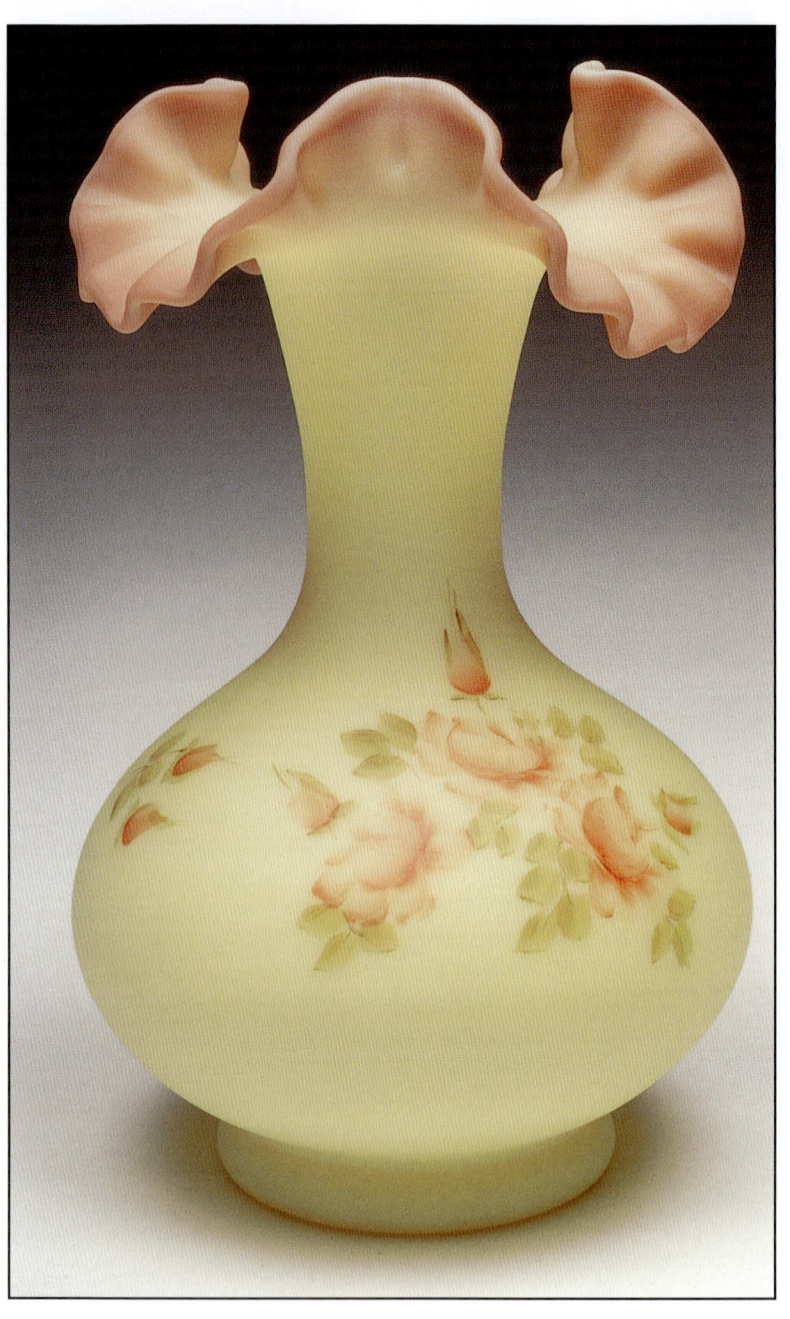

Vase #7251RB, hand painted "Rose" decoration, 11" tall, double crimp, General Catalog 1973-1976, **$165**

Covered candy jar #7284RB, hand painted "Rose" decoration, 7" tall, 5.5" wide, General Catalog 1973, **$275**

Detail of hand painted "Tree Scene" decoration.

The 1970s 43

Student lamp #7411DB, hand painted "Tree Scene" decoration, 21" overall height, 10" double crimp shade, General Catalog 1973-1979, **$595**

The gift shop featured a gloss version of the large vase that had been decorated with roses in the catalog.

Vase #7251BE, plain gloss finish, 10.5" tall, double crimp, From Fenton Gift Shop 1973-1976, **$125**

1974

For 1974, four new pieces of Scene were added to the general catalog.

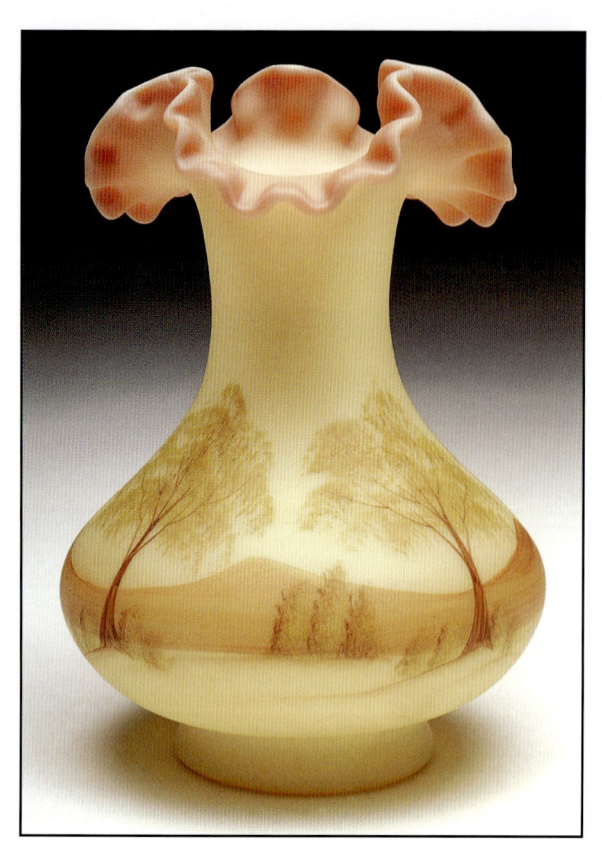

Vase #7252DB, hand painted "Tree Scene" decoration, 7" tall, double crimp, General Catalog 1974-1979, **$125**

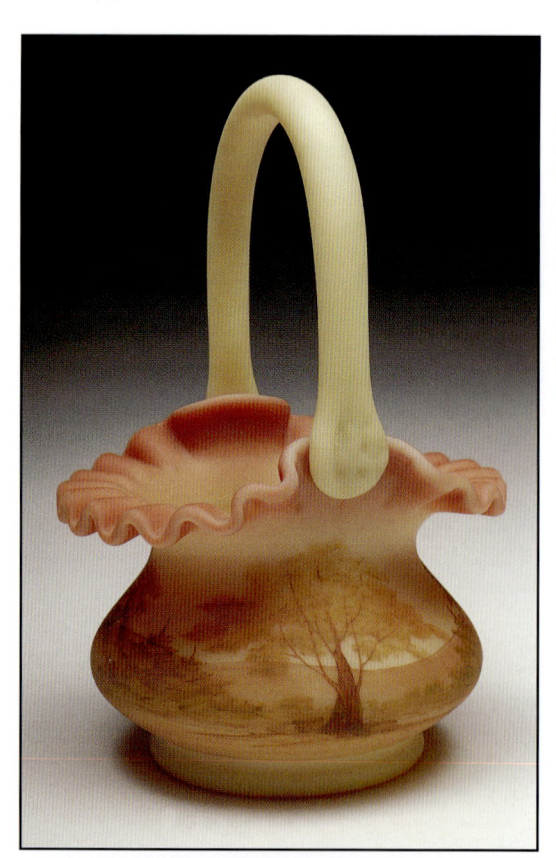

Basket #7437DB, hand painted, "Tree Scene" decoration, 7.5" tall, 5.15" wide, single crimp, General Catalog 1974-1979, **$165**

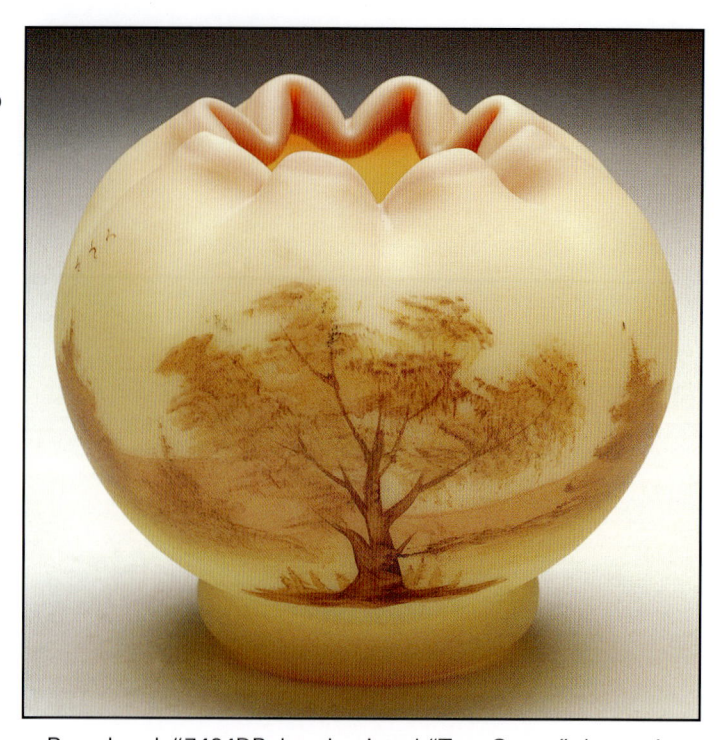

Rose bowl #7424DB, hand painted "Tree Scene" decoration, 4" tall, 4" wide, tight single crimp & cupped in, General Catalog 1974-1978, **$85**

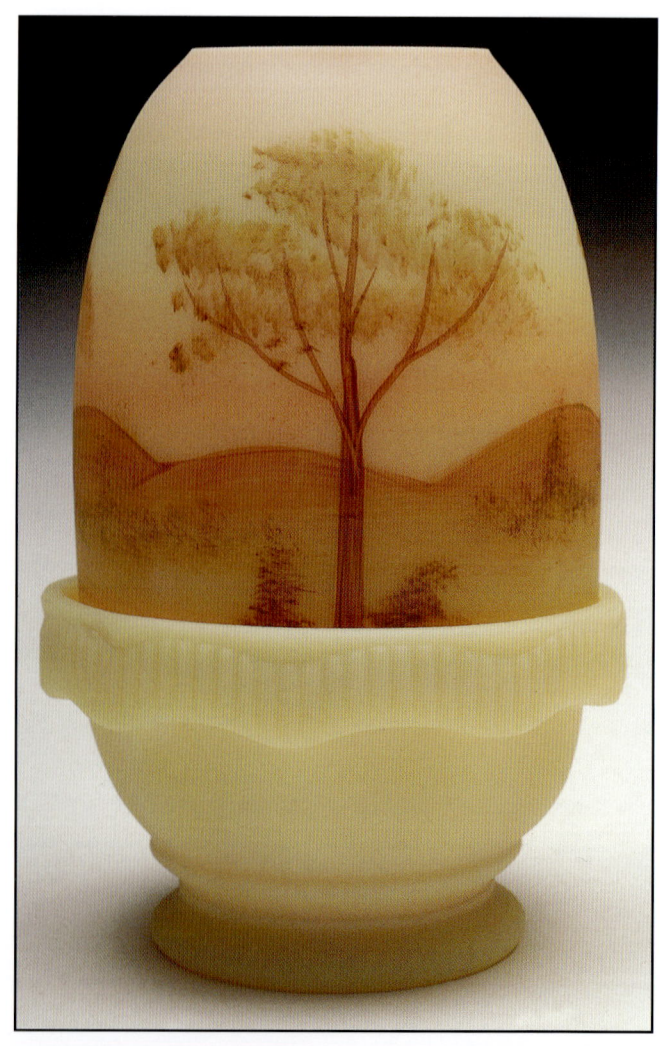

Two piece fairy light #7492DB, hand painted "Tree Scene" decoration, 4.75" tall, 3.15" wide, General Catalog 1974-1977, **$165**

1975

In 1975 there was only one new piece of Scene, the 4" vase. Also that year a new two-piece epergne and a 4" vase were added to the Rose line.

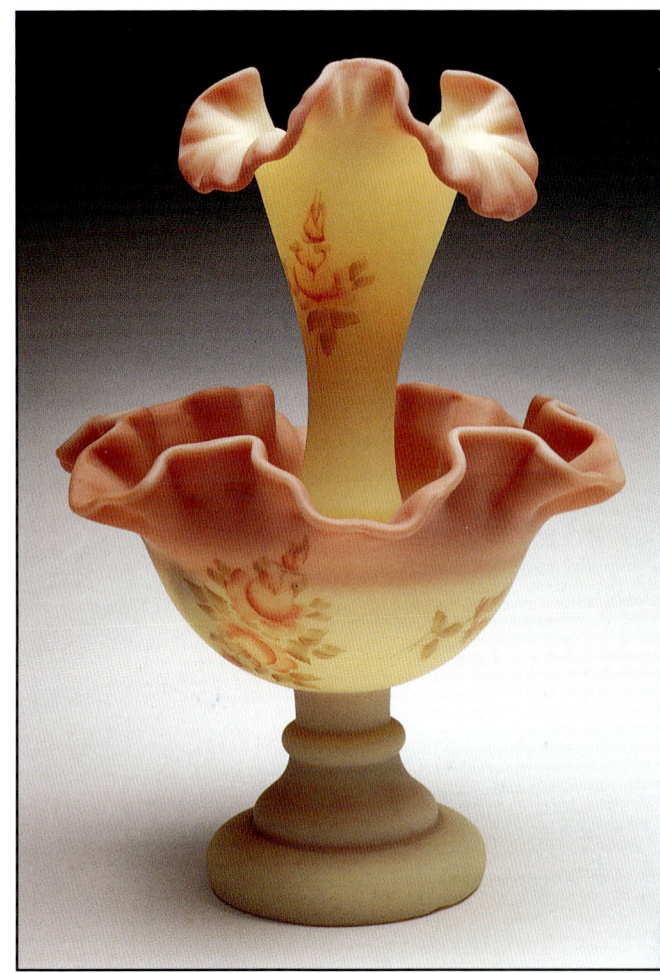

Vase #7457RB, hand painted "Rose" decoration, 5" tall, double crimp, General Catalog 1975-1979, **$65**

Single horn footed epergne #7202RB, hand painted "Rose" decoration, 9.5" tall, 7" wide, double crimp, General Catalog 1975, **$275**

Vase #7457DB, hand painted "Tree Scene" decoration, 4" tall, double crimp, General Catalog 1975-1979, **$85**

46 The 1970s

1976

Even though several pieces were continued for 1976, there were no new pieces offered.

1977

In 1977, two former Verlys moulds, the Mandarin and Empress vases, were used for the first time in Burmese. Two lamps completed the Burmese offering for this year. Rose pieces also came back in full production with two vases and a student lamp.

Detail of 1977 General Catalog, Burmese offering. (Reprinted with permission from the Fenton Art Glass Company).

Vase #8251BR, embossed "Mandarin" plain satin finish, 9.25" tall, General Catalog 1977, **$165**

Vase #8252BR, embossed "Empress" plain satin finish, 7.4" tall, General Catalog 1977, **$165**

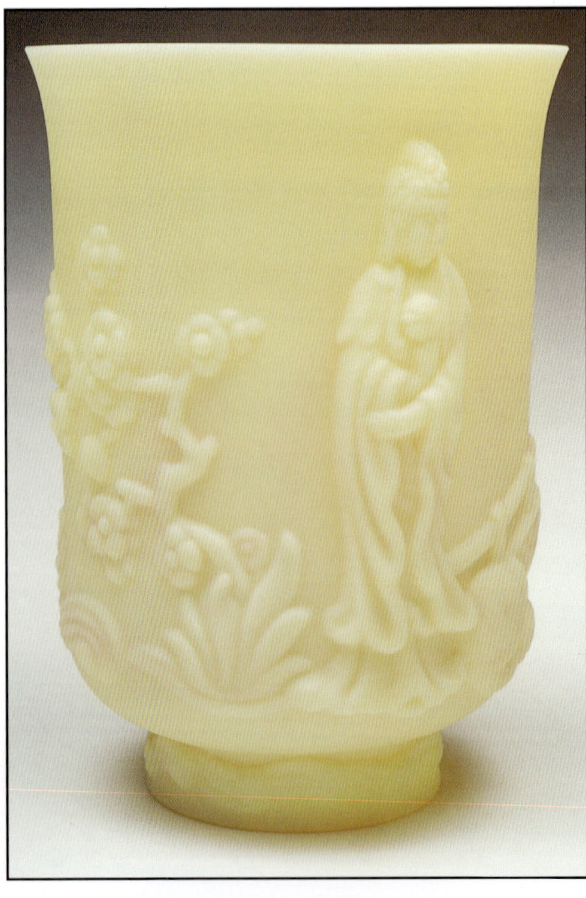

Opposite page, bottom left: Detail comparison of variations in the painting on this decoration. Tulip vase #7255RB, hand painted "Rose" decoration, front view, **Left:** Three roses 10.25" tall; **Right:** Two roses, 10" tall

Opposite page, bottom right: Detail comparison of variations in the painting on this decoration. Tulip vase #7255RB, hand painted "Rose" decoration, back side view, **Left:** Two roses on back 10.25" tall; **Right:** One rose on back, 10" tall

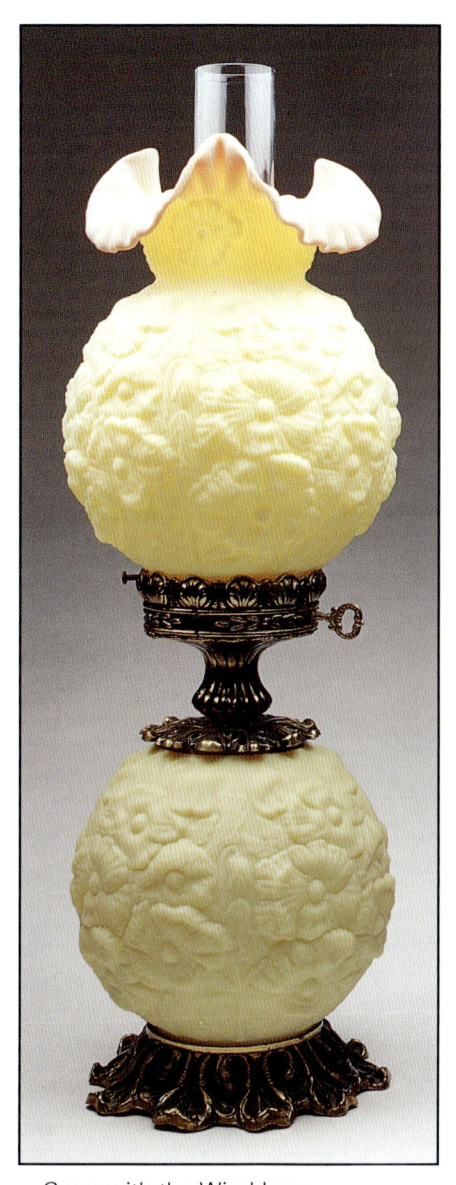

The 1970s   47

Gone with the Wind lamp #9101BR, "Embossed Poppy" pattern, plain satin finish, 23.25" overall height, 10" double crimp ball shade, General Catalog 1977-1981, **$850**

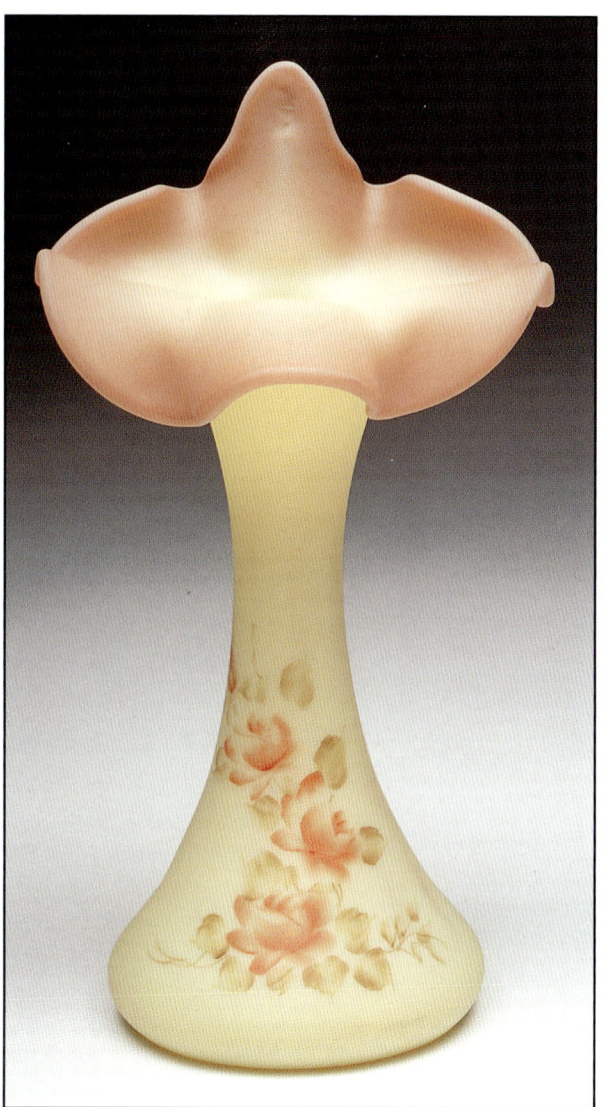

Tulip vase #7255RB, hand painted "Rose" decoration, 10" tall, General Catalog 1977-1980, **$165** Note, also called a Jack In The Pulpit vase.

Gone with the Wind lamp #9200BR, "Embossed Roses" pattern, plain satin finish, 23.25" overall height, 10" double crimp ball shade, General Catalog 1977-1981, **$850** **Note**, this is the almost the same lamp as offered in 1971-1973, but has a short brass base, this time.

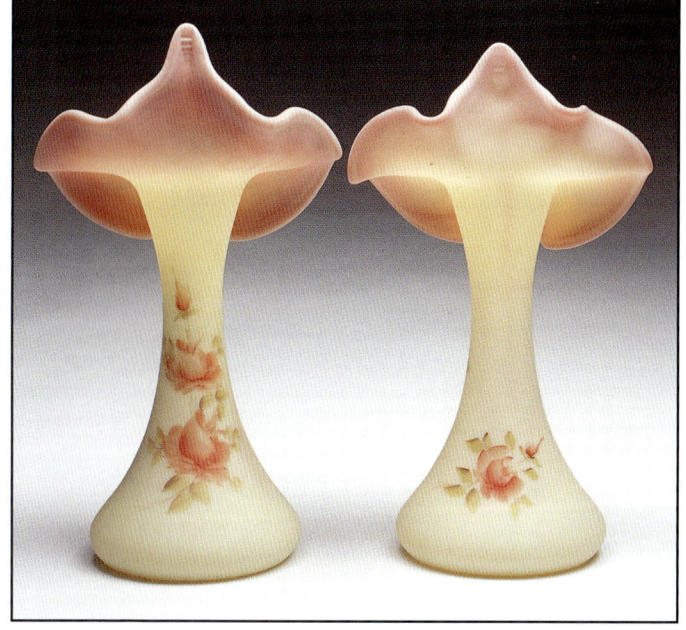

48   The 1970s

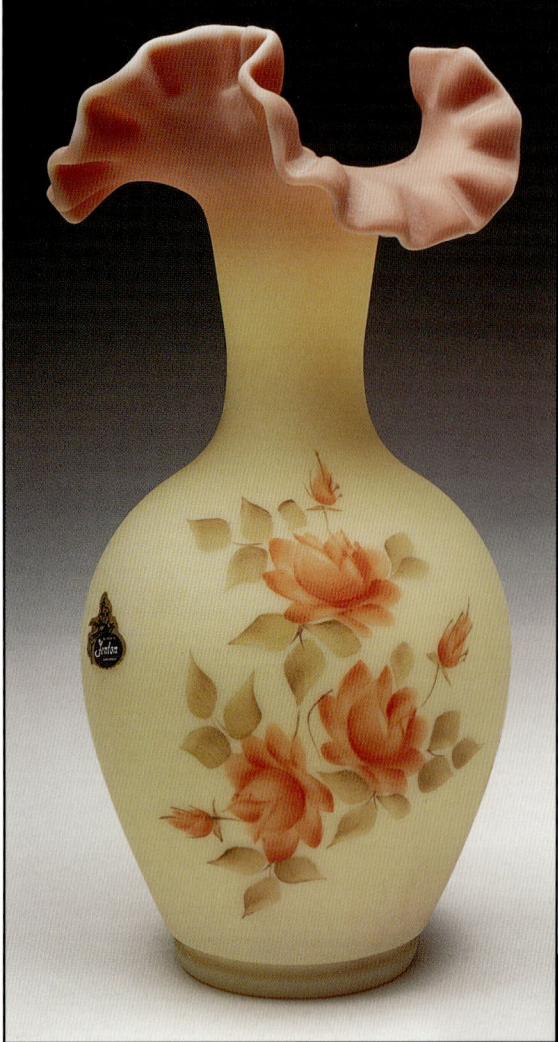

Vase #7257RB, hand painted "Rose" decoration, 10" tall, double crimp, General Catalog 1977-1979, **$125**

The gloss version of the tulip vase was found in the gift shop.

Student lamp #9306RB, hand painted "Rose" decoration, 20" overall height, 7" double crimp shade, General Catalog 1977, **$495**

Tulip vase #7255BE, plain gloss finish, 10" tall, From Fenton Gift Shop 1977, **$95**
Note, also called a Jack In The Pulpit vase.

The 1970s 49

In 1977, for the first time, some pieces were decorated for special orders when Fenton was contacted by the Frederick and Nelson department store of Seattle, Washington. Shapes of Burmese already in production were utilized to develop a special offering for sale in their stores. Louise Piper designed the Pink Butterflies pattern. This unique decoration showed butterflies hovering on a bush.

Detail of hand painted "Pink Butterflies" decoration.

Vase #7252, hand painted "Pink Butterflies" decoration, 7" tall, double crimp, Special order made exclusively for Frederick & Nelson Company of Seattle, Washington 1977, **$195**

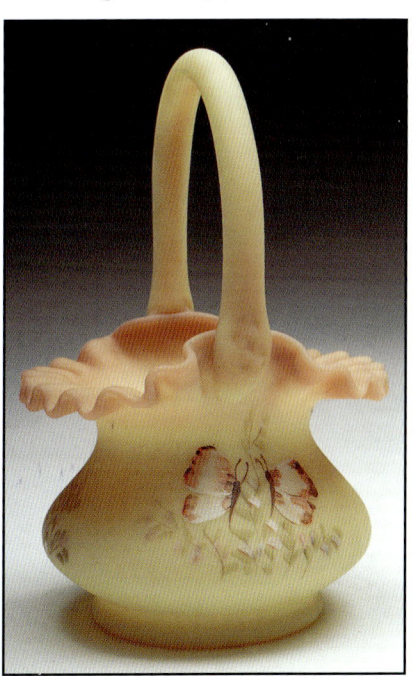

Basket #7437, hand painted "Pink Butterflies" decoration, 7.5" tall, 5" wide, single crimp, signed Louise Piper, Special order made exclusively for Frederick & Nelson Company of Seattle, Washington 1977, **$275**

Rose bowl #7424, hand painted "Pink Butterflies" decoration, 4" tall, 4" wide, tight single crimp & cupped in, Special order made exclusively for Frederick & Nelson Company of Seattle, Washington 1977, **$150**

Student Lamp #9306, hand painted "Pink Butterflies" decoration, 20" overall height, 10" double crimp shade, Special order made exclusively for Frederick & Nelson Company of Seattle, Washington 1977, **$895**

The 1970s

Fenton also made a special offering for the Levay Company of Illinois. Once again, pieces in the line were also used but with a purple violet decoration. Gary Levi, founder of the company, said he loved the Violets in the Snow decoration and thought the violet color would compliment the Burmese very well. The five-piece set was limited to 1000 sets of a basket, cruet, fairy light, rose bowl, and vase. It was decided to include both a cruet and fairy light in the set since these are highly desired by collectors. The other pieces were from shapes already being used that year. The violet decoration had previously been designed by Louise Piper.

Detail of hand painted "Violets" decoration.

Rose bowl #7424BV, hand painted "Violets" decoration, 3" tall, 4" wide, tight single crimp & cupped in, Limited to 1000, Special order made exclusively for Levay 1978, **$95**

Group of entire "Violets" offering, Special order made exclusively for Levay 1978. Back left: Basket #7437BV, 7" tall, 5" wide, **$195**; Back center: Vase #7252BV, 7" tall, **$145**; Back center right: Cruet #7468BV, 7.5" tall, **$300**; Back Right: Fairy Light #7492BV, 4.75" tall, **$225**; Front: Rose bowl, #7424BV, 3" tall, **$95**

1978

Nothing new for the Fenton Burmese line was offered in 1978.

1979

To the Rose line two vases were added in 1979. A Rose bell was sold in the Fenton gift shop rather than in the general catalog. This was the last new piece of Burmese glass to offered in the catalog for a couple of years, even though remaining stock continued to be sold.

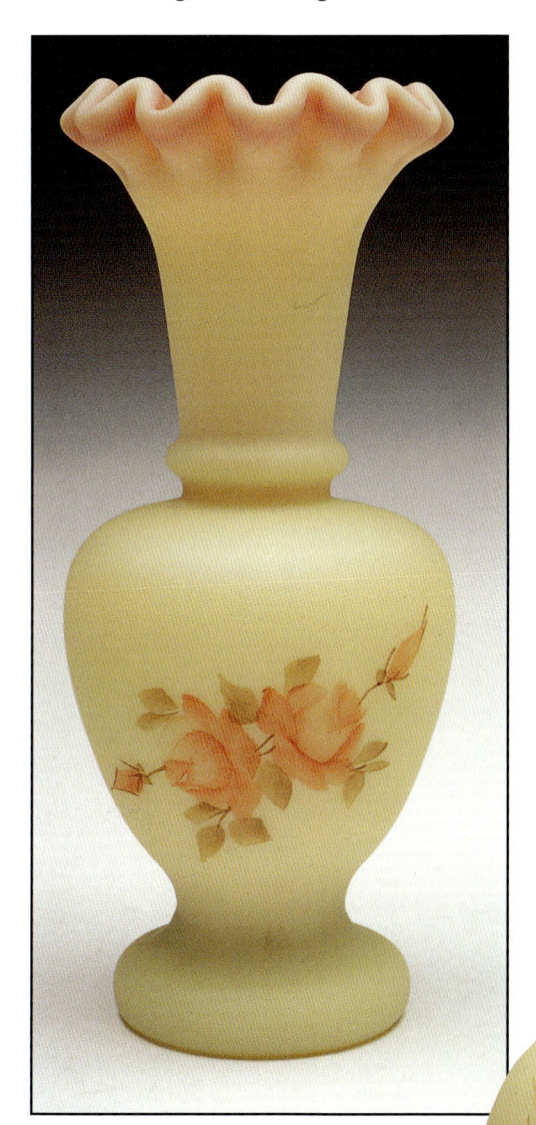

Vase #7460RB, hand painted "Rose" decoration, 6.5" tall, double crimp, General Catalog 1979, **$85**

Bud vase #7348RB, hand painted "Rose" decoration, 6" tall, single crimp, General Catalog 1979-1980, **$65**

Bell #7564RB, hand painted "Rose" decoration, 6" tall, Sample piece from Fenton Gift Shop 1979, **$85**

52   The 1970s

A Special Order was made as a retirement gift for Dr. Fischer, the Fenton plant psychologist, who enjoyed frogs. Fenton decorators Dianna Barbour, Jeanne Brown, Day Haught, and Nancy Gribble joined Louise Piper in decorating a lamp with a swamp scene. Each of the decorators created a special creature on this lamp: a frog striking a fly, a crocodile, a turtle, and a heron and dragonfly. The company acquired the lamp back at Dr. Fischer's estate auction sale.

Another special order was made for Levay in 1979, an undecorated line. Fenton pulled out the moulds for the Wild Rose and Bowknot line because Gary Levi, the company's owner, liked this pattern. These moulds were last used in the early 1960s. Four pieces in this pattern were made in both gloss and satin finish.

Detail of original ad for the Levay "Historic Burmese" collection, embossed "Wild Rose & Bowknot" pattern. (Reprinted with permission from Gary Levi)

Student lamp #7412, Swamp scene with hand painted frog & bird decoration, 20" overall height, 10" double crimp shade, September 1979, Special order for Dr. Fischer's retirement, Value Not determined

Basket #2834BE, embossed "Wild Rose & Bowknot" pattern, plain gloss finish, 9.25" tall, double crimp, Special order made exclusively for Levay 1979, **$145**

The 1970s 53

Rose bowl #2824, embossed "Wild Rose & Bowknot" pattern, plain, 4.75" tall, tight single crimp & cupped in, Special order made exclusively for Levay 1979, **Left**: Gloss finish #2824BE, **$75**; **Right**: Satin finish #2824BR, **$85**

Tulip vase #2854BE, embossed "Wild Rose & Bowknot" pattern, plain gloss finish, 8.3" tall, single crimp, Special order made exclusively for Levay 1979, **$110** Note, also called a Jack In The Pulpit vase.

Vase #2857, embossed "Wild Rose & Bowknot" pattern 7.6" tall, double crimp, Special order made exclusively for Levay 1979,
Left: Satin finish, 2857BR, **$85**; **Right**: Gloss finish, 2857BE, **$75**

The 1980s

This decade also saw Fenton's Burmese glass used in different ways. Burmese was finally brought back as a full line. Changes were being made to the Burmese formula to also allow it to be pressed. The shading was also softened, to be less intense. Many old carnival moulds were now being used in Burmese production. The Connoisseur Collection also made its debut during this decade and the QVC television program brought Fenton glass to the attention of many new collectors.

1981

The Pink Dogwood pattern was designed by Diane Johnson and debuted in 1981. This pattern featured pastel pink dogwood flowers with brown stems. The Dogwood line had 14 pieces and most were offered for two years.

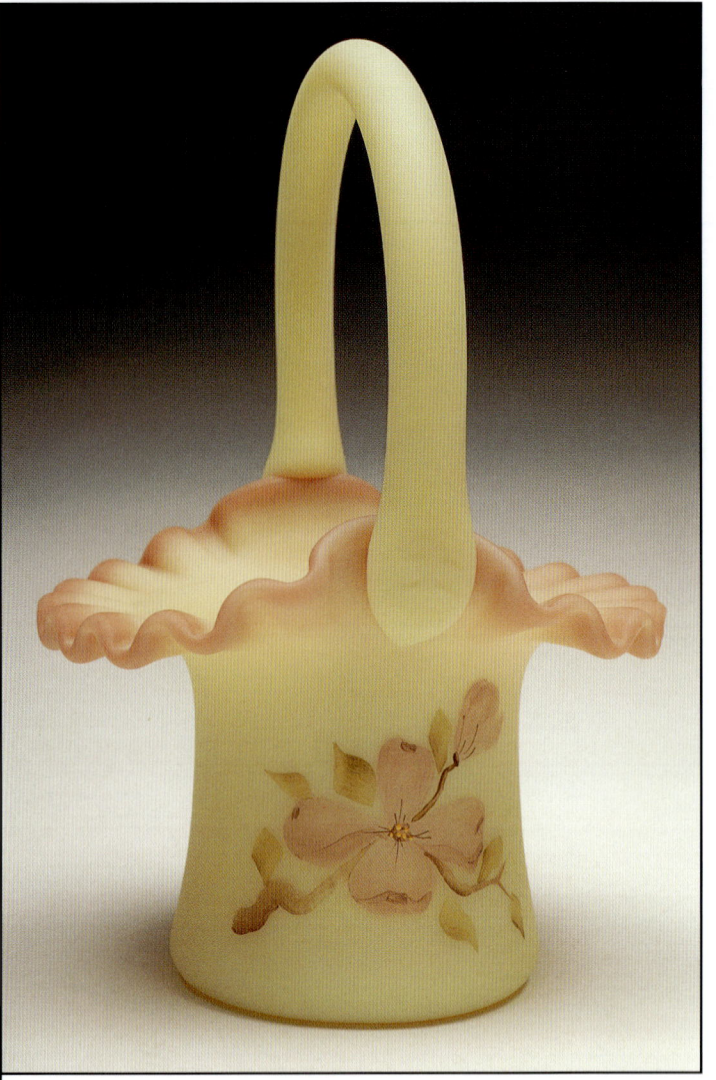

Hat basket #7235PD, hand painted "Pink Dogwood" decoration, 6.6" tall, 4.5" wide, single crimp, General Catalog 1981-1982, **$115**

Hat vase #7442PD, hand painted "Pink Dogwood" decoration, 3.75" tall, double crimp, General Catalog 1981-1982, **$65**

Detail of hand painted "Pink Dogwood" decoration.

The 1980s   55

Tulip vase #7255PD, hand painted "Pink Dogwood" decoration, 10.75" tall, General Catalog 1981-1982, **$165**
Note, also called a Jack In The Pulpit vase.

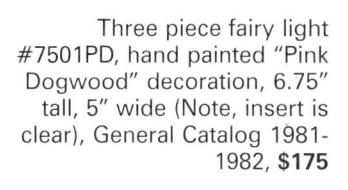

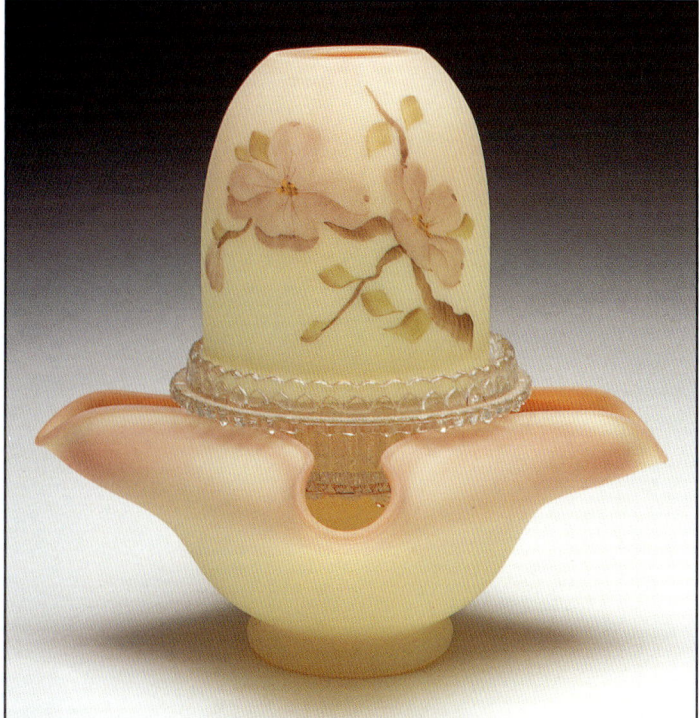

Student lamp #7503PD, hand painted "Pink Dogwood" decoration, 21" overall height, 7" double crimp shade, General Catalog 1981, **$495**

Three piece fairy light #7501PD, hand painted "Pink Dogwood" decoration, 6.75" tall, 5" wide (Note, insert is clear), General Catalog 1981-1982, **$175**

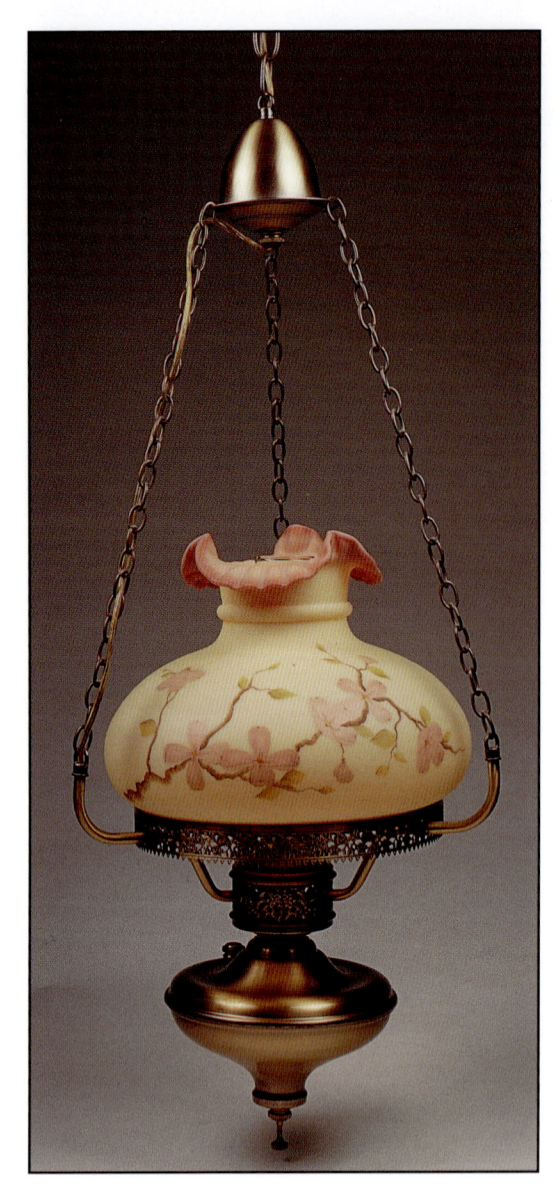

56   The 1980s

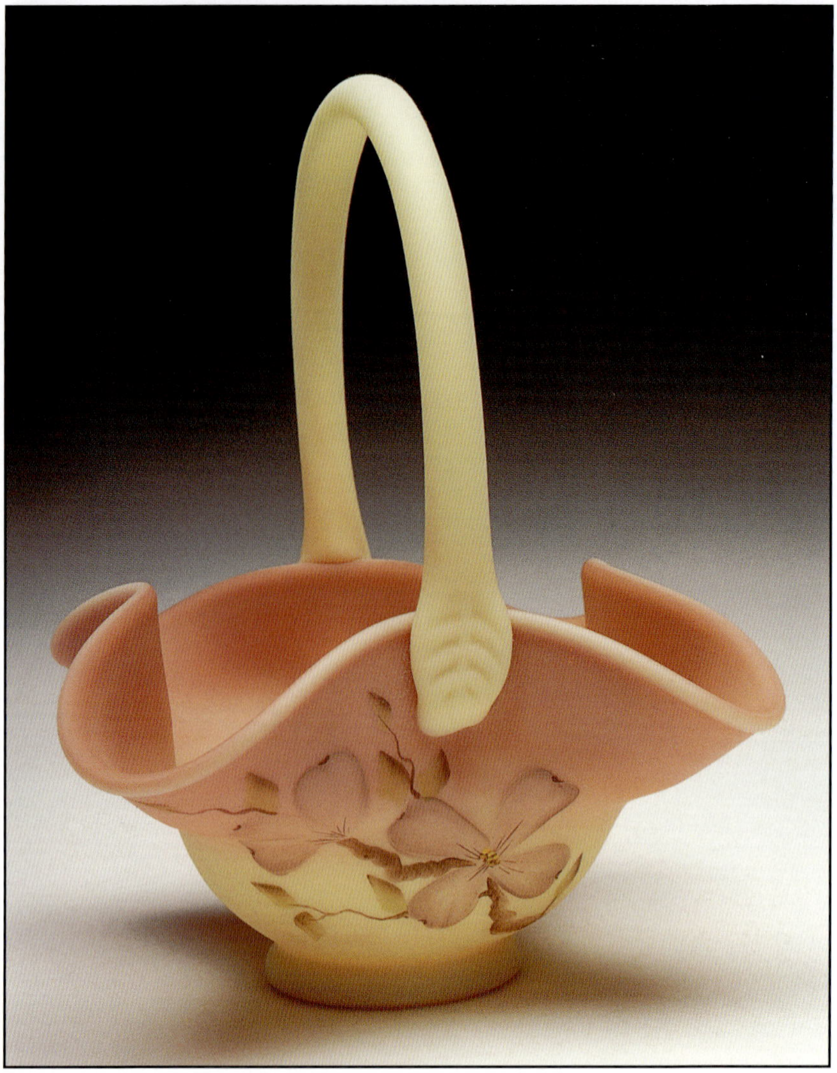

Basket #7535PD, hand painted "Pink Dogwood" decoration, 8" tall, 7.25" wide, single square crimp, General Catalog 1981-1982, **$125**

Hanging lamp #7506PD, hand painted "Pink Dogwood" decoration, 20" overall height, 10" double crimp shade, General Catalog 1981, **$650**

Vase #7546PD, hand painted "Pink Dogwood" decoration, 3.6" tall, double crimp, General Catalog 1981-1982, **$65**

The 1980s 57

Vase #7547PD, hand painted "Pink Dogwood" decoration, 4.8" tall, double crimp, General Catalog 1981-1982, **$80**

Bud vase #7558PD, hand painted "Pink Dogwood" decoration, 6" tall, General Catalog 1981-1982, **$65**

Tulip vase #7552PD, hand painted "Pink Dogwood" decoration, 6.25" tall, General Catalog 1981-1982, **$110**
Note, also called a Jack In The Pulpit vase.

58   The 1980s

Vase #7559PD, hand painted "Pink Dogwood" decoration, 7.5" tall, General Catalog 1981-1982, **$80**

Vase #7560PD, hand painted "Pink Dogwood" decoration, 6.75" tall, General Catalog 1981-1982, **$110**

Column lamp #9301PD, hand painted "Pink Dogwood" decoration, 19.25" overall height, 7" double crimp shade, General Catalog 1981, **$395**

The 1980s 59

A few sample Dogwood designs showed up in the gift shop. The Violet design was used on pieces for the gift shop.

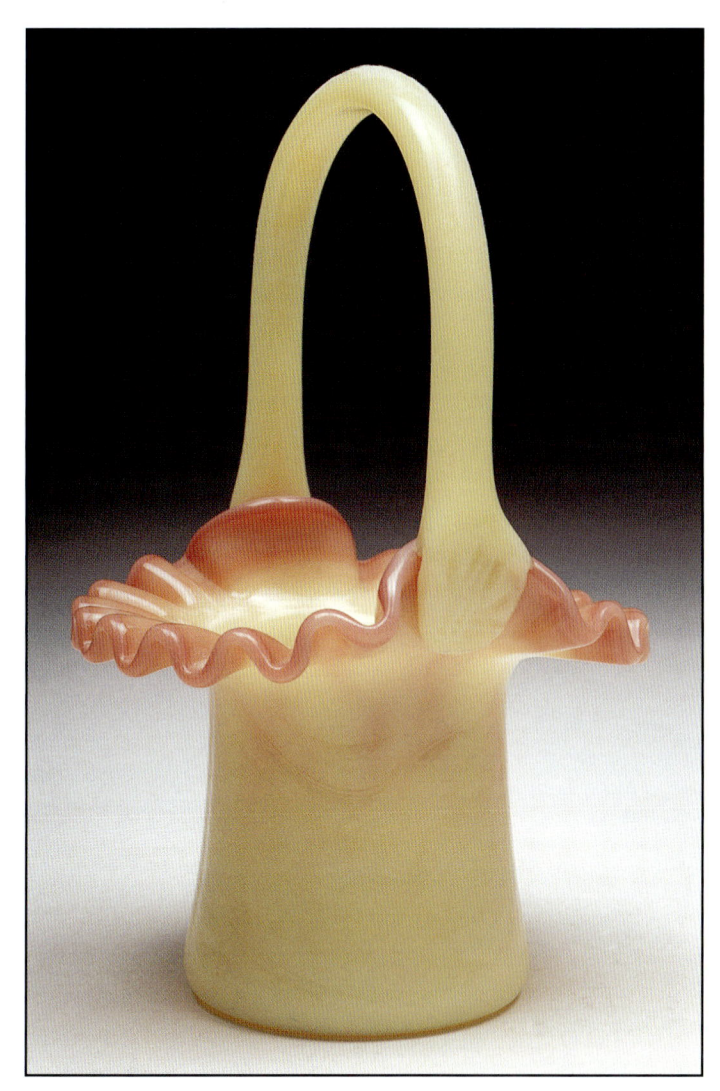

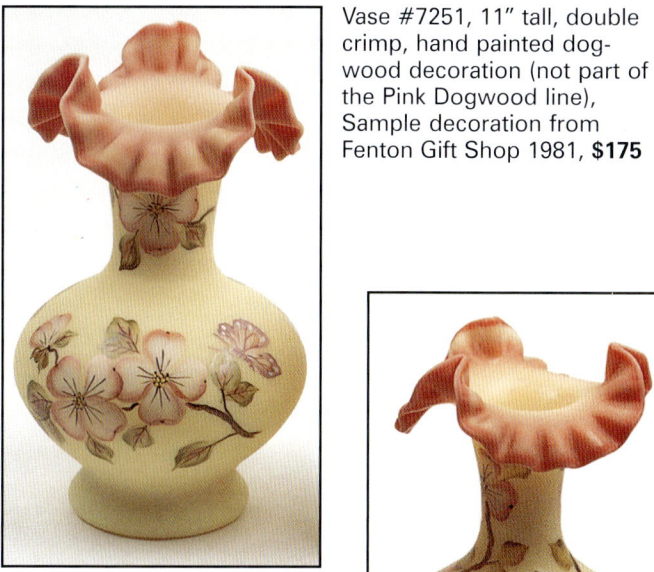

Vase #7251, 11" tall, double crimp, hand painted dogwood decoration (not part of the Pink Dogwood line), Sample decoration from Fenton Gift Shop 1981, **$175**

Vase #7459, 8" tall, double crimp, hand painted dogwood decoration (not part of the Pink Dogwood line), Sample decoration from Fenton Gift Shop 1981, **$125** Note, blue butterfly on vase.

Vase #7252, 7" tall, double crimp, hand painted dogwood decoration (not part of the Pink Dogwood line), Sample decoration from Fenton Gift Shop 1981, **$125**

Hat basket #7235BE, plain gloss finish, 6.75" tall, 4.25" wide, single crimp, From Fenton Gift Shop 1981-1982, **$75**

Creamer #7461, 4.25" tall, 4.25" wide, hand painted dogwood decoration (not part of the Pink Dogwood line), Sample decoration from Fenton Gift Shop 1981, **$85**

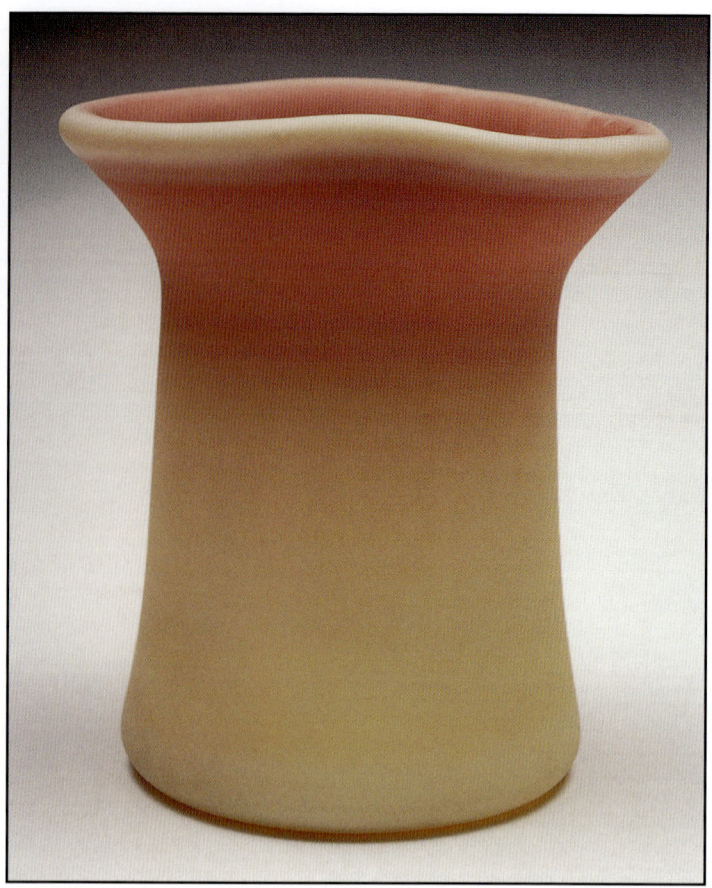

60   The 1980s

Tulip vase #7255BR, plain satin finish, 10.75" tall, From Fenton Gift Shop 1981-1982, **$85**
Note, also called a Jack In The Pulpit vase.

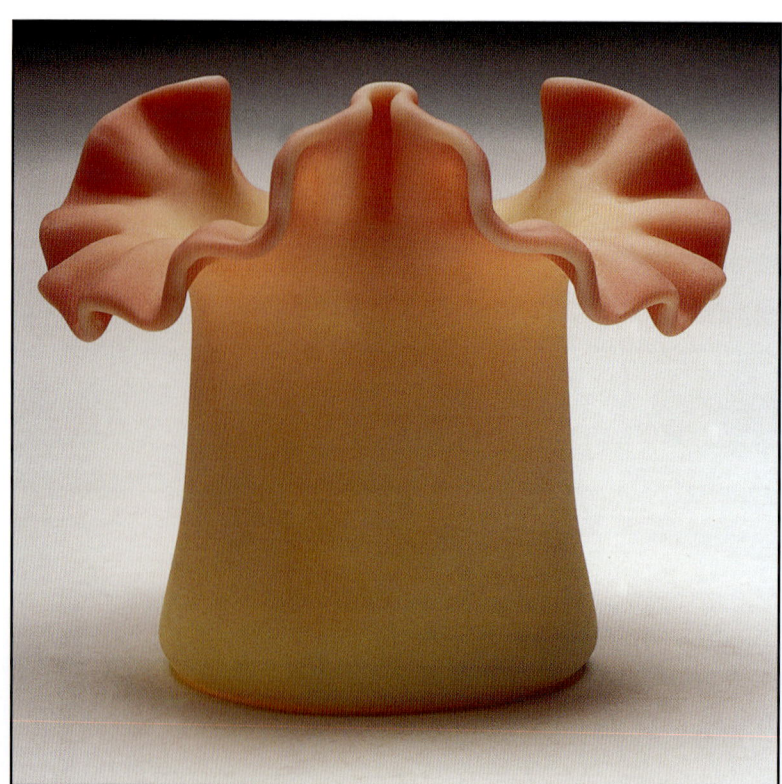

Hat vase #7442BR, 3.75" tall, plain satin finish, slightly flared top, From Fenton Gift Shop 1981-1982, **$50**
Note, this piece was never finished off & is probably a second quality item.

Hat vase #7442BR, plain satin finish, 3.5" tall, double crimp, From Fenton Gift Shop 1981, **$45**

The 1980s 61

Hat vase #7442, hand painted dogwood decoration (not part of the Pink Dogwood line), gloss finish, 3.5" tall, double crimp, From Fenton Gift Shop 1981, **$65**

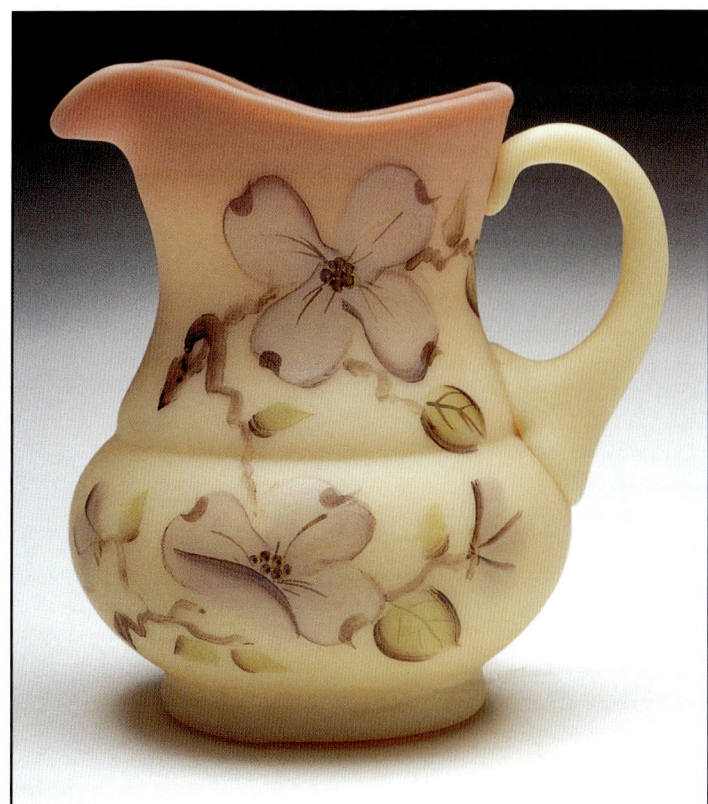

Cream pitcher #7461, hand painted brown dogwood decoration (not part of the Pink Dogwood line), 4.4" tall, 4.25" wide, From Fenton Gift Shop 1981-1982, **$75**

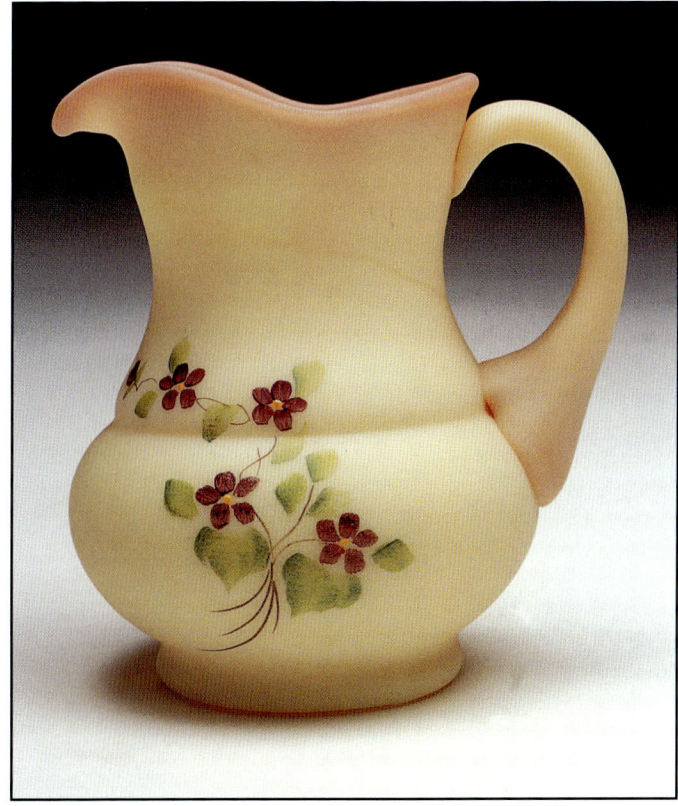

Cream pitcher #7461VB, hand painted violets (not part of Levay "Violets" line), 4.4" tall, 4.25" wide, From Fenton Gift Shop 1981, **$75**

62   The 1980s

Three piece fairy light #7501, 6.75" tall, 5" wide (Note, insert is clear), From Fenton Gift Shop 1981-1982,
Left: Satin finish #7501BR, **$145**; **Right:** Gloss finish #7501BE, **$135**

Three piece fairy light #7501VB, hand painted violets decoration (not part of Levay "Violets" line), 6.75" tall, 5" wide (Note, insert is clear), Decorated by S. (Sue) Lee, From Fenton Gift Shop 1981, **$195**

The 1980s 63

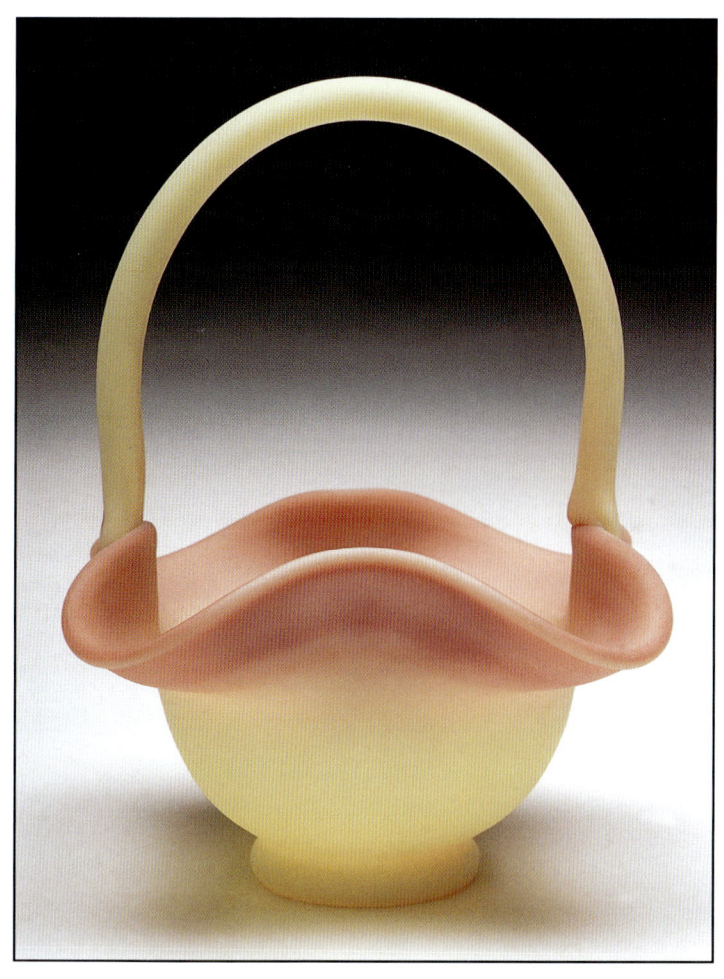

Basket #7535BR, plain satin finish, 8" tall, 7.25" wide, single square crimp, From Fenton Gift Shop 1981, **$85**

Basket #7535BR, plain satin finish, 7" tall, 4.5" wide, unusual plain edge (no crimp treatment), From Fenton Gift Shop 1981, **$135**

Vase #7547BE, plain gloss finish, 4.8" tall, tight ribbon double crimp, From Fenton Gift Shop 1981, **$75**

Doris Lechler, author of reference books on children's dishes, contacted Fenton to produce a series of children's dishes. Lechler's Heirlooms of Tomorrow were mainly children's water sets made in a variety of colors that were limited to 500. Only one set was made in Burmese. The set consisted of a ruffled top miniature water pitcher with six tumblers. This set came out in 1981 and had the Rose pattern on it.

Miniature set #7368RB, hand painted "Rose" decoration, pitcher & tumblers, Limited to 500 sets, Special order made exclusively for Doris Lechler 1981, **$345 set**

The Fenton gift shop featured the bud vase that was used in the Walrath line. The vase was found in satin, gloss and with a crimped top.

Bud Vase #7558, plain, 6" tall, From Fenton Gift Shop 1982, **Left**: Gloss finish, tight ribbon single crimped, **$60**; **Center**: Satin finish, flared top, **$55**; **Right**: Gloss finish, flared top, **$50**

1982

One of the most interesting and certainly inspirational stories about a Burmese offering came in 1982. Mary shared with me her complete story on how her offering of Love Bouquet came into existence.

Mary Walrath at the time was dealing with a spiritual family crisis in her family. She prayed for a direction to take to reach those in need of guidance and felt God was calling her to assist him in his work. After several months of not knowing what to do, she still felt the urge to develop something that would have a special feeling when looked at. Although she felt forces were trying to distract her and defeat her, she persevered to develop a gift for the unbelievers that would make them see the light of the glory of God. Suddenly after many sleepless nights, a plan began to fall into place. She saw how it could be done through a delicate and magnetically simple arrangement of a bouquet of flowers, blessedly revealing and describing our blessed Lord and Redeemer. Mary took her idea to Fenton to have them make the glass for her with this bouquet on the pieces. The name Love Bouquet was decided on since it would convey the greatest love of all time, Jesus dying for sinners. Burmese was chosen because to her Burmese was the "Cadillac" of all glass. She wanted the greatest glass technology as the foundation on which to build her spiritual inspirations.

Fenton agreed to produce six limited edition hand blown pieces, known as the Series I Collection. Each would be hand painted by the artist and bear the inscription "Inspired by Mary Walrath". Deeply involved with this project were Frank and Bill Fenton, Linda Everson (one of the decorating designers), and Howard Seufer (quality control manager). The flowers on these pieces all represent a spiritual meaning. The rose bud shows we are made in his image. The Lily of the Valley is a name attributed to Jesus in the bible. The Forget-me-nots testify that Jesus will never let us down. Mary was also inspired to write a poem to dignify the artwork and include it in filling all orders. Plans are to produce it as a bookmark and on stationary.

The pieces went out to Mary's family. The desire to inspire others led to the collection being offered for sale in her daughter's gift shop. Many customers bought it for gifts. Finally for Mother's Day a young lady came in looking for a gift. This was an unbeliever wanting a gift for her mother. A basket was chosen as a gift to fill with flowers. Before she left though she stated she felt the need to have the whole collection for herself. Mary got it wrapped up, but purposely omitted the poem thinking the girl would not appreciate it. Later, upon unpacking the collection and discovering that the poem was not included, she called Mary asking for it. "I want it," she stressed. At last Mary could see that God does work miracles by having such an affect on an unbeliever, now calling and wanting to have something printed with his word on it.

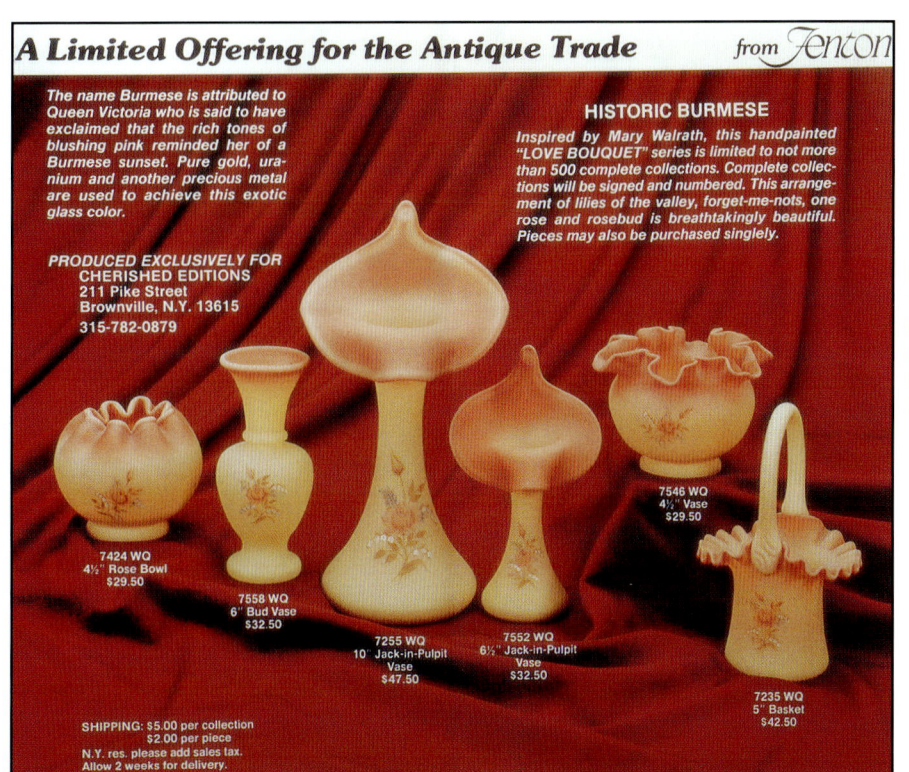

Detail of Mary Walrath - "Love Bouquet" 1982 ad. (Reprinted with permission from Mary Walrath)

66   The 1980s

Detail of Mary Walrath - hand painted "Love Bouquet" decoration.

Hat Basket #7235WQ, hand painted "Love Bouquet" collection, 6" tall, 4.25" wide, single crimp, Limited to 500, marked on bottom #18/500, Special order made exclusively for Mary C. Walrath 1982, **$135**

Tulip Vase #7255WQ, hand painted "Love Bouquet" collection, 10.5" tall, Special order made exclusively for Mary C. Walrath 1982, **$195**
Note, also called a Jack In The Pulpit vase.

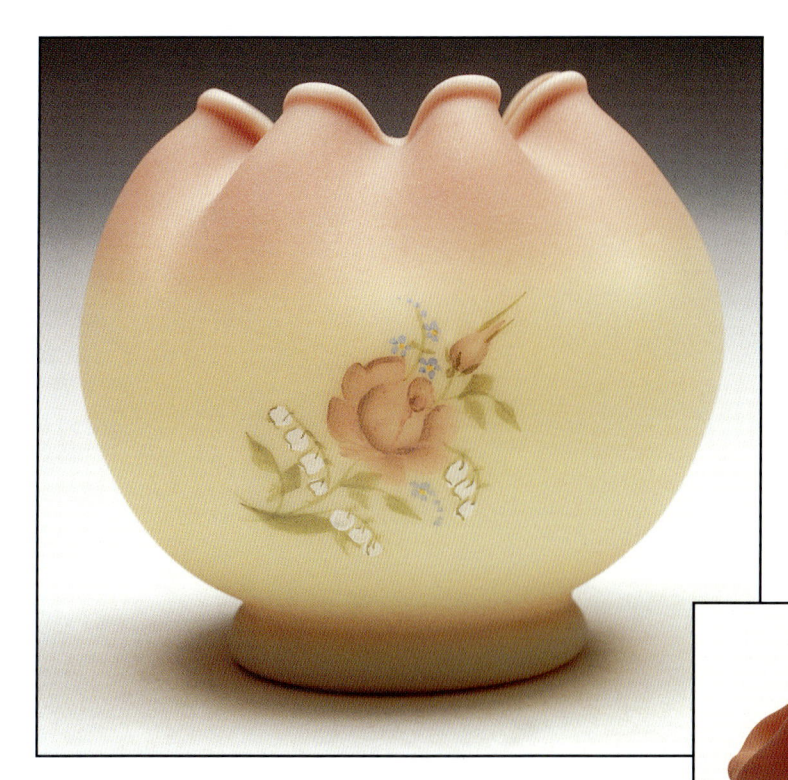

The 1980s 67

Rose Bowl #7424WQ, hand painted "Love Bouquet" collection, 3.5" tall, 4" wide, tight single crimp & cupped in, Special order made exclusively for Mary C. Walrath 1982, **$85**

Vase #7546WQ, hand painted "Love Bouquet" collection, 4.5" tall, double crimp, Special order made exclusively for Mary C. Walrath 1982, **$85**

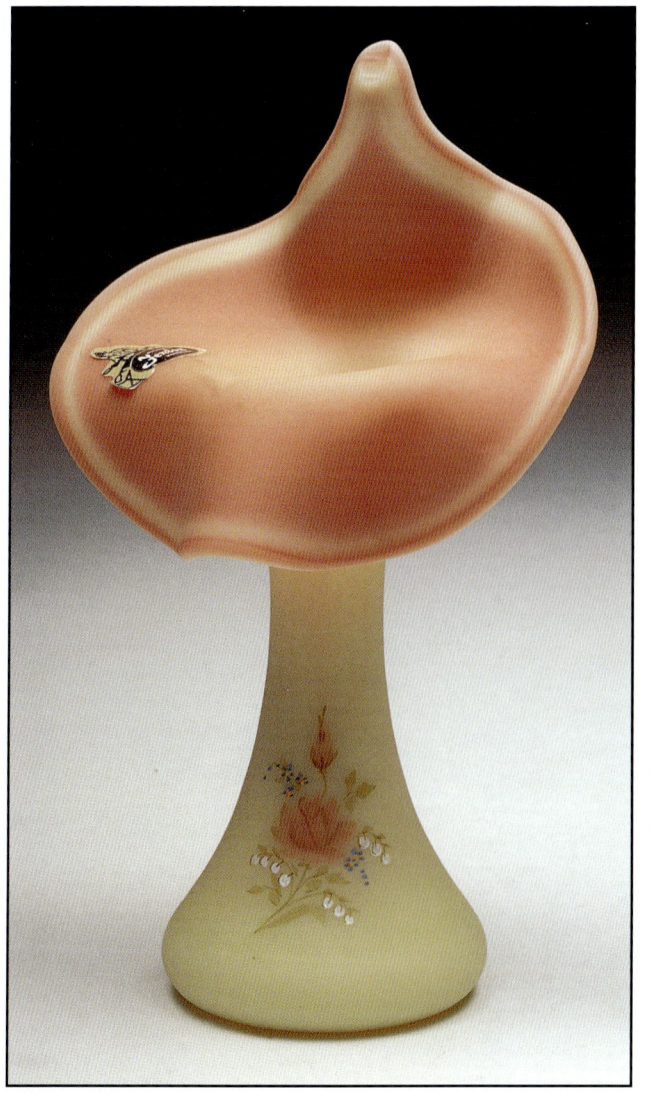

Tulip vase #7552WQ, hand painted "Love Bouquet" collection, 6.75" tall, Special order made exclusively for Mary C. Walrath 1982, **$110** Note, also called a Jack In The Pulpit vase.

68   The 1980s

Detail of Mary Walrath - hand painted "Love Bouquet" decoration, **Left**: back view of decoration; **Right**: front view of decoration.

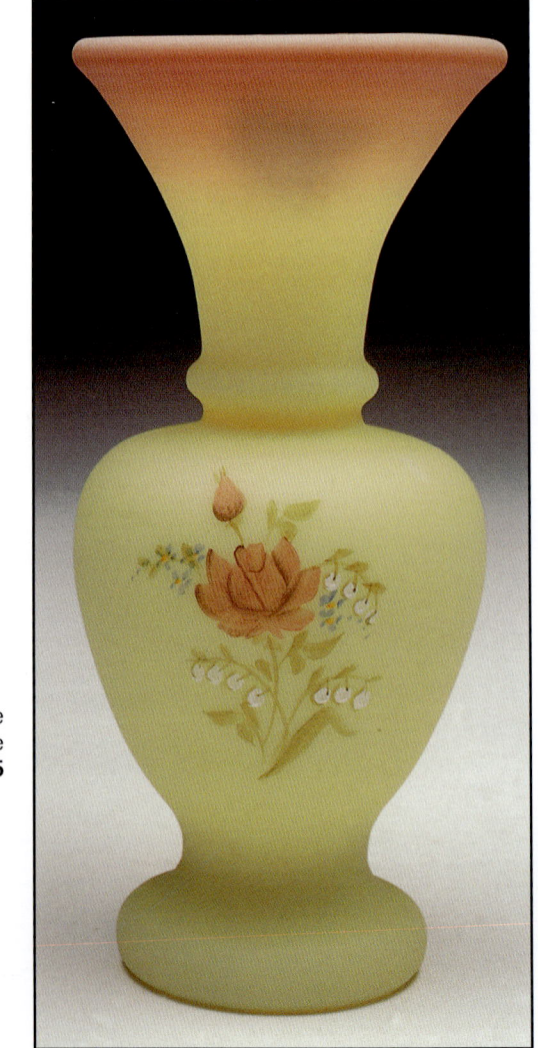

Bud Vase #7558WQ, hand painted "Love Bouquet" collection, 6" tall, Special order made exclusively for Mary C. Walrath 1982, **$75**

The 1980s 69

Bud Vase #7558, hand painted "Love Bouquet" experimental version, 6" tall, From Fenton Gift Shop 1982, **$125**

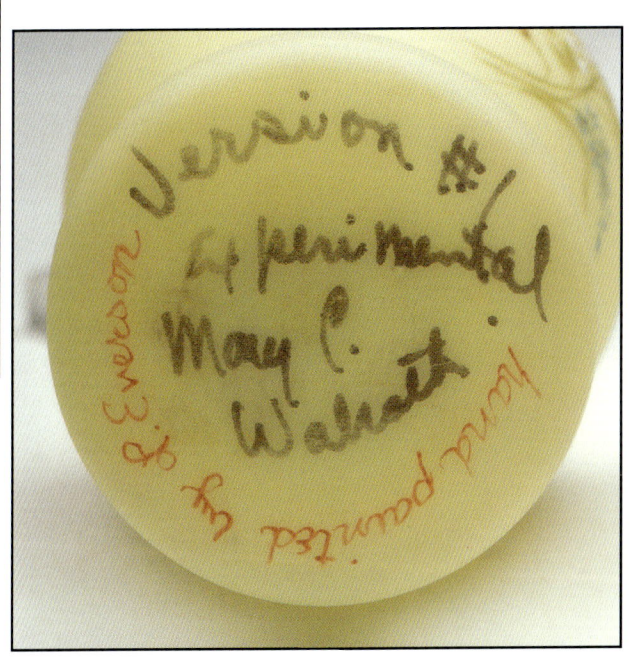

Detail of bud vase bottom #7558, hand painted experimental version of "Love Bouquet"

70   The 1980s

The Fenton Art Glass Collectors of America had a hat vase decorated with butterflies also in 1982. This piece was made as a convention souvenir. This was the first piece made for them in Burmese.

Hat vase #7442, hand painted butterfly & flower, 4.25" tall, 5.75" wide, single crimp with two sides turned up, Special order made exclusively for FAGCA (Fenton Art Glass Collectors of America) convention souvenir piece 1982, **$95**

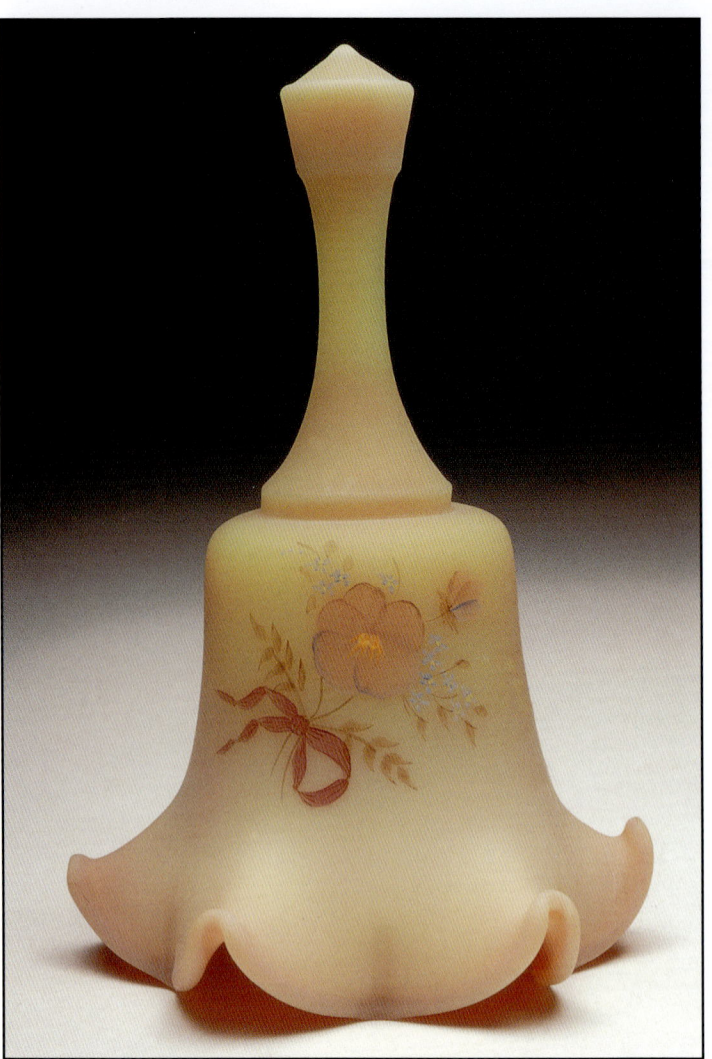

1983

There were no regular in line items made for 1983. The Connoisseur Collection debuted with a limited edition hand painted bell and a plain satin four horn epergne. The bell decoration was designed by Linda Everson.

Bell #7562UF, hand painted pink flower & purple Ribbon, decoration designed by Linda Everson, 6.75" tall, single star crimp, Decorated by Amy S., Limited to 2000, Connoisseur Collection 1983, **$78**

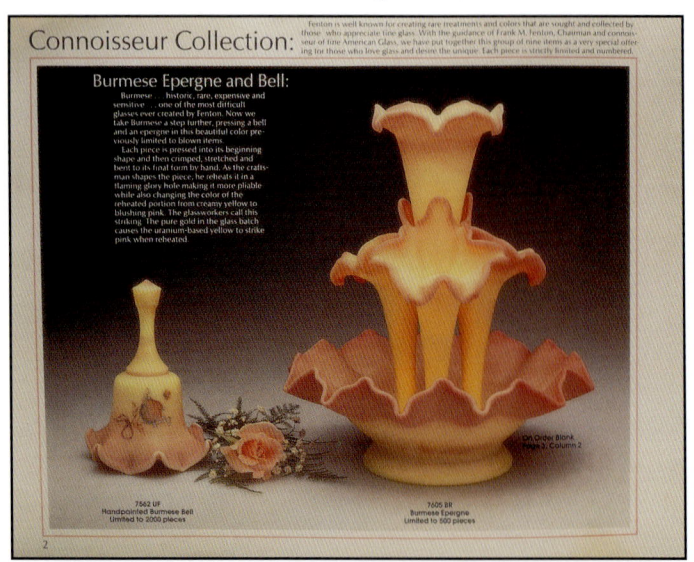

Detail of catalog Connoisseur Collection 1983. (Reprinted with permission from the Fenton Art Glass Company)

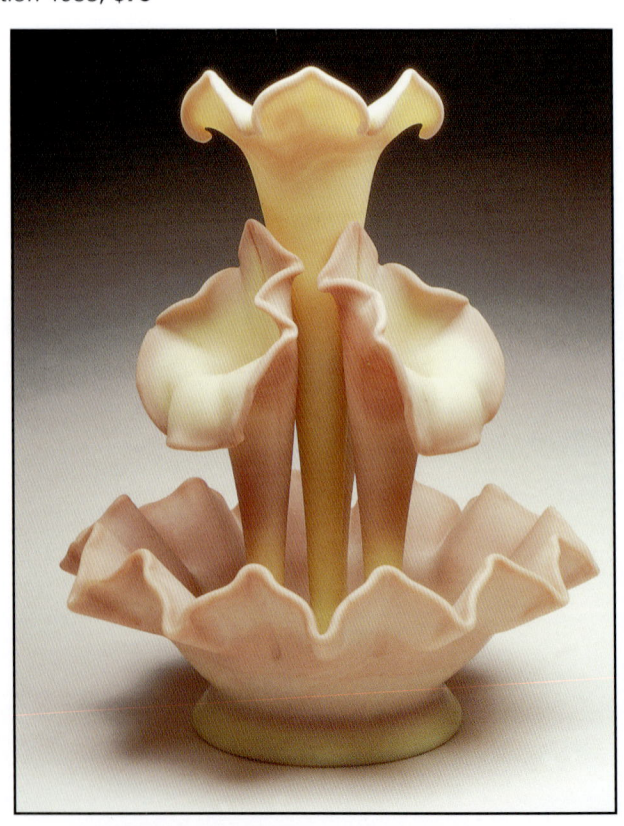

Four horn epergne #7605BR, plain satin finish, 12.5" tall, 11" wide, single star crimp, Connoisseur Collection 1983, **$595**

In the Fenton gift shop there were some different decorated items. The hat shape vase had been used for Fenton Art Glass Collectors of America (FAGCA) and the bell had been in the Connoisseur Collection.

Hat vase #7442, hand painted orange butterflies, 4.25" tall, Sample decorated by Louise Piper & signed 7-22-83 on bottom, From Fenton Gift Shop 1983, **$175**

Detail of hat vase #7442, back side to show other version of butterfly

72   The 1980s

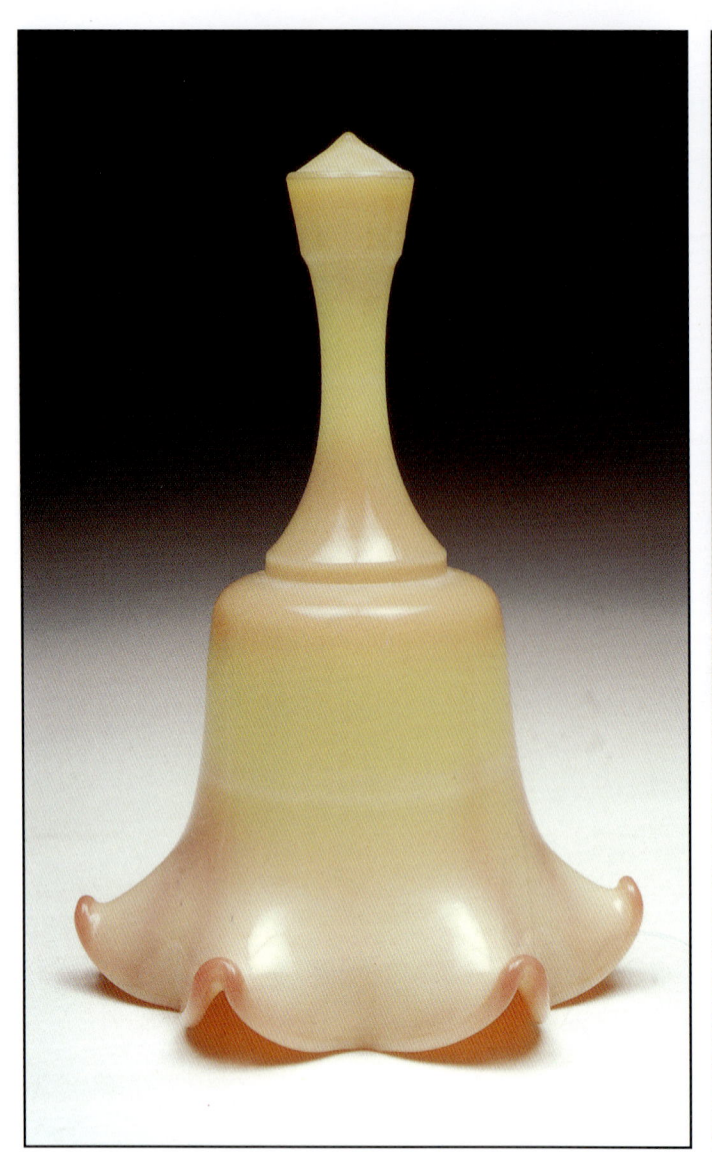

Bell #7562BE, plain gloss finish, 6.8" tall, single star crimp, From Fenton Gift Shop 1983, **$58**

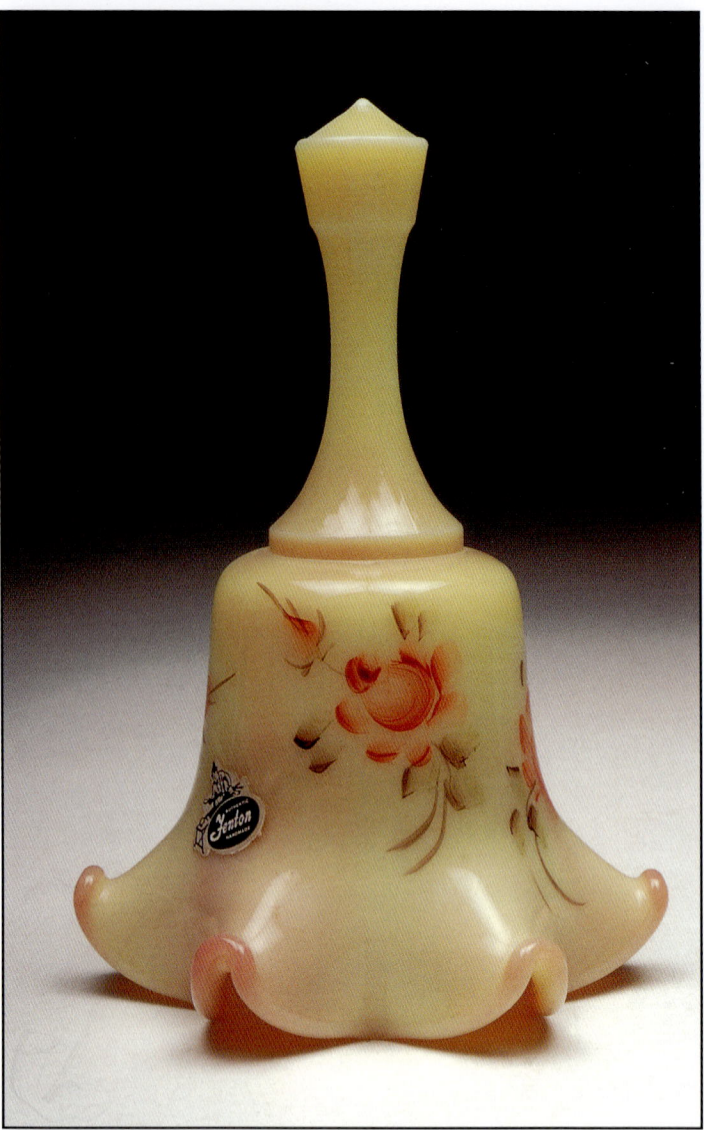

Bell #7562RB, hand painted "Rose" decoration, gloss finish, 7" tall, single star crimp, signed with initials DK, From Fenton Gift Shop 1983, **$80**

The Fenton Art Glass Collectors of America (FAGCA) had a miniature Daisy and Button hat made in both satin and gloss finish.

Miniature hat #1991, "Daisy & Button", 1.75" tall, 2.1" wide, Special order made exclusively for FAGCA (Fenton Art Glass Collectors of America) 1983, **Left:** Satin finish #1991BR, **$38**; **Right:** Gloss finish #1991BE, **$35**

1984

For 1984 there was an absence of any new Burmese.

1985

For the June 1985 Supplement, a limited edition collectible offering was made to honor the 100th anniversary of Burmese glass. The Butterfly and Flowering Branch decoration appeared on three items: lamp, basket, and bell. These were designed by Linda Everson. The Shell vase decorated with shells and under the sea scene also was in this collection. Dianna Barbour developed this new decoration. Frank Fenton relayed this story about the piece. He was sitting in his office looking over a new Shell Oil calendar he had gotten and thought one of the sea shore scenes was so gorgeous. He asked the decorating department to create something similar. The vase was the result of his request.

The bell was the first item to be made in the new pressed Burmese formula developed by Wayne King. A dramatic change was made to the Burmese formula. Bill Fenton had approached Wayne about developing this type of formula and finally after several years of experimenting, he succeeded. All of the previous pieces had been blown into a mould. Fenton decided to try the formula in pressed moulds. This new process made the Burmese act completely different. With blown pieces the glass cools slowly and uniformly. In the pressed pieces, the glass cools at different rates depending on its thickness and the pressure applied to the molten glass in the mould. Adjustments needed to be made to the formula. Finally after much experimentation, the desired affect was achieved.

Detail of catalog Limited Edition Collectible offering 1985. (Reprinted with permission from the Fenton Art Glass Company)

Lamp #7602EB, hand painted "Butterfly & Flowering Branch" decoration, 22" overall height, double crimp shade, Limited to 350, Limited Edition Collectible offering 1985, **$750**

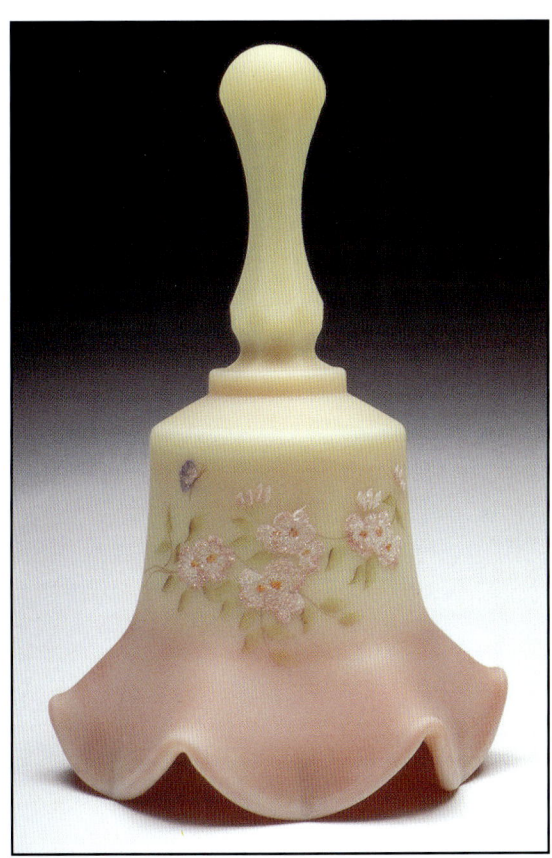

Bell #7666EB, hand painted "Butterfly & Flowering Branch" decoration, 6.25" tall, 4" wide, single star crimp, Limited to 2500, Limited Edition Collectible offering 1985, **$95** Note, this was the first item to be made with the new pressed Burmese formula.

74   The 1980s

Detail of hand painted "Butterfly & Flowering Branch" decoration.

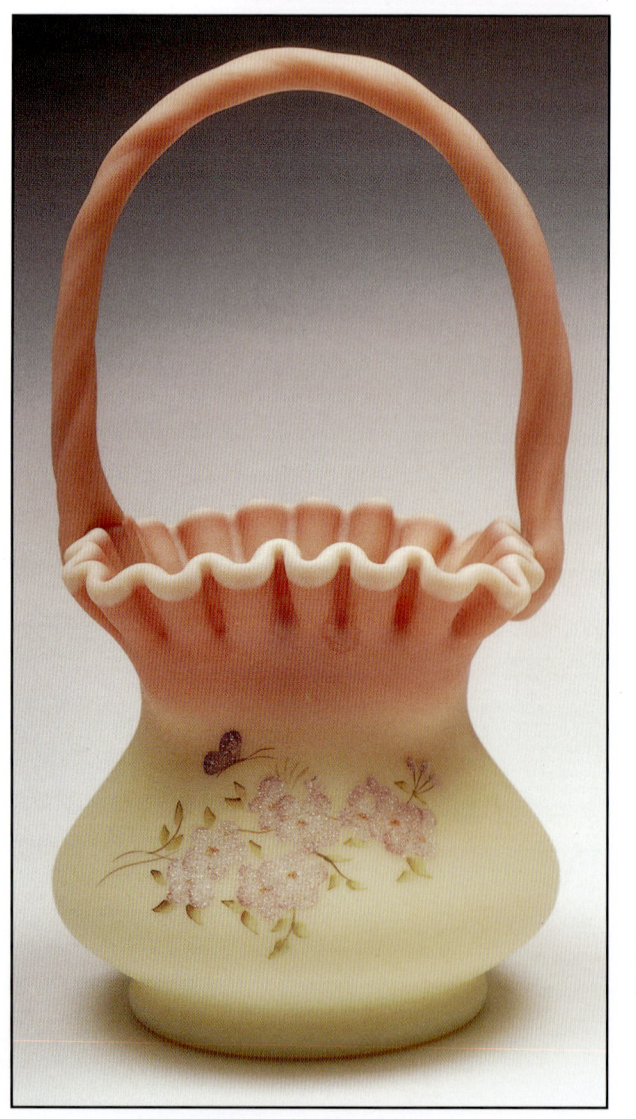

Detail of basket #7634EB, bottom showing artist signature, limited edition number & date.

Basket #7634EB, hand painted "Butterfly & Flowering Branch" decoration, 8.5" tall, 4.25" wide, tight ribbon single crimp, Limited to 1250, Limited Edition Collectible offering 1985, **$165**

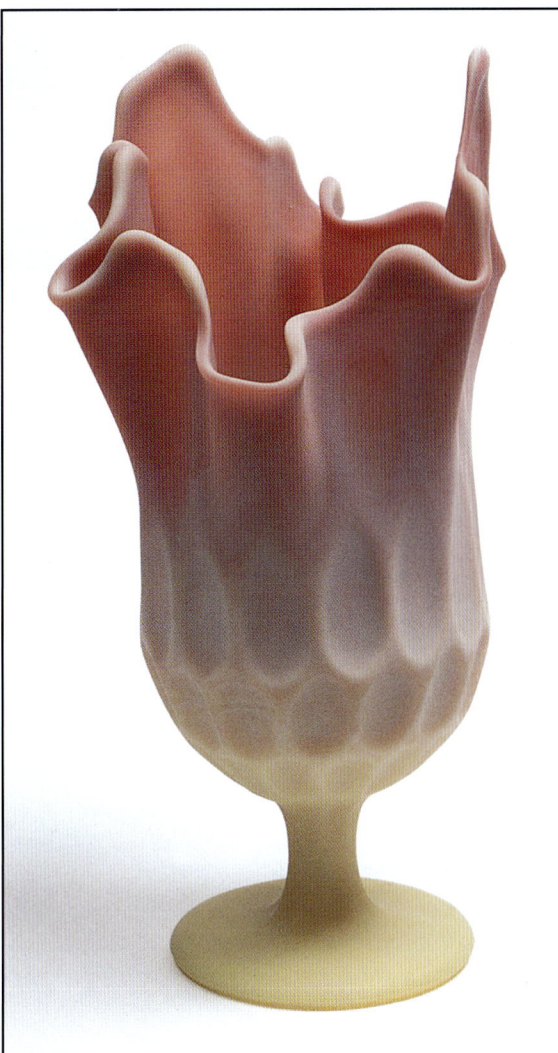

The 1980s 75

While the Thumbprint vase was being made in other colors for the catalog, it was only offered in Burmese in the gift shop. The #8808 vase was decorated in several different ways. Some undecorated items from the Ratcliff offering were also available. Louise Piper decided to decorate some left over epergnes.

Swung vase #4454BR, "Thumbprint" pattern plain satin finish, 8" tall, Sample from Fenton Gift Shop 1985, **$125**

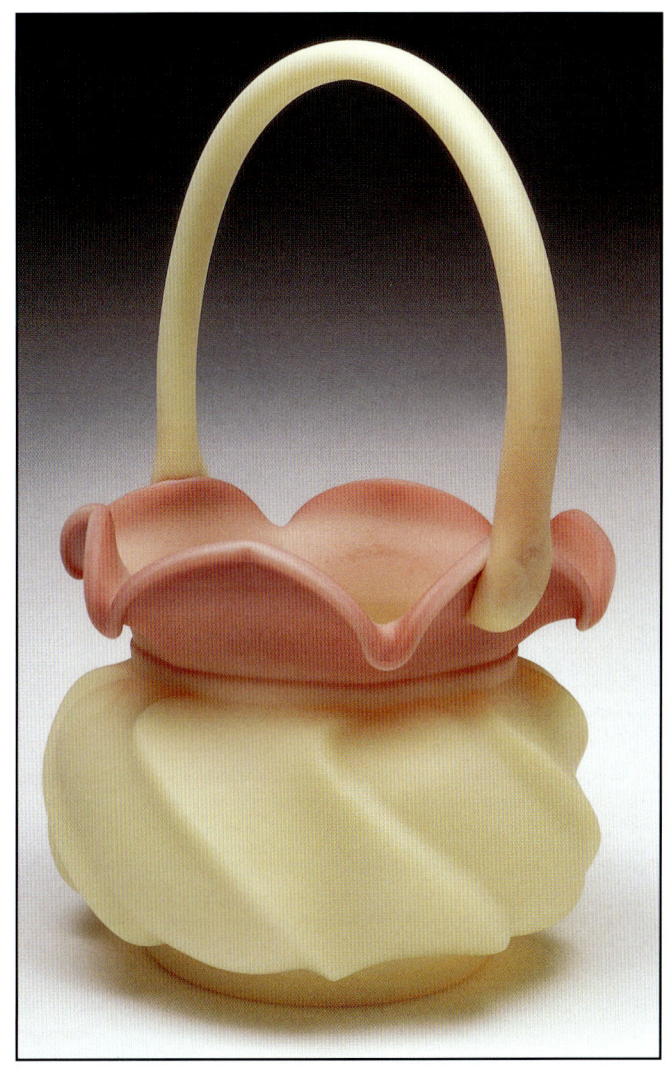

Basket #6037BR, "Wavecrest" pattern plain satin finish, 9.5" tall, 6" wide, single star crimp, From Fenton Gift Shop 1985, **$165**

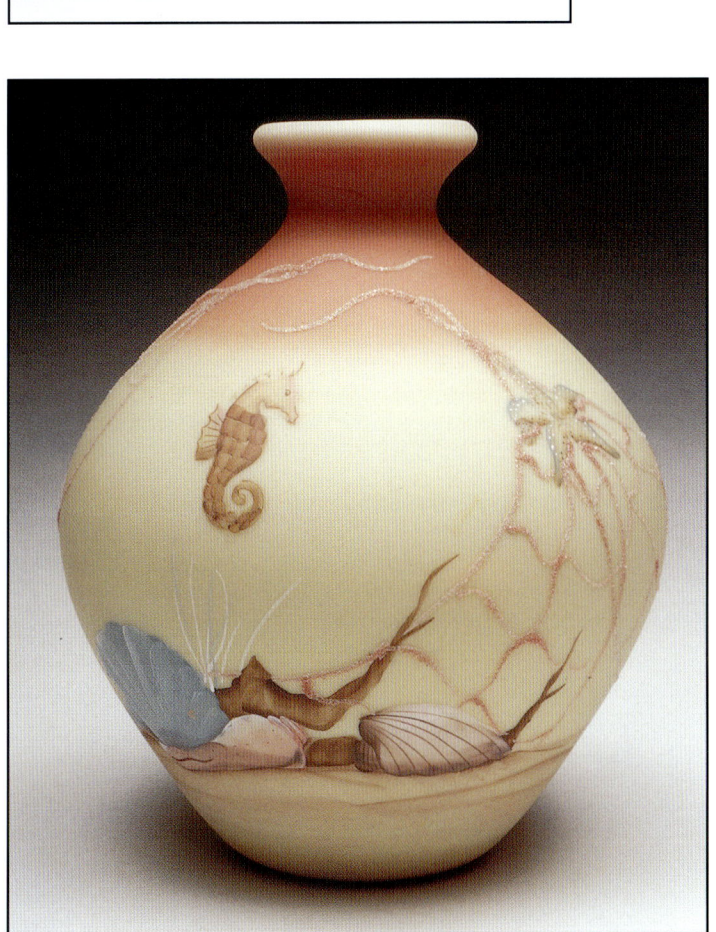

Vase #8808SB, hand painted under sea scene "Shell" decoration, 8" tall, Limited to 950, Limited Edition Collectible offering 1985, **$295**

76　The 1980s

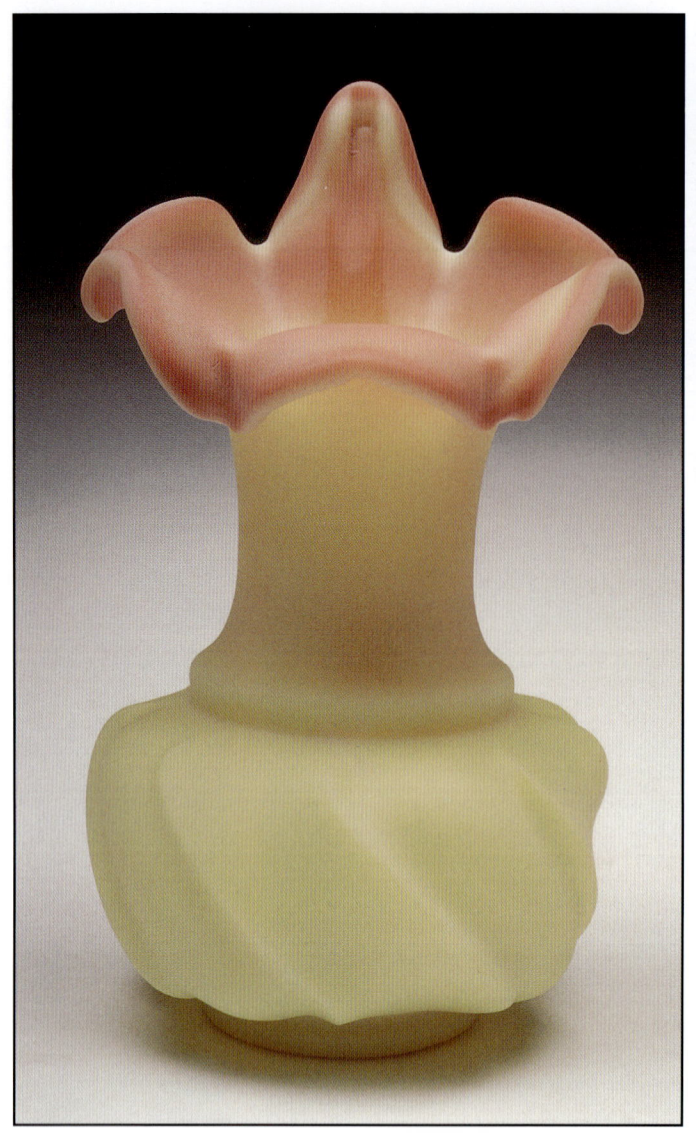

Tulip vase #6058BR, "Wavecrest" pattern plain satin finish, 7.5" tall, single crimp, From Fenton Gift Shop 1985, **$125** Note, also called a Jack In The Pulpit vase.

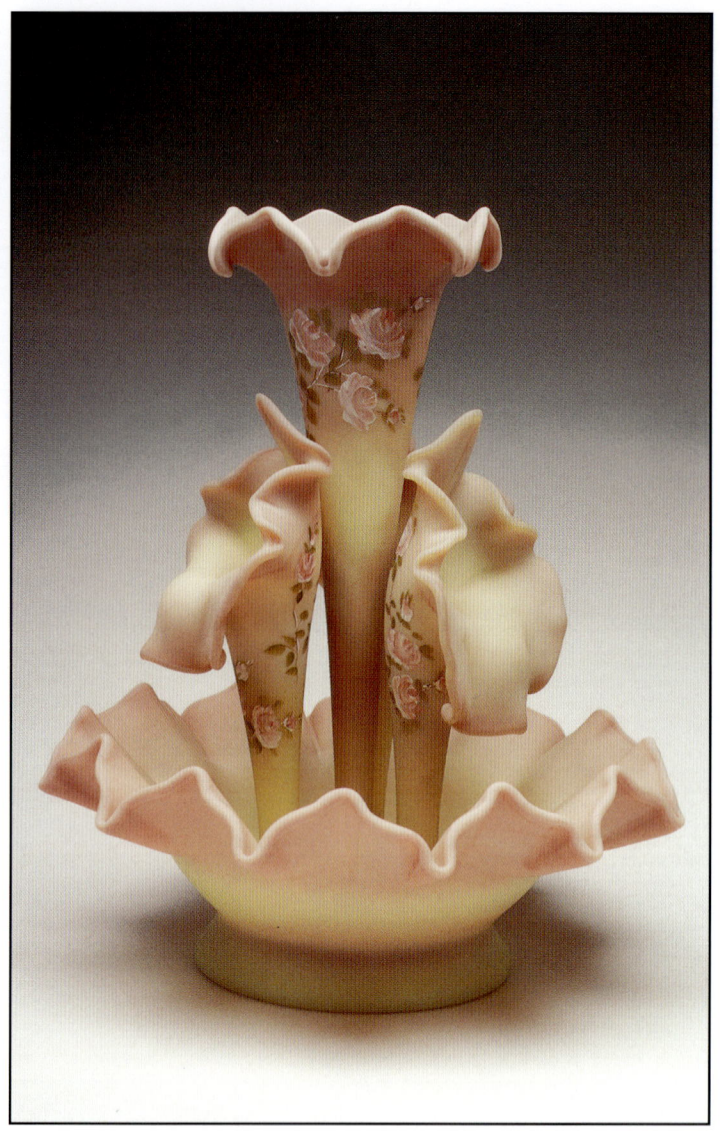

Four horn epergne #7605, hand painted pink roses, 12.5" tall, 11.25" wide, Decorated by Louise Piper & dated 5-15-85 (Note, each piece is signed & dated), From Fenton Gift Shop 1985, **$2,500**

Detail of horn from the four horn epergne #7605, Signed & dated by Louise Piper 5-15-85.

The 1980s   77

Vase #8808BE, plain gloss finish, 7.75" tall, From Fenton Gift Shop 1985, **$95**

A beautiful rose in the garden of life — ever blooming… enriching all she touches.

Bringing a wealth of knowledge and technical brilliance; Louise arrived in 1968 with the task of designing decorations and training the young people who became the nucleus of the present staff of artists in the decorating shop at The Fenton Art Glass Company.

Over the years many young aspiring artists have reflected her dedication — her enthusiasm for ceramic artistry. Each eagerly signs their creation as a master painter signs his canvas, a sign of final approval.

The hands of Louise create new designs on Fenton ware with paint, brush, and with the gentle touch of love.

The Fenton Art Glass Company is proud to offer original limited editions designed and executed by Louise, each displaying a true dedication to ceramic artistry. Her enthusiasm never waivers — truly an act of love to her craft — a credit to past craftsmen who taught and gave her insight and inspiration to pursue her talents in this particular field of endeavor.

No greater love has any artist for her craft…

Detail of brochure on Louise Piper.

Vase #8808, hand painted orange frit flowers & purple frit butterfly, 7.75" tall, Decorated by E. Thomas, From Fenton Gift Shop 1985, **$175**

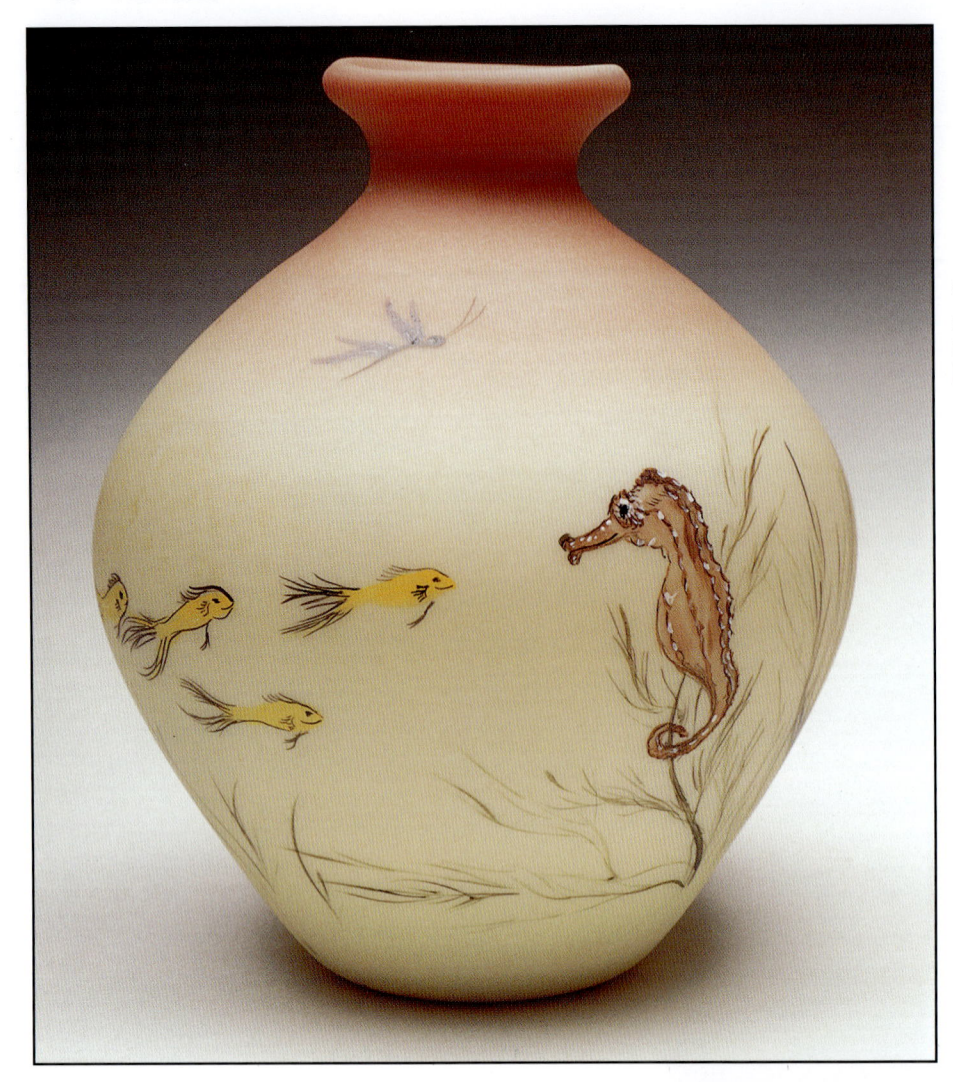

78 The 1980s

Vase #8808, hand painted under sea scene of Seahorse & fish, 7.75" tall, Decorated by E. Thomas, From Fenton Gift Shop 1985, **$195**

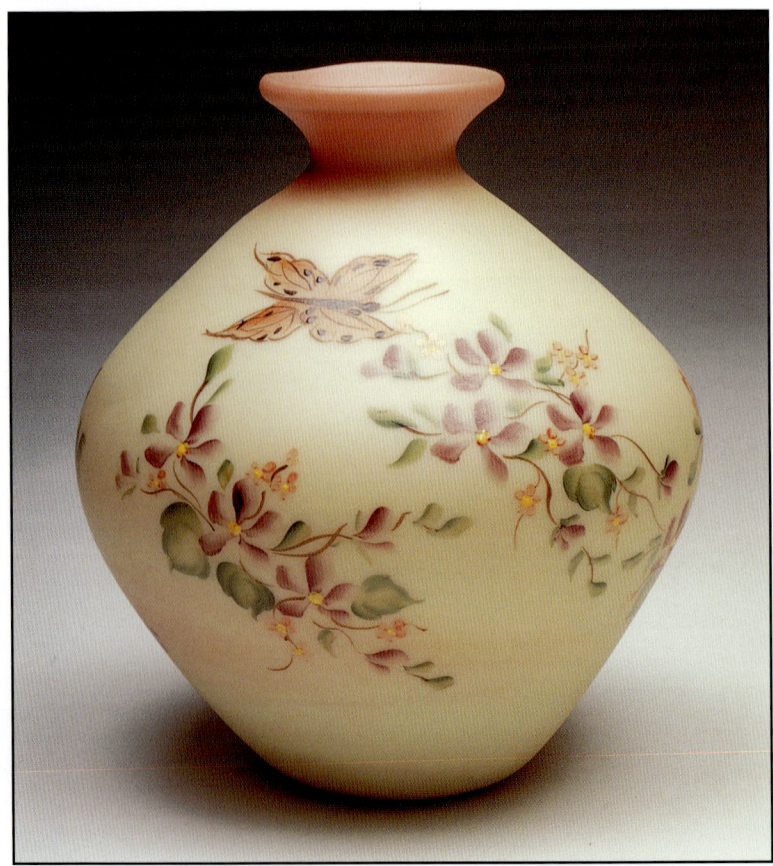

Vase #8808, hand painted purple flowers & orange butterfly, 7.75" tall, Decorated by E. Thomas, From Fenton Gift Shop 1985, **$175**

The 1980s   79

Also for 1985 another piece was made for Fenton Art Glass Collectors of America (FAGCA), the butterfly mug.

Butterfly mug, plain satin finish, 3.15" tall, Limited to 597, Special order made exclusively for FAGCA (Fenton Art Glass Collectors of America) 1985, **$60**

Lois Ratcliff of Elemar Glass from Indiana asked Fenton to make some pieces for her using the Wavecrest moulds. The Rose decoration was used on all of the pieces. These pieces were made with a satin and iridized finish.

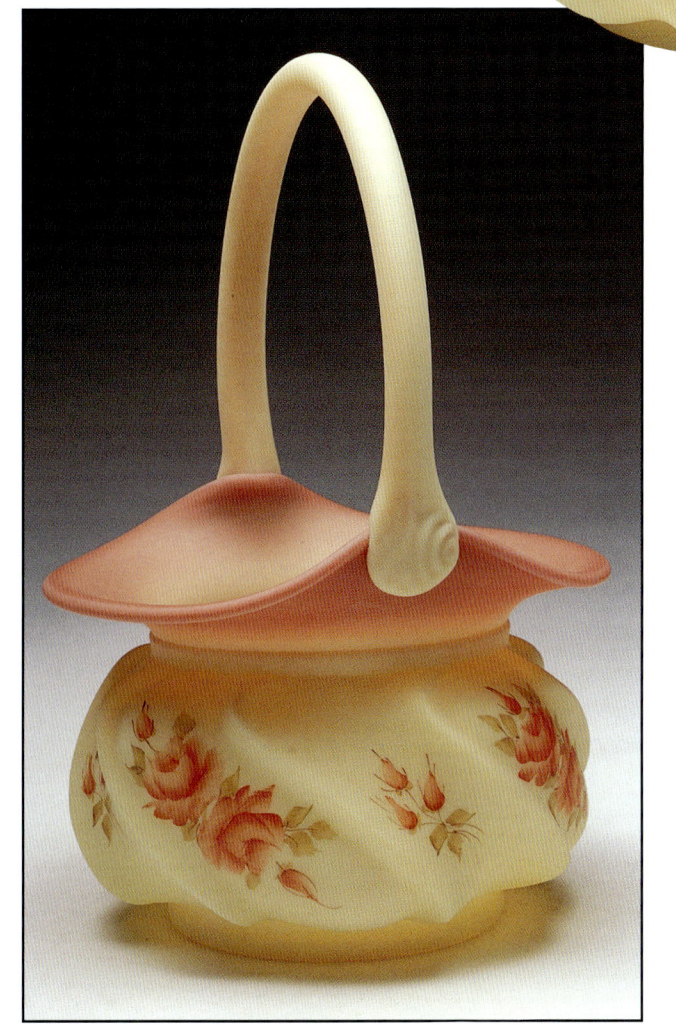

Tulip vase #6058RB, "Wavecrest" pattern hand painted "Rose" decoration, 7.1" tall, single crimp, Limited to 260, Special order made exclusively for Lois Ratcliff 1985, **$165** Note, also called a Jack In The Pulpit vase.

Basket #6037RB, "Wavecrest" pattern hand painted "Rose" decoration, 9.5" tall, 6" wide, Limited to 200, Special order made exclusively for Lois Ratcliff 1985, **$210**

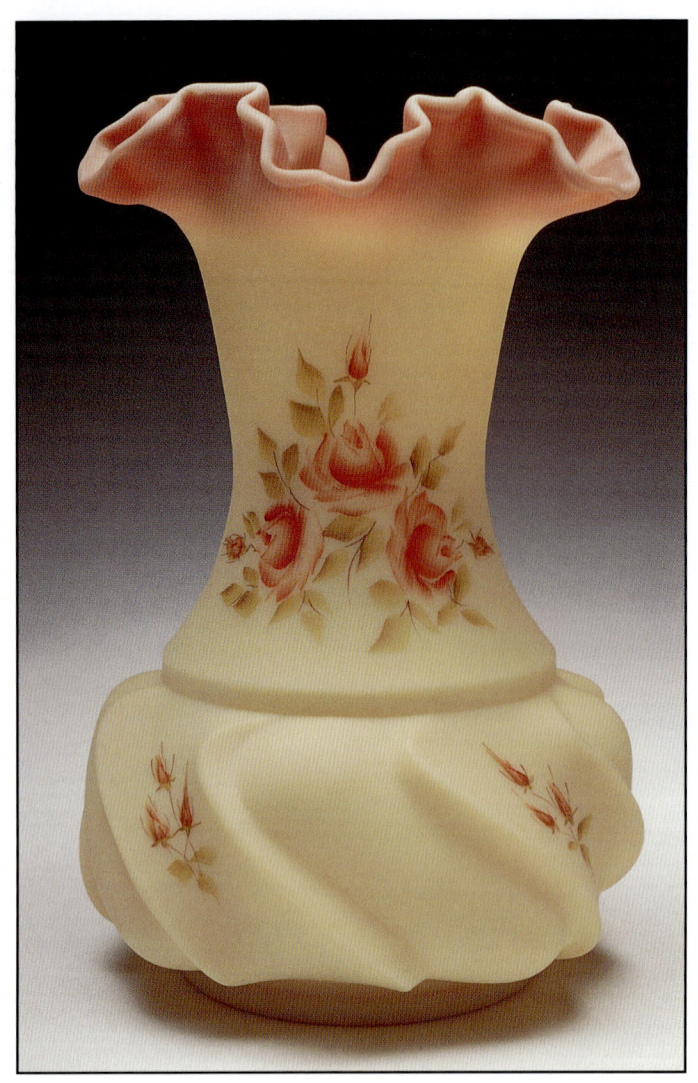

80   The 1980s

1986

With the new pressed Burmese formula now perfected, it was decided to make a whole offering utilizing this technique. There were 15 pieces in this offering for 1986. Interestingly, several of the moulds were last used in the production of early carnival glass. A Mariners lamp based on the previous years Shell vase appeared in the Connoisseur Collection.

Vase #6059RB, "Wavecrest" pattern hand painted "Rose" decoration, 8.5" tall, double crimp, Decorated by Frances Burton, Limited to 112, Special order made exclusively for Lois Ratcliff 1985, **$145**

Detail of signature of decorator, Frances Burton on Wavecrest vase.

Detail of General Catalog 1986 (Reprinted with permission from the Fenton Art Glass Company)

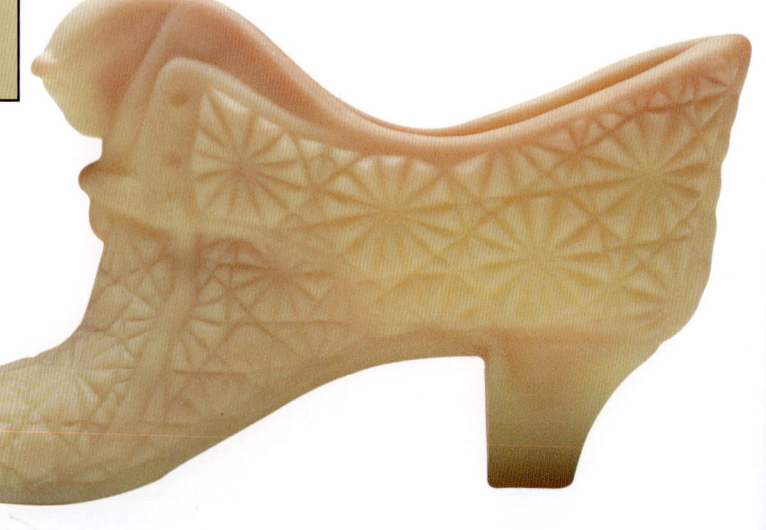

Cat head slipper #1995BR, embossed "Daisy & Button" pattern, plain satin finish, 3" tall, 5.5" long, General Catalog 1986–1987, **$45**

The 1980s 81

Three horn epergne #4809BR, "Diamond Lattice" pattern plain satin finish, three horn, 10" tall, 11" wide, General Catalog 1986, **$395**

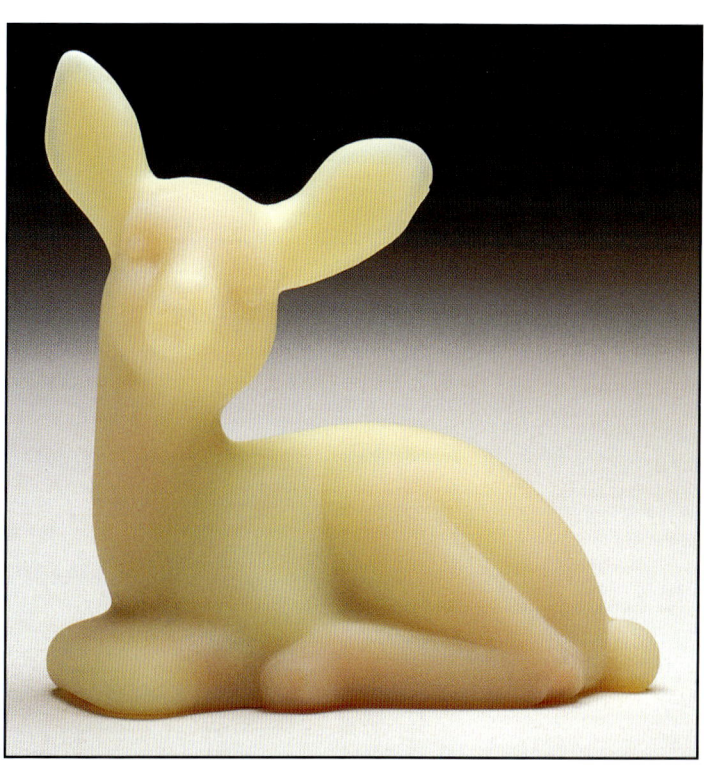

Fawn #5160BR, plain satin finish, 3.75" tall, 3.5" long, General Catalog 1986-1987, **$50**

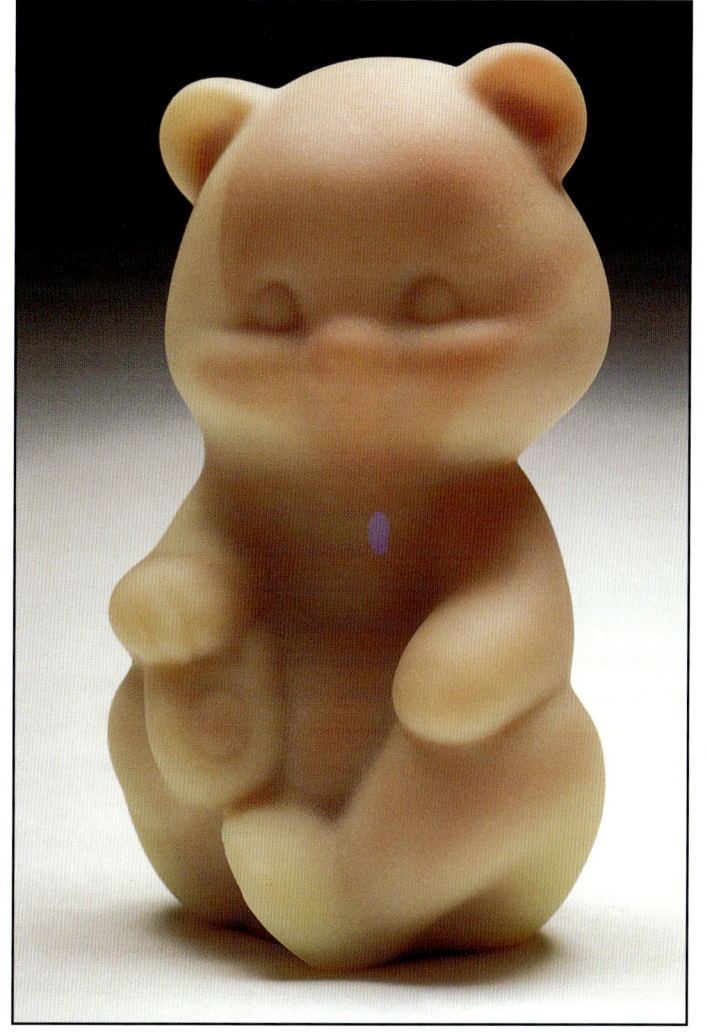

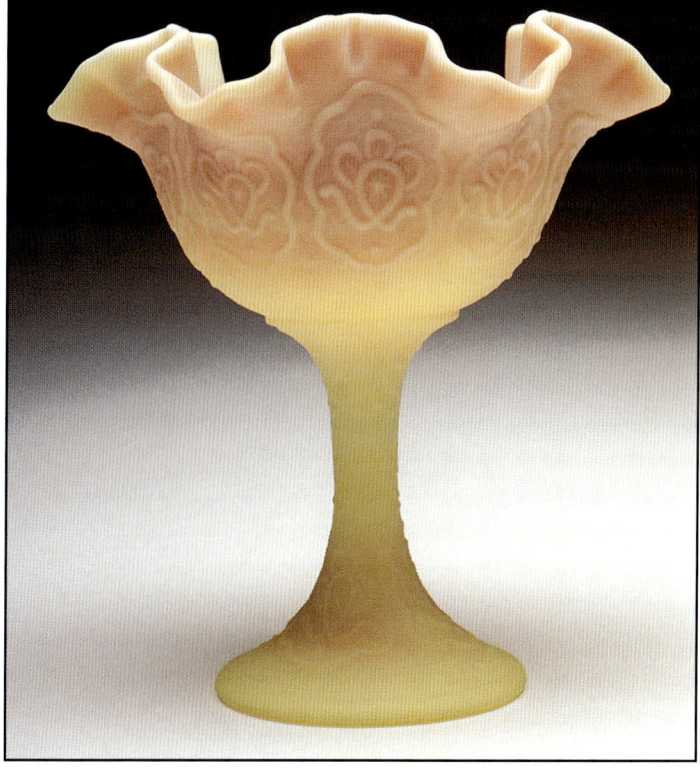

Compote #8234BR, embossed "Persian Medallion" pattern, plain satin finish, 6.5" tall, 6" wide, double crimp, General Catalog 1986-1987, **$58**

Sitting bear #5151BR, plain satin finish, 3.5" tall, 2.25" wide, General Catalog 1986, **$65**

82   The 1980s

Detail of inside bowl #8289BR, embossed "Orange Tree" pattern, showing the inside pattern of embossed "Cherries"

Vase #8257BR, "Peacock" pattern plain satin finish, 7.8" tall, General Catalog 1986-1987, **$115**

Bowl #8289BR, embossed "Orange Tree" pattern (outside) plain satin finish, 3.5" tall, 7.5" wide, single crimp & cupped in, General Catalog 1986, **$85**

The 1980s 83

Toothpick # 8294BR, embossed "Paneled Daisy" pattern, plain satin finish, 3.5" tall, General Catalog 1986-1987, **$35**

Three piece fairy light #8408BR, embossed "Persian Medallion" pattern, satin finish, three piece (Note, insert is clear), 6.75" tall, 5" wide, General Catalog 1986, **$135**

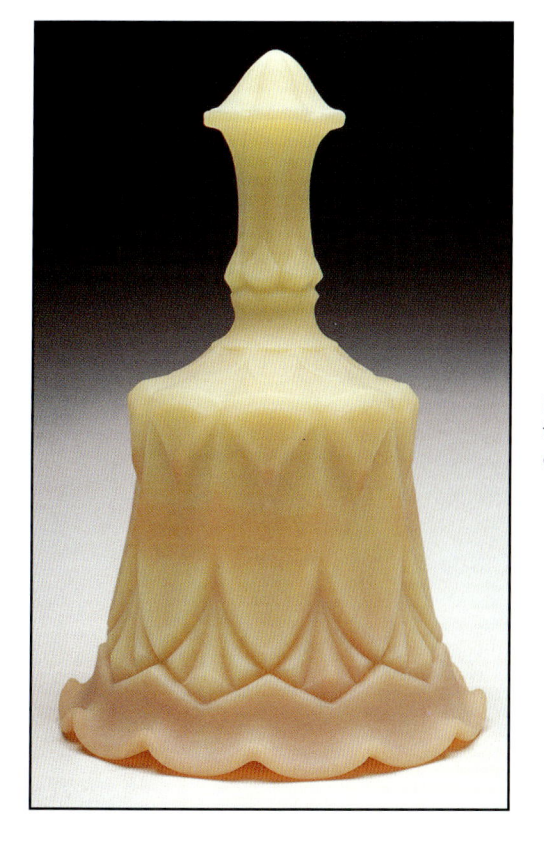

Bell #9066BR, "Whitton" pattern plain satin finish, 6.5" tall, 4.25" wide, slight single crimp, General Catalog 1986-1987, **$60**

84   The 1980s

Dish #9125BR, embossed "Pansy" pattern, plain satin finish, 7.5" long, 5.25" wide, single crimp, General Catalog 1986, **$60**
Note, the scalloped edge gives it almost a look of being a double crimp piece.

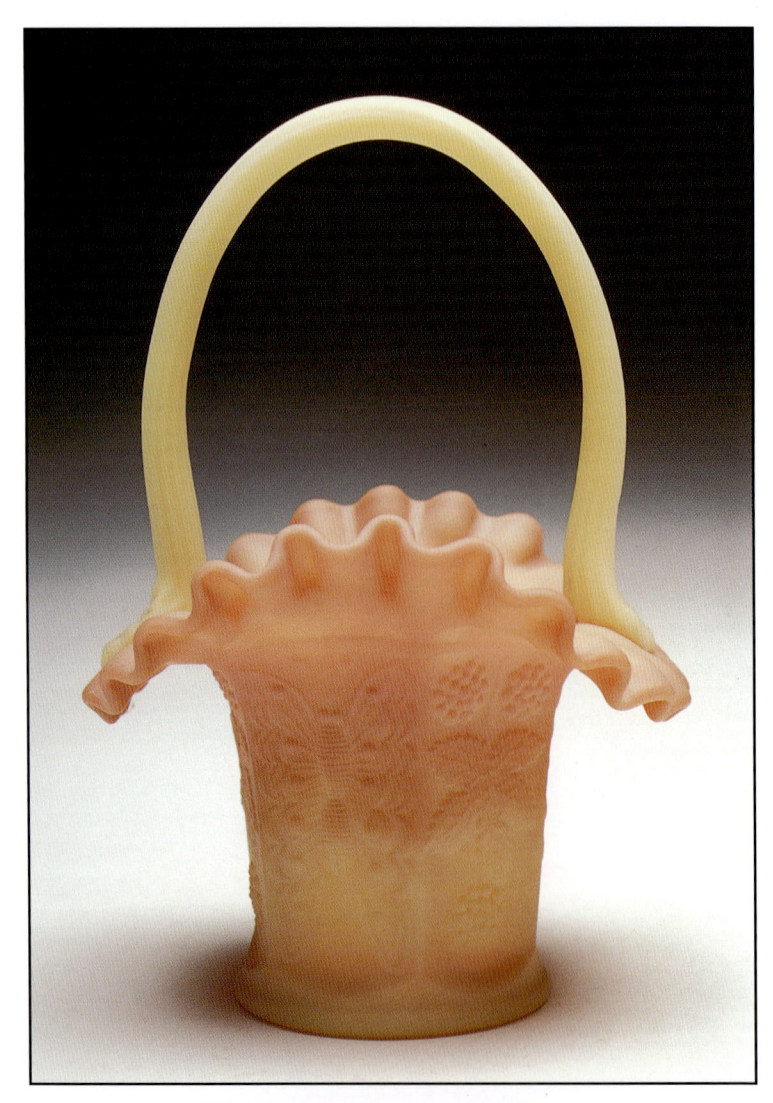

Basket #9234BR, embossed "Butterfly & Berry" pattern, plain satin finish, 6.75" tall, 4.25" wide, single crimp (two sides turned down), General Catalog 1986, **$110**

Covered footed candy #9185BR, embossed "Paneled Daisy" pattern, plain satin finish, 9" tall, 5.25" wide, General Catalog 1986, **$85**

The 1980s   85

Mariners lamp #7400SB, hand painted under sea scene of seahorse & shells decoration designed by Dianna Barbour, 19.5" tall, double crimp, Limited 500, Connoisseur Collection 1986, **$795**

Vase #1742VB, hand painted violets decoration (not part of Levay "Violets" line), 5.4" tall, slight single crimp, Decorated by S. (Sue) Lee, From Fenton Gift Shop 1986, **$65**

The gift shop featured several plain items from the Walrath line. Different decorated peacock vases were also found. The Daisy and Button covered candy was found in other colors for the catalog but was only available in Burmese in the Fenton gift shop.

Left: Vase #1742BR, plain satin finish, 5.25" tall, slight single crimp, From Fenton Gift Shop 1986, **$45**

Right: Covered candy #1980BR, "Daisy & Button" pattern plain satin finish, 5" tall, From Fenton Gift Shop 1986, **$175**

86　The 1980s

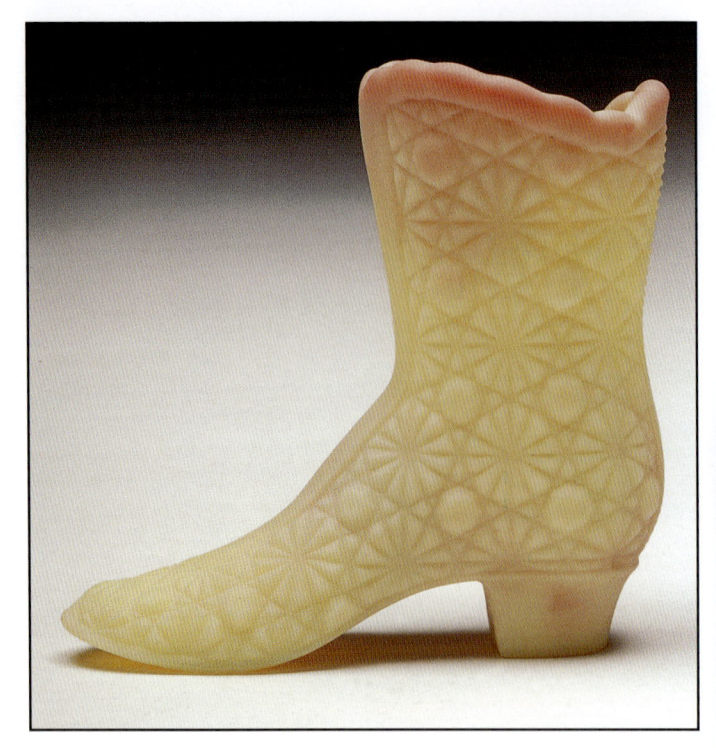

High Boot #1990BR, embossed "Daisy & Button" pattern, 4" tall, From Fenton Gift shop 1986, **$30**

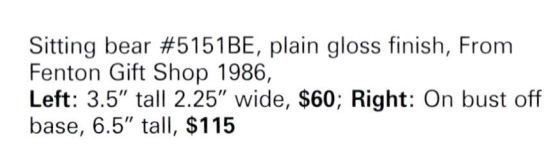

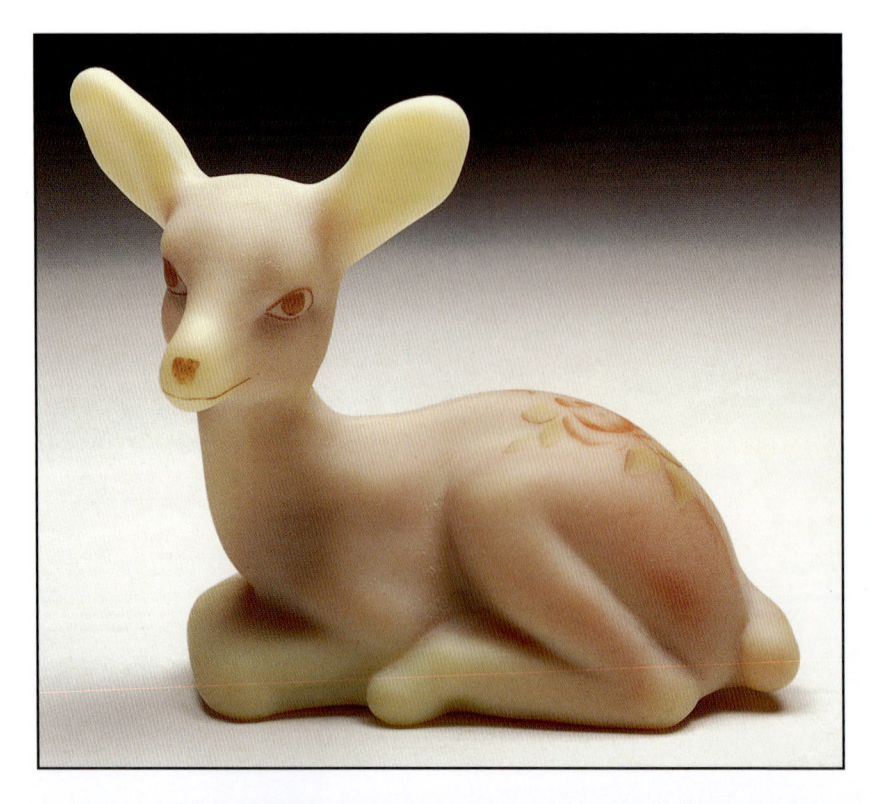

Sitting bear #5151BE, plain gloss finish, From Fenton Gift Shop 1986,
Left: 3.5" tall 2.25" wide, **$60**; **Right**: On bust off base, 6.5" tall, **$115**

Fawn #5160RB, hand painted "Rose" decoration, 3.25" tall, 3.5" long, From Fenton Gift Shop 1986, **$68**

The 1980s 87

Petite bell #7662BR, plain satin finish, 4.5" tall, From Fenton Gift Shop 1986, **$35**

Petite bell #7662, hand painted pink dogwood decoration (not part of the Pink Dogwood line), 4.25" tall, Decorated by S. Bryon, From Fenton Gift Shop 1986, **$48**

Vase #8257BE, "Peacock" pattern plain gloss finish, 7.8" tall, plain, From Fenton Gift Shop 1986, **$100**

88　The 1980s

Vase #8257, "Peacock" pattern hand painted peacock & flowers, 7.5" tall, From Fenton Gift Shop 1986, **$145** Note, the collar base was cut off at the factory before decorating.

Vase #8257, "Peacock" pattern hand painted pastel decoration with frit, 7.8" tall, Decorated by Dianna Barbour, From Fenton Gift Shop 1986, **$165**

Basket #9230, hand painted roses & butterflies, 5.25" tall 3.25" wide, Decorated by Marilyn Wagner, From Fenton Gift Shop 1986, **$110**

Detail of basket #9230, bottom showing artist signature, Marilyn Wagner.

The 1980s 89

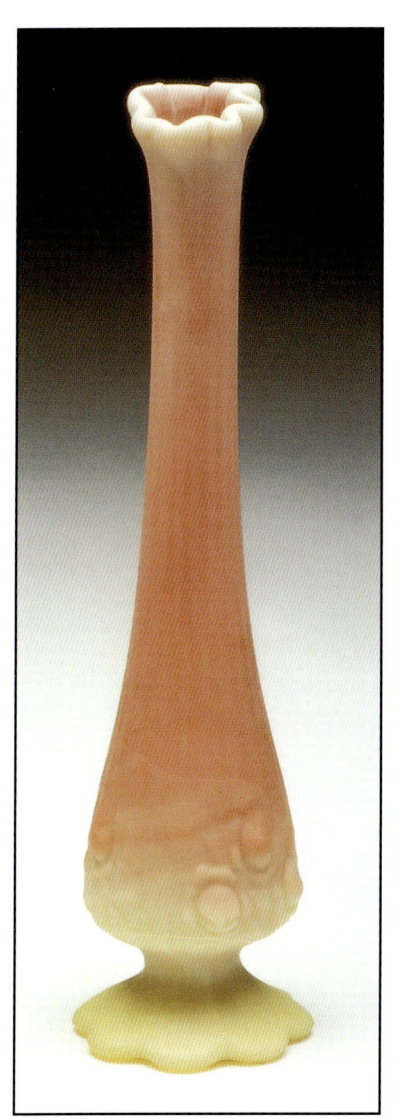

Footed bud vase #9256BR, "Embossed Roses" pattern, plain satin finish, 9.75" tall, From Fenton Gift Shop 1986, **$48**

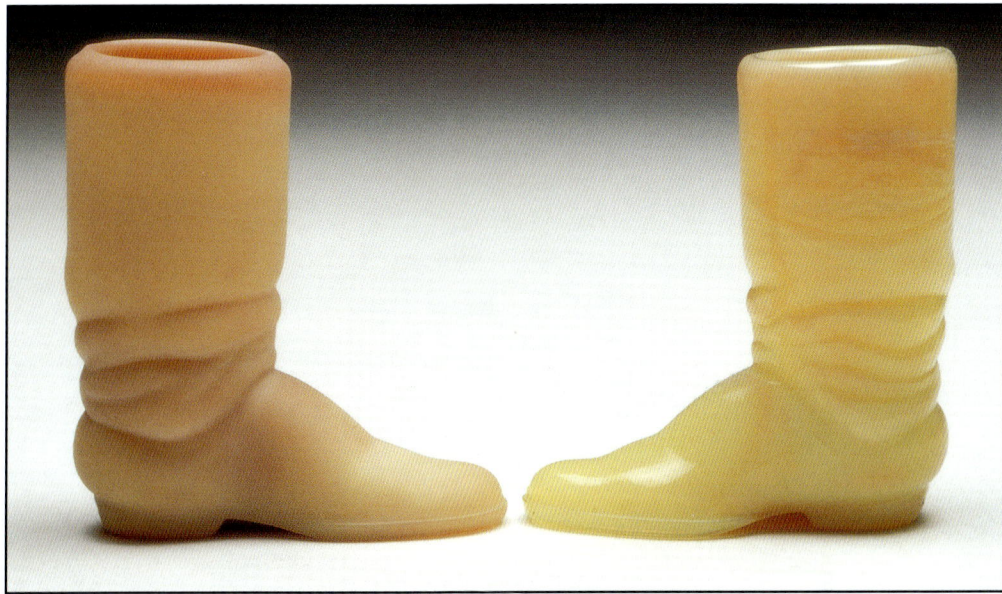

Boot #9590, 2.5" tall, 2.75" long, From Fenton Gift Shop 1986,
Left: Satin finish #9590BE, **$32**; **Right:** Gloss finish #9590BR, **$38**

Miniature rose bowl #9558, 1.75" tall, 3.25" wide, slight single crimp & cupped in, From Fenton Gift Shop 1986,
Left: Gloss finish #9558BE, **$30**; **Right:** Satin finish #9558BR, **$35**

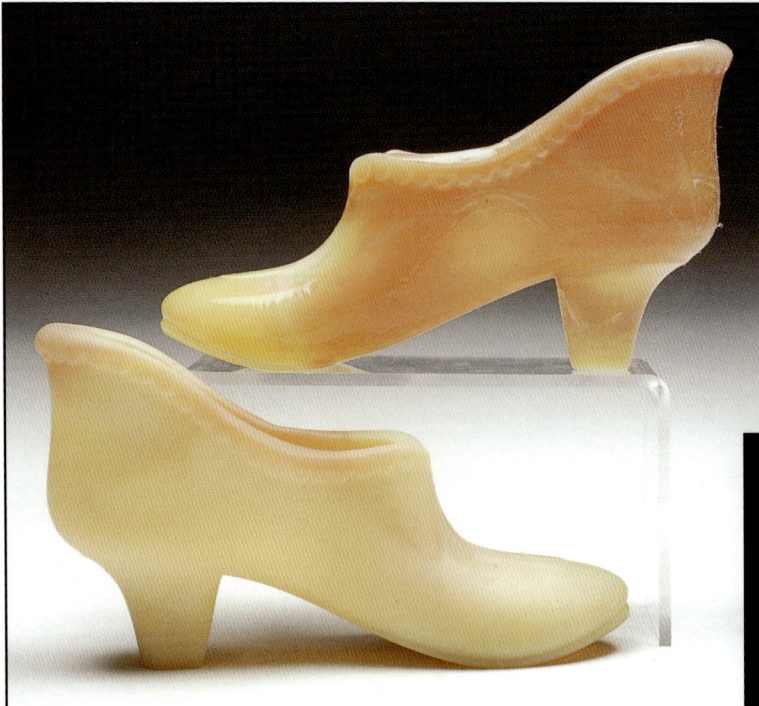

90 The 1980s

Slipper #9591, 2.6" tall, 5.25" long, From Fenton Gift Shop 1986, **Top:** Gloss finish #9591BE, **$40**; **Bottom:** Satin finish #9591BR, **$45**

Toothpick #9592BR, plain satin finish, 2.5" tall, From Fenton Gift Shop 1986, **$30**

Toothpick #9592VB, hand painted violets decoration (not part of Levay "Violets" line), 2.5" tall, Decorated by S. (Sue) Lee, From Fenton Gift Shop 1986, **$48**

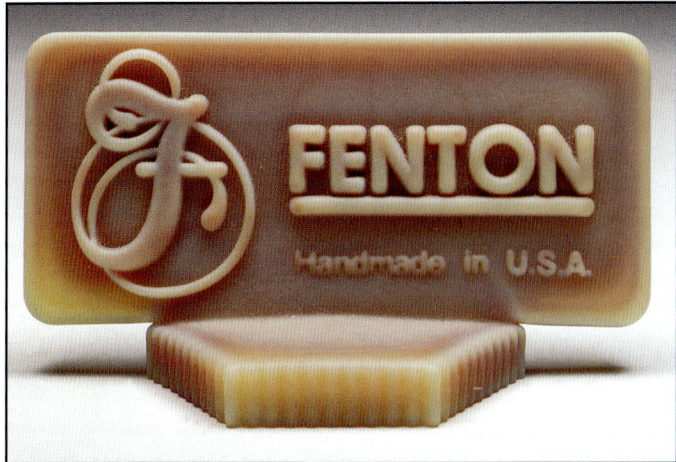

The 1980s   91

Fenton Logo #9797BR, plain satin finish, 2.6" tall, 5" long, From Fenton Gift Shop 1986, **$125**

Mary Walrath once again approached Fenton to make another collection for her based on the Love Bouquet. This time it was decided to make a set of miniatures. The same meticulous detail was given to each piece. The exact same decoration was used, though the Burmese color varied from the previous collection due to all of these pieces being pressed. This was the first special order to be produced with the pressed formula.

Footed bud vase #1752WQ, hand painted "Love Bouquet" Miniature Collection, 5.25" tall, slight single crimp, Special order made exclusively for Mary C. Walrath 1986, **$60**

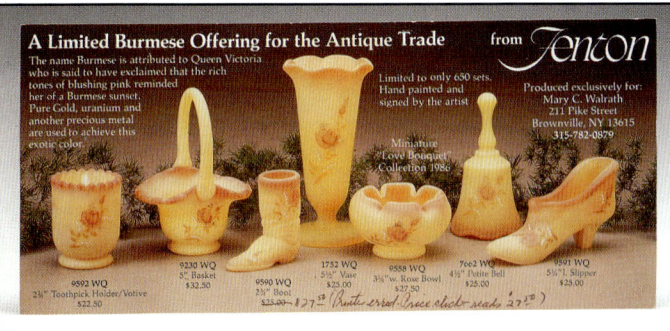

Original brochure of the hand painted "Love Bouquet" Miniature Collection by Mary Walrath 1986. (Reprinted with permission from Mary Walrath)

Petite bell #7662WQ, hand painted "Love Bouquet" Miniature Collection, 4.4" tall, Special order made exclusively for Mary C. Walrath 1986, **$65**

92   The 1980s

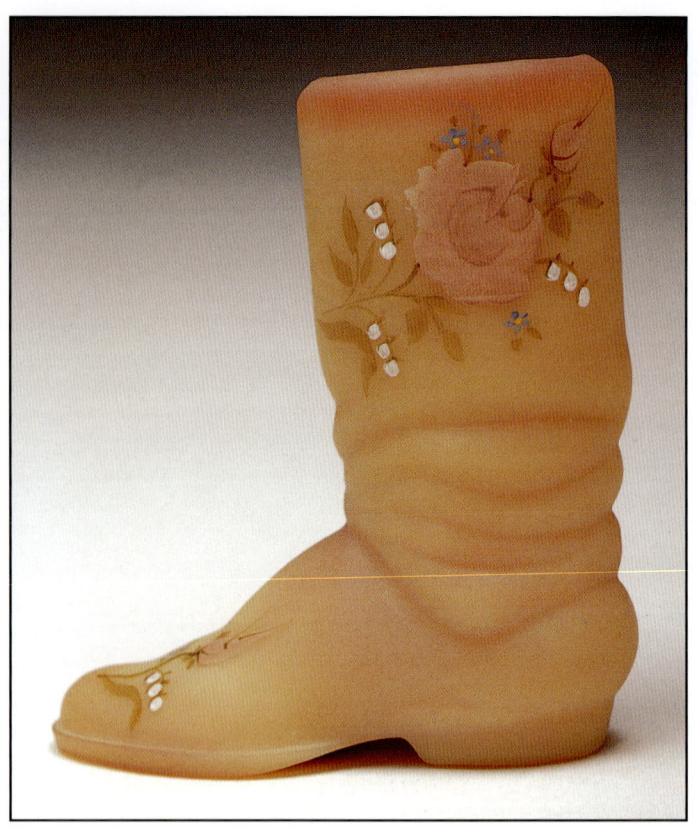

Boot #9590WQ, hand painted "Love Bouquet" Miniature collection, 2.75" tall, 2.4" long, Special order made exclusively for Mary C. Walrath 1986, **$55**

Basket #9230WQ, hand painted "Love Bouquet" Miniature Collection, 4.75" tall, 3.4" wide, very slight crimp, Special order made exclusively for Mary C. Walrath 1986, **$95**

Rose bowl #9558WQ, hand painted "Love Bouquet" Miniature Collection, 1.8" tall, 3" wide, slight single crimp & cupped in, Special order made exclusively for Mary C. Walrath 1986, **$48**

Toothpick #9592WQ, 2.5" tall, hand painted "Love Bouquet" Miniature collection, Special order made exclusively for Mary C. Walrath 1986, **$48**

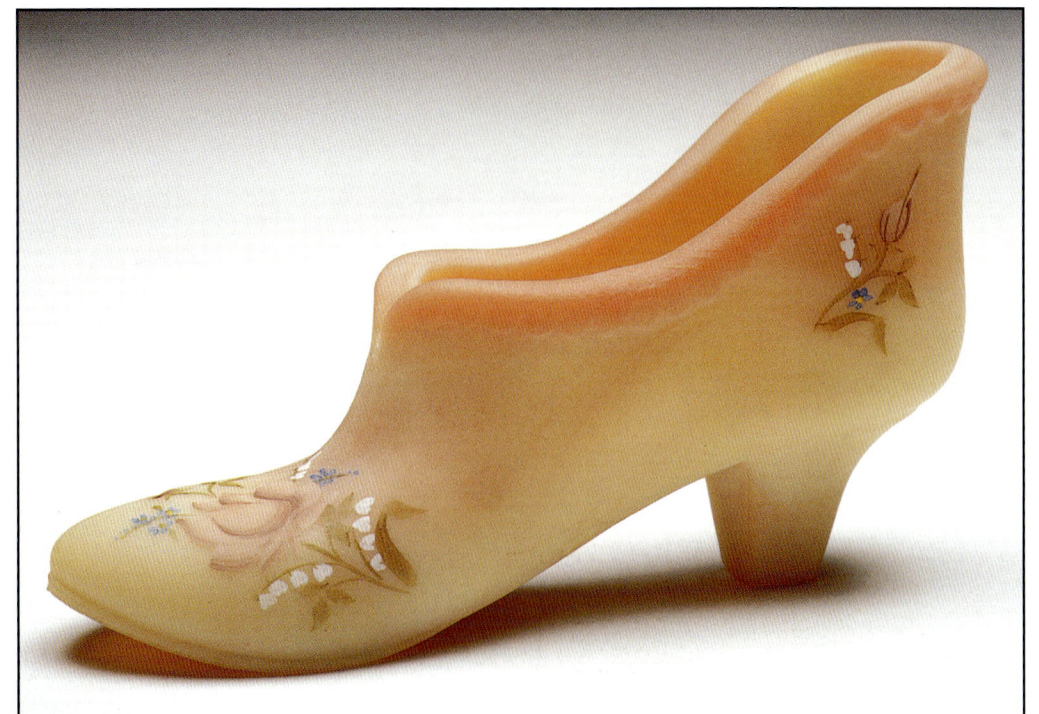

Slipper #9591WQ, hand painted "Love Bouquet" Miniature Collection, 2.5" tall, 5" long, Special order made exclusively for Mary C. Walrath 1986, **$68**

1987

For 1987, only one Burmese item was produced. A bell was made in the previous Shell design and put in the Connoisseur Collection. A limited number of 2500 were scheduled to be made. The following year Fenton decided to try putting some items on QVC. Since the bell hadn't sold out, it was decided to have this piece shown on one of the programs. This was the first piece of Burmese to debut on QVC in 1988 even though it had actually been made in 1987. Every piece of Burmese since has been made exclusively for the show like all the rest of the glass.

Bell #7666SB, hand painted under sea scene of seahorse & shells, 6.25" tall, 3.8" wide, single star crimp, "Shell" decoration designed by Dianna Barbour, Limited to 2500, Connoisseur Collection 1987, **$110**
Note, this bell hadn't sold out and was used as the first Burmese piece on the October 1998 QVC Show.

Detail of hand painted "Shell" decoration.

94   The 1980s

1988

While no new Burmese items were made in 1988, several blanks from previous years were decorated by Louise Piper and offered in the gift shop.

No new items were made for the next couple of years.

Tulip vase #7255, hand painted white doves & pink flowers, 10.75" tall, decorated by Louise Piper, dated Feb. 3, 1988, From Fenton Gift Shop 1988, **$295** Note, also called a Jack In The Pulpit vase.

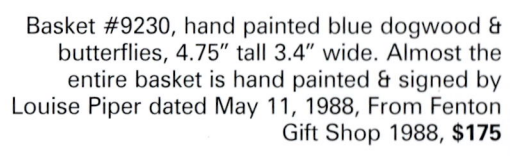

Basket #9230, hand painted blue dogwood & butterflies, 4.75" tall 3.4" wide. Almost the entire basket is hand painted & signed by Louise Piper dated May 11, 1988, From Fenton Gift Shop 1988, **$175**

The 1990s

This new decade also saw more changes to the Fenton Burmese formula and the production of many new types of items. The Burmese formula is continually being adjusted. A creamier yellow was desired on the Burmese to reflect current decorating trends. In addition the National Regulatory Commission (NRC) also has its say in the handling of the uranium oxide. Previously the chemist could physically adjust the amount of uranium that was used. Now the uranium comes in sealed pre-measured packets so no human hands can touch it. Fenton is constantly being monitored, when it uses this chemical in production, for any hazardous spills and contamination. Many regulations must be followed to be able to make the Burmese glass. During this decade, the *Glass Messenger*, Fenton's own publication came into existence. In addition many different special orders of Burmese were also developed during this decade.

1990

In 1990 Fenton celebrated its 85th anniversary of being in business. It was decided to make an elaborate offering of Burmese to celebrate this occasion. All of these items were made in place of the Connoisseur Collection for this year. Sales were limited from May to November only. All were marked 1990 and 85th anniversary on the bottom. Four different designs were used for the first time. The Petite Floral had an epergne and cruet. Linda Everson designed this pattern.

Detail of catalog 85th Anniversary offering "Gold Burmese" 1990. (Reprinted with permission from the Fenton Art Glass Company)

96   The 1990s

Detail of hand painted "Petite Floral" decoration.

One horn epergne #7202QJ, hand painted "Petite Floral" decoration designed by Linda Everson, 9.5" tall, 7" wide, double crimp, Decorated by C. Still, 85th Anniversary offering "Gold Burmese" 1990, **$175**

Detail of epergne bottom showing artist signature & 85th Anniversary.

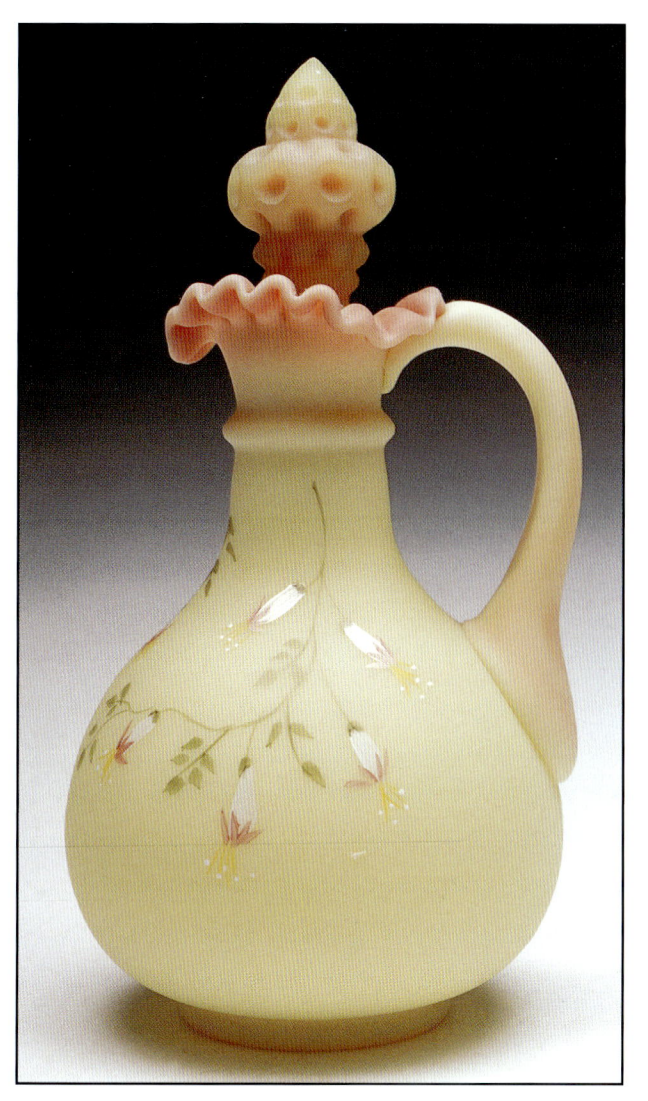

Cruet #7701QJ, hand painted "Petite Floral" decoration designed by Linda Everson, 7" tall, 85th Anniversary offering "Gold Burmese" 1990, **$135**

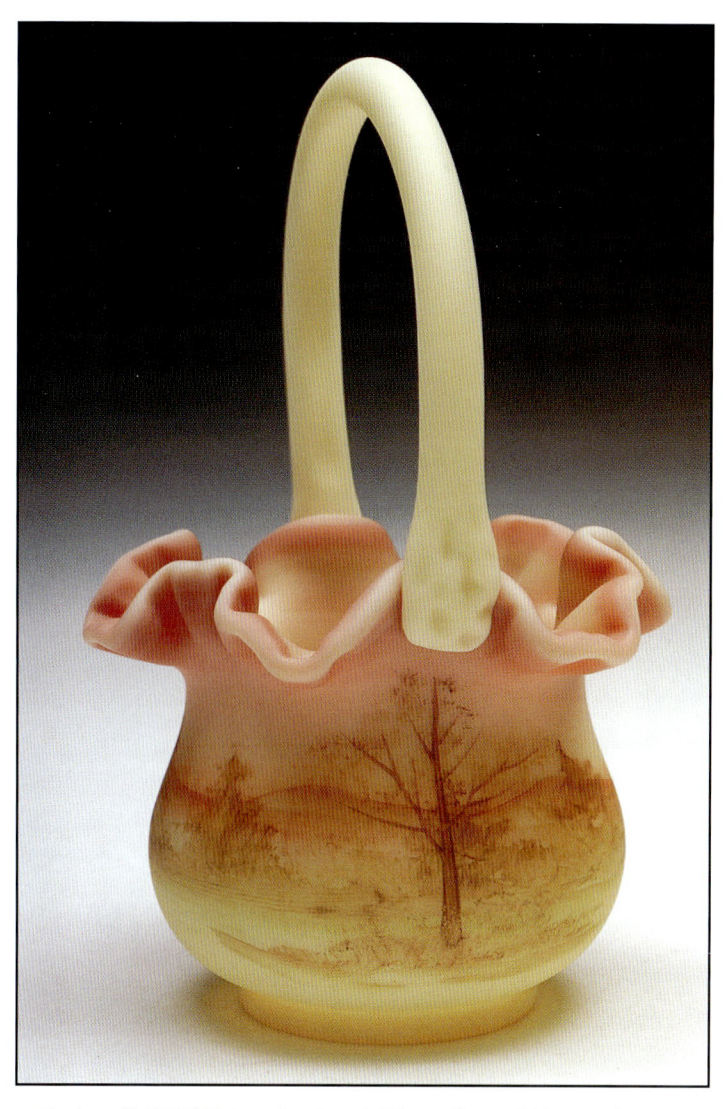

Basket #7732QD, hand painted "Trees Scene" decoration designed by Frances Burton, 6.5" tall, 4" wide, double crimp, 85th Anniversary offering "Gold Burmese" 1990, **$98**

The Rose design was revived by Dianna Barbour and was used on two vases and a lamp. The Trees Scene was on a basket and a vase. Frances Burton worked on the original design of Tree Scene by Louise Piper and slightly altered it.

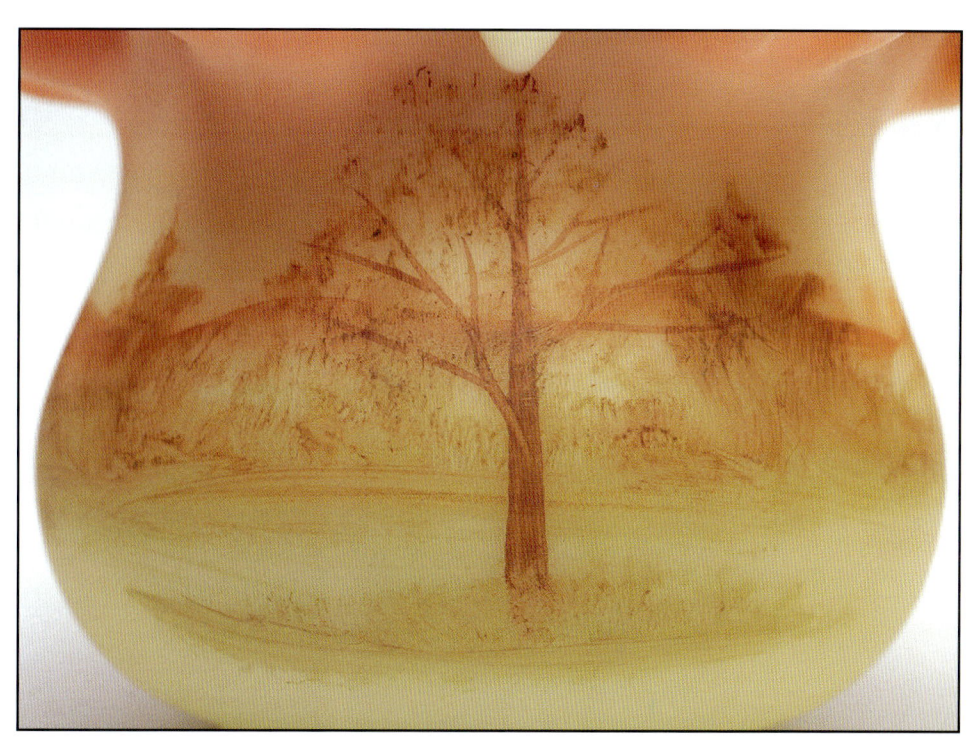

Detail of hand painted "Trees Scene" decoration.

98   The 1990s

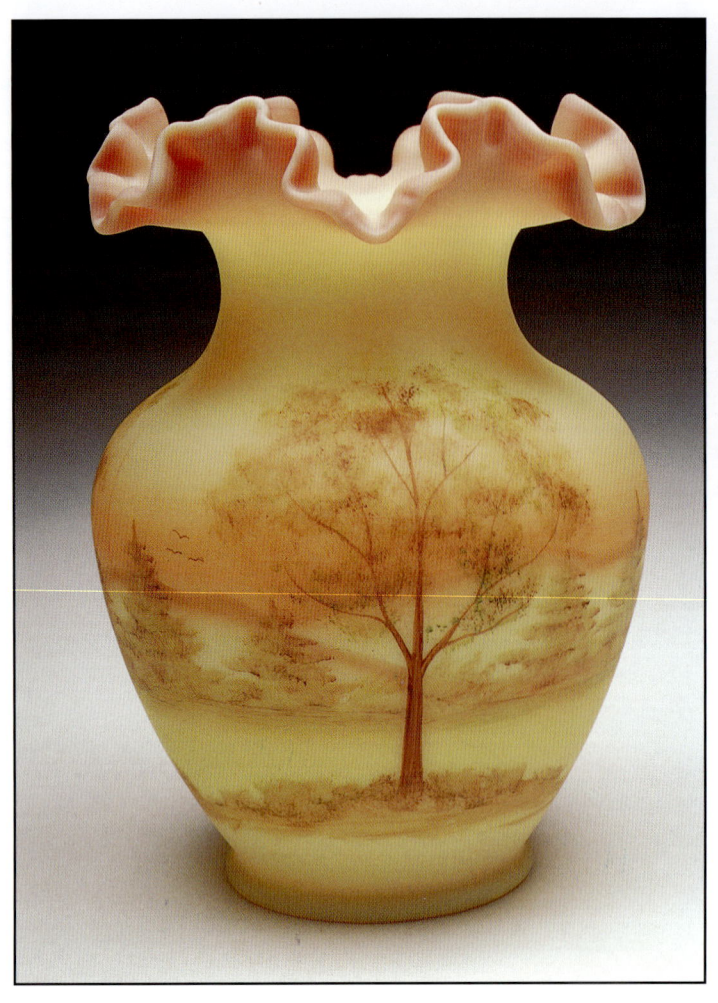

Vase #7792QD, hand painted "Trees Scene" decoration designed by Frances Burton, 8.5" tall, double crimp, 85th Anniversary offering "Gold Burmese" 1990, **$115**

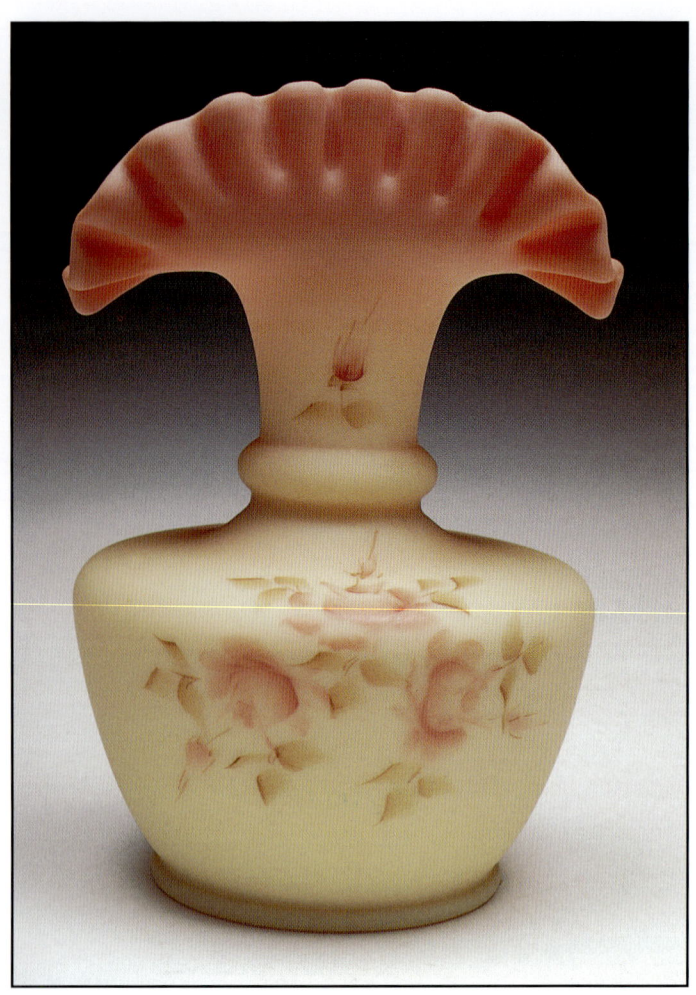

Fan vase #7790RB, hand painted "Rose" decoration designed by Dianna Barbour, 6.4" tall, single crimp (then pulled into a fan shape), 85th Anniversary offering "Gold Burmese" 1990, **$75**

Detail of hand painted "Rose" decoration.

The 1990s 99

Vase #7791RB, hand painted "Rose" decoration designed by Dianna Barbour, 6.5" tall, single crimp, 85th Anniversary offering "Gold Burmese" 1990, **$65**

Classic student lamp #9308RB, hand painted "Rose" decoration designed by Dianna Barbour, 20" overall height, 7" double crimp shade, 85th Anniversary offering "Gold Burmese" 1990, **$325**

100   The 1990s

Another new design was the Raspberry decoration. Linda Everson also came up with this design. This was used on a basket, lamp, and water set. The water set has an interesting story about it. We had ordered the set with the crimped squat pitcher. Later we found another set but with a tankard style pitcher. A couple of years later when Frank came out as a guest at the PNWFA convention in Springfield, Oregon, I asked him about the reason for the two styles of pitchers. He kind of laughed and said there had been a mixup. It had been planned to go with the squat pitcher. Sample pieces were made, decorated and photographed for the supplement. When the actual production was started for the set, another pitcher mould got accidentally pulled. Many pitchers were made before the mistake was discovered. Being the resourceful company they were, Fenton decided to offer the tankard style on the east coast and the squat style on the west coast. Both utilized the same number and no one figured anyone would be the wiser. But as everyone knows, the collector will eventually figure it all out.

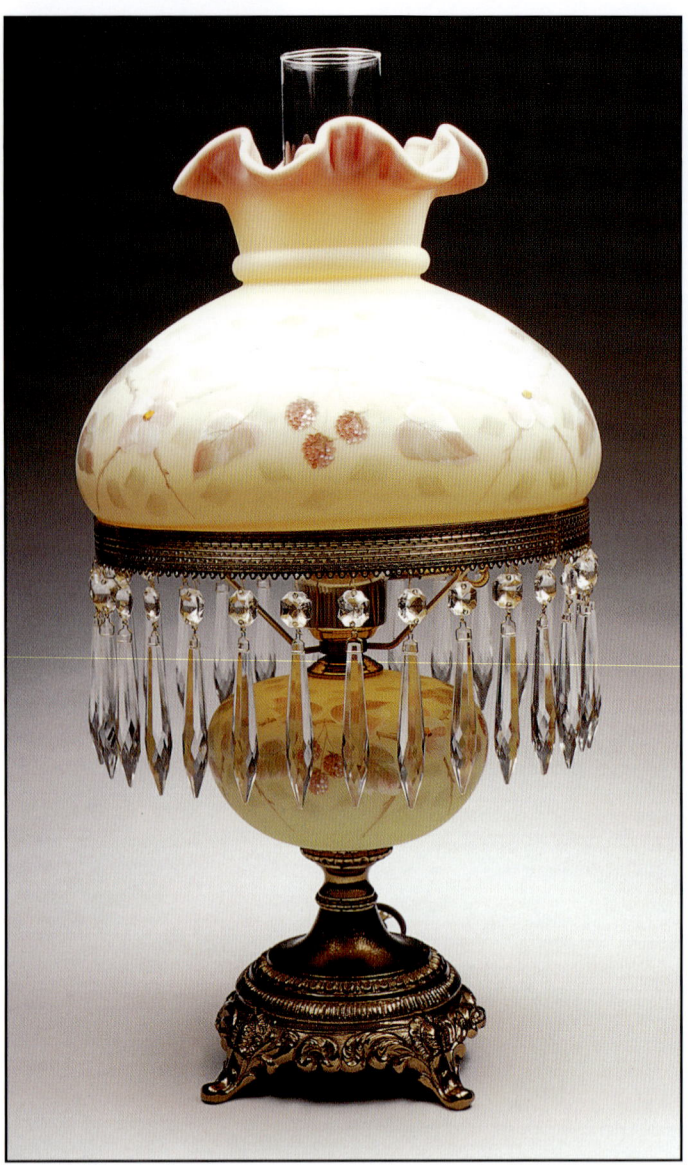

Student lamp #7412QH, hand painted "Raspberry" decoration designed by Linda Everson, 20" overall height, 10" double crimp shade, 85th Anniversary offering "Gold Burmese" 1990, **$395**

Detail of hand painted "Raspberry" decoration.

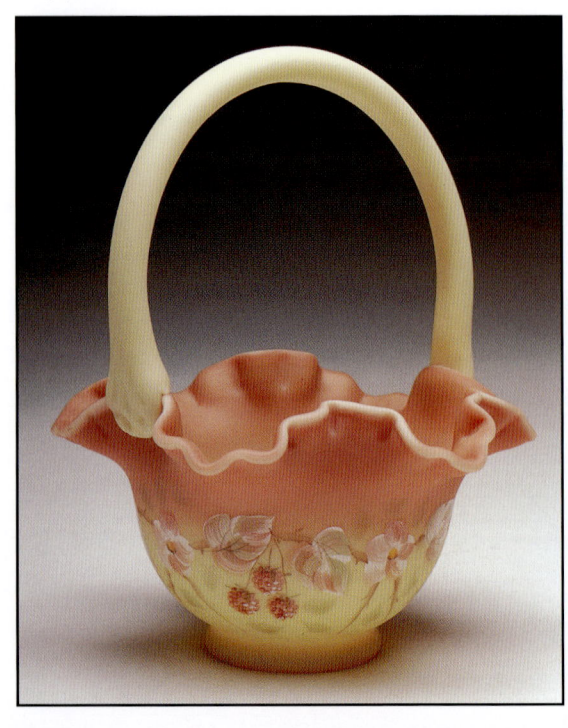

Basket #7731QH, hand painted "Raspberry" decoration designed by Linda Everson, 8" tall, 6.25" wide, double crimp, 85th Anniversary offering "Gold Burmese" 1990, **$98**

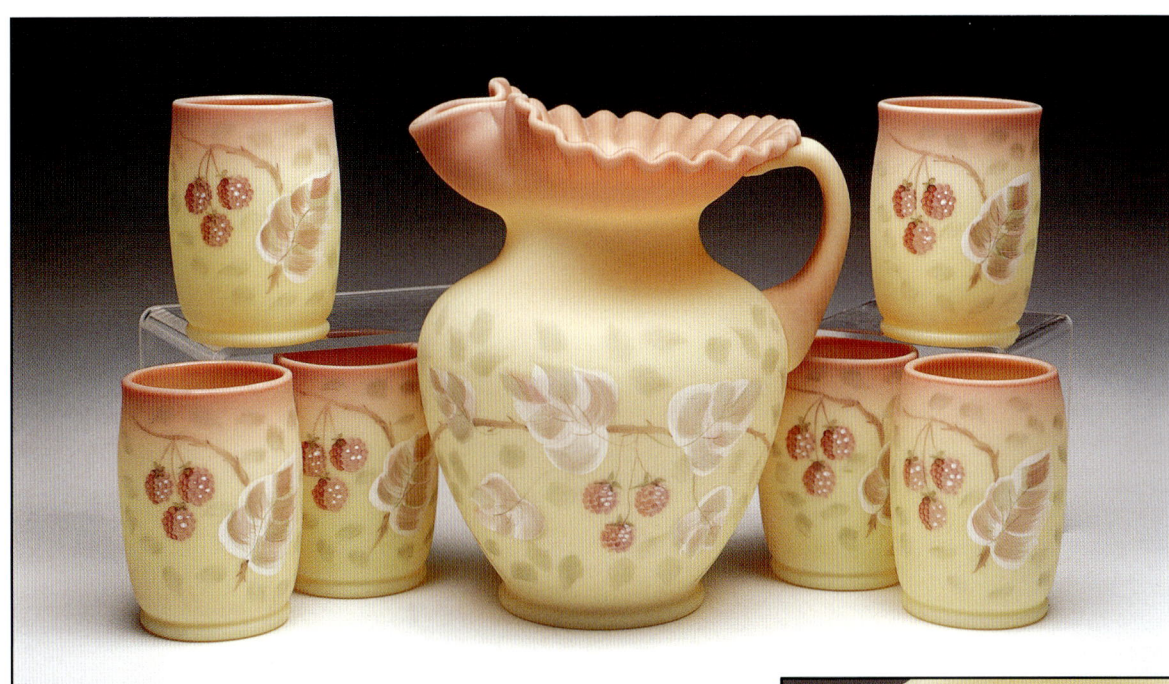

The 1990s 101

Water set #7700QH, hand painted "Raspberry" decoration designed by Linda Everson, 85th Anniversary offering "Gold Burmese" 1990, **$495** Sold on West Coast with squat pitcher, single crimp & ice lip **Left:** Tumblers, 4" tall, 11 ounces; **Center:** Pitcher, 8.6" tall, 64 ounces; **Right:** Tumblers, 4" tall, 11 ounces

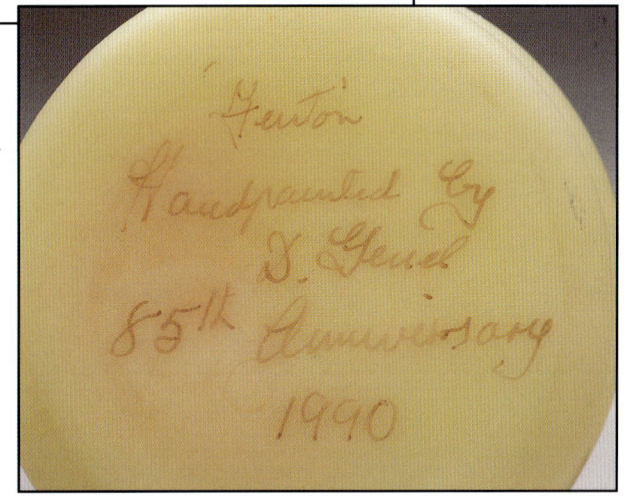

Detail of "Raspberry" tumbler bottom showing artist signature, 85th Anniversary.

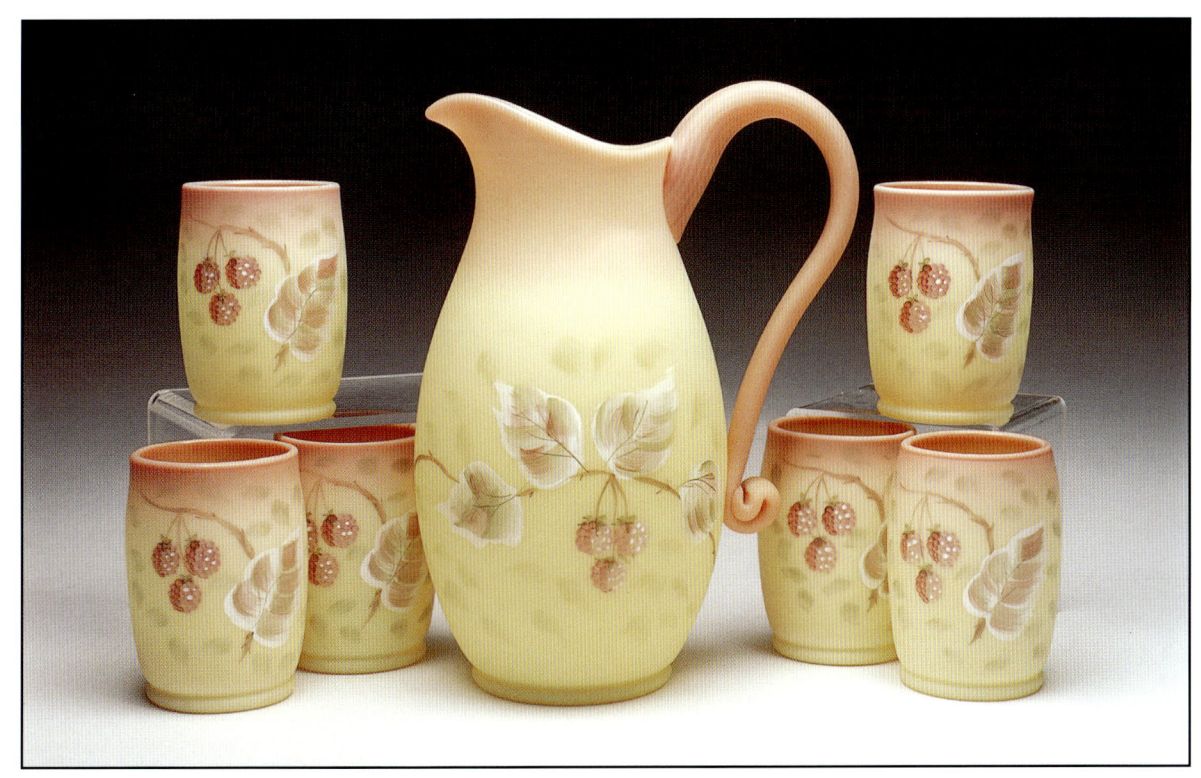

Water set #7700QH, hand painted "Raspberry" decoration designed by Linda Everson, 85th Anniversary offering "Gold Burmese" 1990, **$450** Sold on East Coast with tankard pitcher, no crimp or ice lip, **Left:** Tumblers, 4" tall, 11 ounces; **Center:** Pitcher, 9.75" tall, 64 ounces; **Right:** Tumblers, 4" tall, 11 ounces

The 1990s

The Fenton gift shop once again featured several undecorated versions from the catalog and QVC. A couple of the baskets were found with twist loop handles.

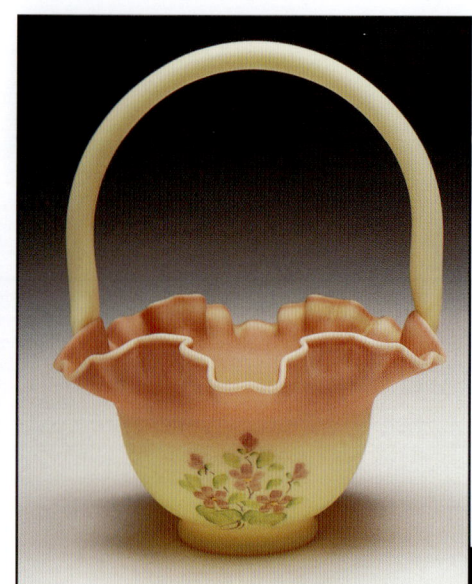

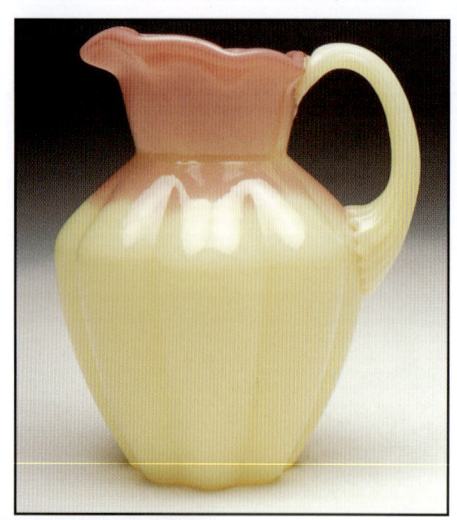

Melon pitcher #4661BE, plain gloss finish, 5.5" tall, slight single crimp, holds 16 ounces, From Fenton Gift Shop 1990, **$40**

Basket #7731VB, hand painted violets decoration (not part of the Levay Violets line), 8" tall, 6.25" wide, double crimp, From Fenton Gift Shop 1990, **$125**

Melon pitcher #4661, hand painted purple berries & blue leaves, 5.5" tall, slight single crimp, holds 16 ounces, From Fenton Gift Shop 1990, **$65**

Cruet #7701BR, plain satin finish, 7.25" tall, tight single crimp, crown stopper, From Fenton Gift Shop 1990, **$125**

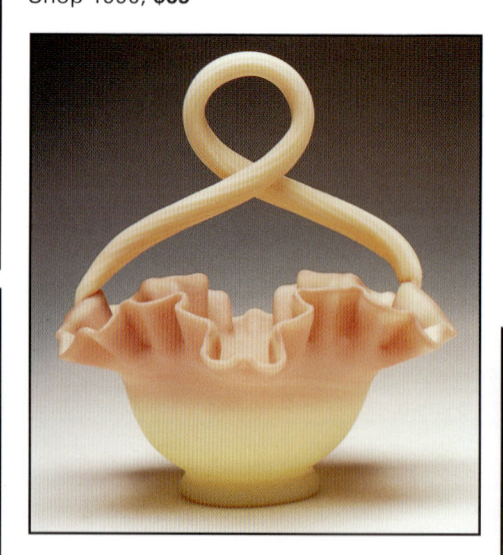

Top right: Basket #7731BR, plain satin finish, 8" tall, 6.25" wide, double crimp with twisted loop rib handle, Sample from Fenton Gift Shop 1990, **$125**

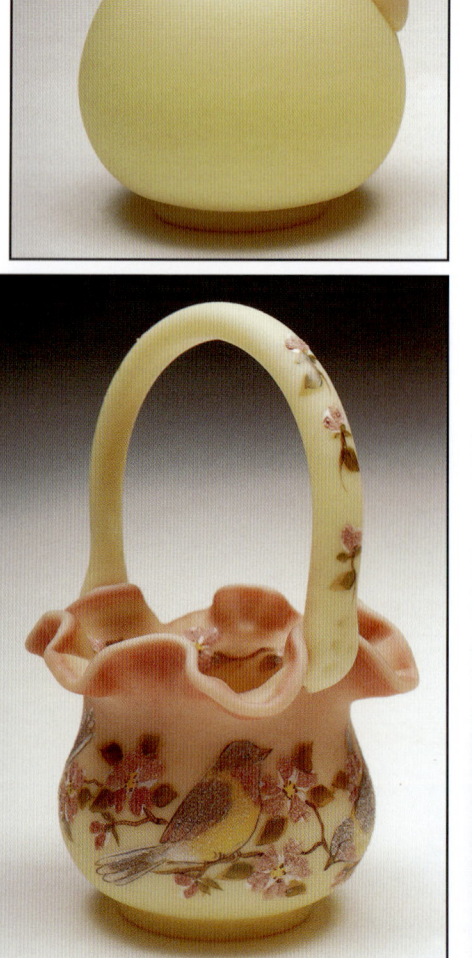

Basket #7732, hand painted frit birds & flowers, 6.25" tall, 4" wide, double crimp, Decorated by Marilyn Wagner, From Fenton Gift Shop 1990, **$135**

Tumbler #7543BR, plain satin finish, 4" tall, holds 11 ounces, From Fenton Gift Shop 1990, **$24**

The 1990s 103

Basket #7732BE, plain gloss finish, 7" tall, 4" wide, double crimp with twisted loop handle (very unusual handle), Sample from Fenton Gift Shop 1990, **$135**

The offering for QVC in 1990 in Burmese only had one item, a melon pitcher. As with other years, a few plain pieces were decorated special for the gift shop.

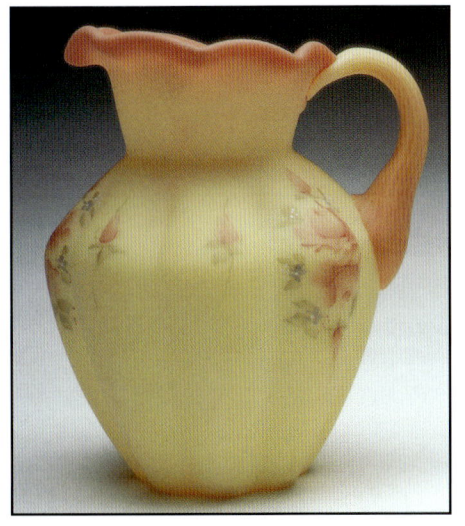

Melon pitcher #C4661RB, hand painted "Roses" decoration, 5.25", slight single crimp, Bill Fenton signature, Made for QVC Show October 1990, **$95**

While shopping back East that year, we found two gloss Burmese vases that were decorated with roses but were signed by Louise Plues. We were confused about this signature. Louise Piper was from the Fenton decorating department but Louise Plues was a decorator for Westmoreland and now Westmoreland was closed. Seeking to satisfy our curiosity about the pieces, we showed them to Frank. He didn't say much except to say that he would look into it. Apparently what had been happening was plain Fenton pieces were being bought and taken over to the Westmoreland gift shop to be sold. Louise Plues was doing contract work for them and was also decorating some pieces. The problem was that the roses, even though larger, looked a lot like the Fenton rose decoration. The similarity of names between Louise Piper and Louise Plues could cause problems to some collectors. No more pieces painted with roses and having Louise Plues' name on them were ever made again.

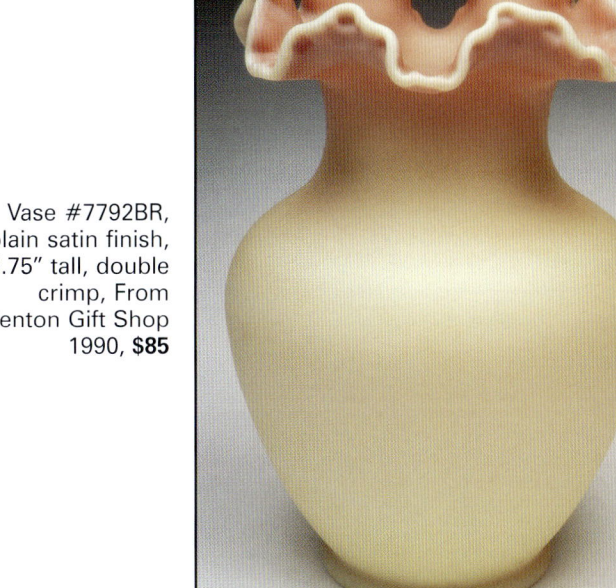

Vase #7791, hand painted flowers on gloss finish, 6.5" tall, tight single crimp, Decorated by Marilyn Wagner, From Fenton Gift Shop 1990, **$65**

Vase #7792BR, plain satin finish, 8.75" tall, double crimp, From Fenton Gift Shop 1990, **$85**

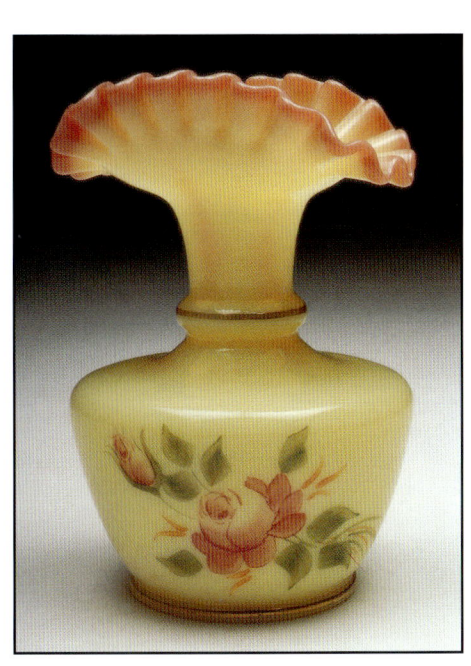

Fan vase #7790, hand painted roses on gloss finish with gold trim, 6" tall, single crimp (then pulled into a fan shape), Decorated by Louise Plues for Westmoreland Museum Gift Shop 1990, **$125** Note, this piece was purchased from the Fenton Gift Shop plain and decorated after leaving the Fenton factory.

104   The 1990s

Detail of signature of Louise Plues former Westmoreland decorator.

A basket with Roses in the melon shape was the only piece to be offered on QVC. While Fenton didn't produce much this particular year for themselves, an avalanche of items were produced for special orders.

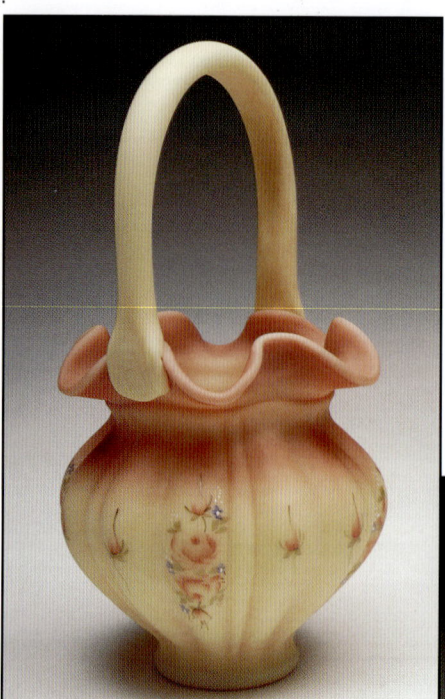

Melon basket #C4648RB, hand painted "Rose" decoration, 9" tall, 4.8" wide, single crimp, Bill Fenton signature, Made for QVC Show June 1991, **$98**

Melon Basket #4648BR, plain satin finish, 9" tall, 4.8" wide, single crimp, From Fenton Gift Shop 1991, **$85**

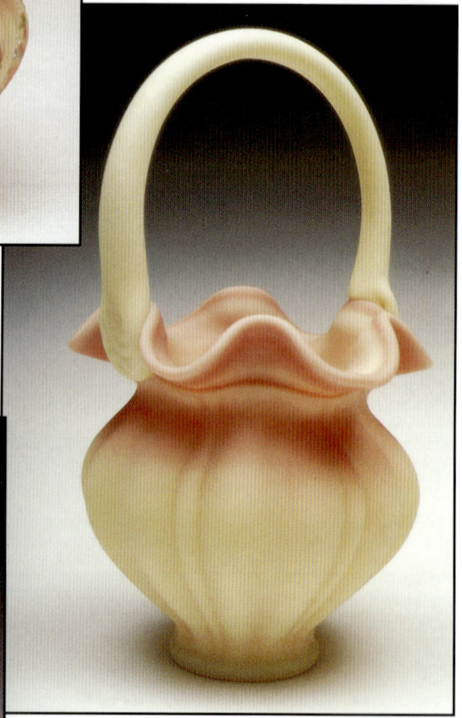

Bottom right: Vase #7792, hand painted roses on gloss finish with gold trim, 8.5" tall, double crimp, Decorated by Louise Plues for Westmoreland Museum gift Shop 1990, **$175**
Note, this piece was purchased from the Fenton Gift Shop plain and decorated after leaving the Fenton factory.

1991

The Connoisseur Collection of 1991 offered a Paisley student lamp in the Rose decoration that was designed by Frances Burton. Another piece of Raspberry, a 7" vase was also made.

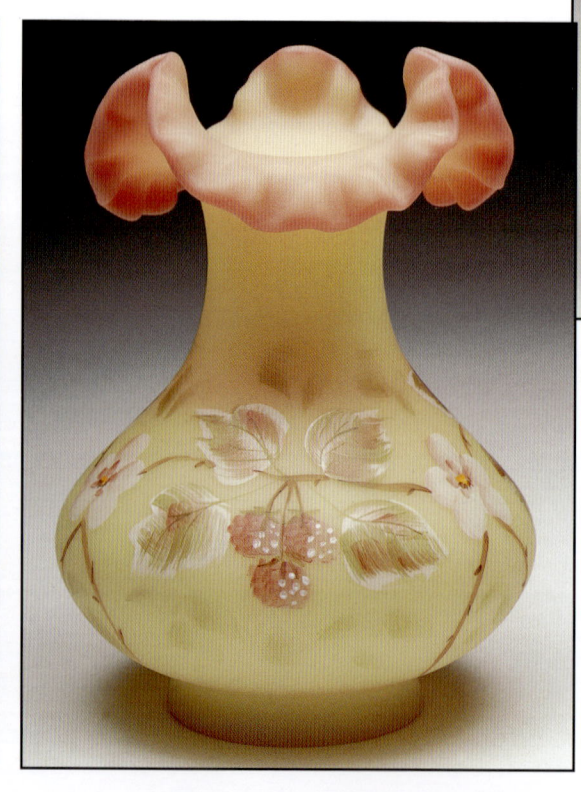

Left: Paisley student lamp #6701RB, hand painted "Rose" decoration designed by Frances Burton, 20" overall height, 7" double crimp shade, Limited edition of 500, Connoisseur Collection 1991, **$395**
Note, this item continued to be offered until Spring 1992.

Right: Vase #7252QH, hand painted "Raspberry" decoration designed by Linda Everson, 7" tall, double crimp, Connoisseur Collection 1991, **$85**
Note, this item continued to be offered until Spring 1992.

The 1990s   105

Some plain heart nappies were sampled for a special order. When they were not chosen to be used, the decorators went all out and did some beautiful decorations on these pieces exclusively for the gift shop. Several of the Fenton decorators also decided to decorate them for the annual tent sale in June. Most were painted with flowers but one was decorated with a kitten and daisies.

Heart handled nappy #3733BR, embossed "Hobnail" pattern, plain satin finish, 8" long, 6.25" wide, tight ribbon single crimp, From Fenton Gift Shop 1991, **$125**

Vase #7252, hand painted roses, gloss finish, 7" tall, double crimp, Decorated by D. Kennedy, From Fenton Gift Shop 1991, **$85**
Note, this decoration is similar to but not the same as "Rose" decoration.

Vase #7252, hand painted pink rose with two rose buds, gloss finish, 7" tall, double crimp, From Fenton Gift Shop 1991, **$95**
Note, this decoration totally different from the "Rose" decoration.

The 1990s

Tulip vase #7255, hand painted pink wild roses, 10.75" tall, Decorated by Dianna Barbour, From Fenton Gift Shop 1991, **$135**
Note, also called a Jack In The Pulpit vase.

Tulip vase #7255, hand painted palm tree & white frit accents, 10.75" tall, Decorated by Dianna Barbour, From Fenton Gift Shop 1991, **$145**
Note, also called a Jack In The Pulpit vase.

Heart handled nappy #7333, hand painted ivy & pink frit flowers, 8" long, 6.5" wide, tight single crimp, From Fenton Gift Shop 1991 **Left:** Satin finish, Decorated by Dianna Barbour, **$135**; **Right:** Gloss finish, Decorated by1 Dianna Barbour, **$125**

Heart handled nappy #7333, plain, 8" long, 6.5" wide, tight single crimp, From Fenton Gift Shop 1991,
Left: Gloss finish #7333BE, **$75**; **Right:** Satin finish #7333BR, **$85**

Heart handled nappy #7333, hand painted mauve frit flowers & frit hummingbirds with gold accents, 8" long, 6.5" wide, tight single crimp, Decorated by Marilyn Wagner, From Fenton Gift Shop 1991, **$165**

Heart handled nappy #7333, hand painted pink rose, gloss finish, 8" long, 6.5" wide, tight single crimp, Decorated by Dianna Barbour, From Fenton Gift Shop 1991, **$135**

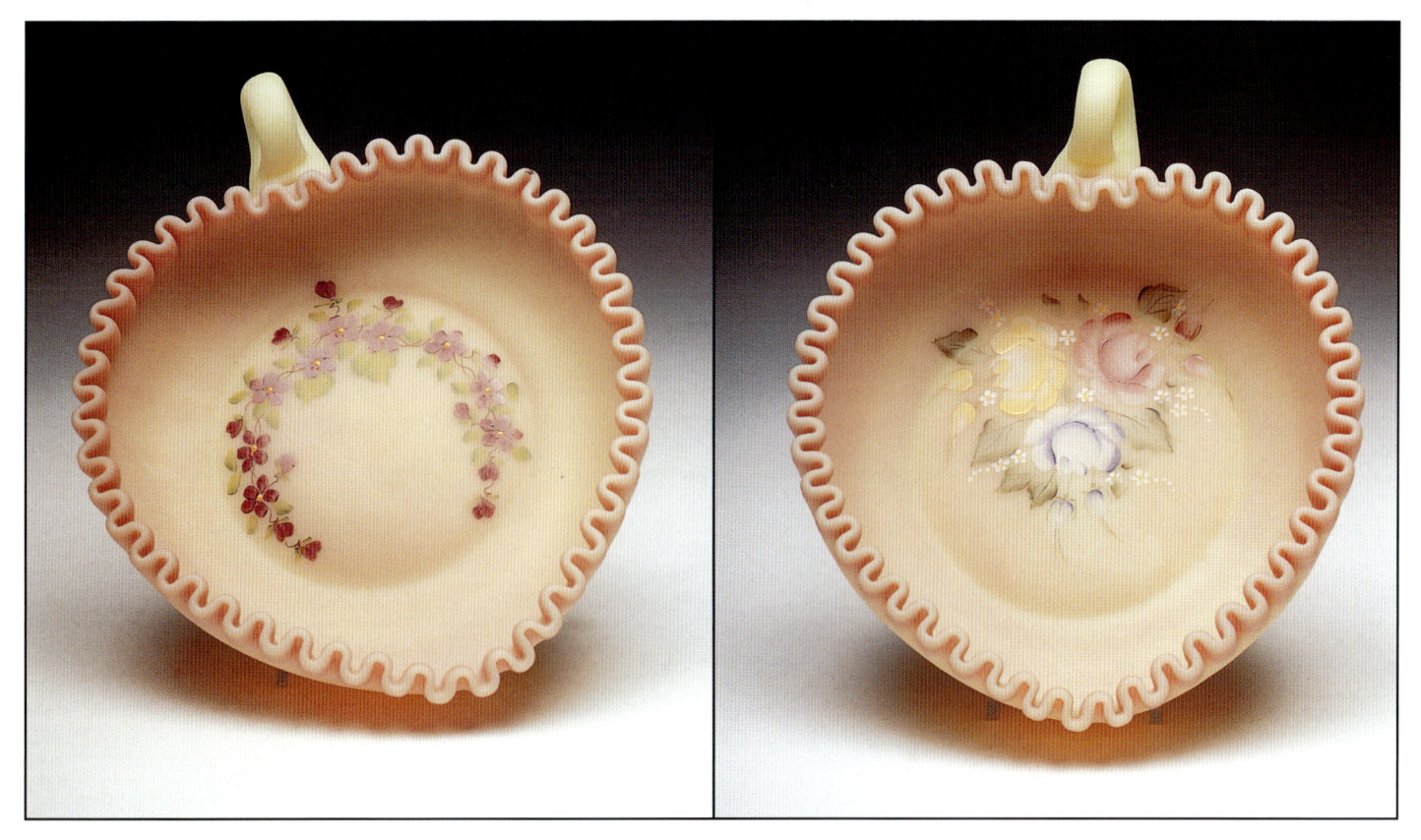

The 1990s 107

Heart handled nappy #7333VB, hand painted violets decoration (not part of Levay "Violets" line), 8" long, 6.5" wide, tight single crimp, Decorated by S. (Sue) Lee, From Fenton Gift Shop 1991, **$150**

Heart handled nappy #7333, hand painted three roses (yellow, pink & blue), 8" long, 6.5" wide, tight single crimp, Decorated by K. Lauderman, From Fenton Gift Shop 1991, **$150**

Heart handled nappy #7333, hand painted kittens & daisies, 8" long, 6.5" wide, tight single crimp, Decorated by Marilyn Wagner, From Fenton Gift Shop 1991, **$175**

Heart handled nappy #7333, hand painted purple flowers & butterfly, 8" long, 6.5" wide, tight single crimp, From Fenton Gift Shop 1991, **$145**

The 1990s

Crail and Son of Indiana had Fenton make two items for them in Burmese. The first was the #3480 Cactus Jar. Only 143 pieces were made of this candy. The other item was made from a former Verlys mould. The #8254BR Mermaid vase was a heavily sculpted vase featuring mermaids dancing around the entire outside of the vase. Out of the four hour turn, only 57 were actually made.

Shirley Griffith, author of the Milk Glass Hobnail book had Fenton produce for her the #5202 donkey and cart set. There were only 120 sets made.

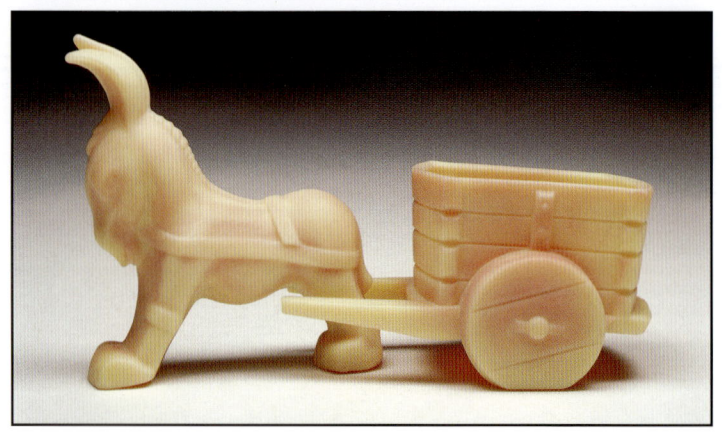

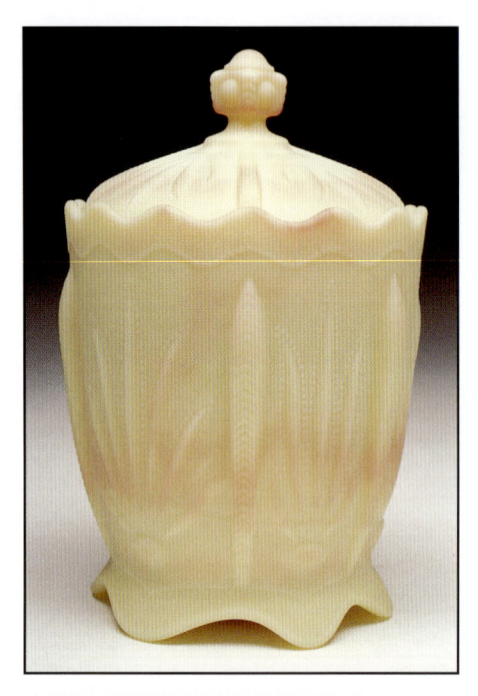

Cactus covered jar #3480BR, plain satin finish, 8" tall, 5.25" wide, Limited to 143, Special order made exclusively for Crails 1991, **$250**

Donkey & Cart, plain satin finish, Limited to 120 sets, Special order made exclusively for Shirley Griffith 1991, **$250 pair** **Left:** Donkey #5125BR, 5" tall, 4.25" long; **Right:** Cart #1524BR, 2.8" tall, 5.25" long

McMillen and Husband of Michigan first had the #8208 Little Brown Church covered candy made in both a gloss and satin finish. There were 113 items produced in gloss and 308 in satin. Next up was a blown egg #8990 featuring the Hanging Heart treatment. They had previously produced a series of these eggs in different colors. The egg was offered in both a gloss and stain finish. A limited edition of 80 were made in gloss while 400 were made in satin.

Little Brown Church #8208, plain, 8.25" tall, 4.4" wide, Special order made exclusively for McMillin & Husband 1991, **Left:** Satin finish #8208BR, Limited to 308, **$125**; **Right:** Gloss finish #8208BE, Limited to 113, **$145**

Mermaid vase #8254BR, plain satin finish, 6.5" tall, mould originally from Verlys, Limited to 57, Special order made exclusively for Crails 1991, **$395**

Blown Egg #8990, with "Hanging Heart" treatment, 5" tall, Special order made exclusively for McMillin & Husband 1991, **Left:** Satin finish, Limited to 400, **$165**; **Right:** Gloss finish, Limited to 80, **$250**

The 1990s   109

Singleton Bailey, who operates the Loris Drug Store in South Carolina made several items in the Farmyard pattern. The interesting thing with these pieces is they actually have two patterns on them. The Farmyard is the inside pattern and the outside pattern is the Jeweled heart. A double crimped bowl was made. The spittoon was made in a crimped and plain edge version.

Bowl, embossed "Jeweled Heart" outside pattern, embossed "Farmyard" pattern inside, satin finish, 9.5" wide, double crimp, Marked on bottom DBS, Special order made exclusively for Singleton Bailey 1991, **$125**

Spittoon shape, embossed "Jeweled Heart" outside pattern, embossed "Farmyard" pattern inside, plain gloss finish, 4" tall, 6.25" wide, slight single crimp, Marked on bottom DBS, Special order made exclusively for Singleton Bailey 1991 **$95**

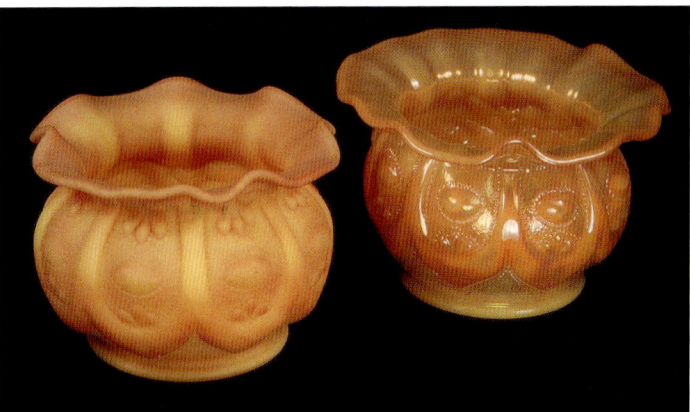

Spittoon shape, embossed "Jeweled Heart" outside pattern, embossed "Farmyard" pattern inside, 4" tall, 6.25" wide, slight single crimp, Marked on bottom DBS, Special order made exclusively for Singleton Bailey 1991,
Left: Satin finish, **$125**; **Right**: Iridized (Carnival) finish, **$125**
Note, when Burmese is photographed on black background it appears to be more yellow than it really is.

Spittoon shape, embossed "Jeweled Heart" outside pattern, embossed "Farmyard" pattern inside, plain satin finish, 4" tall, 6" wide, flared top, Marked on bottom DBS, Special order made exclusively for Singleton Bailey 1991, **$125**

The 1990s

Dorothy Taylor of Kansas City was the leading authority on new carnival glass. She published a series of books called Encore that listed the different pieces of new carnival made from American glass companies. She choose to produce the kittens miniature basket in various colors. This basket is very hard to find in the old carnival. The #9639 basket was issued in three finishes: gloss, satin, and iridized (carnival). Each of the pieces is marked Encore KC MO 1991 Taylor. Her extra care in having the basket marked enabled it not to be confused with the older versions.

The Buckeye Bash, a glass club located in Zanesville, Ohio decided to make a special toothpick holder to honor Bill Heacock. They selected the #9592 toothpick to have his picture on. There were 400 produced and each were individually numbered. The design on this toothpick was applied by the pad printing process. Bill Heacock had long worked with this club and they wanted to do something to honor his memory.

Toothpick (front view) #9592, Pad printing process on satin finish, 2.5" tall, Limited to 400, Special order made exclusively for National Toothpick Holder Collectors Society 1991, **$48** Note, this is front side of toothpick showing; depiction of Bill Heacock. It also has the following printed on it; "William R. Heacock 1947-1988".

Detail of toothpick back view (Heacock toothpick) #9592, Showing; depiction of a pattern glass toothpick (in red). It also has the following printed on it; "Buckeye Bash, National Toothpick Holder Collectors Society".

Kittens basket #9639BI, Iridized (Carnival) finish, 5" tall, 4.5" wide, single crimp, marked on bottom ENCORE K.C. MO 1991 & next to the marie base is the word TAYLOR, Special order made exclusively for Dorothy Taylor 1991, **$75**

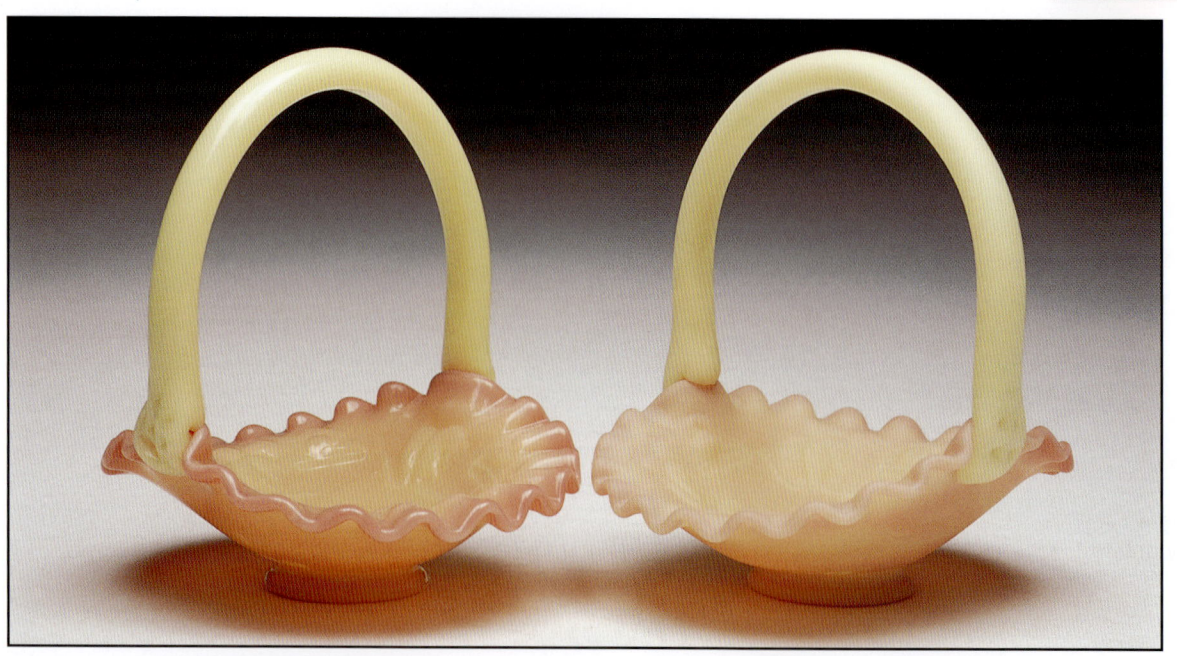

Kittens basket #9639, 5" tall, 4.5" wide, single crimp, marked on bottom ENCORE K.C. MO 1991 & next to the marie base is the word TAYLOR, Special order made exclusively for Dorothy Taylor 1991, **Left:** Gloss finish, BE, **$85**; **Right:** Satin finish, BR, **$95**

Tom Collins of Akron, Ohio decided to have a set of decorated heart dishes made. Tom decided to go with the #7333 heart dish with the Hobnail pattern on the outside. Each heart dish was decorated with different types of flowers. Beverly Cumberledge designed all of these decorations.

Heart handled nappy #7333, embossed "Hobnail" pattern, hand painted Pink Dogwood, satin finish, 8" long, 6.5" wide, tight single crimp, Decorated by Beverly Cumerledge, Special order made exclusively for Tom Collins 1991, **$195**

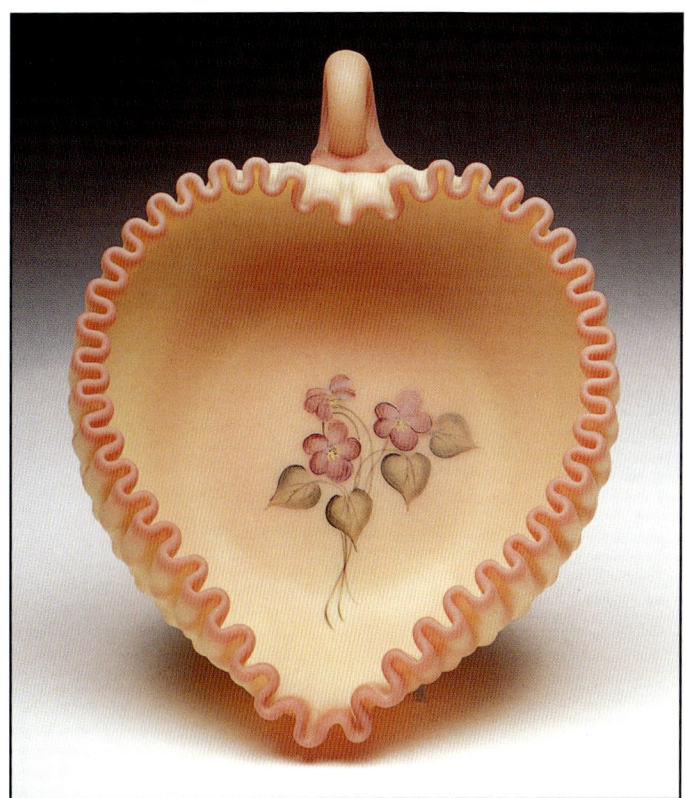

Heart handled nappy #7333VB, embossed "Hobnail" pattern, hand painted Violets, satin finish, 8" long, 6.5" wide, tight single crimp, Decorated by Beverly Cumerledge, Special order made exclusively for Tom Collins 1991, **$195**

Lois Ratcliff once again went to Fenton to have another item made for her in Burmese. This time it was a #5019 blown apple. The apple had an applied stem and leaf. It was available in both gloss and satin.

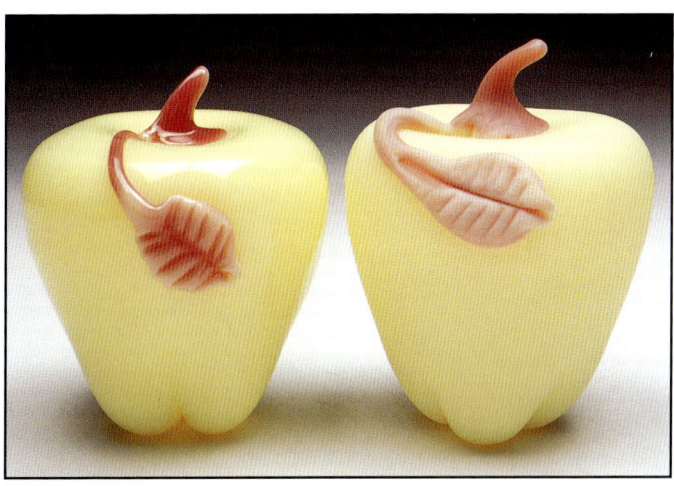

Heart handled nappy #7333, embossed "Hobnail" pattern, hand painted yellow butterfly & pink thistles, satin finish, 8" long, 6.25" wide, tight single crimp, Decorated by Beverly Cumberledge, Special order made exclusively for Tom Collins 1991, **$195**

Apple paperweight, plain, 3.75" tall, 3.15" wide, Applied stem & leaf, Special order made exclusively for Lois Ratcliff 1991,
Left: Gloss finish, BE, **$145**; **Right:** Satin finish, BR, **$145**

1992

In June 1992, there were two pieces made for the Connoisseur Collection, another Raspberry piece, and a Leaf pattern, designed by Martha Reynolds, on a new style of creamer. These were both limited to 1500 pieces.

Many undecorated items appeared in the Fenton gift shop. The decorators also really expressed themselves on the numerous vases they hand painted.

Detail of hand painted "Leaf" decoration.

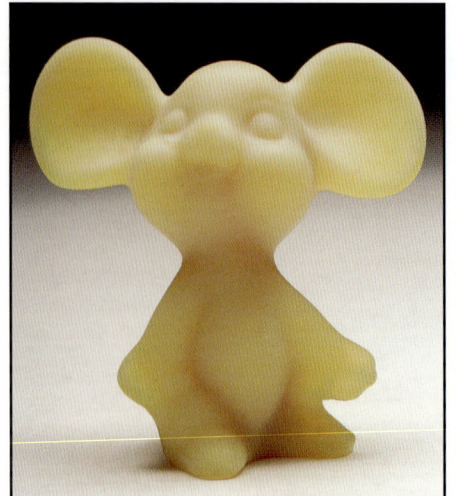

Mouse #5148BR, plain satin finish, 2.8" tall, 2.75" wide, From Fenton Gift Shop 1992, **$40**

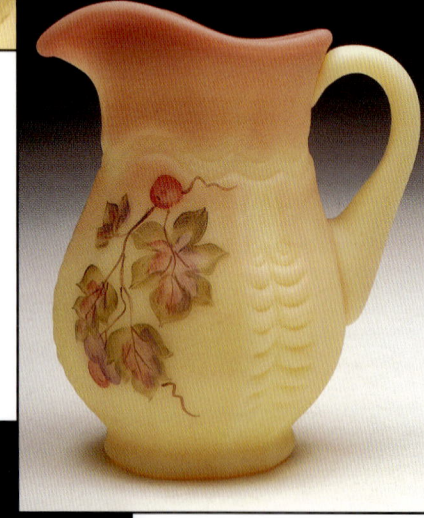

Cream pitcher #5531QP, hand painted "Leaf" decoration designed by Martha Reynolds, 4.6" tall, holds 8 ounces, Limited to 1500, Connoisseur Collection 1992, **$58**

Mouse #5148RB, hand painted "Rose" decoration, 2.8" tall, 2.75" wide, From Fenton Gift Shop 1992, **$60**

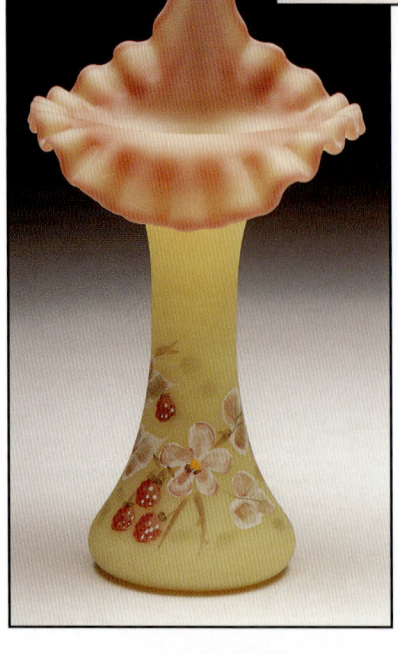

Tulip vase #5541QH, hand painted "Raspberry" decoration designed by Linda Everson, 7.5" tall, single crimp, Limited to 1500, Connoisseur Collection 1992, **$75** Note, also called a Jack In The Pulpit vase.

Sitting Cat #5165, hand painted purple frit flowers, 3.75" tall, 2.6" wide, Decorated by Marilyn Wagner, From Fenton Gift Shop 1992, **$85**

The 1990s   113

Cream pitcher #5531, plain, 4.5" tall, holds 8 ounces, From Fenton Gift Shop 1992, **Left:** Satin finish #5531BR, **$40**; **Right:** Gloss finish #5531BE, **$35**

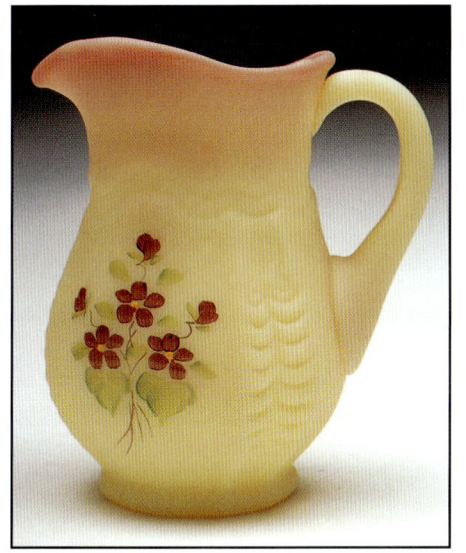

Cream pitcher #5531VB, hand painted violets decoration (not part of Levay "Violets" line), 4.5" tall, holds 8 ounces, Decorated by S. (Sue) Lee, From Fenton Gift Shop 1992, **$60**

Tulip vase, 5541BE, plain gloss finish, 6.4" tall, From Fenton Gift Shop 1992, **$40**
Note, also called a Jack In The Pulpit vase.

Tulip vase, 5541BR, plain satin finish, 6.4" tall, From Fenton Gift Shop 1992, **$45**
Note, also called a Jack In The Pulpit vase.

114   The 1990s

Tulip Vase #7552, hand painted tree scene decoration (not part of "Trees Scene" line), 6.75" tall, From Fenton Gift Shop, 1992, **$75**

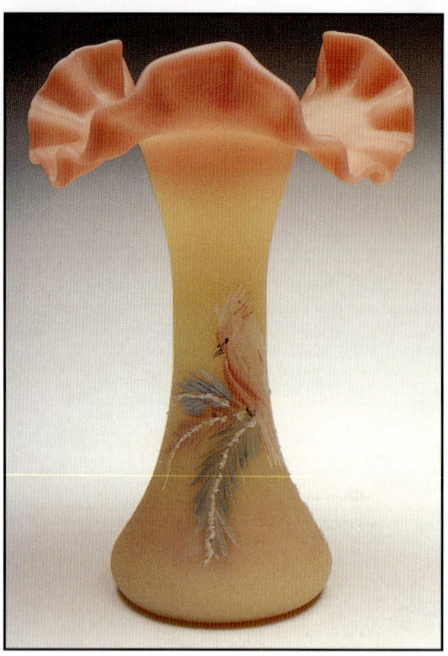

Tulip vase #7552, hand painted pink flamingo by palm tree & frit accents, 7" tall, not artist signed, From special glass room at Fenton factory 1992, **$75**
Note, also called a Jack In The Pulpit vase.

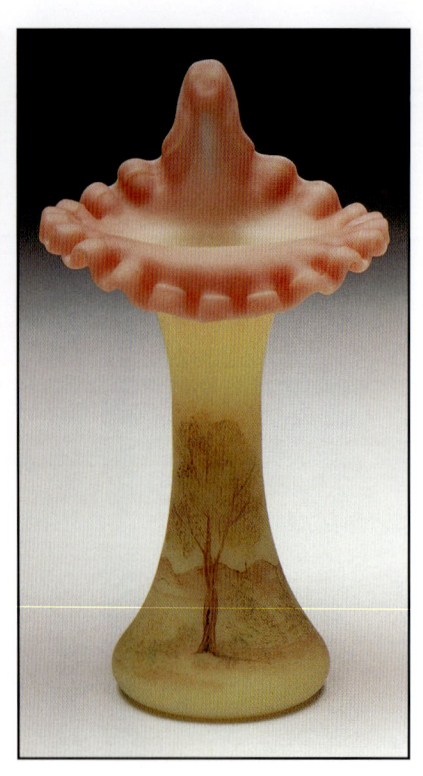

Vase #7552, hand painted pink cockatoo & palm leaves, 5.75" tall, double crimp, not artist signed, From special glass room at Fenton factory 1992, **$65**

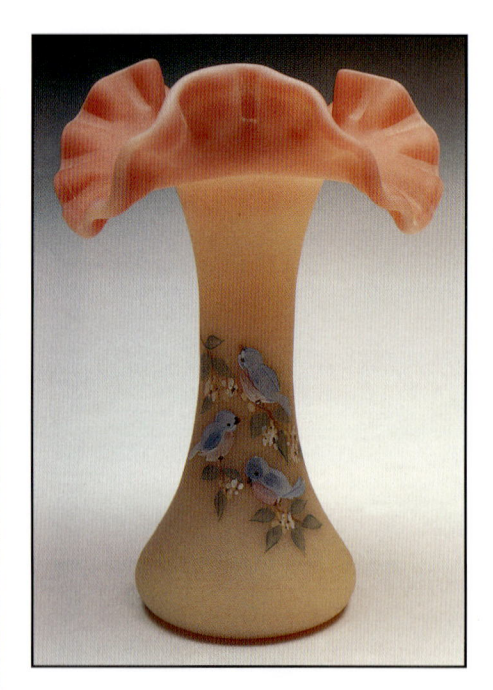

Vase #7552, hand painted small blue birds in a bush, 5.6" tall, double crimp, not artist signed, From special glass room at Fenton factory 1992, **$65**

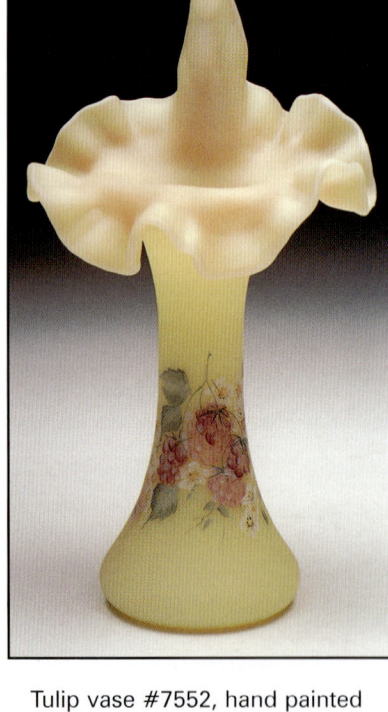

Tulip vase #7552, hand painted blackberries & flowers, 7.5" tall, double crimp, Decorated by Dianna Barbour, From special glass room at Fenton factory 1992, **$75**
Note, also called a Jack In The Pulpit vase.

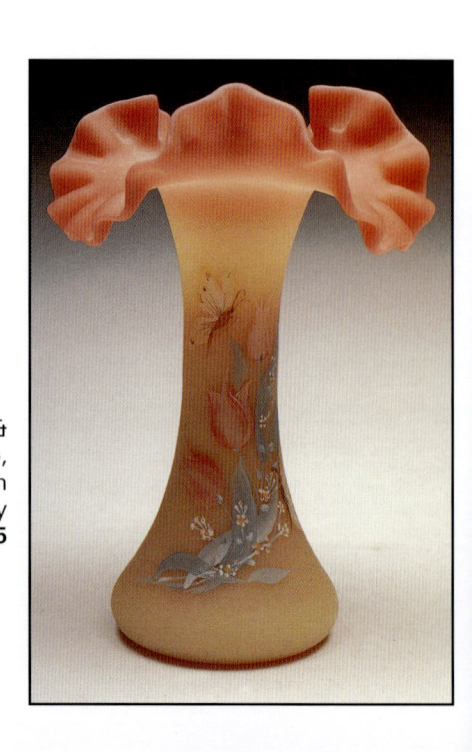

Vase #7552, hand painted pink tulips & white butterfly, 5.4" tall, double crimp, Decorated by Dianna Barbour, From special glass room at Fenton factory 1992, **$65**

The 1990s   115

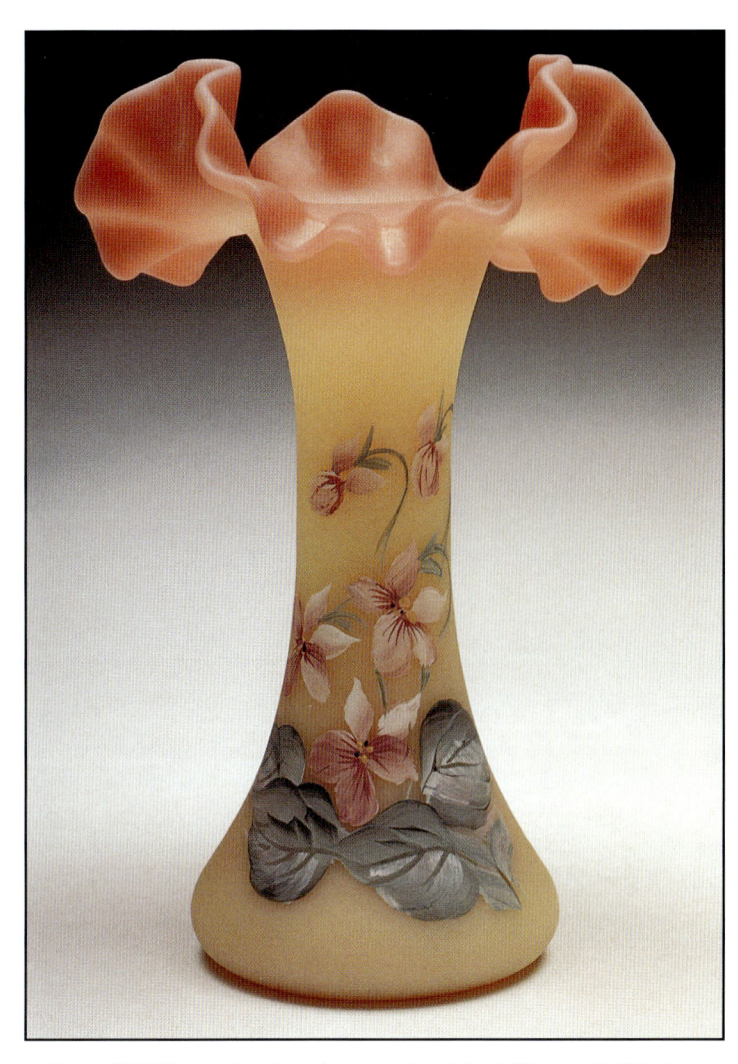

Vase #7552, hand painted purple & white trilliums, 5.5" tall, double crimp, Decorated by Dianna Barbour, From special glass room at Fenton factory 1992, **$65**

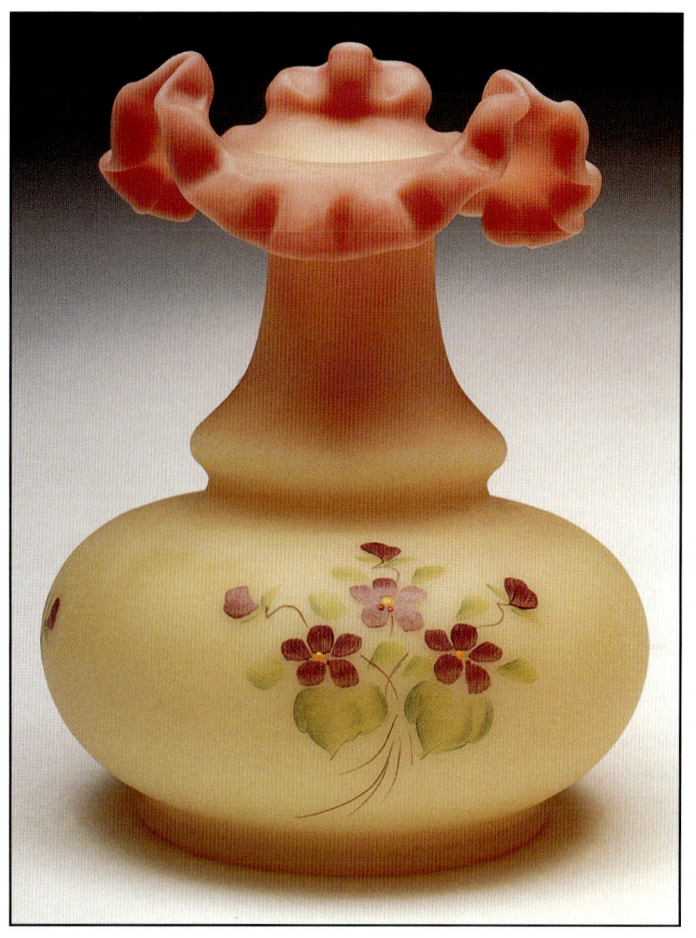

Vase #2454VB, hand painted violets decoration (not part of Levay "Violets" line), 5.75" tall, double crimp, From Fenton Gift Shop 1992, **$75**

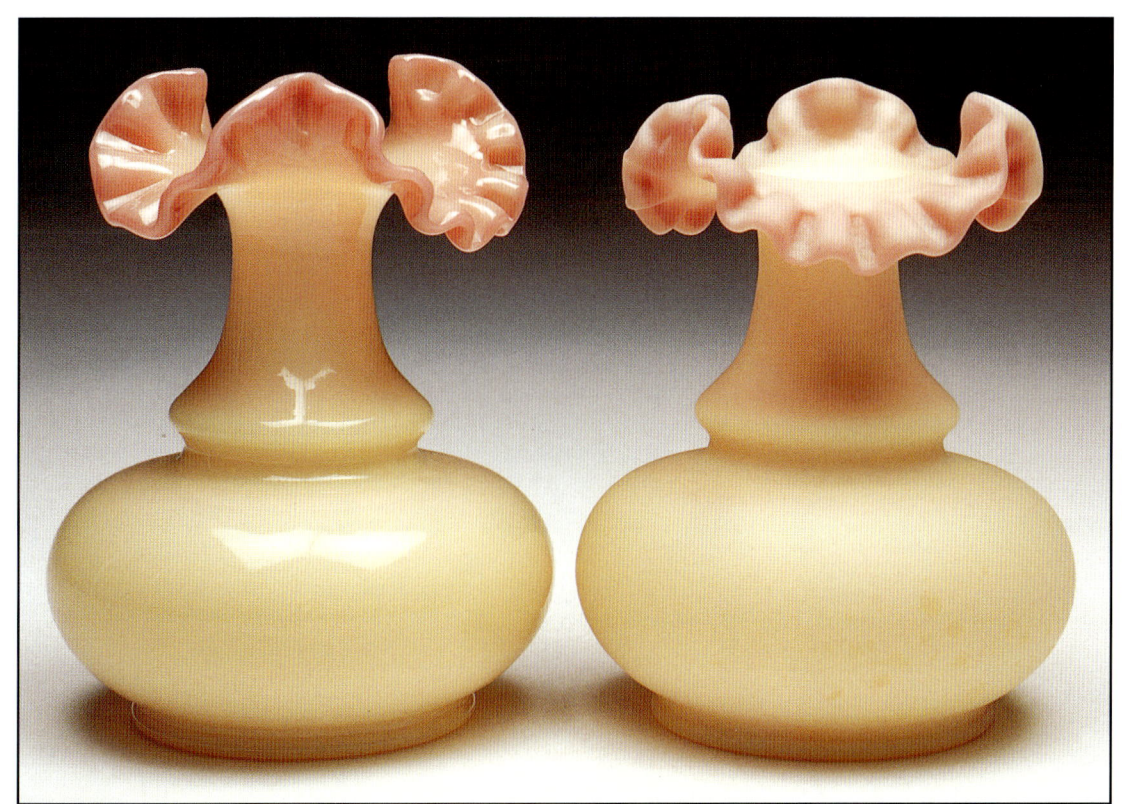

Vase #2454, plain, 5.75" tall, double crimp, From Fenton Gift Shop 1992, **Left**: Gloss finish #2454BE, **$45**; **Right**: Satin finish #2454BR, **$48**

116   The 1990s

The QVC program had one vase decorated with Roses. This piece also had Bill Fenton's signature on it.

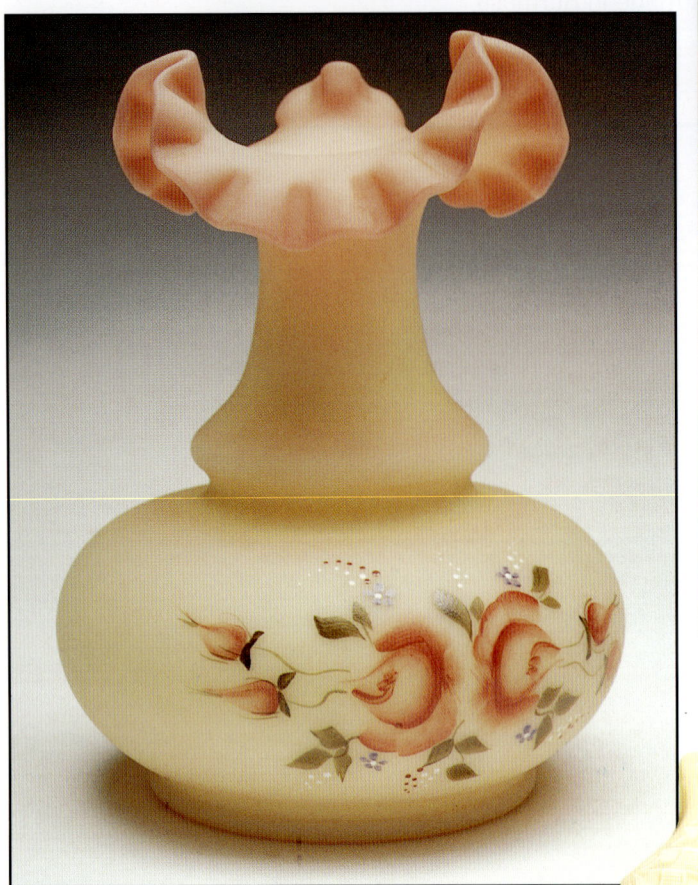

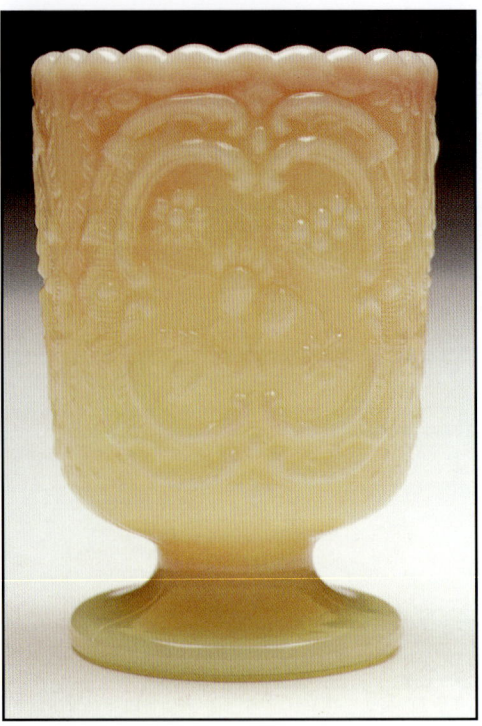

Toothpick #8295BE, "Embossed Strawberry" pattern plain gloss finish, 3" tall, Special Order made for FAGCA banquet favor 1992 1986, **$45**

Vase #2454RB, hand painted "Rose" decoration, 5.75" tall, double crimp, Bill Fenton signature, Made for QVC May 1992, **$70**

The Fenton Art Glass Collectors of America had the satin finish butterfly on a stand made for their convention display table favor. The gloss version along with the butterflies with cut off bases were used as fund raisers. The strawberry toothpick was used as the convention banquet favor.

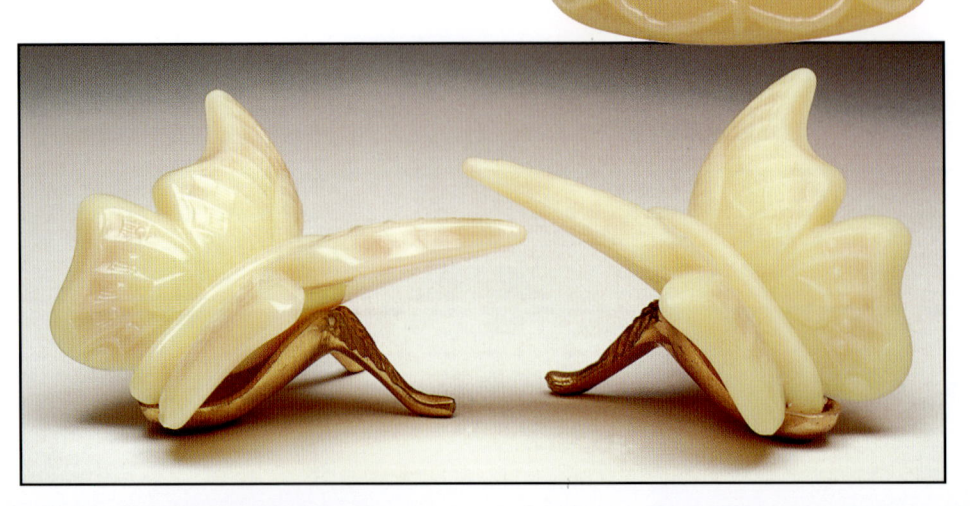

Butterfly on stand #5171, 5" tall, 4" wide, Special Order made for FAGCA Display Table Favor 1992
Left: Gloss finish #5171BE, **$68;**
Right: Satin finish #5171BR, **$70**

Butterfly #5170, plain, 3.5" long, 4.24" wide, on brass base, Special Order made for FAGCA 1992,
Left: Gloss finish #5170BE, **$40;**
Right: Satin finish #5170BR, **$45**

The Heisey Club of America (HCA) came to Fenton to have one of the former Heisey moulds produced in Burmese. The Plug Horse was being issued each year in different colors and this year the HCA wanted to have it made in Burmese.

Plug horse #1540 (Heisey mould number), plain, 4.25" tall, 3.75" long, Mould originally from Heisey, Special order made exclusively for HCA (Heisey Club of America) 1992, **Left**: Gloss finish, BE, **$45**; **Right**: Satin finish, **$50**
Note, mould is owned by HCA and they have pieces made from original Heisey moulds as fund raisers (never done in original Heisey colors).

Plug horse on bust off base #BE, plain gloss finish, 6.25" tall, 3.75" long, Mould originally from Heisey, Special order made exclusively for HCA (Heisey Club of America) 1992, **$125**
Note, when Burmese is photographed on black background it appears to be more yellow than it really is.

1993

For 1993, Fenton didn't offer any Burmese in their own lines. At the Fenton Art Glass Collectors of America (FAGCA) August convention, the Atlantis vase, another former U.S. Glass mould (probably from their Duncan Glass division), was offered in the Special Glass room in both gloss and satin. The hand painted version was designed by Dianna Barbour.

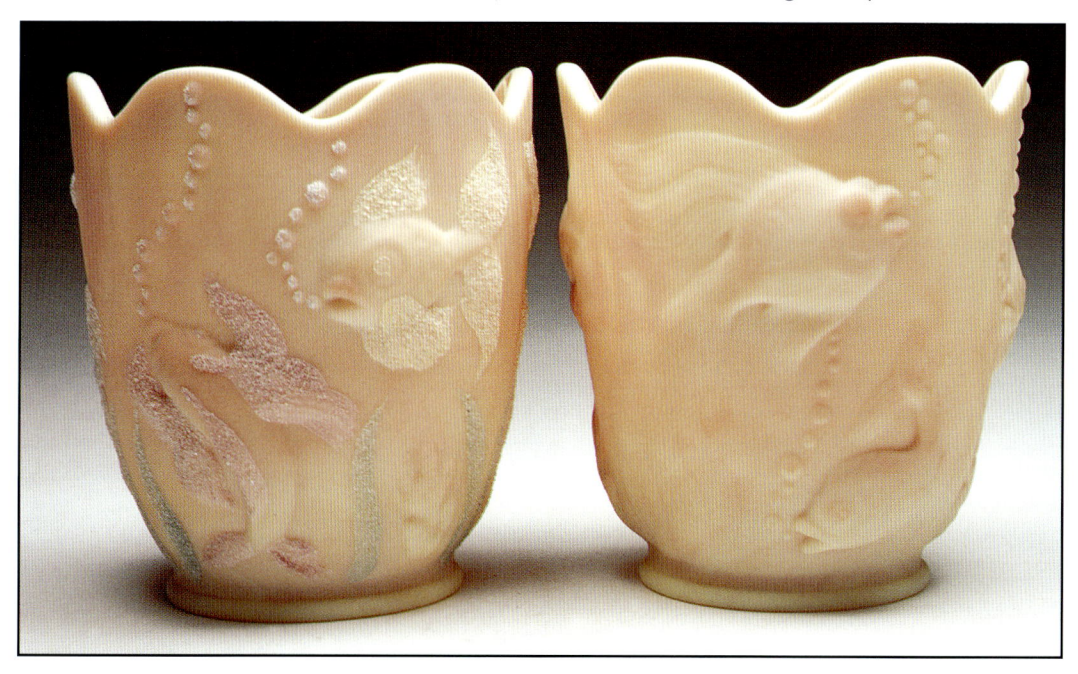

Atlantis vase #5150, 6.5" tall, From special glass room at Fenton factory 1993, **Left**: Hand painted frit accents **$250**; **Right**: Plain satin finish #5150BR, **$195**
Note, originally considered a Verlys mould, it is actually one from U.S. Glass Company.

118   The 1990s

1994

At the annual Gift Shop sale in February of 1994, there were several items made for this event. The #5167 Sunfish was made as one of the special items.

Sunfish on bust off base #5167, plain, 4.25" tall, 2.75" long, From Fenton Gift Shop annual February sale 1994, **Left:** Gloss finish #5167BE, **$75**; **Right:** Satin finish #5167BR, **$85**

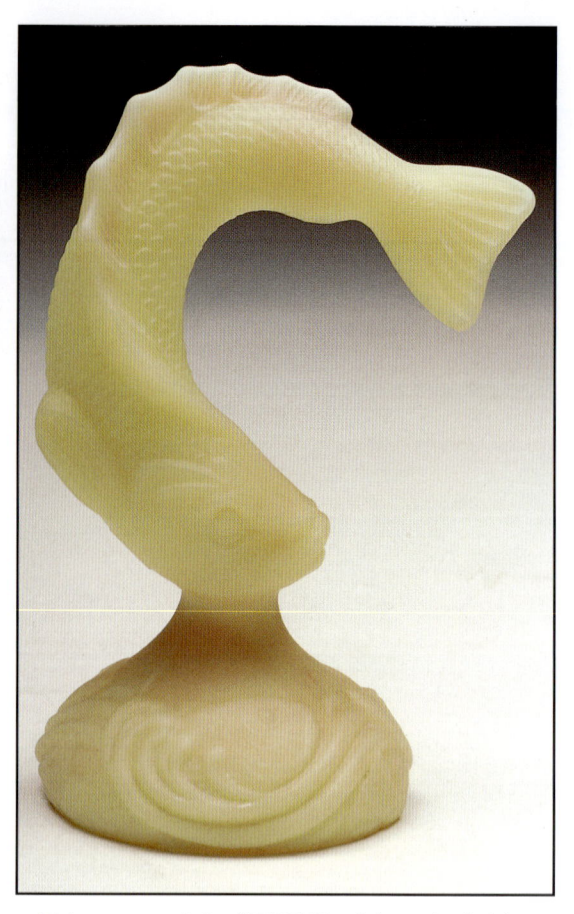

Fish paperweight #5193BR, plain satin finish, 4.75" tall, 3" wide, From Fenton Gift Shop 1994, **$70**

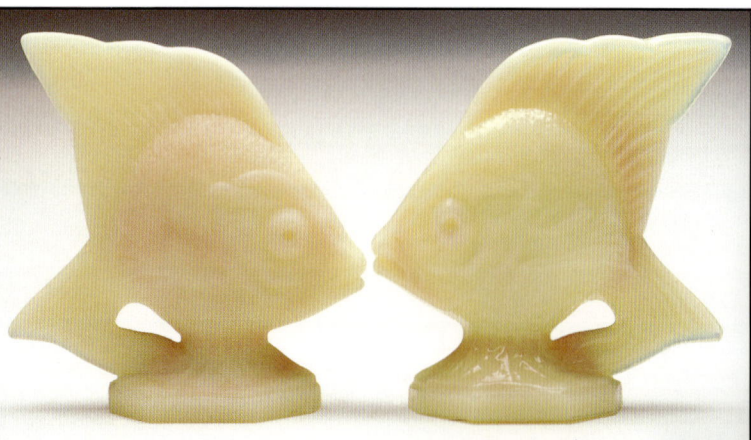

Sun Fish #5167, plain, 2.6" tall, 2.75" long, From Fenton Gift Shop annual February sale 1994, **Left:** Satin finish #5167BR, **$48**; **Right:** Gloss finish #5167BE, **$45**

Fox #5226BR, plain satin finish, From Fenton Gift Shop 1994, **Left:** Regular 4.5" tall, **$70**; **Right:** On bust off base, 8" tall, **$125**

The 1990s   119

Another special piece was the #9752BR Daffodil vase. On the bottom of this particular vase was the signatures of second and third generation family members. The third item was the #9754 Caprice vase. This vase was adapted from a former Cambridge mould with the addition of a bow at the top. The fourth item was the #5226 Fox.

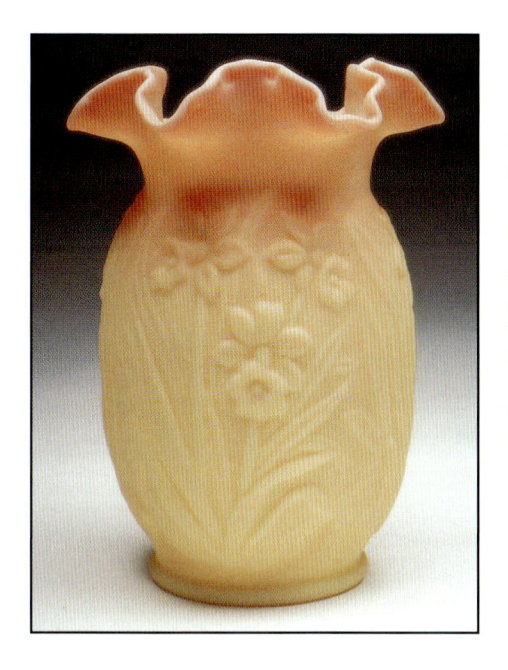

Vase #9752BR, embossed "Daffodil" pattern, plain satin finish, 8" tall, double crimp, second & third generation Fenton family signatures, From Fenton Gift Shop annual February sale, 1994, **$95**

Caprice Vase #9754, 6.5" tall, double crimp, From Fenton Gift Shop 1994, **Left:** Satin finish #9754BR, **$68**; **Right:** Gloss finish #9754BE, **$60**

Usually what appears in the Fenton gift shop is plain versions of whatever appears decorated in the line, from QVC, or special order work. This particular summer while making the ewer, there was some leftover molten Burmese in the pot that needed to be used and a couple of Hobnail moulds were pulled out.

The Lattice Rose ewer was the only piece for the Connoisseur Collection this year. The decoration was designed by Frances Burton.

Detail of hand painted "Lattice Rose" decoration.

Ewer #2729JI, hand painted "Lattice Rose" decoration designed by Frances Burton, 10.25" tall, Limited to 750, Connoisseur Collection 1994, **$225**

Ewer #2729BE, "Diamond Optic" treatment, plain gloss finish, 10.25" tall, ribbed handle, From Fenton Gift Shop 1994, **$95**

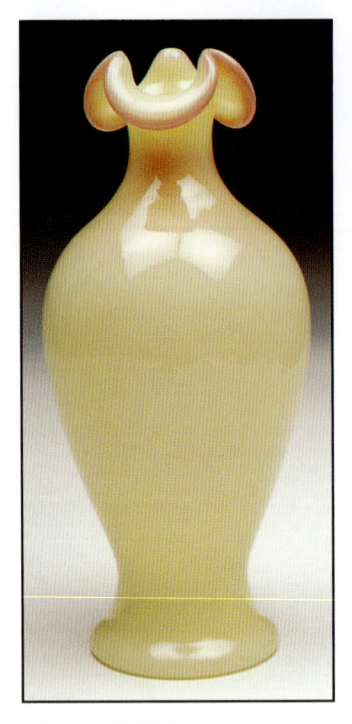

120　The 1990s

Vase #2758BE, plain gloss finish, 8.5" tall, single crimp, From Fenton Gift Shop 1994, **$75**

Vase #2758, hand painted Dogwood flower with frit, 8.75" tall, single crimp, Decorated by Marilyn Wagner, From Fenton Gift Shop 1994, **$95**

Ewer #3163, plain, 6.25" tall, From Fenton Gift Shop 1994, **Left:** Satin finish #3163BR, **$70**; **Right:** Gloss finish #3163BE, **$65**

Miniature hand vase #5153BR, plain satin finish, 3.65" tall, tight single crimp, From Fenton Gift Shop 1994, **$48**

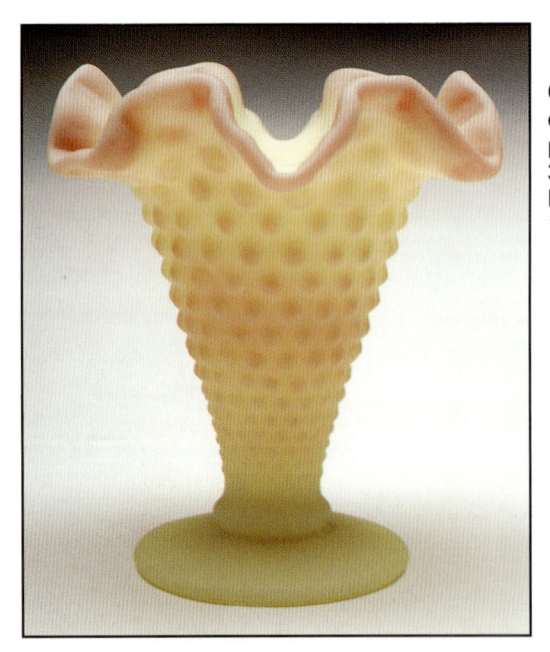

Cone vase #3952BR, embossed "Hobnail" pattern, plain satin finish, 3.75" tall, double crimp, From Fenton Gift Shop 1994, **$45**

The #3854 vase and #3952 vase, were a complete surprise to find in the gift shop. In visiting the gift shop you never know what you will find.

Vase #3854, embossed "Hobnail" pattern, plain, 3" tall, double crimp, From Fenton Gift Shop 1994, **Left:** Satin finish #3854BR, **$48**; **Right:** Gloss finish #3854BE, **$42**

The 1990s

For the first time, more than one item was made for QVC. Public interest had really picked up on the Burmese items and the decision was made to offer more. All of the items sold out quickly.

Wheat Vase #5858, plain, 7.1" tall, double crimp, From Fenton Gift Shop 1994, **Left:** Satin finish #5858BR, **$65**; **Right:** Gloss finish #5858BE, **$55**

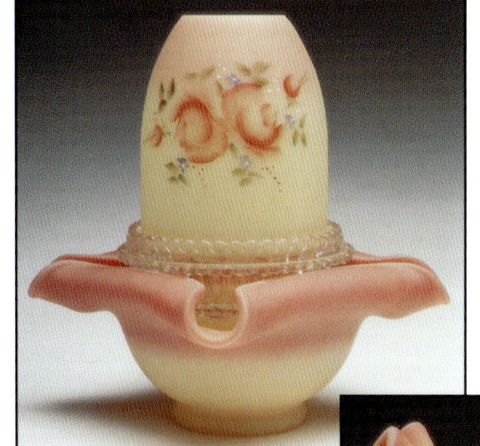

Three piece fairy light #C7501RB, hand painted "Rose" decoration designed by Sue Jackson, 6.75" tall, 5" wide (Note, insert is clear), Made for QVC Show January 1994, **$185**

Pitcher #3163RB, hand painted "Rose" decoration designed by Kim Plauche, 6.5" tall, Made for QVC Show January 1994, **$85**

Rose bowl #8453BR, embossed "Lily of Valley" pattern, plain satin finish, 3.75" tall, 5.25" wide, cupped in, Sample from Fenton Gift Shop 1994, **$48**

Miniature hand vase #5153IE, Iridized (Carnival) finish, 3.65" tall, tight single crimp, Made for QVC Show October 1994, **$38**

Pillar vase #9655RB, hand painted "Rose" decoration around shoulder of piece, 7.3" tall, single crimp, Sample from Fenton Gift Shop 1994, **$80**

Paisley student lamp #C67014N, hand painted "Rose" decoration designed by Frances Burton, 20" overall height, 7" double crimp shade, Made for QVC Show August 1994, **$395**

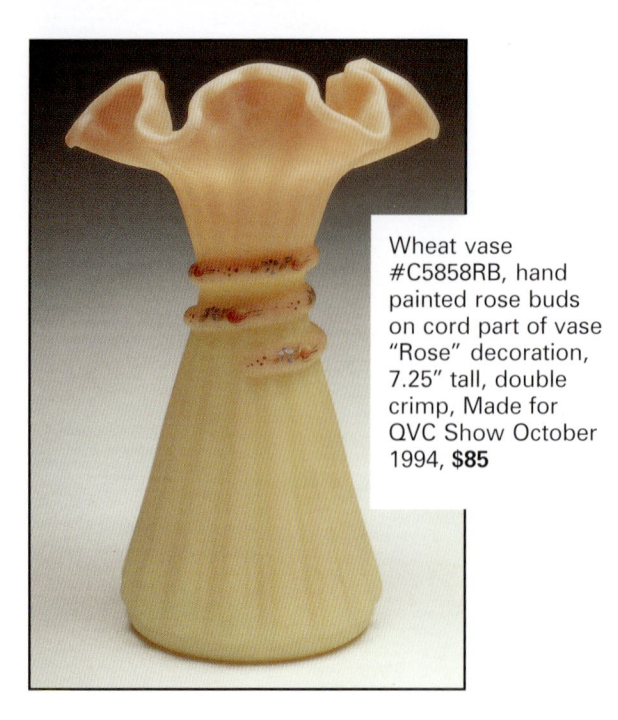

Wheat vase #C5858RB, hand painted rose buds on cord part of vase "Rose" decoration, 7.25" tall, double crimp, Made for QVC Show October 1994, **$85**

Detail of hand painted "Butterfly" decoration.

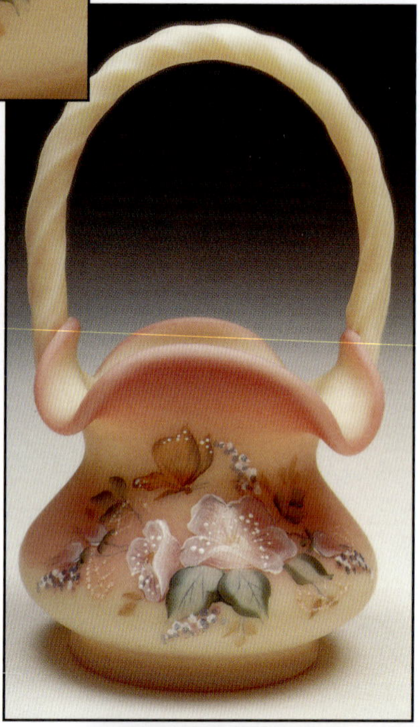

Basket #2932UL, hand painted "Butterfly" decoration designed by Martha Reynolds, 8.25" tall, 5.25" wide, Limited to 790, Decorated by J. Crenshaw, 90th Anniversary Historical Collection 1995, **$185**
Note, this mould was developed in 1962.

1995

In celebration of their 90th anniversary, Fenton issued the Historical Collection in 1995. This collection features five different pieces to honor the original creator of Burmese, Frederick Shirley of the Mt. Washington Glass Company. Martha Reynolds designed the decorations on four of the pieces and each was limited to 790. Frances Burton designed the lamp, which was limited to only 300. This was the first Historical Collection to offer all items as numbered limited editions.

Vase #2955UU, hand painted morning glories & "Hummingbird" decoration designed by Martha Reynolds, 9.5"T, Family signature piece, 90th Anniversary Historical Collection 1995, **$195**
Note, this mould was purchased in 1991 from the Chicago Art Glass Company.

Detail of catalog 90th Anniversary Historical Collection 1995. (Reprinted with permission from the Fenton Art Glass Company)

Bowl #2909UK, hand painted "Vintage" decoration designed by Martha Reynolds, 10" diameter, rolled edge, Limited to 790, 90th Anniversary Historical Collection 1995, **$175**
Note, this mould was developed in 1980.

Pitcher #2968UN, hand painted butterfly & "Cherry Blossom" decoration, 9.75" tall, Heart shape spout, Limited to 790, 90th Anniversary Historical Collection 1995, **$225**
Note, this mould was developed in 1948.

The 1990s 123

Pillar Lamp #7502UQ, hand painted tree scene "Daybreak" decoration designed by Frances Burton, 33" overall height, 10" ball double crimp shade, Limited to 300, 90th Anniversary Historical Collection 1995, **$550.00** Note, this mould was developed in 1959.

The Fenton showroom this year featured a swan vase that had been decorated with pastel paints and frit to add to the detail. Dianna Barbour designed this decoration.

Swan vase #9458, hand painted with frit accents, 8" tall, Decoration designed by Dianna Barbour, double crimp, Made for Fenton representatives at show room 1995, **$125**

The previous year saw the introduction of the Showcase Dealer Exclusive. For this year, was a seashore theme vase called Sea of Dreams. This type of decoration hadn't been used in many years. Frances Burton designed this decoration.

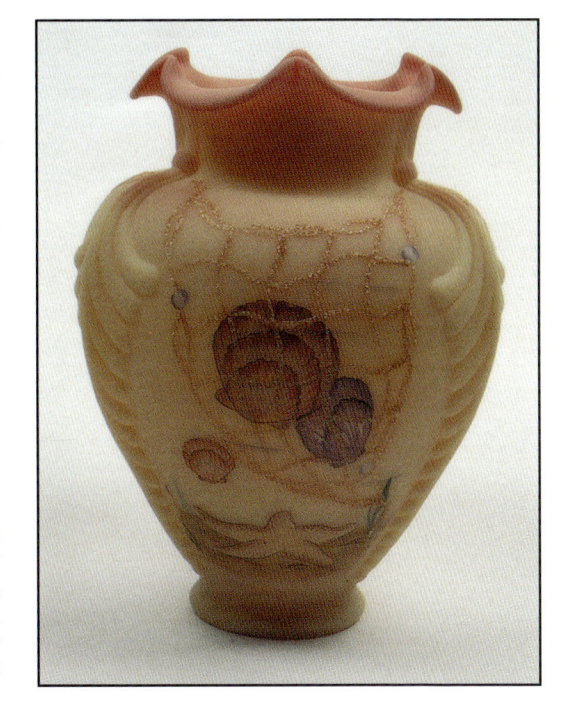

Feather vase #1649UY, hand painted under sea scene "Sea of Dreams" decoration designed by Frances Burton, 9.5" tall, single star crimp, Limited to 790, Showcase dealer exclusive 1995, **$295**

The 1990s

The Fenton gift shop had many pieces of undecorated items that were either from the Connoisseur Collection or a QVC program. A unique table lamp was made from the Connoisseur vase.

Feather vase #1649, plain, 9.5" tall, single star crimp, From Fenton Gift Shop 1995, **Left:** Gloss finish #1649BE, **$125**; **Right:** Satin finish #1649BR, **$145**

Bowl #2922BE, plain gloss finish, 10" wide, rolled edge, From Fenton Gift Shop 1995, **$75**

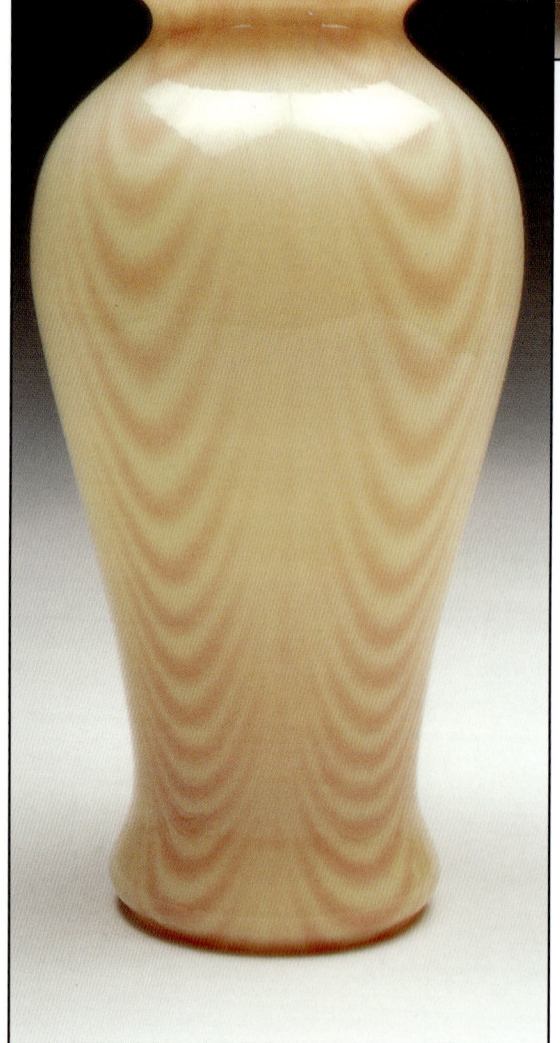

Vase #1559, plain gloss finish on "Drapery Optic" treatment, 9.5" tall, From Fenton Gift Shop 1995, **$115**

Paisley slipper #2931BE, plain gloss finish, 3" tall, 4.75" long, From Fenton Gift Shop 1995, **$30**

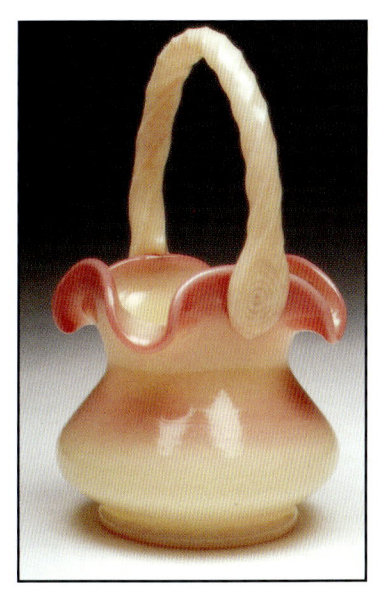

The 1990s   125

Basket #2932BE, plain gloss finish, 8.25" tall, 5.25" wide, single square crimp with twist handle, From Fenton Gift Shop 1995, **$85**

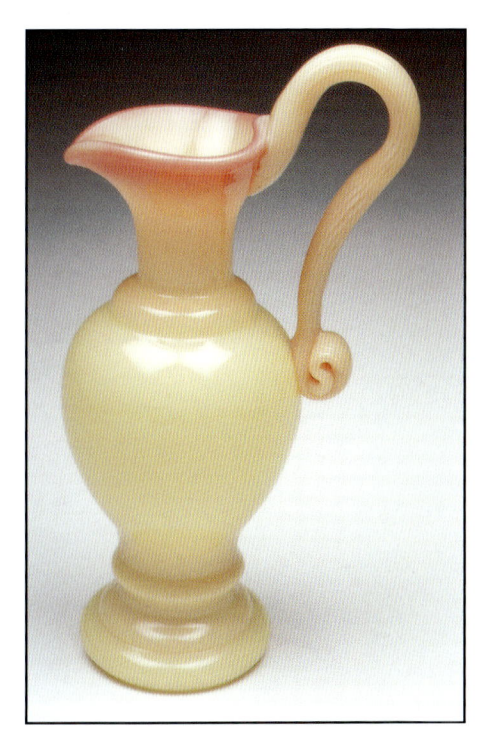

Pitcher #2968BE, 8.75" tall, plain gloss finish, Heart shape spout, From Fenton Gift Shop 1995, **$110**

Pinch vase #6450BS, "Diamond Optic" treatment, plain gloss finish, 8.5" tall, double crimp, From Fenton Gift Shop January 1995, **$85**

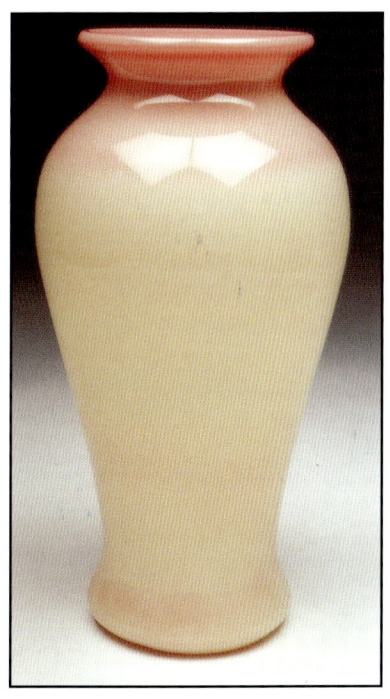

Vase #2955BE, plain gloss finish, 9.5" tall, From Fenton Gift Shop 1995, **$90**

Bridesmaid Doll figurine #5228, plain, 6.75" tall, From Fenton Gift Shop 1995, **Left:** Gloss #5228BE, **$60**; **Right:** Satin #5228BR, **$68**

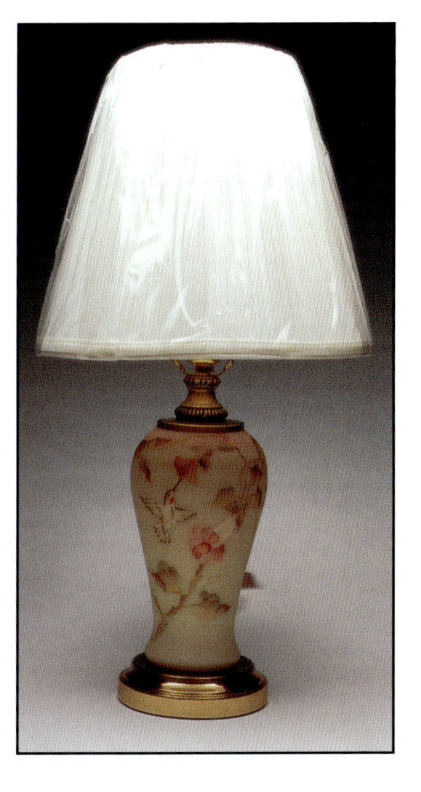

Lamp #2955UU, hand painted morning glories & "Hummingbird" decoration designed by Martha Reynolds, overall height 22.5" tall, made from the Family signature piece, 90th Anniversary Historical Collection 1995, From Fenton Gift Shop 1995, **$395**
Note, this mould was purchased in 1991 from the Chicago Art Glass Company.

126   The 1990s

The QVC program featured seven different items over the course of the year. More people were discovering the beauty of the Burmese glass by shopping on television.

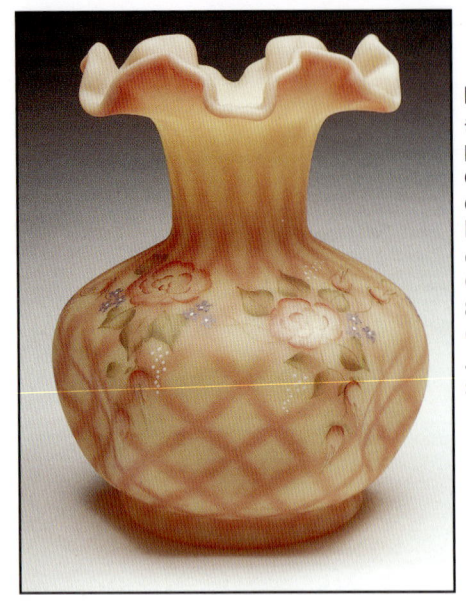

Pinch vase #C1146RB, hand painted "Rose" decoration designed by Martha Reynolds on "Diamond Optic" treatment, 8" tall, Made for QVC Show January 1995, **$135**

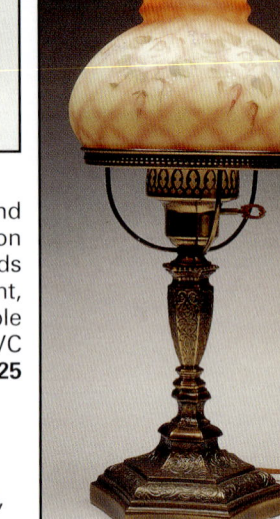

Bridesmaid Doll figurine #C5228RB, hand painted rose buds "Rose" decoration designed by Martha Reynolds, 6.75" tall, Shelly Fenton signature, Made for QVC Show August 1995, **$85**

Student lamp #C2793RB, hand painted "Rose" decoration designed by Martha Reynolds on "Diamond Optic" treatment, 20" overall height, 7" double crimp shade, Made for QVC Show August 1995, **$325**

Paisley slipper, C2931T2, hand painted "Roses" decoration designed by Kim Plauche, 3" tall, 4.75" long, Made for QVC Show April 1995, **$45**

Two piece fairy light #C16390, hand painted "Rose" decoration designed by Martha Reynolds on "Diamond Optic" treatment, 4.75" tall, 3.15" wide, Made for QVC Show April 1995, **$110**

Sitting cat #51654N, hand painted "Daisies" decoration designed by Frances Burton, 3.75" tall, 2.6" wide, Made for QVC Show August 1995, **$69**

Swan vase #9458BR, plain satin finish, 8" tall, double crimp, Made for QVC Show April 1995, **$95**

There were three special orders for this year. The Fenton Art Glass Collectors of America (FAGCA) had the #9206BR embossed Rose shakers made for them. The National Fenton Glass Society (NFGS) produced the miniature basket in a gloss Burmese.

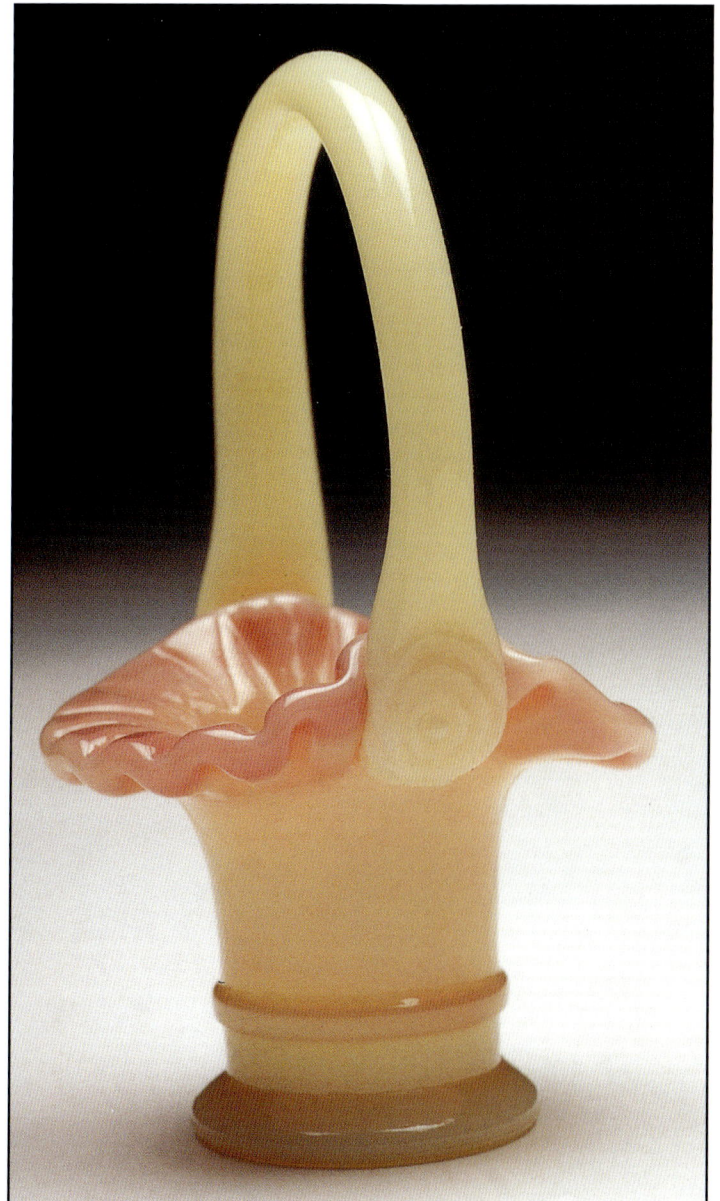

Miniature basket #7567BE, plain gloss finish, 4." tall, 2.25" wide, slight single crimp, Limited to 180, Special order made exclusively for NFGS (National Fenton Glass Society) 1995, **$60**

Footed shakers #9206BR, "Embossed Roses" pattern, plain satin finish, 3.5" tall, Special order made exclusively for the FAGCA (Fenton Art Glass Collectors of America) 1995, **$60 pair**

Singleton Bailey also had Fenton produce the swan vase with an iridized finish for him.

Swan vase #9458BI, Iridized (Carnival) finish, 8" tall, double crimp, Special order made exclusively for Singleton Bailey 1995, Only 107 made, **$95**
Note, when Burmese is photographed on black background it appears to be more yellow than it really is.

1996

For 1996, there were three items in the Connoisseur Collection. Each of these were magnificent works of art. Two of the moulds used were designed by Jon Saffell, the #9866TR vase and #2960WQ pitcher. With having a love of fishing, the Trout vase seemed a natural for Robin Spindler to create. Martha Reynolds developed the elegant Queen's Bird. The mould for this was first used in 1935. Frances Burton also obtains ideas from nature and developed the dragonfly and waterlilies for the pitcher. The fall lamp sale, for the first time had a Burmese lamp. Martha Reynolds designed this floral decoration with a buzzing bee.

Detail of hand painted floral & bee decoration.

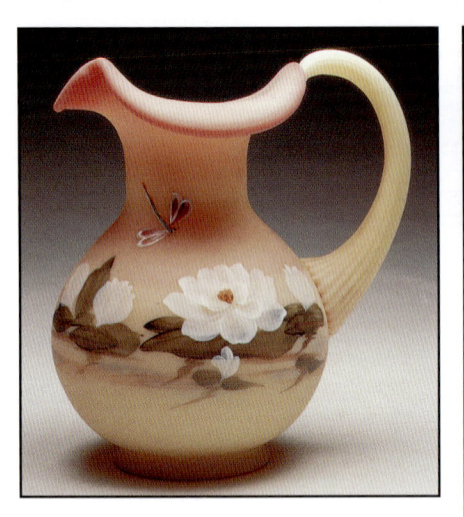

Pitcher #2960WQ, hand painted water lilies & "Dragonfly" decoration designed by Frances Burton, 8" tall, Mould designed by Jon Saffell, Limited to 1450, Connoisseur Collection 1996, **$165**

Vase #3254QJ, hand painted "Queen's Bird" decoration designed by Martha Reynolds, 11" tall, single crimp, Limited to 1350, Connoisseur Collection 1996, **$295**

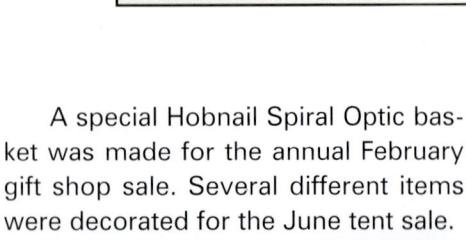

Lamp #75555X, hand painted floral & bee, 12.5" tall, 6.75" wide, Decoration designed by Martha Reynolds, Made as a special promotional piece for Fenton's fall lamp sale 1996, **$295**

Vase #9866TR, hand painted dragonfly & "Trout" decoration designed by Robin Spindler, 8" tall, Mould designed by Jon Saffell, Limited to 1450, Connoisseur Collection 1996, **$145**

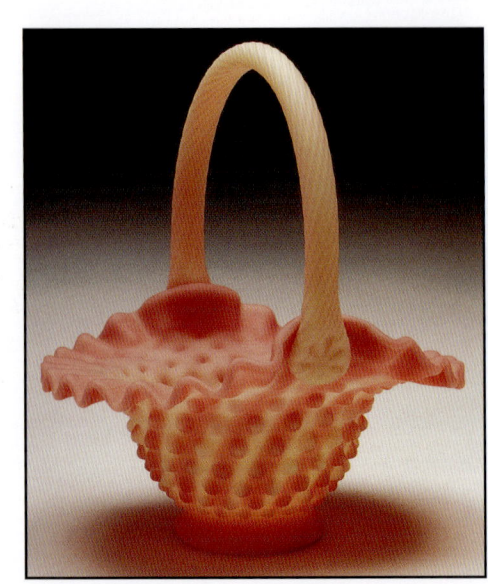

A special Hobnail Spiral Optic basket was made for the annual February gift shop sale. Several different items were decorated for the June tent sale.

Basket #GS007BR, embossed "Hobnail" pattern struck with "Spiral Optic", satin finish, 7.75" tall, 7" wide, tight single crimp, Bill Fenton signature, From Fenton Gift Shop annual February sale 1996, **$125**

Pitcher #1132, "Diamond Optic" treatment, 7.25" tall, double crimp, From Fenton Gift Shop 1996, **Left:** Gloss finish #1132BE, **$65**; **Right:** Satin finish #1132BR, **$75**

Angels, plain gloss finish, 5.75" tall, From Fenton Gift Shop 1996, **Left:** Girl #5114BE, **$40**; **Right:** Boy #5113BE, **$45**

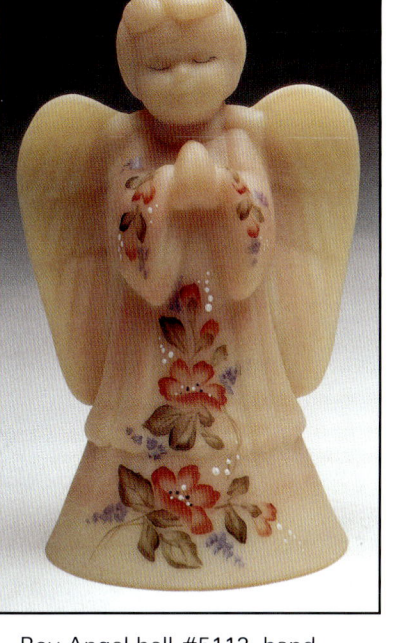

Boy Angel bell #5113, hand painted red flowers, 5.75" tall, From Fenton Gift Shop 1996, **$60**

Left: Sitting cat #5165BE, plain gloss finish, 3.75" tall, 2.6" wide, From Fenton Gift Shop 1996, **$40**

Right: Sitting cat #5165BR, plain satin finish, 3.75" tall, 2.6" wide, From Fenton Gift Shop 1996, **$45**

Left: Alley cat #5177BE, plain gloss finish, 10.25" tall, From Fenton Gift Shop 1996, **$165**

Right: Alley cat #5177, hand painted multicolored wildflowers, 10.75" tall, From Fenton Gift Shop 1996, **$225**

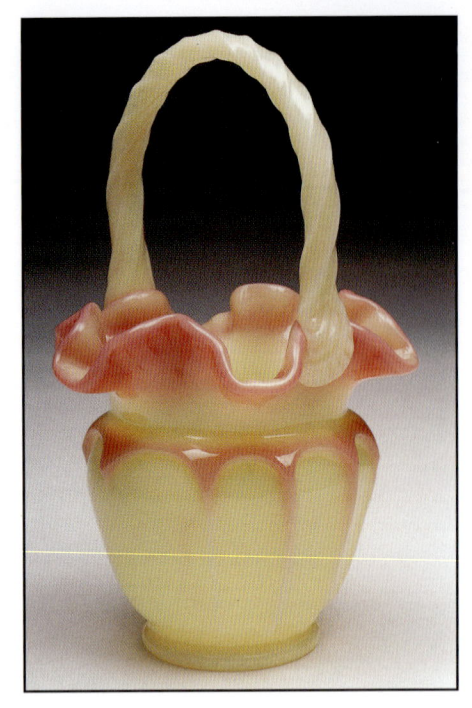

The 1990s

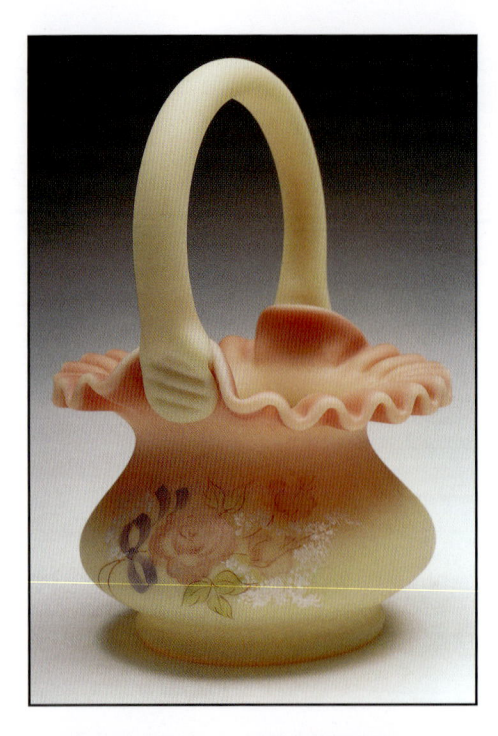

Basket #7437, hand painted roses with purple bow, 7" tall, 5" wide, single crimp, From Fenton Gift Shop 1996, **$110**

Open Heart Arches basket #6540BE, plain gloss finish, 8.25" tall, 4.8" wide, double crimp, From Fenton Gift Shop 1996, **$85**
Note, the Fenton mould was inspired by "Open Heart Arches" pattern created by Nicholas Kopp circa 1900-1905 while with Consolidated of Pittsburgh Lamp, Brass & Glass Co.

Bell #7668, 6.4" tall, hand painted pink & white apple blossoms, single star crimp, Decorated by C. Griffith, From Fenton Gift Shop 1996, **$50**

Bell #7668, 6.4" tall, hand painted purple & blue pansies, single star crimp, Decorated by C. Griffith, From Fenton Gift Shop 1996, **$55**

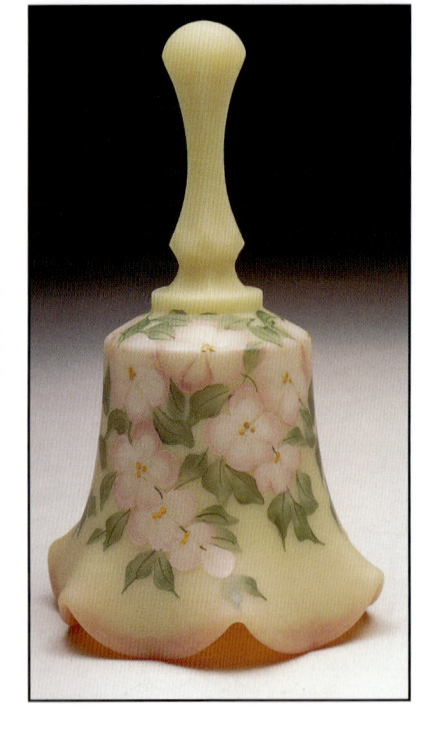

Bell #7668BR, plain satin finish, 6.4" tall, single star crimp, From Fenton Gift Shop 1996, **$35**

Bell #7668, 6.4" tall, hand painted small pink flowers, single star crimp, Decorated by C. Griffith, From Fenton Gift Shop 1996, **$45**

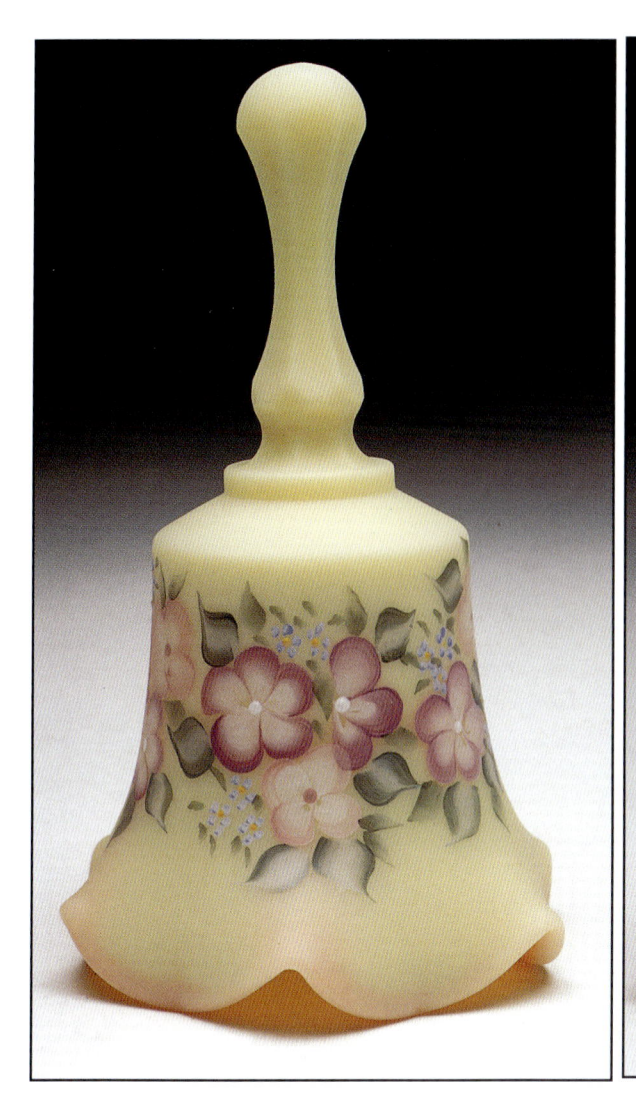

The 1990s   131

Left: Bell #7668, 6.4" tall, hand painted purple & pink flowers, single star crimp, Decorated by C. Griffith, From Fenton Gift Shop 1996, **$50**

Right: Bell #7668, 6.4" tall, hand painted red rose, single star crimp, Decorated by C. Smith, From Fenton Gift Shop 1996, **$48**

Left: Bell #7668, 6.4" tall, hand painted blue & purple pansies, single star crimp, Decorated by C. Griffith, From Fenton Gift Shop 1996, **$50**

Right: Bell #7668, 6.4" tall, hand painted purple cornflowers, single star crimp, Decorated by C. Griffith, From Fenton Gift Shop 1996, **$50**

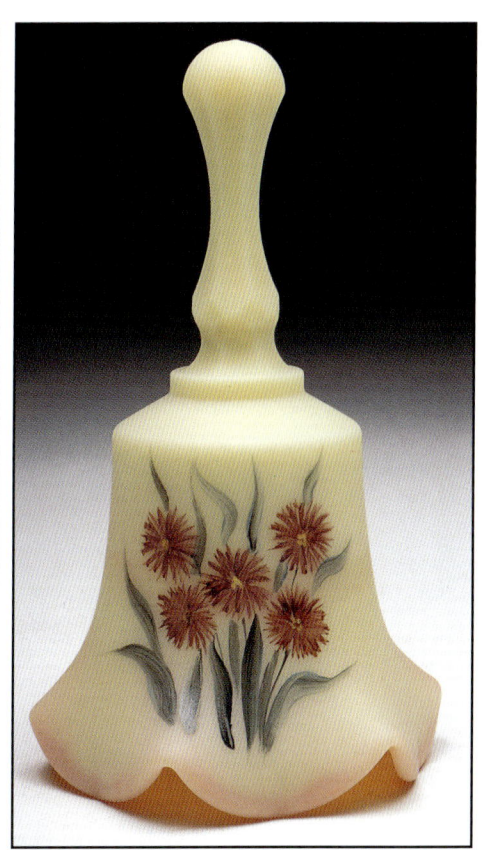

The QVC program offered nine pieces during the year. The collection was continuing to grow with many new collectors falling in love with Burmese.

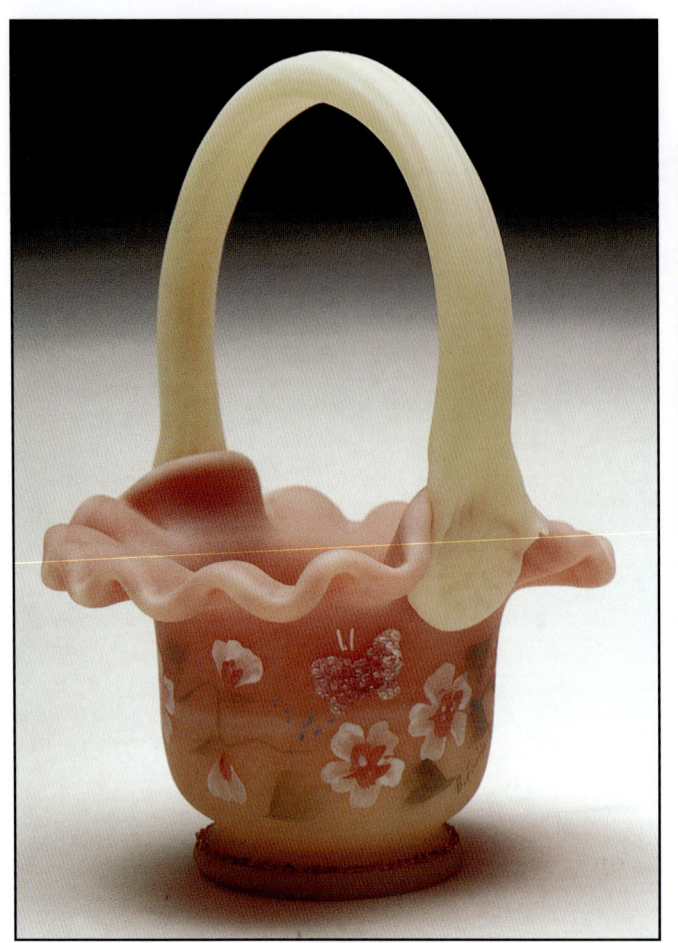

Detail of hand painted "Rose" decoration on "Diamond Optic" treatment.

Basket #9230, hand painted floral with pink frit butterfly, 4.5" tall, 3.25" wide, From Fenton Gift Shop 1996, **$85**

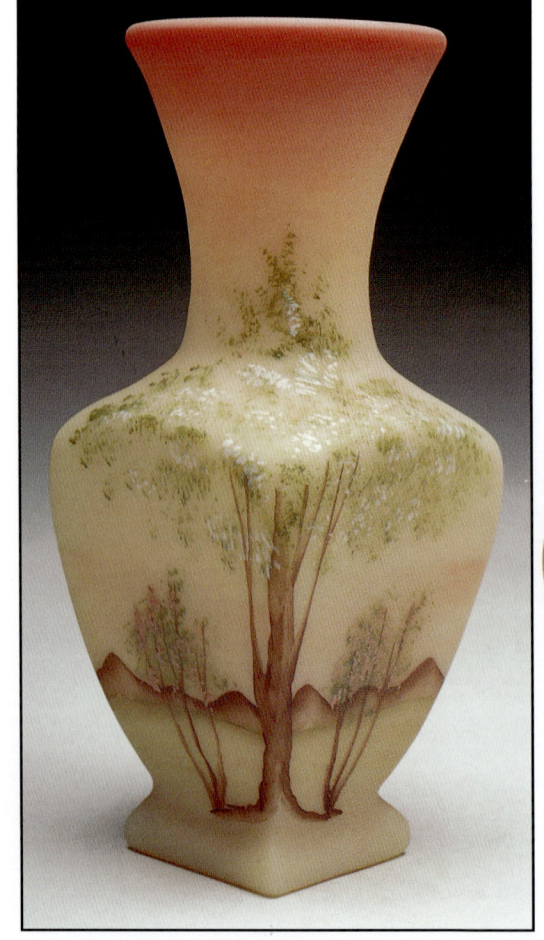

Vase #9866YE, hand painted tree & background scene, 8" tall, Decoration designed by Robin Spindler, Mould designed by Jon Saffell, Frank Fenton signature, Limited Edition piece, From Fenton Gift Shop 1996, **$135**

Cruet #CV120RB, hand painted "Rose" decoration designed by Martha Reynolds on "Diamond Optic" treatment, 7" tall, rib stopper, Made for QVC Show January 1996, **$135**

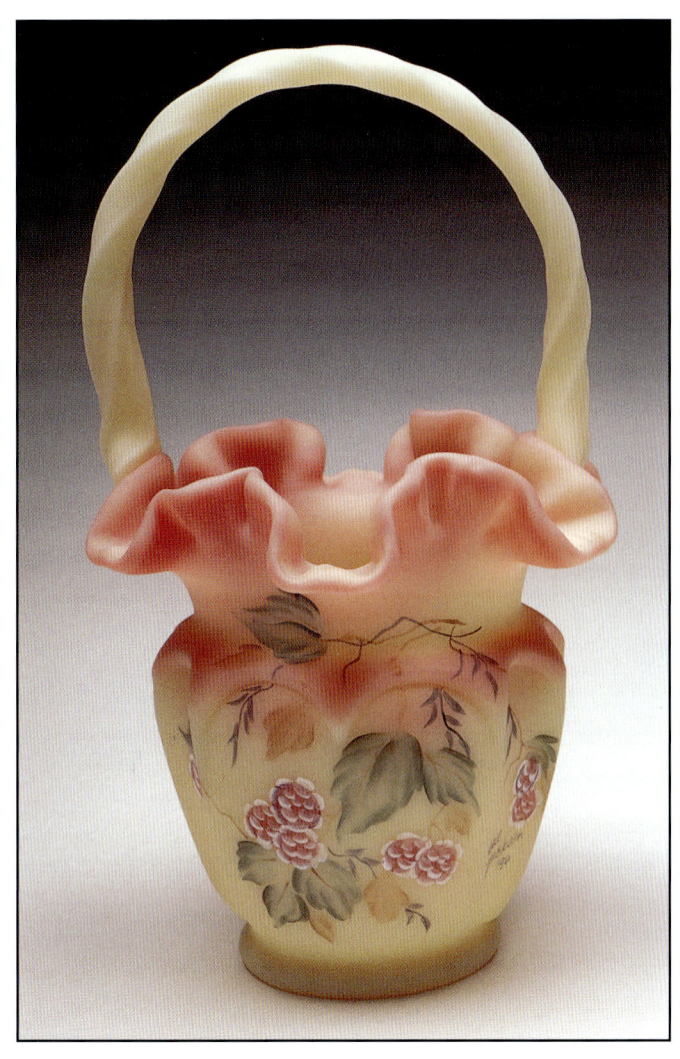

The 1990s   133

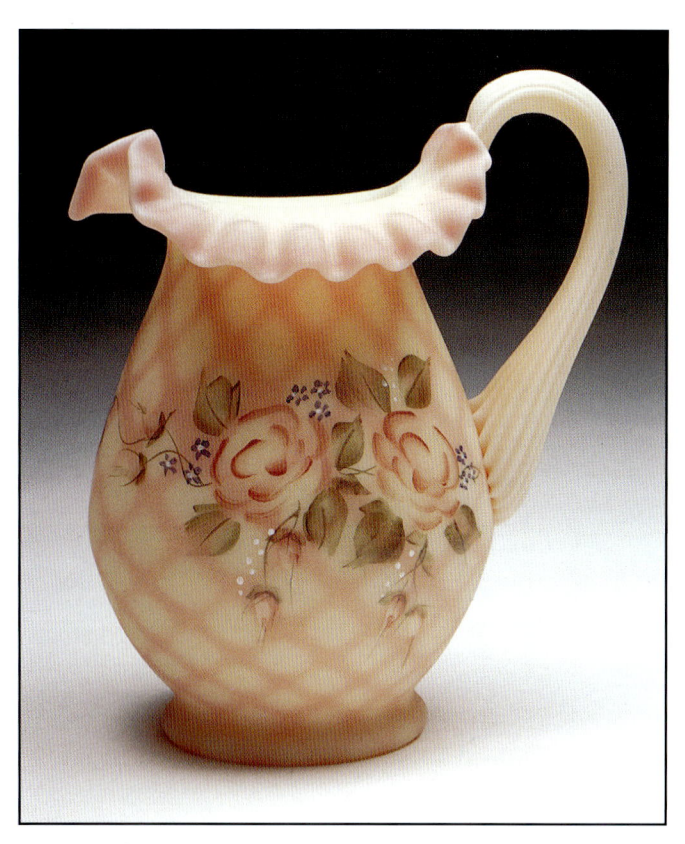

Pitcher #C1132RB, hand painted "Rose" decoration designed by Martha Reynolds on "Diamond Optic" treatment, 6.75" tall, double crimp, Don Fenton signature, Made for QVC Show March 1996, **$98**

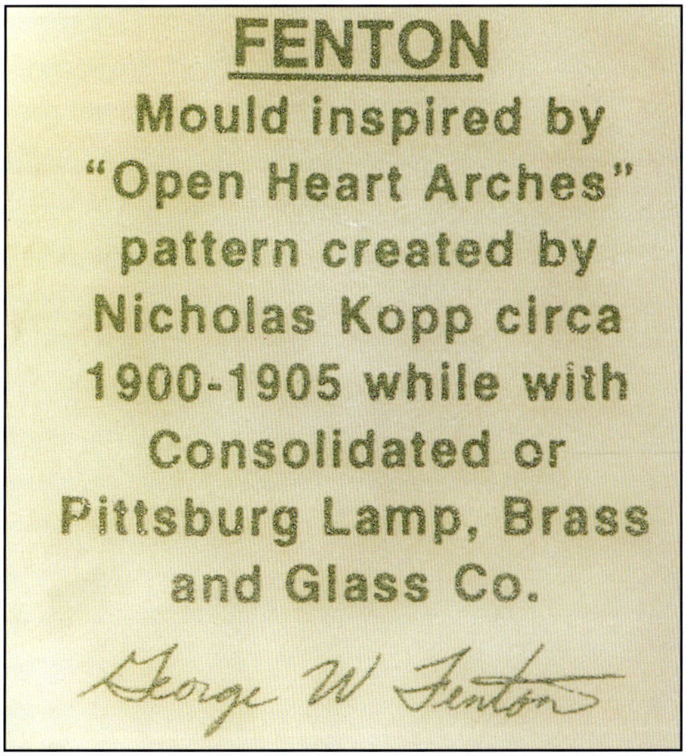

Open Heart Arches basket #CV0701F (#6540), hand painted purple berries, 8.25" tall, 4.8" wide, double crimp, George Fenton signature, Made for QVC Show January 1996, **$145**

Basket #CV1324X, hand painted star flowers & butterfly, 4.25" tall, 3.25" wide, single crimp, 10th Anniversary item, Bill & George Fenton signatures, Made for QVC Show June 1996, **$69**

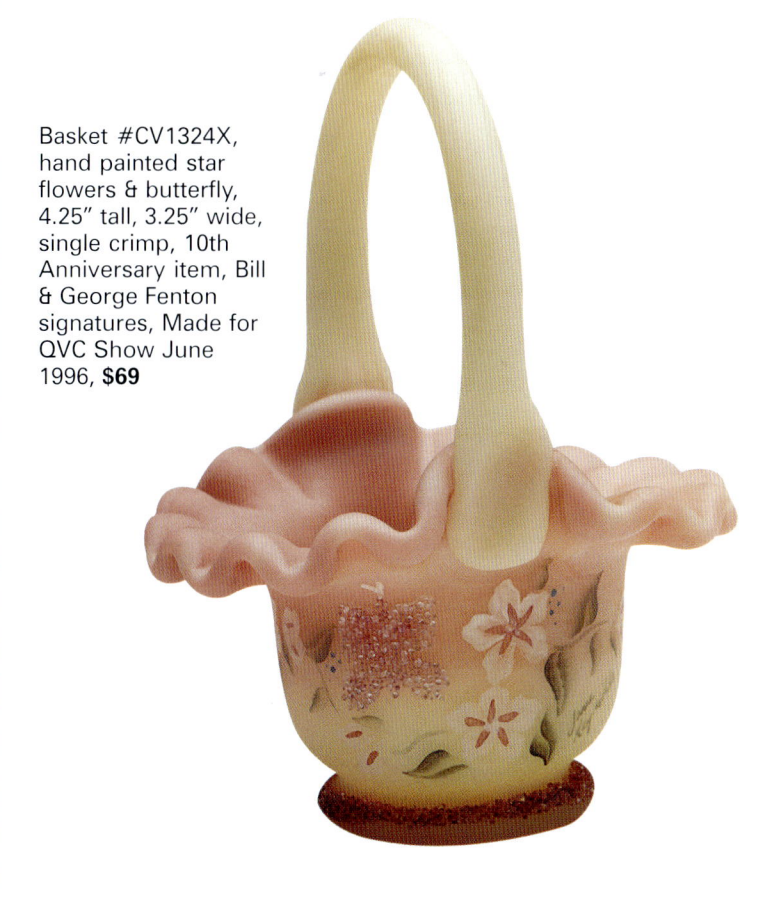

FENTON
Mould inspired by "Open Heart Arches" pattern created by Nicholas Kopp circa 1900-1905 while with Consolidated or Pittsburg Lamp, Brass and Glass Co.

George W Fenton

Detail of basket bottom explaining about the mould & George Fenton signature.

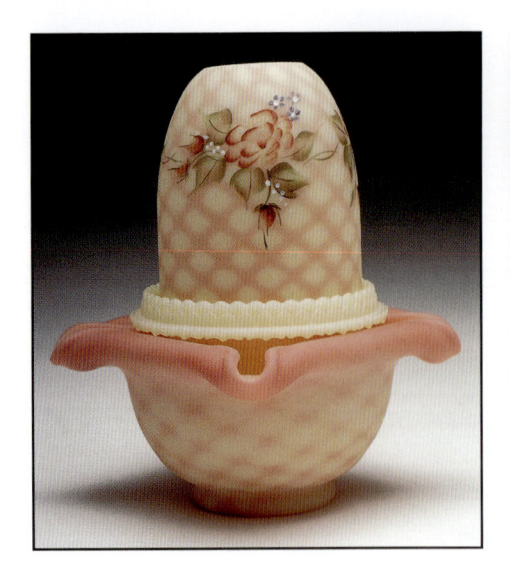

134   The 1990s

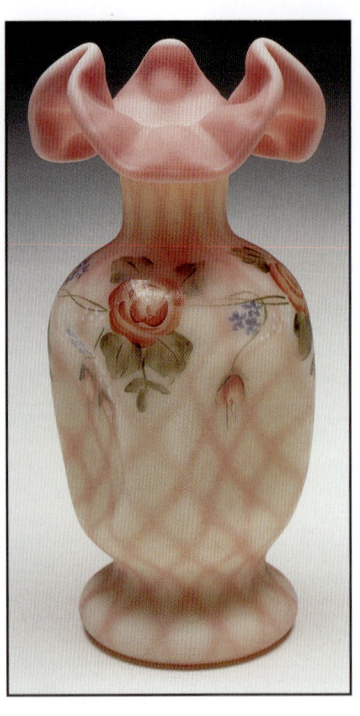

Pinch vase #C1146RB, hand painted "Rose" decoration designed by Martha Reynolds on "Diamond Optic" treatment, 7" tall, double crimp, Made for QVC Show August 1996, **$85**

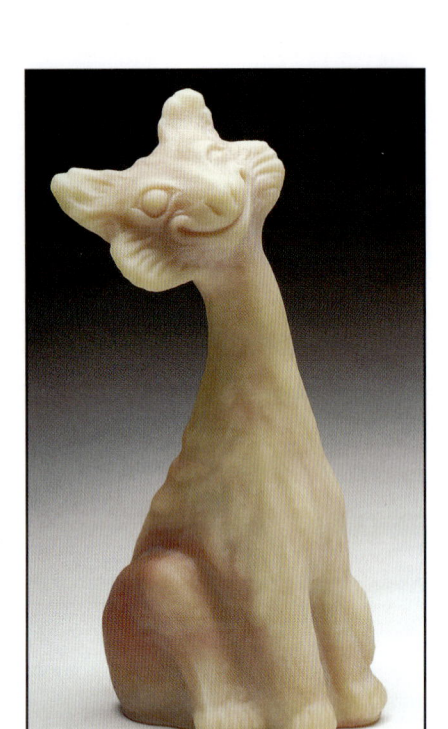

Three piece fairy light #CV142RB (#7501), hand painted "Rose" decoration designed by Martha Reynolds on "Diamond Optic" treatment, 6.75" tall, 5" wide, Made for QVC Show June 1996, **$175** Note, the insert was done in Burmese.

Alley Cat #5177BR, plain satin finish, 10.25" tall, Made for QVC Show December 1996, **$145**

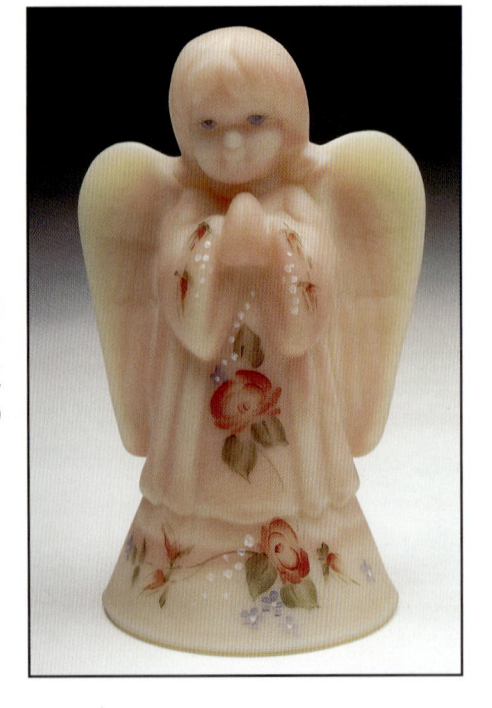

Girl angel #C5114RB, hand painted "Rose" decoration designed by Martha Reynolds, 5.75" tall, Made for QVC Show August 1996, **$60**

Boy angel #C5113RB, hand painted "Rose" decoration designed by Martha Reynolds, 5.75" tall, Made for QVC Show November 1996, **$60**

The 1990s 135

Two special orders were made for the Fenton Art Glass Collectors of America (FAGCA). The #5277 Happy Cat was issued in Burmese. A mould for this cat was adapted from an old Tiffin design. The #7488 Temple Jar featured beautiful butterflies. The National Fenton Glass Society (NFGS) produced another Burmese miniature basket, this time with a satin finish.

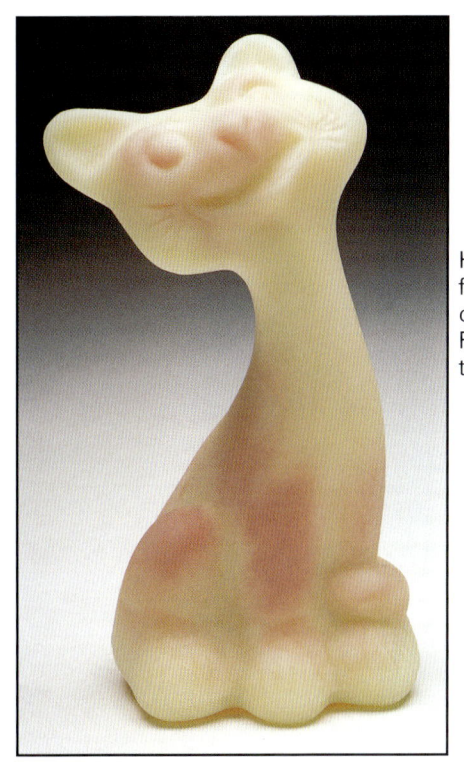

Happy cat #5277BR, plain satin finish, 6" tall, 2.75" wide, Special order made exclusively for FAGCA (Fenton Art Glass Collectors of America) 1996, **$115**

Detail of temple jar bottom showing artist signature & date.

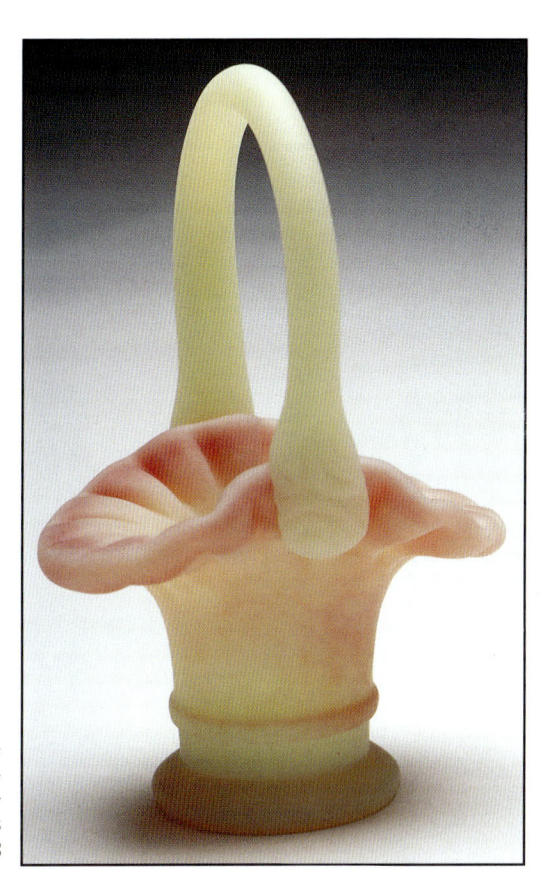

Temple jar #7488, hand painted apple blossom & large butterfly, 6" tall, Decorated by Diane Gessel, Special order made exclusively for FAGCA (Fenton Art Glass Collectors of America) April/May 1996, **$135**

Miniature basket #7567BR, plain satin finish, 4." tall, 2.25" wide, slight single crimp, Limited to 179, Special order made exclusively for NFGS (National Fenton Glass Society) 1996, **$68**

The 1990s

Ten years after her last offering of the Love Bouquet, Mary Walrath decided to issue one last offering. After so many people writing to her through the years and expressing how all the Love bouquet pieces were exhibited as a special collection, apart from all other Burmese pieces and with the poem hanging above the collection, now at age 80, she finally decided it was time to express a personal tribute to all those who had supported her through the years from her family and close friends to the collectors that had become new friends. This collection was called fittingly, Farewell. She elaborated on her original Love Bouquet design by adding more roses and rose buds. There was a limited edition of 150 made. Each piece was marked "Love Bouquet produced exclusively for Mary C. Walrath 1996". In addition, they were each numbered sequentially and also personally signed by Mary.

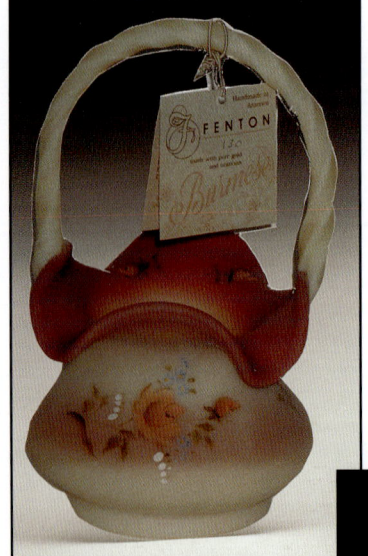

Basket #2932WQ, hand painted "Farewell Love Bouquet" decoration, 8.25" tall, 5.25" wide, single square crimp, Limited to 150, Special order made exclusively for Mary Walrath 1996, **$165**

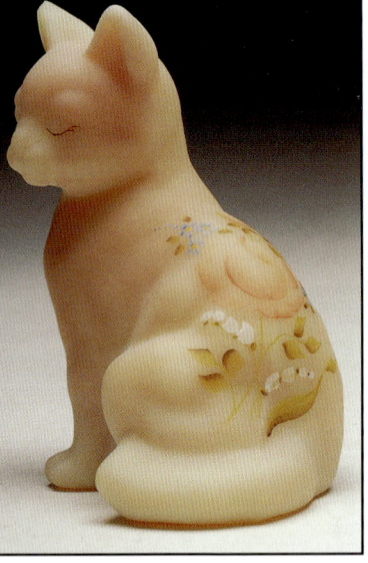

Sitting cat #5165, Sample hand painted version of "Farewell Love Bouquet" decoration, 3.75" tall, 2.6" wide, From Fenton Gift Shop 1996, **$98**

Detail of hand painted "Farewell Love Bouquet" decoration.

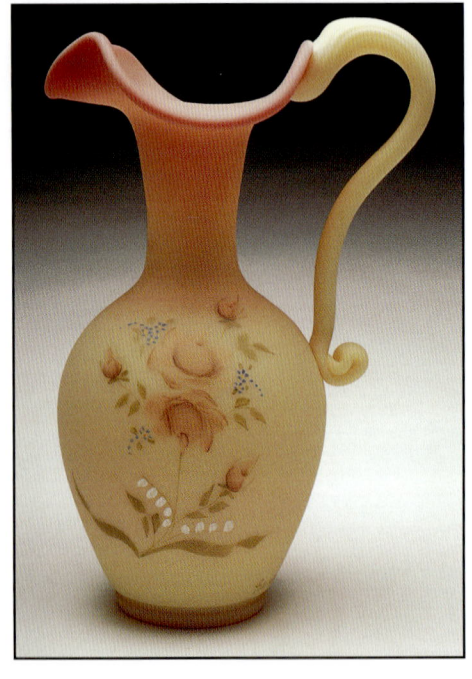

Pitcher #2729WQ, hand painted "Farewell Love Bouquet" decoration, 10" tall, Limited to 150, Special order made exclusively for Mary Walrath 1996, **$195**

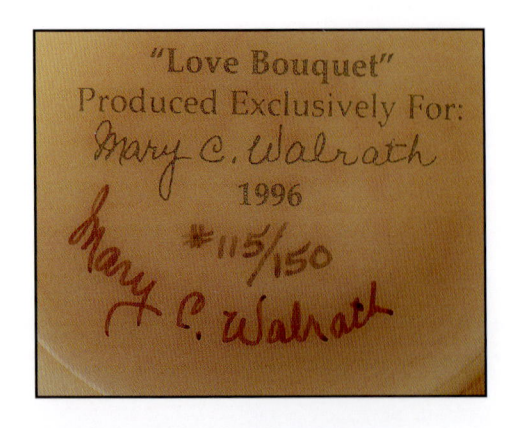

Detail of Pitcher bottom showing Mary Walrath signature.

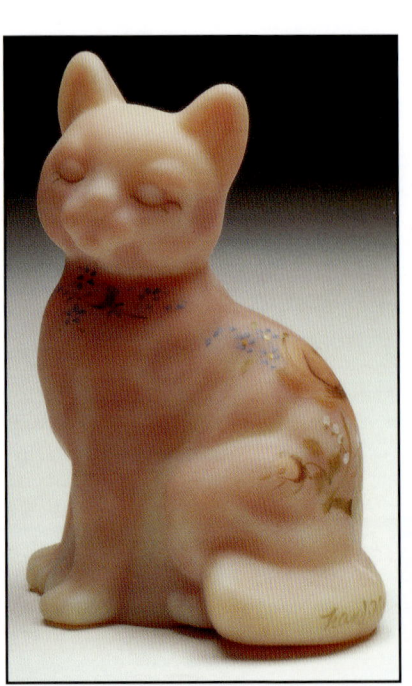

Sitting cat #5165WQ, hand painted "Farewell Love Bouquet" decoration, 3.75" tall, 2.6" wide, Limited to 150, Special order made exclusively for Mary Walrath 1996, **$95**

Another special order was from Memories in Glass located in Tulsa, Oklahoma. Mary Jane Sparkman and Cathy Warren shared a love of collecting Depression glass and Christmas ornaments. They decided to combine these two interests by making ornaments based on Depression glass patterns and call their company, Memories in Glass. They took their ideas to the Fenton Art Glass Company to make the glass ornaments. Each ornament is given a name to go with each particular color of glass. They produced each in limited editions and packed in a special box. The first ornament was made in 1995. All of the ornaments have the company trademark of MG on them along with the Fenton private mould mark. The Snowflake Surprise was based on the the Horseshoe pattern originally made by Indiana Glass.

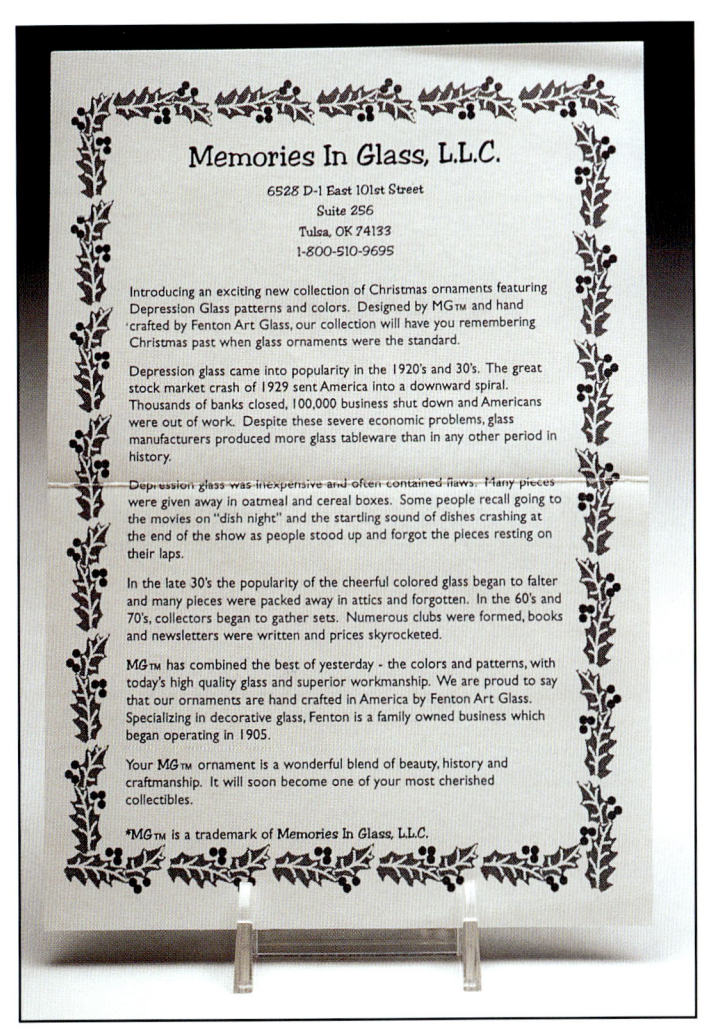

Detail of Memories in Glass brochure.

Ornament, #HS154BR"Snowflake Surprise", 4" long, 4" wide, Limited edition of 500, designed from Horseshoe (a Depression Era) pattern, Special order made exclusively for Memories in Glass 1996, **$45**

1997

The Spring Supplement of 1997 offered for the first time some Burmese items. The Southern Belle was hand painted with a design by Robin Spindler. A new vanity set thrilled perfume collectors. A matching perfume and powder were displayed on a round tray. This set was also designed by Robin Spindler. The Designer Series of four bells featured one of the bells being made of Burmese. Frances Burton designed the decoration on this bell.

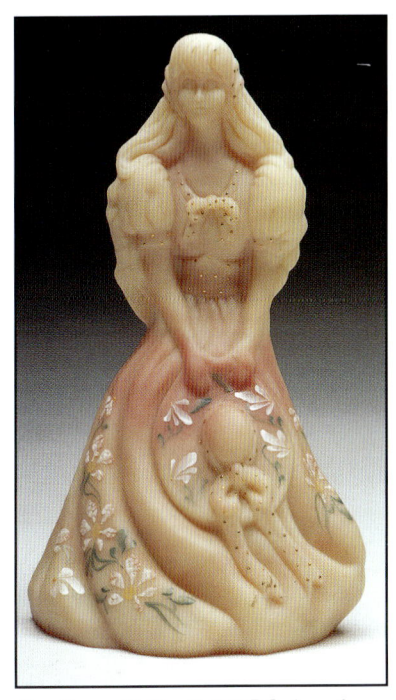

Southern Belle #5141BG, hand painted floral decoration, 8" tall, Decoration designed by Robin Spindler, Limited to 2000, Spring Supplement 1997, **$98**

138   The 1990s

Detail of hand painted "Floral & Butterfly" decoration.

Detail of hand painted "Forest Cottage" decoration.

Vanity set #2905BG, hand painted "Floral & Butterfly" decoration designed by Robin Spindler, Limited to 2000, Spring Supplement 1997, **$250 set**, **Left:** Powder box & cover, 4" tall, 4.25" wide; **Right:** Perfume bottle & stopper: 5.75" tall; **Bottom:** Vanity tray, 7.25" diameter

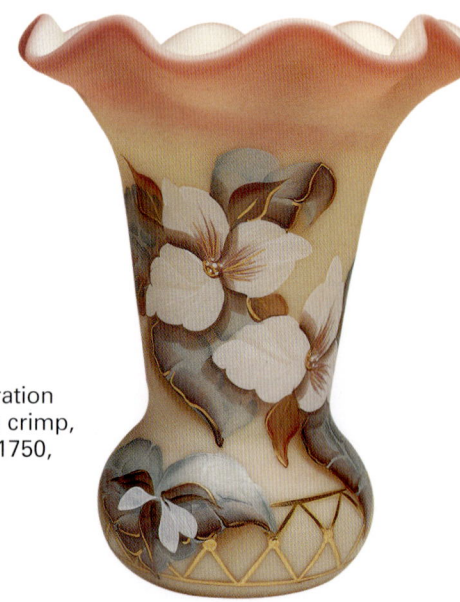

Vase #2961BY, hand painted "Trillium" decoration designed by Robin Spindler, 9.25" tall, single crimp, Eleven Fenton Family signatures, Limited to 1750, Connoisseur Collection 1997, **$225**
Note, this mould was first used in 1932.

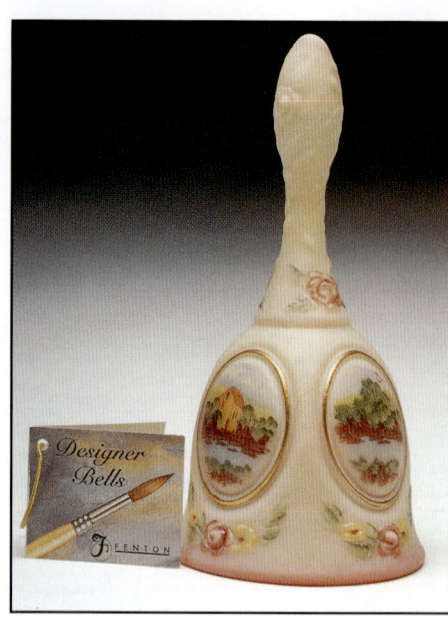

Medallion bell #8267CF, hand painted "Forest Cottage" decoration designed by Frances Burton, 7" tall, Decorated by J. Crenshaw, Limited to 2500, Designer Series 1997, **$85**

Detail of hand painted "Trillium" decoration.

By June, the Connoisseur Collection featured two more pieces of Burmese, Fenced Garden basket and Trillium vase. The designs were both from Robin Spindler. To add extra elegance the basket had frit (crushed glass) applied to the paint. The basket was another new creation from Jon Saffell. The vase featured signatures from 11 family members. This was the first Connoisseur piece to bear these signatures. The vase was made from a mould that was created in 1932.

The 1990s   139

Detail of hand painted "Fenced Garden" decoration.

Vase #1658BE, plain gloss finish (Bulging neck), 8" tall, double crimp, From Fenton Gift Shop 1997, **$60**

Detail of basket bottom showing artist signature & limited edition number.

Vase #2905, hand painted floral decoration & butterfly, 4.25" tall, slight single crimp, made from perfume bottle blank, From Fenton Gift Shop 1997, **$60**

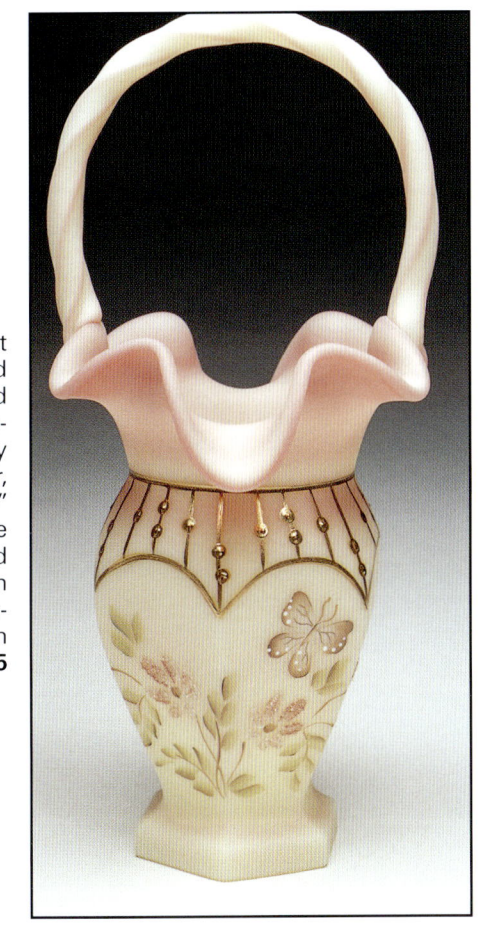

Basket #7632BQ, hand painted "Fenced Garden" decoration designed by Robin Spindler, 11" tall, 5.75" wide, single crimp, Mould designed by Jon Saffell, Connoisseur Collection 1997, **$175**

Perfume bottle & rib stopper #2905, hand painted rust colored poppy, 5.75" tall, tight single crimp, From Fenton Gift Shop 1997, **$95**

140   The 1990s

Kitten #5119BR, plain satin finish, 2.1" tall, 3.75" long, From Fenton Gift Shop 1997, **$48**

Southern Belle #5141BR, plain satin finish, 8" tall, From Fenton Gift Shop 1997, **$65**

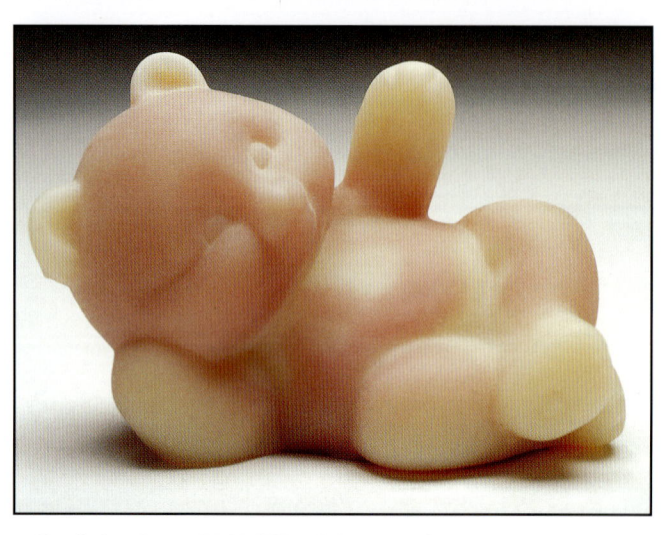

Reclining bear #5233BR, plain satin finish, 2.75" tall, 3.75" long, From Fenton Gift Shop 1997, **$45**

Mini Rooster #5265BR, plain satin finish, 2.75" tall, From Fenton Gift Shop 1997, **$38**

Rose bowl #9126BR, "Embossed Poppy" pattern, plain satin finish, 4.75", From Fenton Gift Shop 1997, **$39** Note, this is the same piece that was sold on QVC, only without the brass stand.

Santa holding a list #5299, plain, 8" tall, Mould designed by Jon Saffell, From Fenton Gift Shop 1997, **Left:** Satin finish #5299BR, **$68**; **Right:** Gloss finish #5299BE, **$60**

The 1990s 141

Grape & Cable tobacco jar #9188BR, plain satin finish, 7" tall, From Fenton Gift Shop annual February sale 1997 **$195**

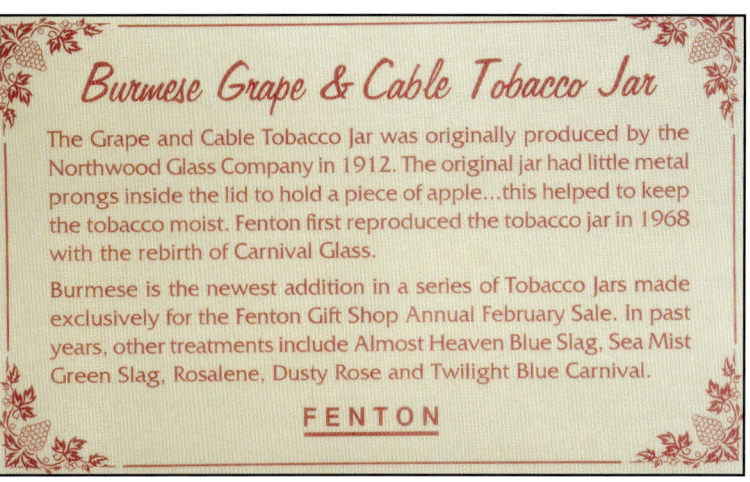

Detail of original brochure on "Grape & Cable" tobacco jar offering.

Burmese Grape & Cable Tobacco Jar

The Grape and Cable Tobacco Jar was originally produced by the Northwood Glass Company in 1912. The original jar had little metal prongs inside the lid to hold a piece of apple...this helped to keep the tobacco moist. Fenton first reproduced the tobacco jar in 1968 with the rebirth of Carnival Glass.

Burmese is the newest addition in a series of Tobacco Jars made exclusively for the Fenton Gift Shop Annual February Sale. In past years, other treatments include Almost Heaven Blue Slag, Sea Mist Green Slag, Rosalene, Dusty Rose and Twilight Blue Carnival.

FENTON

The Grape and Cable tobacco jar was made for the annual February gift shop sale. Numerous undecorated items were also available during the year.

Powder Box, hand painted "Rose" decoration, 4.25" tall, 4.25" wide, From Fenton Gift Shop 1997, **$75**

Powder Box, hand painted wild flowers, 4.25" tall, 4.25" wide, From Fenton Gift Shop 1997, **$75**

142   The 1990s

Each of the QVC shows during the year featured Burmese items with the total being ten. The kitten, bear and clock each had a daisy decoration. A new Santa and group of Christmas trees were in the ending show of the year.

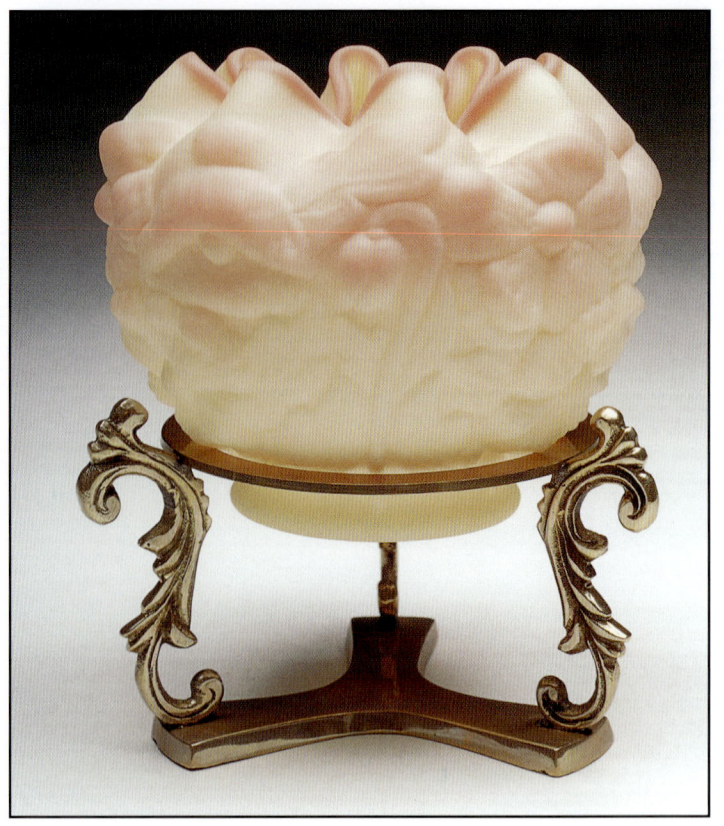

Rose bowl #CV175BR, "Embossed Poppy" pattern set in a brass base, plain satin finish, 4.75", single crimp & cupped in, Made for QVC Show March 1997, **$48**

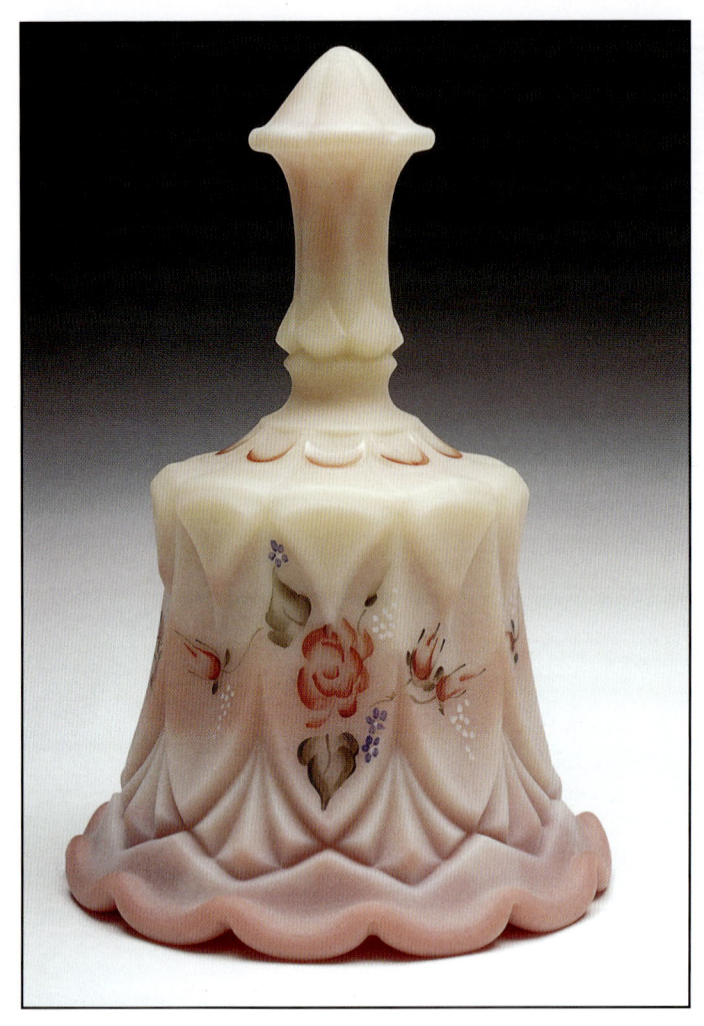

Whitton bell #C9066RB, hand painted "Rose" decoration designed by Martha Reynolds, 6.5" tall, 4" wide, slight single crimp, Shelley Fenton-Ash signature, Made for QVC Show January 1997, **$85**

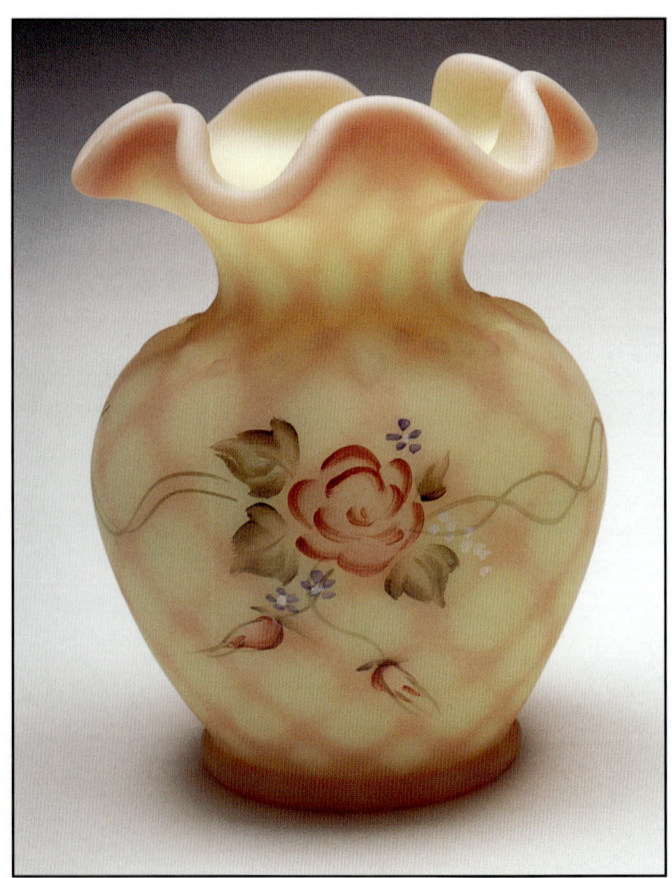

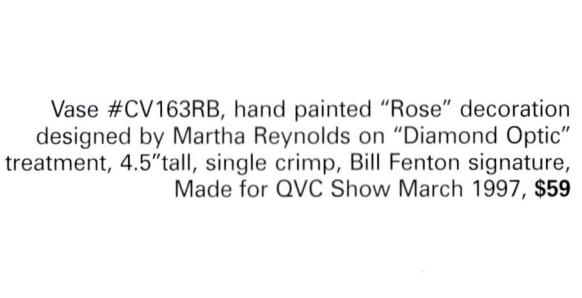

Vase #CV163RB, hand painted "Rose" decoration designed by Martha Reynolds on "Diamond Optic" treatment, 4.5"tall, single crimp, Bill Fenton signature, Made for QVC Show March 1997, **$59**

The 1990s   143

Clock #C86914N, hand painted "Daisies" decoration designed by Frances Burton, 4.5" tall, 5.5" wide, Made for QVC Show March 1997, **$145**

Kitten #C51194N, hand painted "Daisies" decoration designed by Frances Burton, 2" tall, 4" long, Made for QVC Show June 1997, **$65**

Reclining bear #C52334N, hand painted "Daisies" decoration designed by Kim Plauche, 2.25" tall, 4" long, Made for QVC Show October 1997, **$65**

Guest set #CV180RB (#5904), hand painted "Rose" decoration designed by Martha Reynolds on "Diamond Optic" treatment, 7.25" tall, Made for QVC Show August 1997, **$195** Also called a night set or tumble up set.

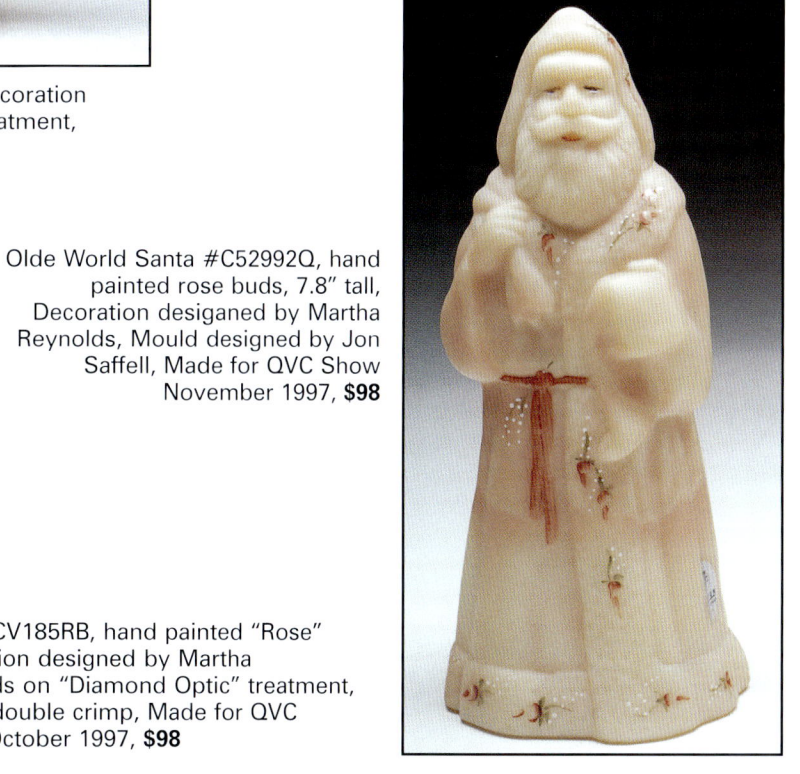

Olde World Santa #C52992Q, hand painted rose buds, 7.8" tall, Decoration desiganed by Martha Reynolds, Mould designed by Jon Saffell, Made for QVC Show November 1997, **$98**

Vase #CV185RB, hand painted "Rose" decoration designed by Martha Reynolds on "Diamond Optic" treatment, 6" tall, double crimp, Made for QVC Show October 1997, **$98**

Tree set #5550, plain satin finish, Made for QVC Show November 1997, **$125 set, Left:** #5557BR, 3" tall, **$28; Center:** #5535BR, 6.25" tall, **$48; Right:** #5556BR, 4" tall, **$36**

There were numerous special orders for the year. One of them was for Joyce Colella. Not wanting to let her mother's legacy of inspirational messages on glass disappear, Joyce came up with a new design. Circle of Love was born utilizing the Love Bouquet and then adding a bouquet of white roses along with lilac Forget-me-nots. The two are then joined by a dove with a white ribbon. This decoration was designed by Kim Plauche. There were six items in this new collection but only five were Burmese. The following items were made: crimped rose bowl, cupped rose bowl, lamp, nymph in a bowl, and pitcher. An unusual item in the set was the Rosalene nymph sitting in a Burmese bowl. This was the first time the two types of glasses had been used together to form a set. All the pieces were made in very limited quantities. Every piece is numbered and signed by both Joyce and Mary.

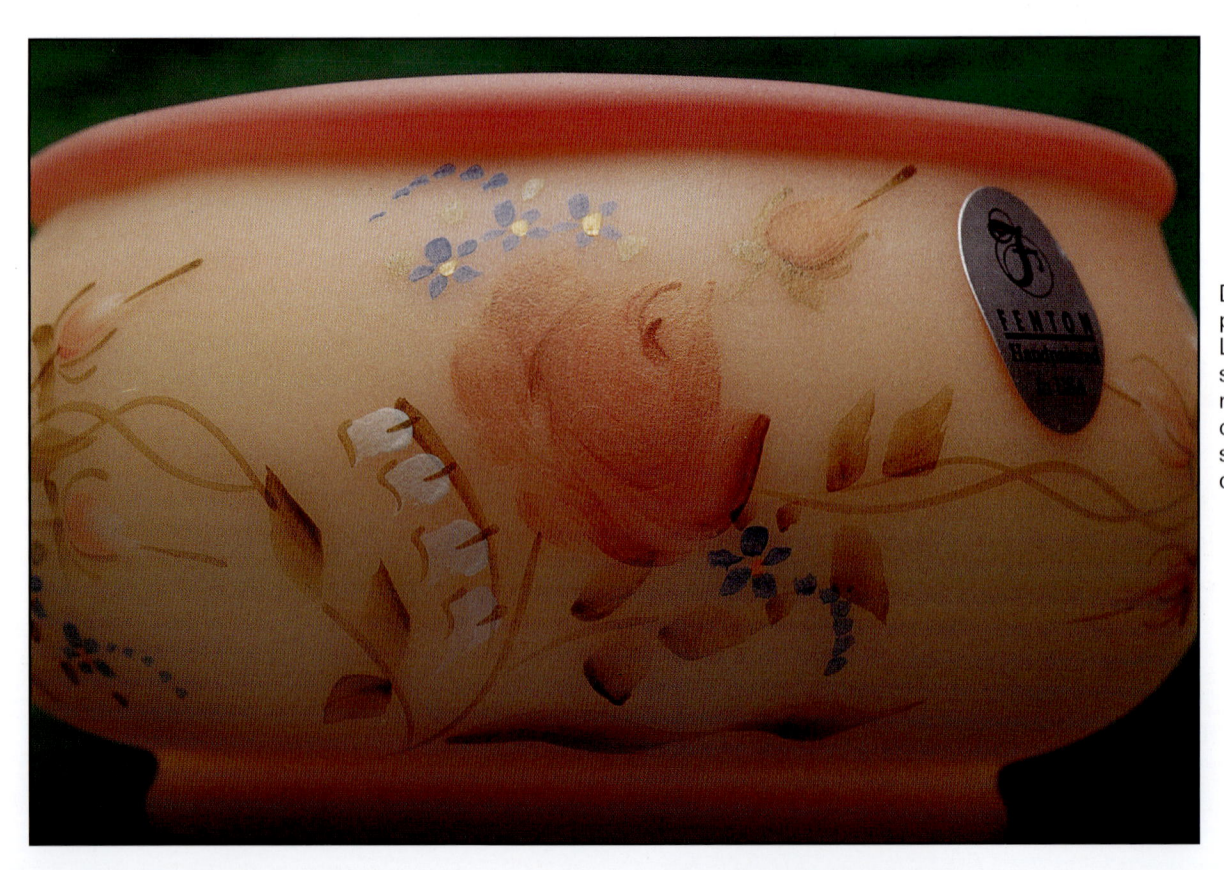

Detail of hand painted "Circle of Love" decoration, showing pink roses. Note, first of four photos to show the entire decoration.

Detail of hand painted "Circle of Love" decoration, showing white & pink flowers. Note, second of four photos to show the entire decoration.

Detail of hand painted "Circle of Love" decoration, showing two white flowers. Note, third of four photos to show the entire decoration.

146 The 1990s

Detail of hand painted "Circle of Love" decoration, showing the white dove. Note, fourth & last of four photos to show the entire decoration.

Group of hand painted "Circle of Love" decoration, Special order made exclusively for Joyce Colella 1997, **Back:** Sample vase made from pitcher, **Market Value**; Pitcher, Limited to 53, **$295**; Sample vase made from pitcher, **Market Value**; **Front:** Cupped rose bowl, Limited to 80, **$100**; Crimped rose bowl, Limited to 163 **$90**

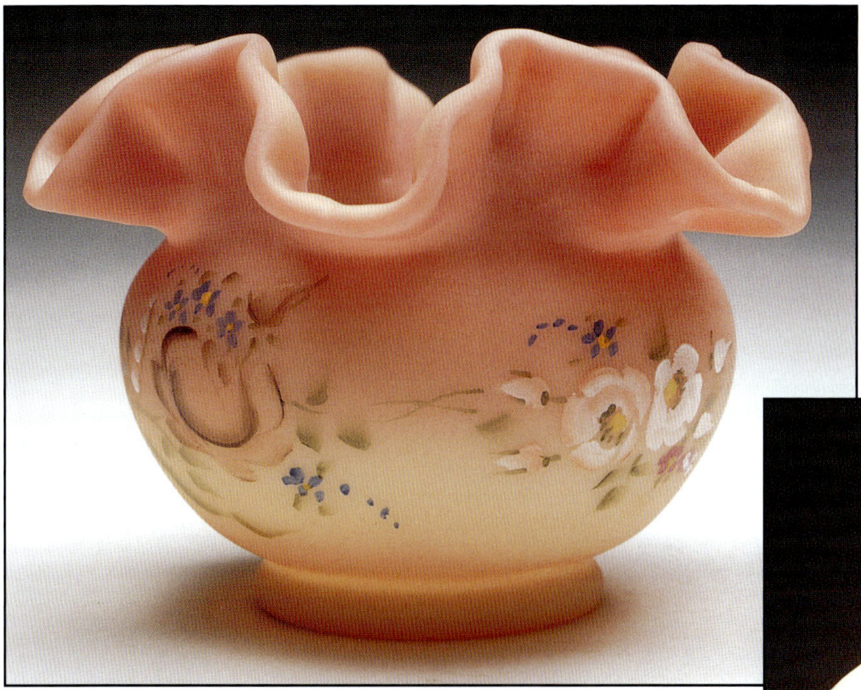

The 1990s   147

Rose bowl #7546, hand painted "Circle of Love" decoration, 3.6" tall, double crimp, Limited to 163, Special order made exclusively for Joyce Colella 1997, **$90**

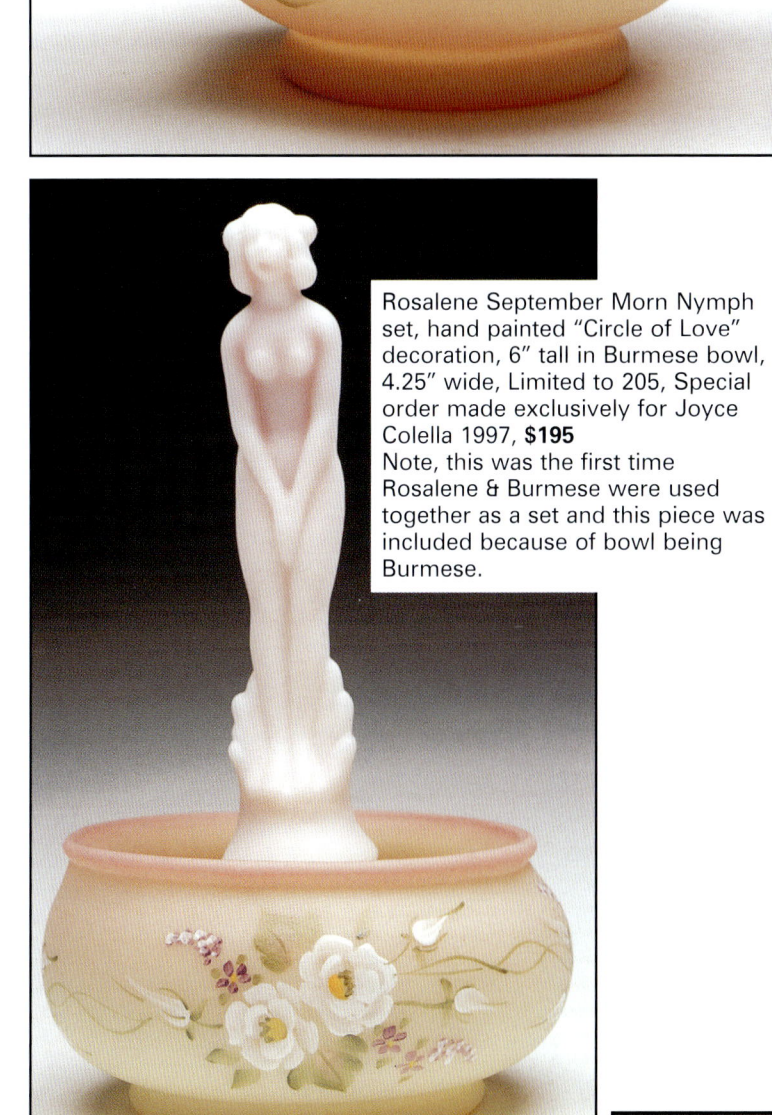

Rosalene September Morn Nymph set, hand painted "Circle of Love" decoration, 6" tall in Burmese bowl, 4.25" wide, Limited to 205, Special order made exclusively for Joyce Colella 1997, **$195**
Note, this was the first time Rosalene & Burmese were used together as a set and this piece was included because of bowl being Burmese.

Student Lamp, hand painted "Circle of Love" decoration, 18" overall height, 10" double crimp shade, Limited to 60, Special order made exclusively for Joyce Colella 1997, **$750**

Detail of "Circle of Love" student lamp back side.

148 The 1990s

Four other special orders were also available. The Fenton Art Glass Collectors of America (FAGCA) had the Bulging Tear Drop shakers hand painted for them.

Bulging Tear Drop shakers #6906, hand painted floral, 2.75" tall 2.5" wide, Special order made exclusively for FAGCA (Fenton Art Glass Collectors of America) April/May 1997, **$75 pair**

Bulging Tear Drop shakers #6906, hand painted floral & butterfly, 2.75" tall 2.5" wide, Special order made exclusively for FAGCA (Fenton Art Glass Collectors of America) April/May 1997, **$75 pair**

Aladdin Lamp contracted with Fenton to make another Grand Vertique lamp for them. This time the lamp would be made in Burmese. The lamps would come in either styles of kerosene or electric. Sue Jackson hand painted the shades on all of these lamps. There were only 500 produced and each were individually numbered on the base. In addition each lamp is also marked Aladdin Fenton 1997 in embossed letters near the number.

Another special order this year was from Memories in Glass. This year's edition is the Kelly Angel. The ornament is based on the Depression Butterflies and Roses pattern originally made by Jeannette Glass Company. This is only the second ornament to be made in Burmese.

Detail of original ad for Aladdin "Grand Vertique" lamp in 1997. **Note,** this lamp is really Burmese, but the photo makes it look more like Rosalene.

Aladdin "Grand Vertique" lamp #EGV2397, hand painted floral shade, 25.25" overall height, 10" shade, double crimp, Limited to 500 lamps with shades decorated by Sue Jackson and 250 lamps without shades, Special order made exclusively for Aladdin Industries 1997, **$500** with shade; **$300** without shade
Note, when each lamp was ordered, you could request either kerosene or electric.

Ornament, #DS146BR, "Kelly Angel", 4.25" long, 3.75" wide, Limited edition of 700, designed from Roses & Butterflies pattern, Special order made exclusively for Memories in Glass 1997, **$45**

The 1990s 149

Kirlins Hallmark store featured the last special order. A decorated, #8267 bell was designed to be sold only in their shop.

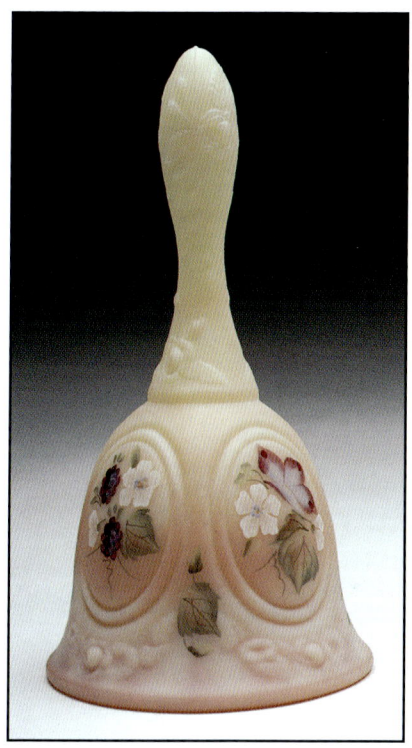

Medallion bell #82679R, hand painted butterflies & blackberries, 6.5" tall, Special order made exclusively for Kirlins Hallmark store 1997, **$65**

1998
The year of 1998 saw the continuation of the Designer Series of bells. Another Burmese limited edition was offered. This one was decorated with Bleeding Hearts and designed by Robin Spindler. Only 2500 were produced.

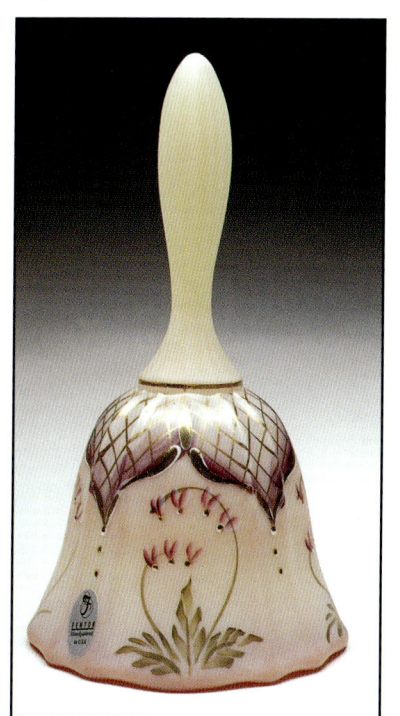

Aurora Bell #9667UJ, hand painted "Bleeding Hearts" decoration designed by Robin Spindler, 6.8" tall, Limited to 2500, Catalog Designer Series 1998, **$60**

The Connoisseur Collection in June had four limited edition pieces. The designs on each reflected the individual interests of the decorators. Kim Plauche created a beautiful butterfly on a vase and blackberries on a basket. Martha Reynolds created a simple floral garland for the lamp. Robin Spindler created a bunch of freshly harvested fruit. Robin was honored for this decoration by being selected as a finalist for the annual decorative award. This was sponsored by the National Association of Limited Edition Dealer (NALED).

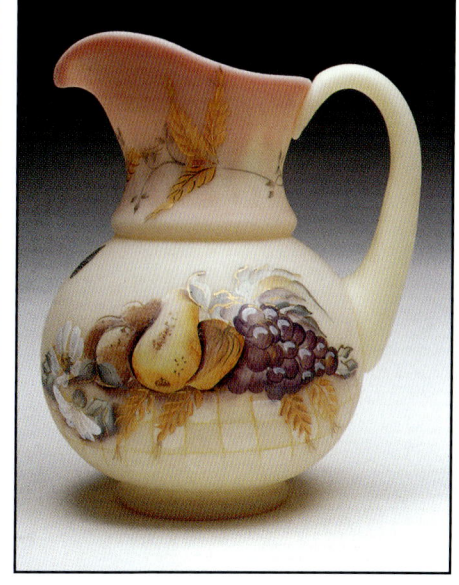

Pitcher #2998YZ, hand painted "Bountiful Harvest" decoration designed by Robin Spindler, 7.25" tall, Limited to 2250, Connoisseur Collection 1998, **$150**

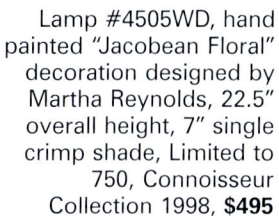

Lamp #4505WD, hand painted "Jacobean Floral" decoration designed by Martha Reynolds, 22.5" overall height, 7" single crimp shade, Limited to 750, Connoisseur Collection 1998, **$495**

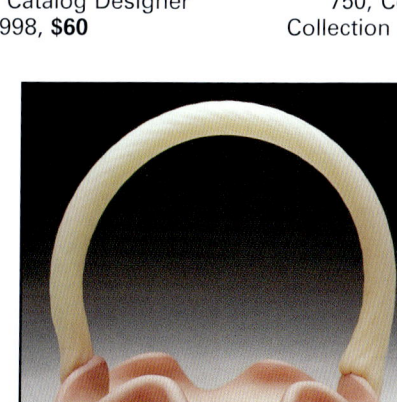

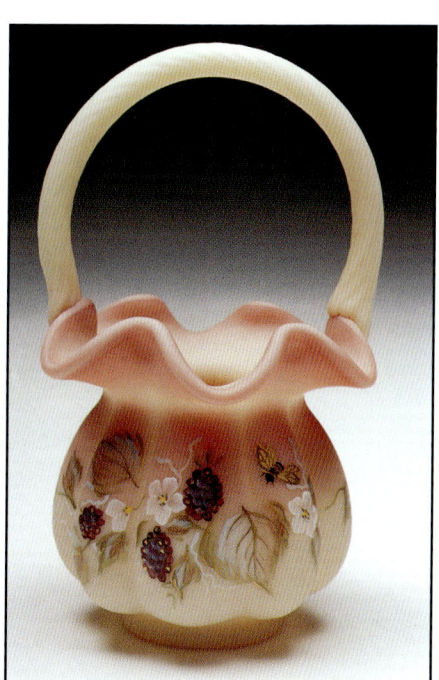

Basket #7139NP, hand painted "Blackberry Bouquet" decoration designed by Kim Plauche, 7.25" tall, 4.5" wide, single crimp, Limited to 2250, Connoisseur Collection 1998, **$135**

150 The 1990s

Detail of hand painted "Butterfly" decoration.

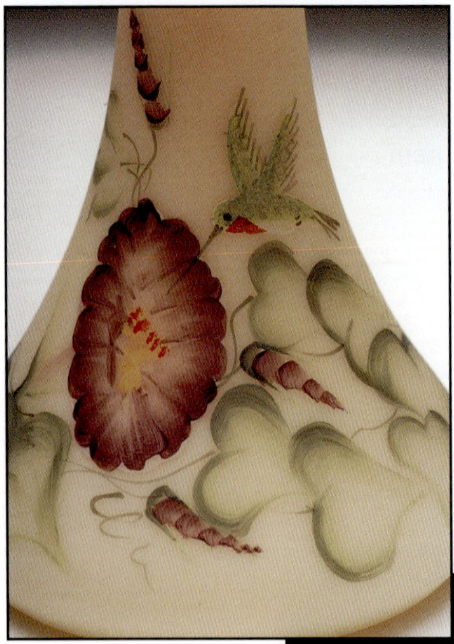

Detail of hand painted "Morning Glories" decoration.

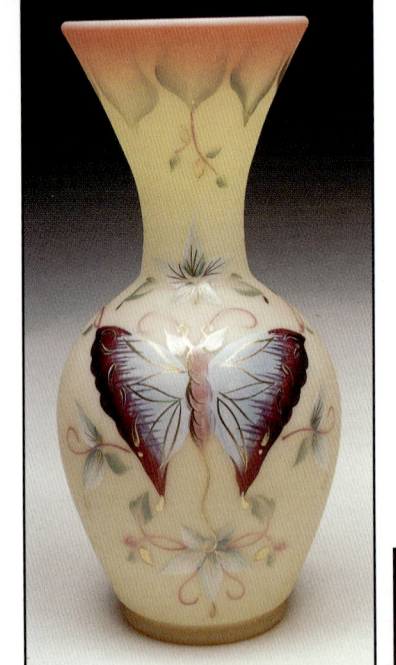

Papillon vase #7557UW, hand painted "Butterfly" decoration designed by Kim Plauche, 9.5" tall, Limited to 2500, Connoisseur Collection 1998, **$185**

Tulip vase #7255UZ, hand painted "Morning Glories" decoration designed by Frances Burton, 10.75" tall, Frank Fenton signature, Glass Messenger Exclusive 1998, **$165** Note, also called a Jack In The Pulpit vase.

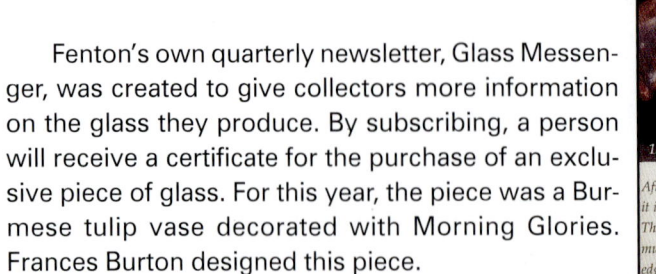

Fenton's own quarterly newsletter, Glass Messenger, was created to give collectors more information on the glass they produce. By subscribing, a person will receive a certificate for the purchase of an exclusive piece of glass. For this year, the piece was a Burmese tulip vase decorated with Morning Glories. Frances Burton designed this piece.

After the vase is blown in the mould (1), it is reheated to bring out the pink color. Then Bill Close, a skilled finisher (2), must work quickly to shape the topmost edge with a crimp (3) before using his pincer to pull up the back edge (4). The pucellas, a traditional glassworkers' tool, is used to gently shape the folds at the front of the vase (5).

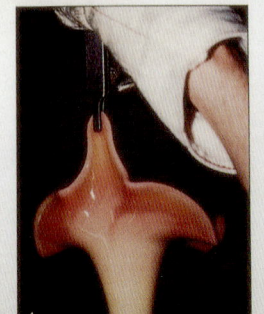

Detail from "Glass Messenger" Publication on the making of the tulip vase. (Reprinted with permission from the Fenton Art Glass Company)

The Fenton gift shop had the puppy decorated in different ways for the June tent sale. Also the ginger jar from the QVC program was made into a table lamp.

Perfume stopper on bust off #2906BE, plain gloss finish, 6" tall, Mould designed by Jon Saffell, From Fenton Gift Shop 1998, **$75**

Puppy #5225BR, plain satin finish, 3.5" tall, 3.75" long, From Fenton Gift Shop 1998, **$58**

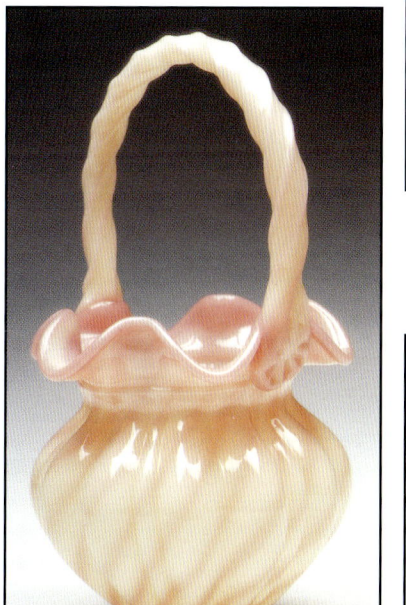

Melon basket #225BE, "Spiral Optic" treatment, gloss finish, 8.75" tall 5" wide, From Fenton Gift Shop 1998, **$115**

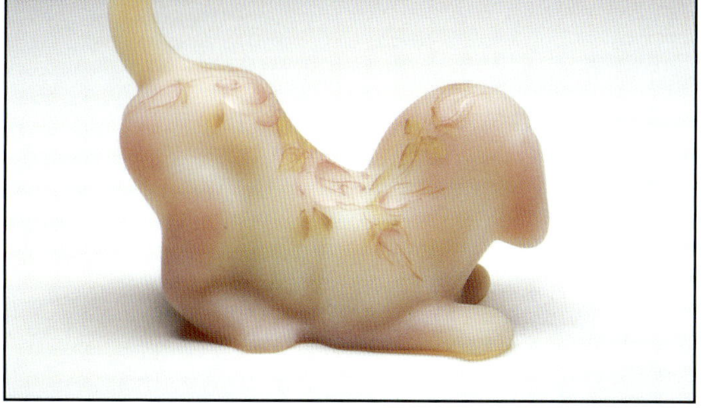

Puppy #5225, hand painted "Log Cabin" scene, 3.5" tall, 3.75" long, Decorated by S. (Sue) Lee, From Fenton Gift Shop 1998, **$75**

Puppy #5225, hand painted "Rose" decoration, 3.5" tall, 3.75" long, Decorated by S. (Sue) Lee, From Fenton Gift Shop 1998, **$68**

152   The 1990s

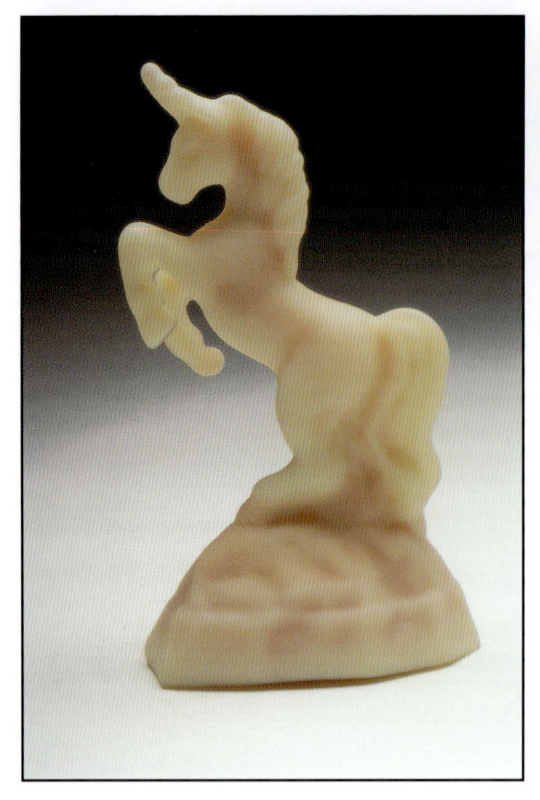

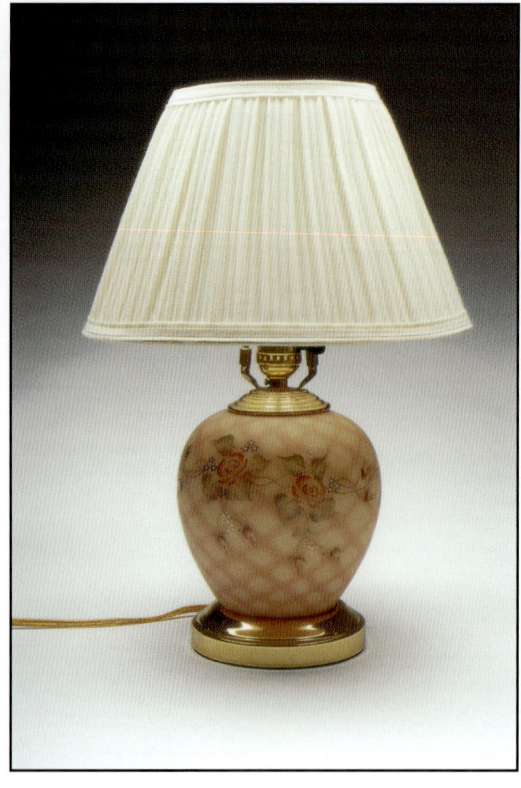

Lamp #5302, hand painted "Rose" decoration on "Diamond Optic" treatment, 21" overall height, made from a ginger jar, From Fenton Gift Shop 1998, **$195**

Unicorn #5253BR, plain satin finish, 5.3" tall, 3.25" long, From Fenton Gift Shop 1998, **$45**

The QVC programs offered a record number of Burmese pieces in 1998, with the total being 14. There were four animals and two baskets made. A new Santa by Jon Saffell also debuted. The Orange Tree bowl was a mould used on the early carnival glass.

Basket #CV204RB, hand painted "Rose" decoration designed by Kim Plauche on "Diamond Optic" treatment, 7.75" tall, 4.75" wide, tight double crimp, Don Fenton signature, Made for QVC Show January 1998, **$125**

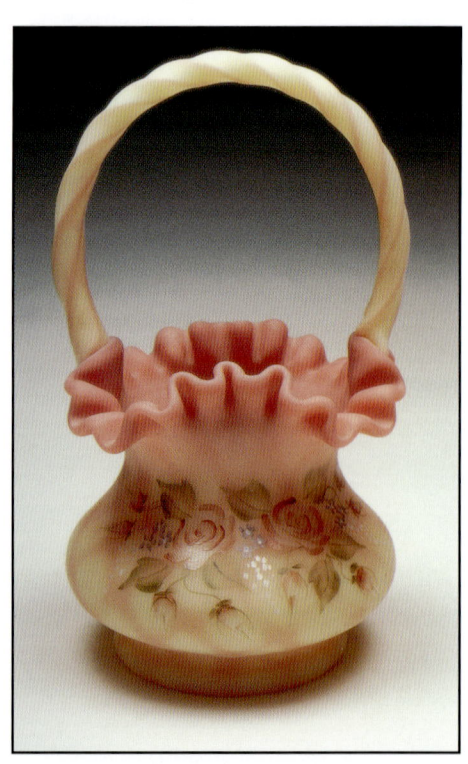

Ginger jar #5302BR, "Diamond Optic" treatment, satin finish, 8.25" tall, three piece set (jar, cover & base), From Fenton Gift Shop 1998, **$145**

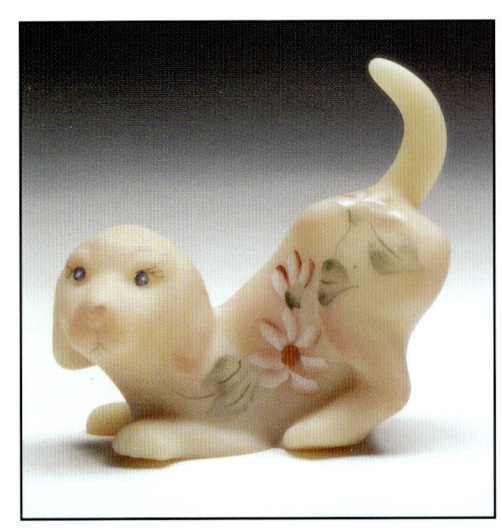

The 1990s   153

Puppy #C52254N, hand painted "Daisies" decoration designed by Martha Reynolds, 3.5" tall, 3.75" long, Made for QVC Show January 1998, **$65**

Melon basket #CV225BR, "Spiral Optic" treatment, satin finish, 8.75" tall, 5" wide, single crimp, Made for QVC Show June 1998, **$95**

Covered Butterfly Box #C92804N, hand painted "Daisies" decoration designed by Frances Burton, 5" tall, 5.1" wide, Made for QVC Show April 1998, **$85**

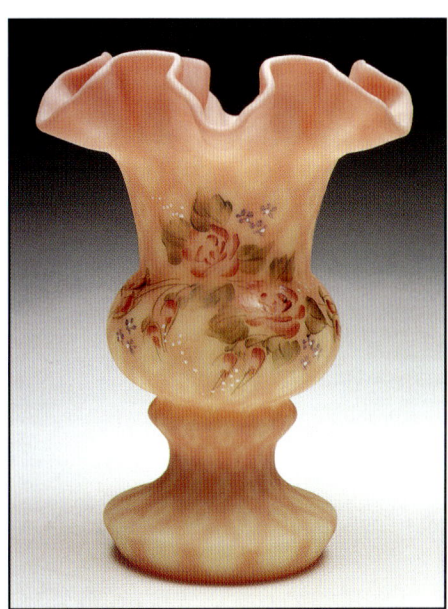

Urn vase #CV228RB, hand painted "Rose" decoration designed by Martha Reynolds on "Diamond Optic" treatment, 6.5" tall, double crimp, Made for QVC Show June 1998, **$99**

Day dreaming bear #C52394N, hand painted "Daisies" decoration designed by Frances Burton, 2.5" tall, 4" long, Made for QVC Show April 1998, **$65**

Bird #C51634N, hand painted "Daisies" decoration designed by Frances Burton, 2.75" tall, 4" long, Made for QVC Show June 1998, **$55**

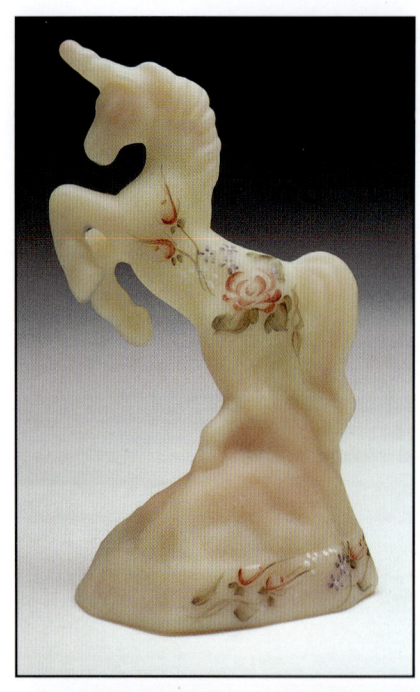

154   The 1990s

Unicorn #C5253RB, hand painted "Roses" decoration designed by Martha Reynolds, 5.3" tall, 3.25" long, Made for QVC Show August 1998, **$75**

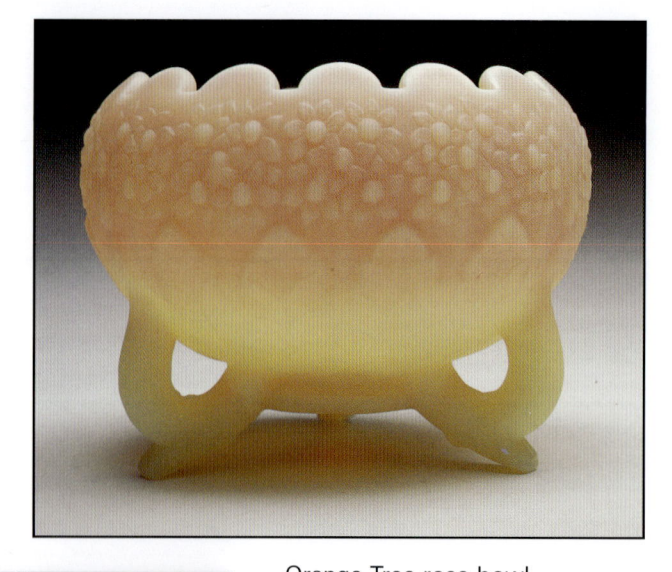

Orange Tree rose bowl #C8223BR, plain satin finish, three tree bark looped feet, 3.8" tall, Made for QVC Show October 1998, **$68**

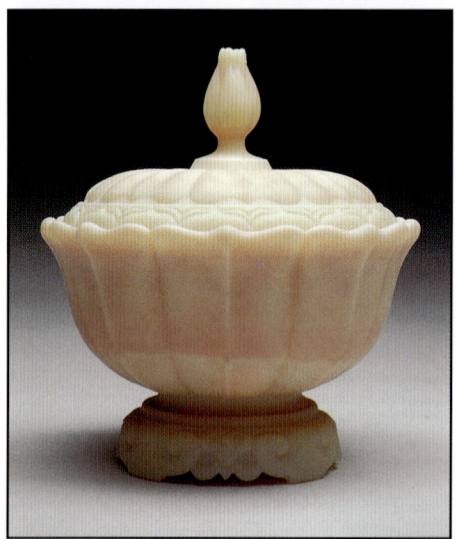

Ginger jar #CV233RB (#5302), hand painted "Rose" decoration designed by Martha Reynolds on "Diamond Optic" treatment, 8.25" tall, three piece set (jar, cover & base), George Fenton signature, Made for QVC Show October 1998, **$195**

Ogee candy box #C9394BR, plain satin finish, 7" tall, 7.25" wide, three piece set (candy, cover & special base), Made for QVC Show August 1998, **$145**

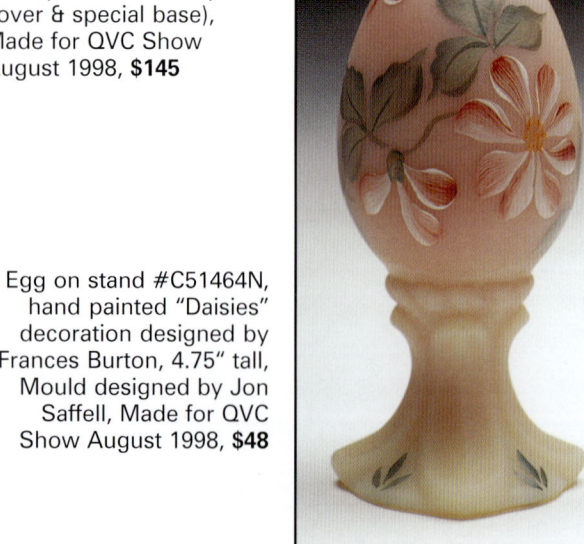

Egg on stand #C51464N, hand painted "Daisies" decoration designed by Frances Burton, 4.75" tall, Mould designed by Jon Saffell, Made for QVC Show August 1998, **$48**

Perfume bottle #CV241RB, hand painted "Rose" decoration designed by Martha Reynolds on "Diamond Optic" treatment, 5.75" tall, Stopper mould designed by Jon Saffell, Bill & Elinor Fenton signatures, Made for QVC Show November 1998, **$98**

Santa holding kitten #C52492Q, hand painted rose buds, 8.5" tall, Decoration designed by Martha Reynolds, Mould designed by Jon Saffell, Made for QVC Show November 1998, **$125**

Joyce Colella continued with her Circle of Love offering. There were two small tulip vases made, one with a plain top and the other with a crimped top. The unusual thing about these is that they had a ebony crest. This was a very different type of treatment to be used in conjunction with Burmese.

Tulip vase #7552, hand painted "Circle of Love Bouquet" decoration, 6.75" tall, plain Ebony Crest, Limited to 120, Special order made exclusively for Joyce Colella 1998, **$135** Note, also called a Jack In The Pulpit vase.

Three special orders were created this year. A pitcher, #2998, the same shape as the one used in the Connoisseur Collection was decorated differently for the National Association of Limited Edition Dealer Association (NALED). This decoration was designed by Robin Spindler.

Tulip vase #7552, hand painted "Circle of Love Bouquet" decoration, 6.75" tall, single crimp Ebony Crest, Limited to 69, Special order made exclusively for Joyce Colella 1998, **$165** Note, also called a Jack In The Pulpit vase.

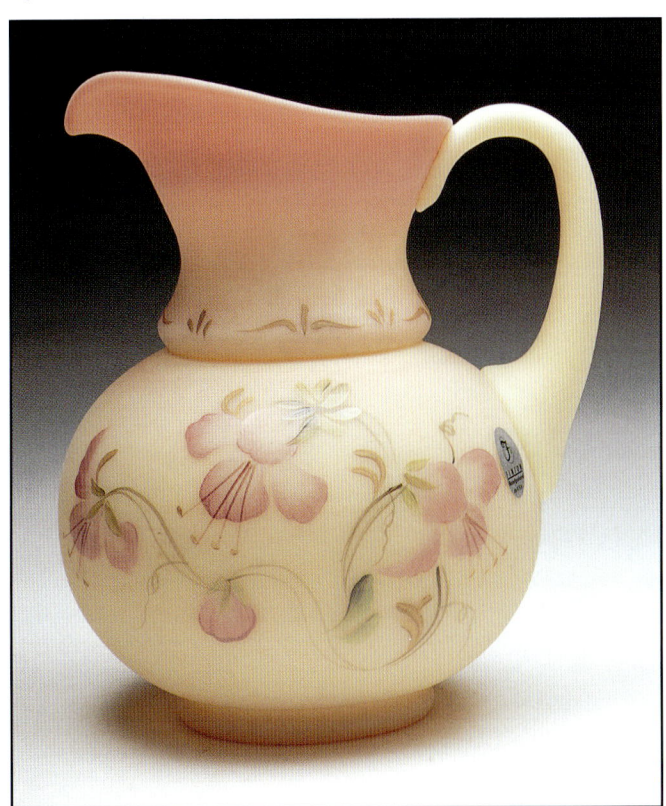

Pitcher #29982G, hand painted lavender flowers, Lynn Fenton Erb signature, Special order made exclusively for National Association of Limited Edition Dealers (NALED), 1998, **$145**

1999

The Connoisseur Collection of 1999 continued with several Burmese items. A beautiful basket with bluebirds was designed by Robin Spindler. Jon Saffell also designed this new basket shape. The Golden Gourds and Poppies vase had decorations by Martha Reynolds. These would be the last items she did for the Connoisseur Collection before retiring from Fenton. The Golden Gourds ewer was created from an old bottle mould. The Poppies vase was another new mould designed by Jon Saffell. The Memories lamp was designed by Robin Spindler and featured hibiscus flowers. Since these were favorite flowers of Robin's late husband, it was decided to call the lamp Memories in honor him.

Vase #6359WS, hand painted "Poppies" decoration designed by Martha Reynolds, 12.5" tall, single crimp, Mould design by Jon Saffell, Limited to 2500, Connoisseur Collection 1999, **$195**

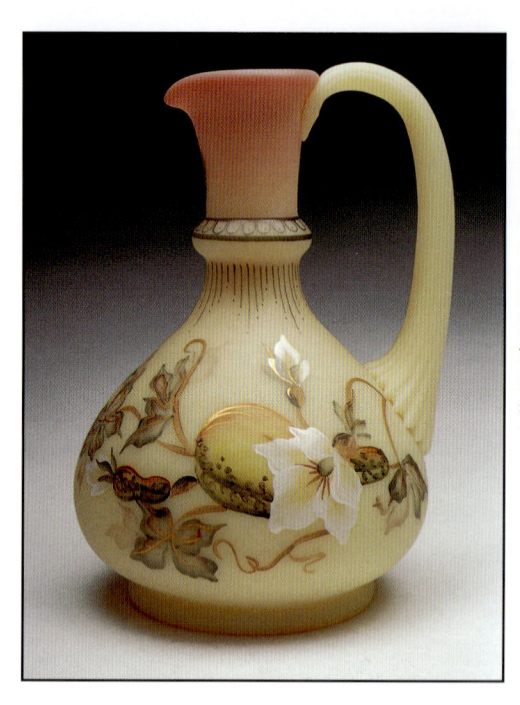

Ewer #1862VV, hand painted "Golden Gourds" decoration designed by Martha Reynolds, 6.75" tall, Limited to 2500, Connoisseur Collection 1999, **$165**

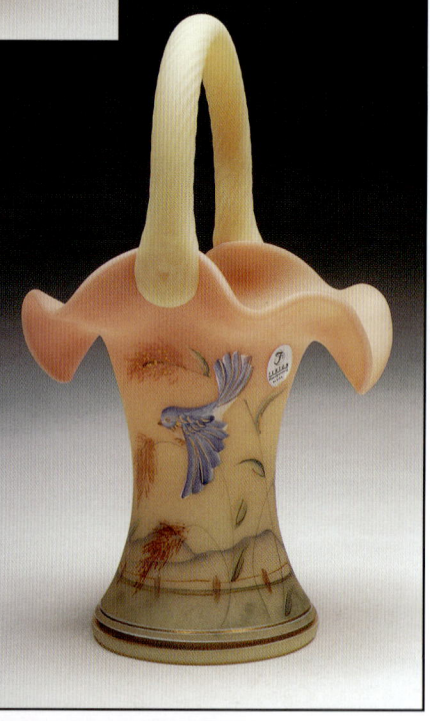

Basket #6831U5, hand painted "Bluebird" decoration designed by Robin Spindler, 9.5" tall, 5.5" wide, single crimp & ends pulled down, Mould designed by Jon Saffell, Limited to 2950, Twelve Fenton family signatures, Connoisseur Collection 1999, **$165** Note, the basket handler mark on this piece shows that Terry Deuley put the handle on this basket.

Memories lamp #6200HW, hand painted white flowers & lace, 17" overall height, Decoration designed by Robin Spindler, Limited to 950, Connoisseur Collection 1999, **$695**

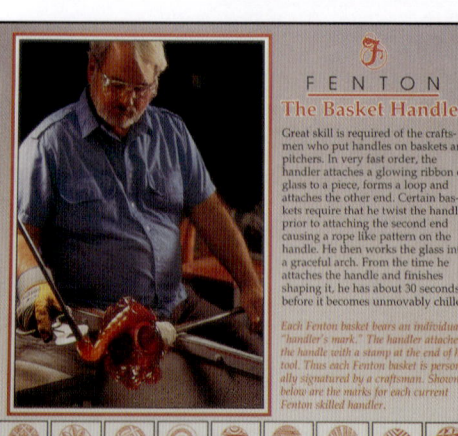

Detail of Fenton paper display sign showing the basket handlers marks. **Note**, you can use the information in this display sign to check the basket handler that has put the handle on your piece.

The 1990s 157

The mini-catalog used by retailers for their mail order customers featured two hand painted Burmese pieces for 1999. The basket and stylized cat each had matching floral decorations designed by Martha Reynolds. Both had Bill Fenton signatures on them.

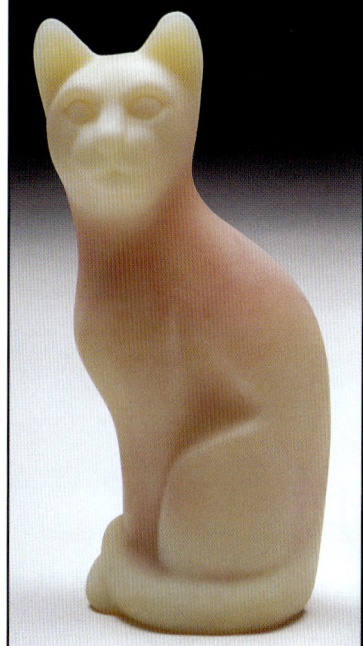

The Fenton gift shop had several of the large vases and basket decorated in different ways. There was also a sample lamp offered.

Stylized cat #5065BR, plain satin finish, 5.25" tall, Mould designed by Jon Saffell, Fenton Gift Shop 1999, **$45**

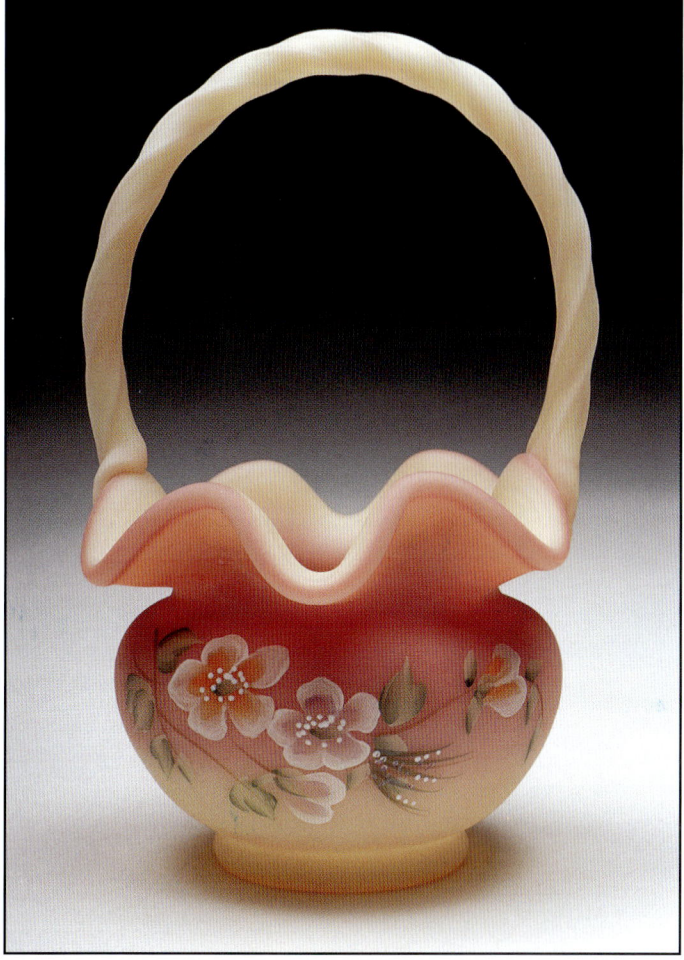

Vase #6359BE, plain gloss finish, 12.5" tall, single crimp, Mould designed by Jon Saffell, From Fenton Gift Shop 1999, **$145**

Basket #2915S3, hand painted floral decoration, 7.5" tall, 5" wide, single crimp, Decoration designed by Martha Reynolds, Bill Fenton signature, Catalog exclusive 1999, **$125**

Stylized cat #5065S3, hand painted floral decoration, 5" tall, 2.5" wide, Decoration designed by Martha Reynolds, Mould designed by Jon Saffell, Bill Fenton signature, Catalog exclusive 1999, **$75**

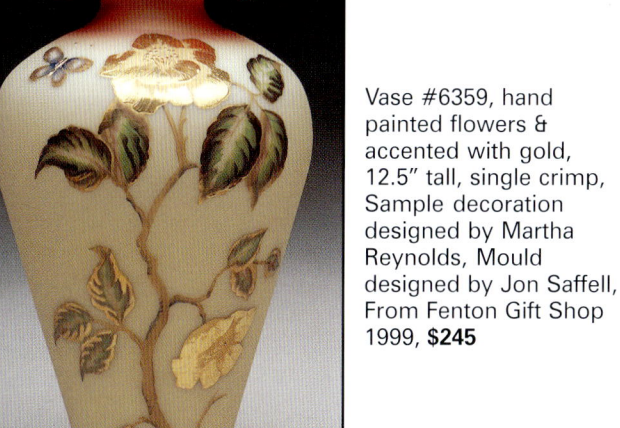

Vase #6359, hand painted flowers & accented with gold, 12.5" tall, single crimp, Sample decoration designed by Martha Reynolds, Mould designed by Jon Saffell, From Fenton Gift Shop 1999, **$245**

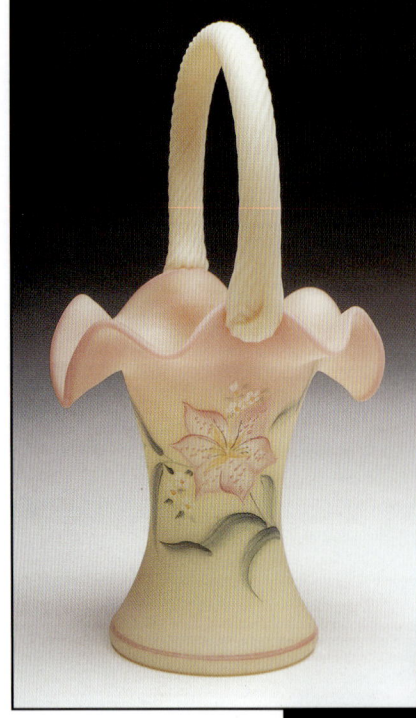

158   The 1990s

Basket #6831, hand painted wild flowers, 9.5" tall, 5.5" wide, single crimp & ends pulled down, Mould designed by Jon Saffell, From Fenton Gift Shop 1999, **$125**

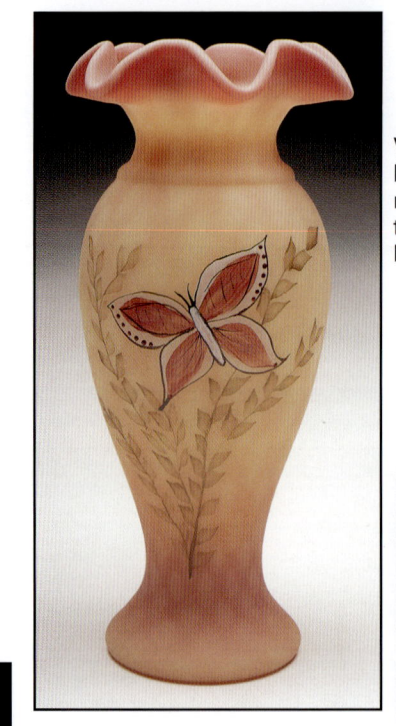

Vase, hand painted pink butterfly on branch "Diamond Optic" treatment, 10.5" tall, single crimp, From Fenton Gift Shop 1999, **$185**

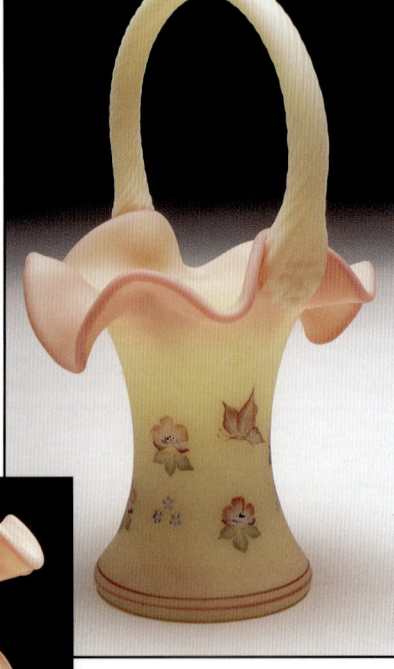

Basket #6831, hand painted small pink flowers & purple butterfly, 9.5" tall, 5.5" wide, single crimp & ends pulled down, Mould designed by Jon Saffell, From Fenton Gift Shop 1999, **$125**

Vase, hand painted lavender daisies on "Diamond Optic" treatment, 10.5" tall, single crimp, Sample decoration, From Fenton Gift Shop 1999, **$145**

Vase, "Diamond Optic" treatment, plain satin finish, 10.5" tall, single crimp, plain version of decorated QVC piece, From Fenton Gift Shop 1999, **$95**

Lamp, hand painted purple pansies decoration, 22.5" tall, From Fenton Gift Shop 1999, **$595**

The QVC programs offered several more Burmese pieces. Half of the items featured the Diamond Optic pattern. A hand painted bell was part of the New Century Collection and it was designed by Kim Plauche. This collection focused on the special skills associated with our glass making heritage. Shelley Fenton Ash designed a unique logo that appeared on every piece. A card describing the glass making technique used was included with every piece. The Burmese bell described the technique of the presser.

Colonial vase #CV266RB, hand painted "Rose" decoration designed by Martha Reynolds on "Diamond Optic" treatment, 10" tall, double crimp, Made for QVC Show June 1999, **$135**

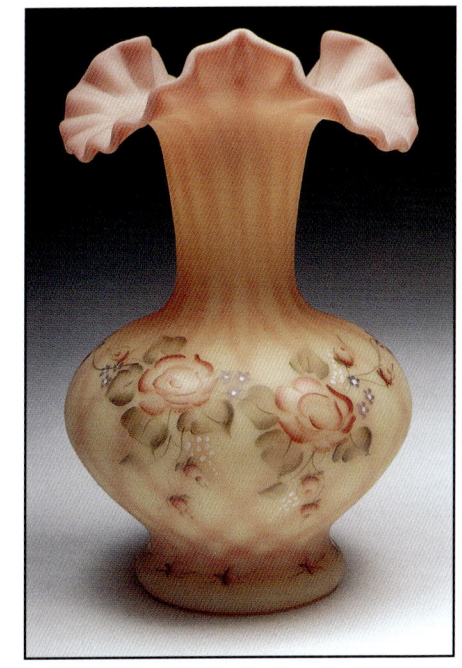

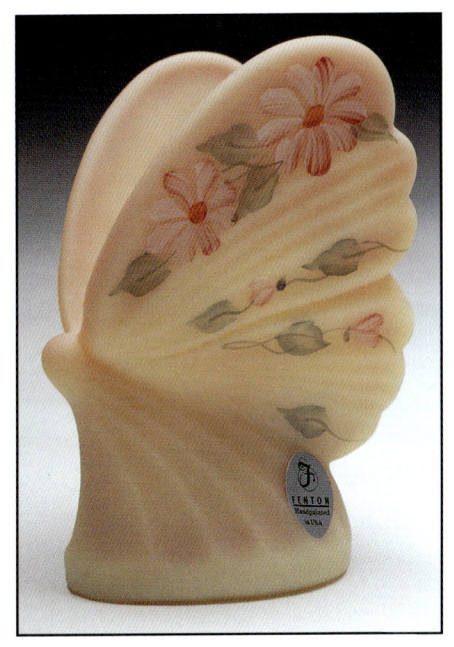

Butterfly #C52714N, hand painted pink daisies, 4.4" tall, Decoration designed by Frances Burton, Made for QVC Show January 1999, **$60**

Blown egg #CV262RB, hand painted "Rose" decoration designed by Jenny Cunningham on "Diamond Optic" treatment, Made for QVC Show March 1999, **$99**

Rose bowl #C1724RB, hand painted "Rose" decoration designed by Martha Reynolds on "Diamond Optic" treatment, 3.25" tall, tight crimp & cupped in, Shelley Fenton-Ash signature, Made for QVC Show August 1999, **$65**

Rooster #C5292WF, hand painted pink petals, 5.25" tall, Decoration designed by Martha Reynolds, Made for QVC Show March 1999, **$65**

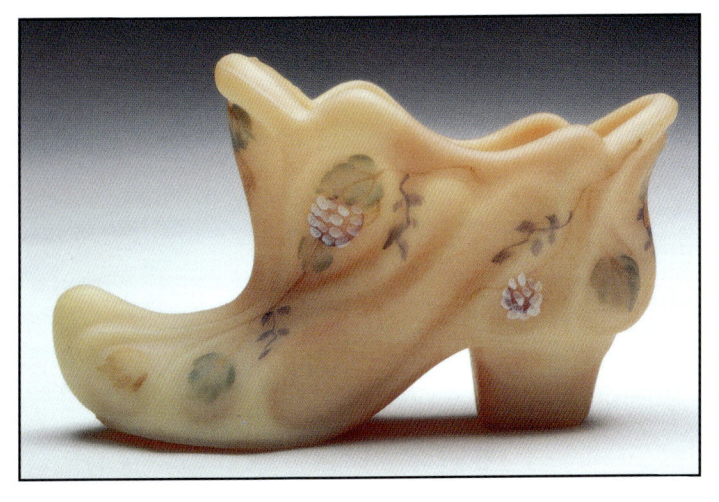

Paisley slipper #C29313F, hand painted purple grapes, 2.8" tall, 4.75" long, Decoration designed by Martha Reynolds, Made for QVC Show August 1999, **$45**

160   The 1990s

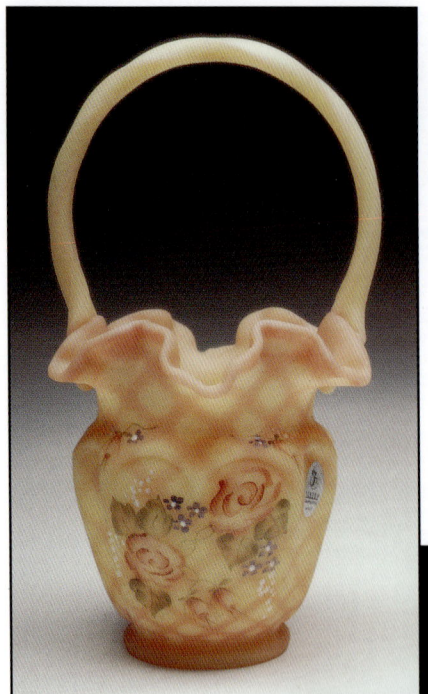

Open Heart Arches basket #CV070RB (#6540), hand painted "Rose" decoration designed by Martha Reynolds on "Diamond Optic" treatment, 8.25" tall, 4.8" wide, double crimp, Made for QVC Show October 1999, **$125**
Note, the Fenton mould was inspired by "Open Heart Arches" pattern created by Nicholas Kopp circa 1900-1905 while with Consolidated of Pittsburgh Lamp, Brass & Glass Co.

The only Special Order this year was from Joyce Colella. She continued with her Circle of Love collection. Her same devotion to detail created another wonderful offering. There were eight pieces in this collection, but only five were made in Burmese. A sitting bear and sitting cat were offered in both gloss and satin versions. Production problems caused not all the needed cats to be made. There were only 35 gloss and 53 satin. This very limited amount received, sold out very quickly. The perfume was only offered in satin with only 60 being made. Notice the stopper is also hand painted with petite flowers.

New Century bell #CV196HF, hand painted "Grape" decoration designed by Kim Plauche, 6.2" tall, star crimp edge with milk glass crest, Bill Fenton signature, Made for QVC Show October 1999, **$89**

Perfume, hand painted "Circle of Love Bouquet" decoration, 5.75" tall, signed by both Mary Walrath & Joyce Colella, Limited to 60, Special order made exclusively for Joyce Colella 1999, **$145**

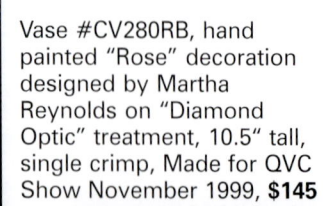

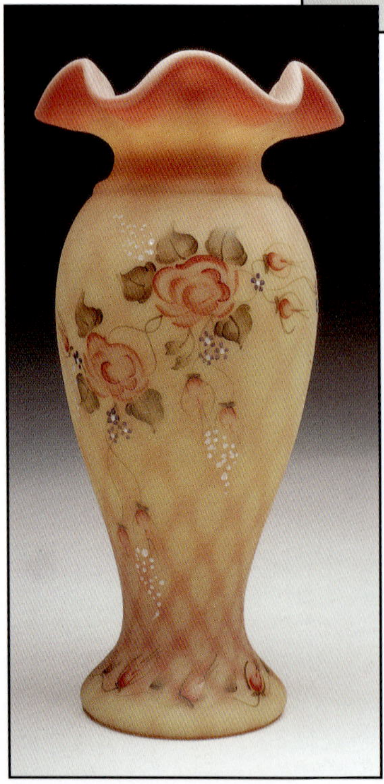

Vase #CV280RB, hand painted "Rose" decoration designed by Martha Reynolds on "Diamond Optic" treatment, 10.5" tall, single crimp, Made for QVC Show November 1999, **$145**

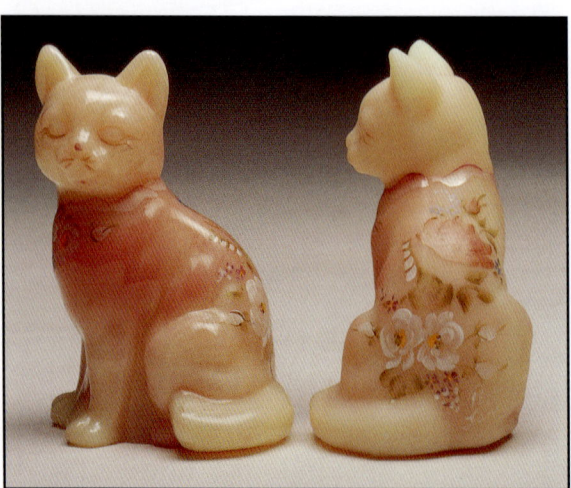

Sitting bear #5151, hand painted "Circle of Love Bouquet" decoration, 3.5" tall, 2.25" wide, signed by both Mary Walrath & Joyce Colella, Limited to 50, Special order made exclusively for Joyce Colella 1999, **$85**

Sitting cat #5165, hand painted "Circle of Love Bouquet" decoration, 3.75" tall, 2.6" wide, signed by both Mary Walrath & Joyce Colella, Special order made exclusively for Joyce Colella 1999,
Left: Gloss finish, Limited to 35, **$95**; **Right:** Satin finish, Limited to 53, **$85**

The New Century

As we reach the dawn of a new century, I am sure many additions are in store with Burmese. The Centennial Collection was started to highlight certain types of glass, as Fenton heads towards their 100th anniversary. Another event would be the first full line of Burmese back in the general catalog.

2000

A special family event was held in 2000. On December 1, Frank celebrated his 85th birthday. A surprise party was planned for him as he came into work that morning. His office was specially decorated with cards sent from collectors across the country.

An assortment of decorated eggs was in the 2000 Spring Supplement. One of these eggs was Burmese that was decorated with the Portland Head lighthouse. It was limited to 3000. Kim Plauche designed the decoration on this egg.

a Rose Poppy. Bill's signature plus the Centennial Collection logo is on the piece. The Poppy design was created by Frances Burton.

Detail of Centennial Collection 2000, Burmese offering. (Reprinted with permission from the Fenton Art Glass Company)

Egg on stand #5146Y7, hand painted "Portland Head Lighthouse" decoration designed by Kim Plauche, 3.75" tall, Mould designed by Jon Saffell, Limited to 3000 pieces, Spring Supplement 2000, **$65**

The Centennial Collection made its debut in 2000. As Fenton heads towards its 100th anniversary, it was decided to honor family members with their favorite types of glass. Each year leading up to 2005, will have two family members select a type of glass they love. The piece would be limited and have a card that tells why the piece is special to that person. Bill and Frank have pieces that will lead the series. Bill chose a Diamond Optic Burmese vase that was decorated with

Detail of hand painted "Rose Poppy" decoration.

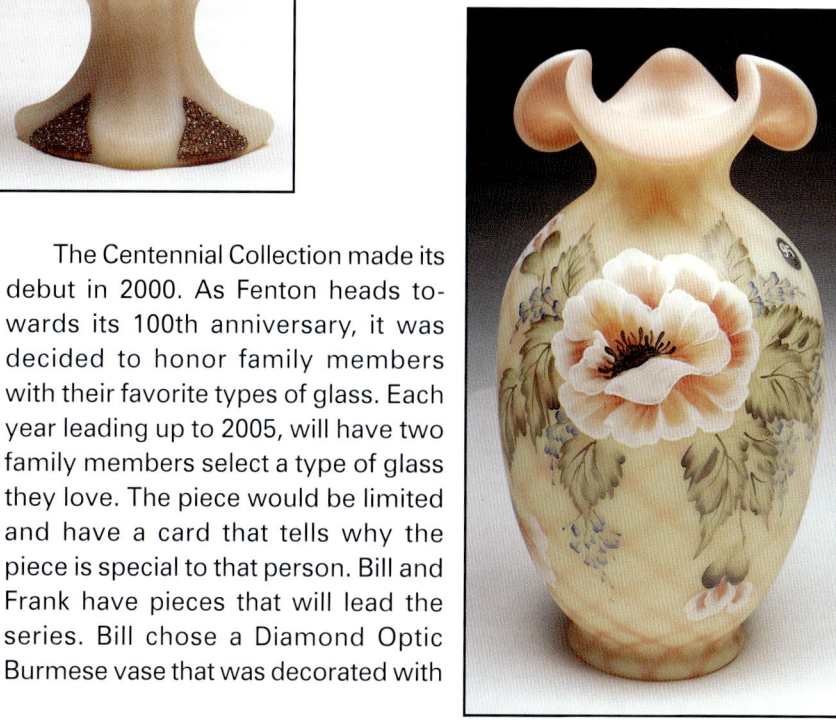

Vase #4855WL, hand painted "Rose Poppy" decoration on "Diamond Optic" treatment, designed by Frances Burton, 9" tall, single crimp, Bill Fenton signature, Centennial Collection 2000, **$170**

162 The New Century

Detail of bottom of "Rose Poppy" vase showing Bill Fenton signature.

Detail of hand painted "Rose Bed" decoration.

The Connoisseur Collection featured only two items this year. The ewer was made from an old Dugan mould. Frances Burton designed the wild roses that are mixed with lattice. Robin Spindler designed the Daisy ginger jar which features large daisy petals that encircle the top with butterflies below. The signatures of 12 family members are also on this piece.

Detail of hand painted butterflies & leaves "Daisy" decoration.

Ginger jar #5302BS, hand painted butterflies & leaves "Daisy" decoration designed by Robin Spindler, 8.5" tall, three piece set (jar, cover & base), twelve Fenton family signatures, Limited to 2750, Connoisseur Collection 2000, **$245**

Ewer #5339EB, hand painted "Rose Bed" decoration designed by Frances Burton, 8.5" tall, Limited to 2750, Connoisseur Collection 2000, **$185**
Note, the mould originally came from the Dugan Glass company.

The highlight for the annual February Gift Shop sale was a matched set of limited edition cats. The mini cat, sitting cat, and stylized cat were each hand painted with matching flowers. The set was numbered and only 350 sets were made. Jon Saffell designed both the mini and stylized cats.

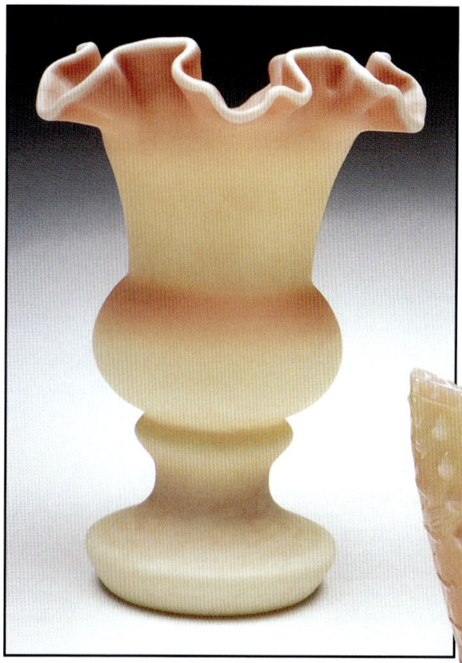

Urn vase #1553BR, plain satin finish, 6.5" tall, double crimp, From Fenton Gift Shop 2000, **$60**

Detail of annual Fenton February Gift Shop sale 2000 ad. (Reprinted with permission from the Fenton Art Glass Company)

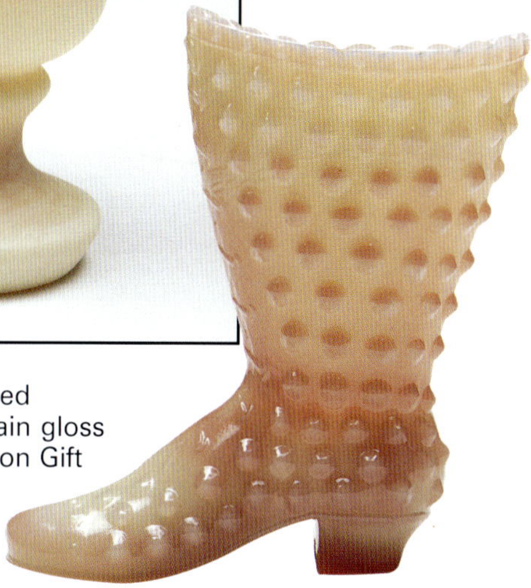

Boot #3992, embossed "Hobnail" pattern, plain gloss finish, 4.25" tall, Fenton Gift Shop 2000, **$40**

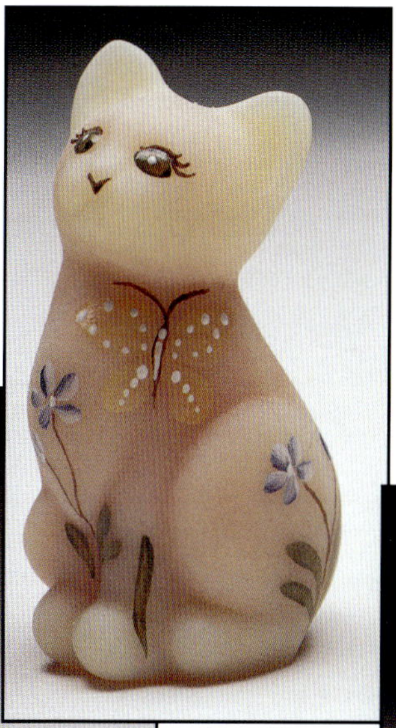

Mini kitten #5365, hand painted butterfly & flowers decoration, 2.75" tall, 1.5" wide, Mould designed by Jon Saffell, Limited to 350 matched sets (all three cats), Made for annual Fenton February Gift Shop sale 2000, **$40**

Stylized cat #5065, hand painted butterfly & flowers decoration, 5.25" tall, 2.5" wide, Mould designed by Jon Saffell, Limited to 350 matched sets (all three cats), Made for annual Fenton February Gift Shop sale 2000, **$75**

Sitting cat #5165, hand painted butterfly & flowers decoration, 3.6" tall, 2.6" wide, Limited to 350 matched sets (all three cats), Made for annual February Gift Shop sale 2000, **$65**

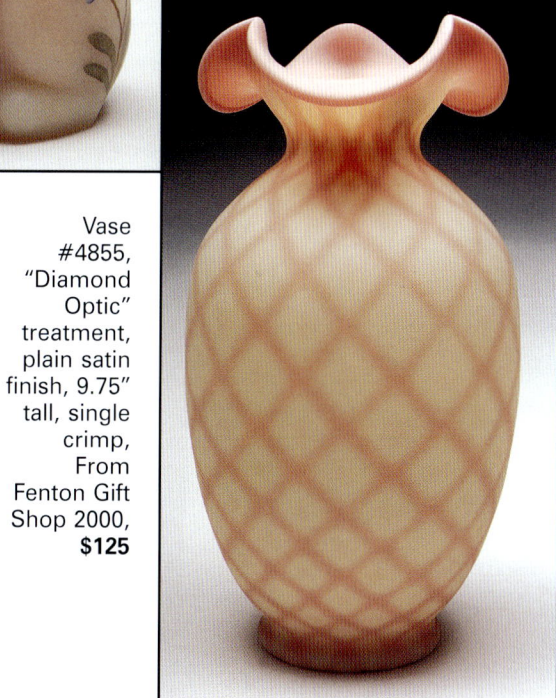

Vase #4855, "Diamond Optic" treatment, plain satin finish, 9.75" tall, single crimp, From Fenton Gift Shop 2000, **$125**

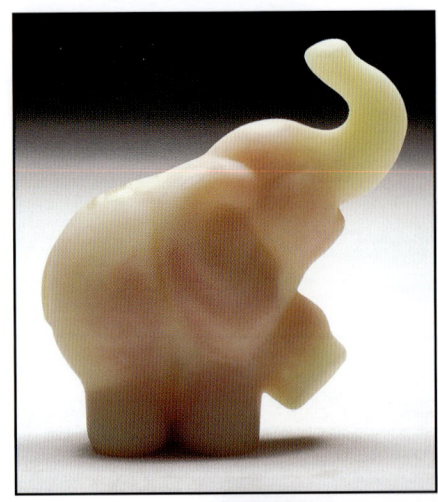

Circus elephant #5136BR, plain satin finish, 3.8" tall, From Fenton Gift Shop, 2000 **$35**

Mini bear #5251BR, plain satin finish, 2.75" tall, 1.75" wide, From Fenton Gift Shop 2000, **$35**

Duckling #5169BR, plain satin finish, 3.4" tall, 2.25" long, From Fenton Gift Shop 2000, **$45**

Of the 12 items from the QVC, four of the pieces featured the Diamond Optic pattern. There were four items to delight the animal collector.

Aurora vase #CV298RB, hand painted "Rose" decoration designed by Martha Reynolds on "Diamond Optic" treatment, 7" tall, double crimp, George Fenton signature, Made for QVC Show January 2000, **$98**

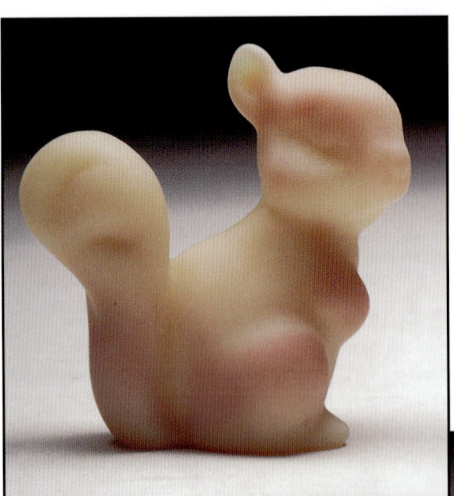

Squirrel #5215BR, plain satin finish, 2.75" tall, 2.75" long, From Fenton Gift Shop 2000, **$45**

Squirrel #5215BI, plain Iridized (Carnival) finish, 2.75" tall, 2.75" long, From Fenton Gift Shop 2000, **$39**

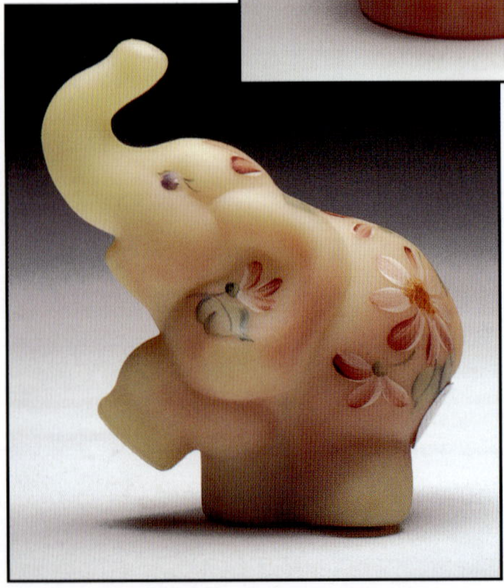

Elephant #C51364N, hand painted "Daisies" decoration designed by Frances Burton, 3.75" tall, 3.25" long, Made for QVC Show May 2000, **$65**

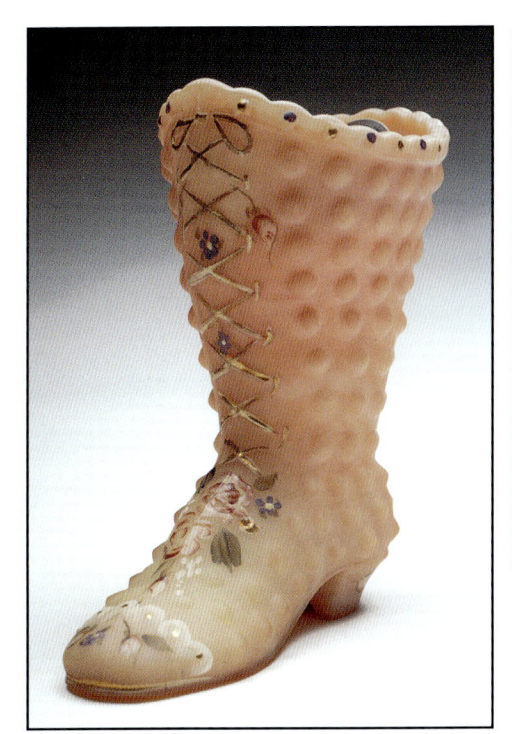

The New Century 165

Boot #E399245 (#3992), embossed "Hobnail" pattern hand painted roses decoration designed by Kim Plauche, 4.25" tall, Victorian Shoe Collection, George Fenton signature, Made for QVC Show February 2000, **$48**

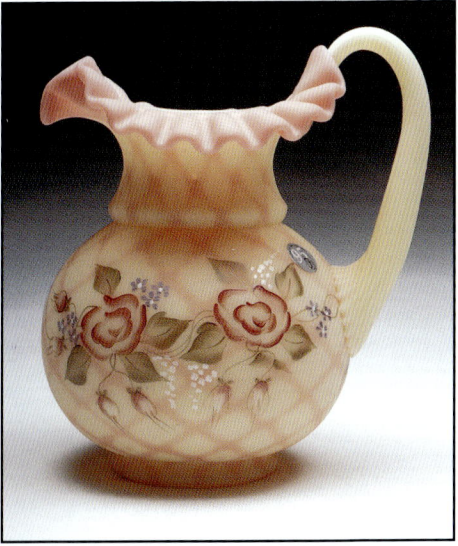

Pitcher #C4761RB, hand painted "Rose" decoration designed by Martha Reynolds on "Diamond Optic" treatment, 7.25" tall, single crimp, with Don Fenton signature, Made for QVC Show April 2000, **$125**

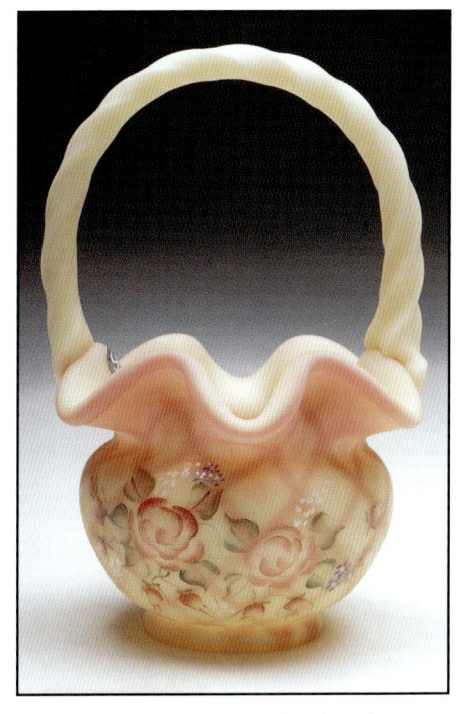

Basket #CV323RB, hand painted "Rose" decoration designed by Martha Reynolds on "Diamond Optic" treatment, 7.25" tall, 5" wide, single crimp, Don Fenton signature, Made for QVC Show August 2000, **$125**

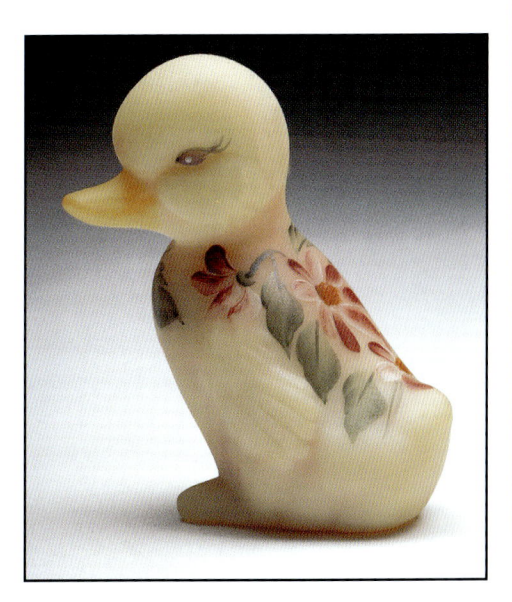

Duckling #C51694N, hand painted "Daisies" decoration designed by Frances Burton, 3.4" tall, 2.25" long, Made for QVC Show April 2000, **$60**

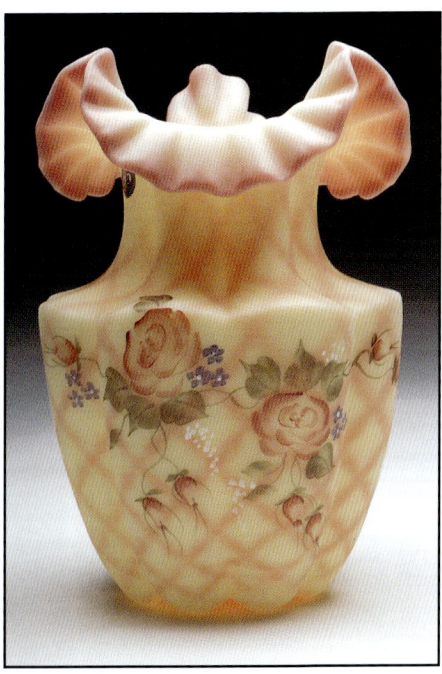

Melon vase #CV325RB, hand painted "Rose" decoration designed by Martha Reynolds on "Diamond Optic" treatment, 9.25" tall, double crimp, Made for QVC Show June 2000, **$135**

Stylized cat #C50654N, hand painted "Daisies" decoration designed by Frances Burton, 5.25" tall, 2.5" wide, Mould designed by Jon Saffell, Made for QVC Show August 2000, **$69**

166　The New Century

Squirrel #C5215P1, hand painted "Acorns & Vine" decoration designed by Robin Spindler, 2.75" tall, 2.75" long, Made for QVC Show September 2000, **$48**
Left: Detail of decoration on right side; **Right:** Detail of decoration on left side

Detail of hand painted "Hibiscus" decoration.

Three piece fairy light #CV327BR (#7501), embossed "Hobnail" pattern satin finish, 8.5" tall, single crimp (top cupped in & base rolled over), Made for QVC Show October 2000, **$125**

Kneeling Santa #C5279RB, hand painted rose buds decoration designed by Martha Reynolds, 6.3" tall, 4.75" wide, Mould designed by Jon Saffell, Made for QVC Show October 2000, **$98**

Guest set #CV314N2 (#5904), hand painted "Hibiscus" decoration designed by Robin Spindler on "Rib Optic" treatment, 6.75" tall, Made for QVC Show October 2000, **$160 set**
Also called a night set or tumble up set

The New Century 167

Joyce continued with her Circle of Love Collection. For this year, the stylized cat was made in both a gloss and satin version. The gloss was limited to 69 and the satin to 145. Each piece is personally signed by Joyce and her mother, Mary. It also bears the edition number of XVIII for gloss and XIX for satin plus the sequential number above the precise production number. There were also production problems in 1999 and not all of the sitting cats were produced. The remainder were made in 2000 and marked to set them apart from the 1999 ones. The edition number I-A is on the gloss (limited to 68) and I-B for the satin (limited to 132). This set was called Circle of Love Bouquet.

Sitting cat #5165, hand painted "Circle of Love Bouquet" decoration, 3.75" tall, 2.6" wide, signed by both Mary Walrath & Joyce Colella, Special order made exclusively for Joyce Colella 2000, **Left:** Gloss finish, Limited to 68, (marked 1-A #40/68), **$85**; **Right:** Satin finish, Limited to 132, (marked 1-B #40/132), **$70**

Stylized cat #5065, hand painted "Circle of Love Bouquet" decoration, 5" tall, 2.5" wide, Mould designed by Jon Saffell, signed by both Mary Walrath & Joyce Colella, Special order made exclusively for Joyce Colella 2000, **Left:** Gloss finish, Limited to 64, XVIII 40/69, **$125**; **Right:** Satin finish, Limited to 145, XIX 40/145, **$95**

Detail of markings on bottom of Circle of Love Bouquet #5165 cat, **Left:** Gloss finish; **Right:** Satin finish

For the Fenton Art Glass Collectors of America (FAGCA) convention a plain Burmese vase was specially painted with a lighthouse for their auction. The National Fenton Glass Society (NFGS) had a blown free hand cane made for their auction.

Detail of markings on bottom of Circle of Love Bouquet #5065 cats, **Left:** Gloss finish; **Right:** Satin finish

Vase #2955, hand painted with lighthouse scene decoration designed by Kim Plauche, 9.5" tall, FAGCA (Fenton Art Glass Collectors of America) special order for their convention auction in 2000, **$295**

168   The New Century

Free Hand cane, twisted "Rib Optic" pattern gloss finish, 7.25" long, NFGS (National Fenton Glass Society) special order for their convention auction in 2000, **$75**

2001

The Veil Tail Habitat vase was the only Burmese item in the 2001 Connoisseur Collection. On one side was swimming gold fish and on the other was a frog. This unique scene from nature was created by Stacy Williams. The vase was inscribed with 12 family member signatures. Jon Saffell was the creator of this vase.

Detail of hand painted frog "Veil Tail Habitat" decoration.

Vase #6151BN, hand painted under water scene "Veil Tail Habitat" decoration designed by Stacy Williams, 9" tall, single crimp, Inscribed with twelve Fenton family members, Limited to 2500, Connoisseur Collection 2001, **$175**
Note, back of "Veil Tail Habitat" vase showing a frog.

Detail of hand painted goldfish "Veil Tail Habitat" decoration.

Vase #6151BN, hand painted under water scene "Veil Tail Habitat" decoration designed by Stacy Williams, 9" tall, single crimp, Mould designed by Jon Saffell, Inscribed with twelve Fenton family members, Limited to 2500, Connoisseur Collection 2001, **$175**
Note, front of "Veil Tail Habitat" vase showing a goldfish.

The New Century 169

The dolphin redesigned by Jon Saffell appeared in the Gift Shop. After many years absence, the work elephant finally made a reappearance. The mould had been reworked so the trunk wouldn't break during production. While the elephant appeared in Topaz Iridized in the line, the elephant was only offered in Burmese through the gift shop.

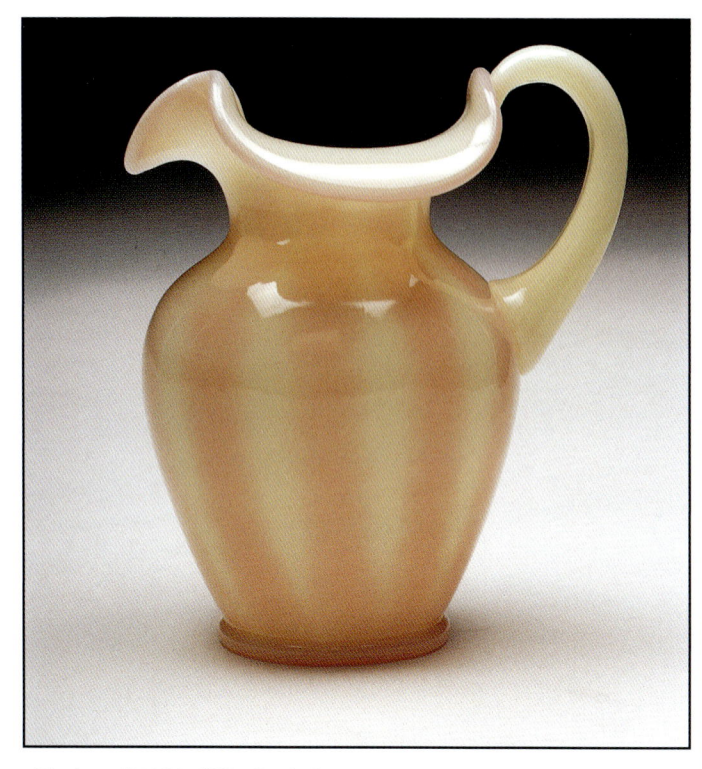

Pitcher #1132, "Rib Optic" treatment, plain gloss finish, 6.75" tall, From Fenton Gift Shop 2001, **$75**

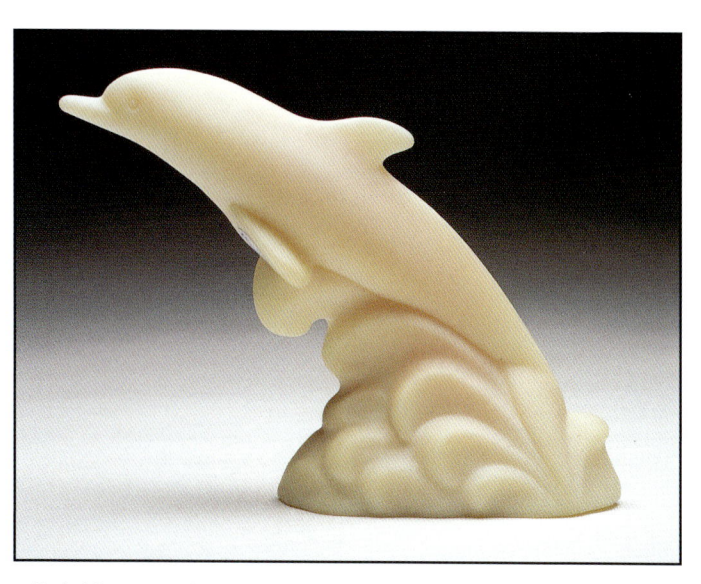

Dolphin #5137BR, plain satin finish, 5.75" tall, 9" long, Mould redesigned by Jon Saffell, From Fenton Gift Shop Annual February Sale 2001, **$60**

Mallard #5147BR, plain satin finish, 2.25" tall, 5" long, From Fenton Gift Shop 2001, **$35**

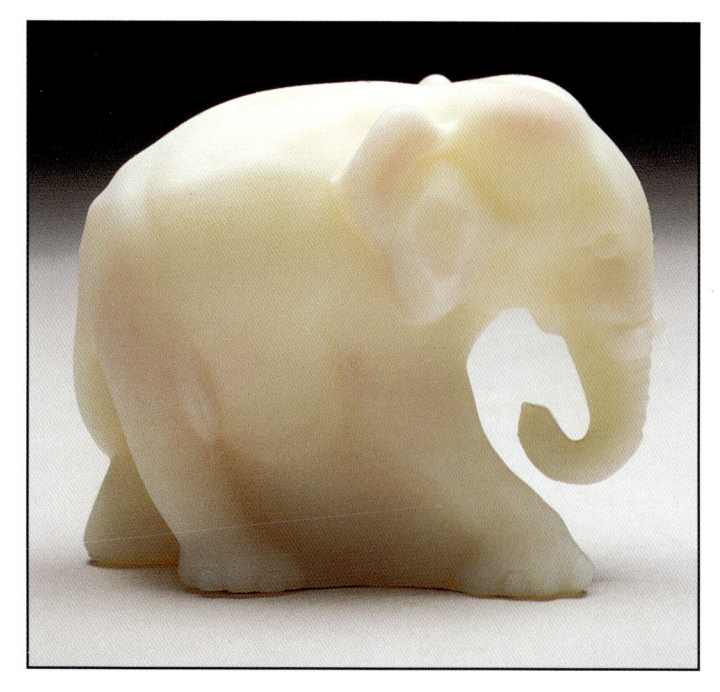

Work elephant #5123BR, plain satin finish, 3" tall, 3.75" long, From Fenton Gift Shop 2001, **$45**

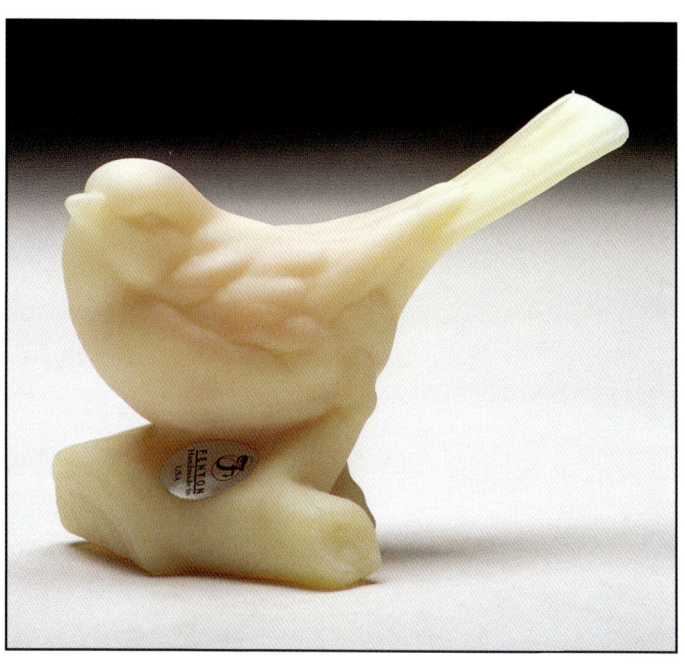

Bird on log #5238BR, plain satin finish, 3" tall, 4.5" long, From Fenton Gift Shop 2001, **$50**

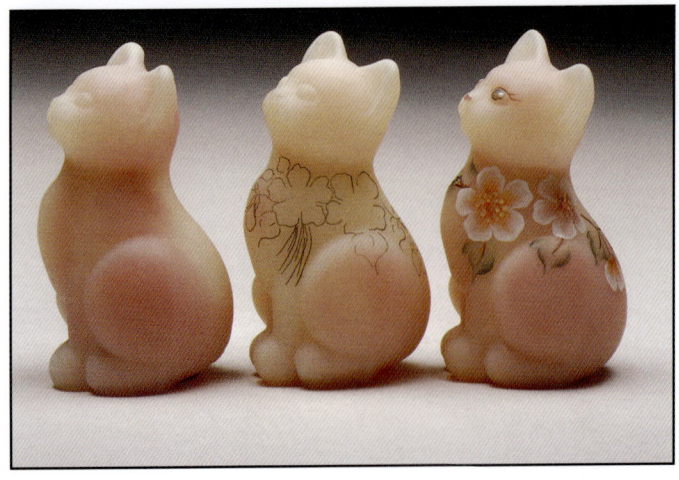

The New Century

Mini Kitten #5365, 2.75" tall, 1.5" wide, Mould designed by Jon Saffell, From Fenton Gift Shop 2001, **Left:** Undecorated, **$30**; **Center:** Sketched out for decoration placement, **$45**; **Right:** Hand Painted, **$40**
Note, detail of steps in decorating, shown for comparison.

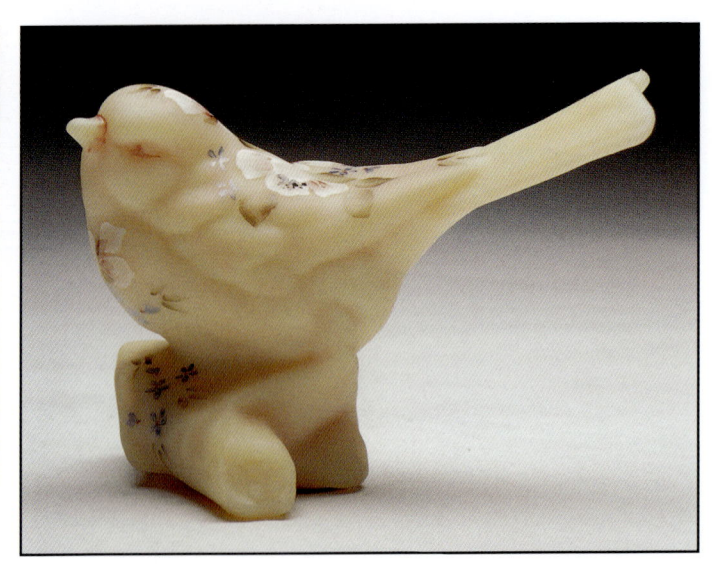

Bird on log #C52383C (#5238), hand painted white "Hibiscus" decoration designed by Stacy Williams, 3" tall, 4.25" long, Scott Fenton signature, Made for QVC Show April 2001, **$69**

Mirrored Rose bell #5762, plain, 5.5" tall, From Fenton Gift Shop 2001, **Left:** Gloss finish #5762BE, **$38**; **Right:** Satin finish #5762BR, **$40**

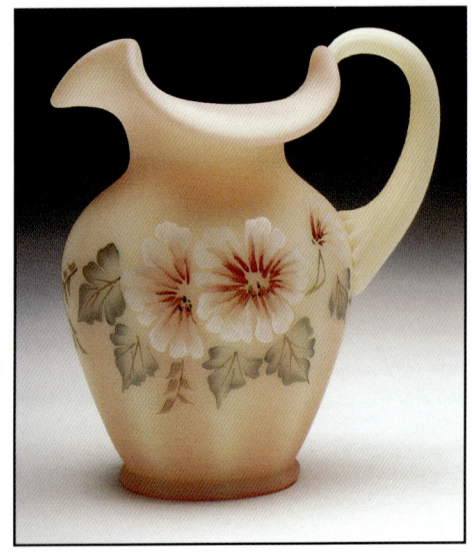

The QVC programs continued to offer many choices for Burmese collectors. The new Atlantis fairy light by Jon Saffell was hand painted. Three family members also put their signatures on pieces. Scott signed the bird on the log. Shelley signed the pitcher. Don put his signature on the melon vase.

Fairy light #C5204BW, embossed "Atlantis" pattern, hand painted fish decoration designed by Robin Spindler, 4.6" tall, Mould designed by Jon Saffell, Made for QVC Show January 2001, **$98**

Pitcher #CV367N2, hand painted "Hibiscus" decoration designed by Robin Spindler on "Rib Optic" treatment, 5.5" tall, Shelley Fenton-Ash signature, Made for QVC Show June 2001, **$98**

The New Century 171

Mirrored Rose bell **#CV368RB**, hand painted "Rose" decoration designed by Kim Plauche, 5.4" tall, Made for QVC Show June 2001, **$69**

Mallard **#C5147HD**, hand painted features decoration designed by Robin Spindler, 2.25" tall, 5" long, Made for QVC Show October 2001, **$65**

Mini kitten **#C5365S3**, hand painted flowers decoration designed by Kim Plauche, 2.75" tall, 1.5" wide, Mould designed by Jon Saffell, Made for QVC Show October 2001, **$48**

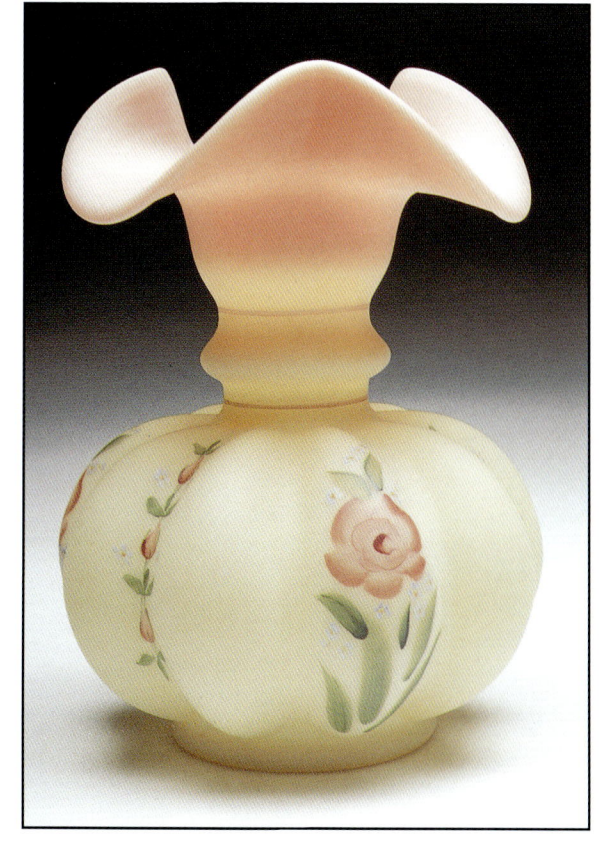

Melon vase **#CV371BC**, hand painted flowers decoration designed by Stacy Williams, 7.75" tall, single crimp, Don Fenton signature, Made for QVC Show August 2001, **$125**

Hand vase **#CV1784A**, hand painted roses decoration designed by Stacy Williams, 10.25" tall, slight single crimp & flared out, Made for QVC Show December 2001, **$125**

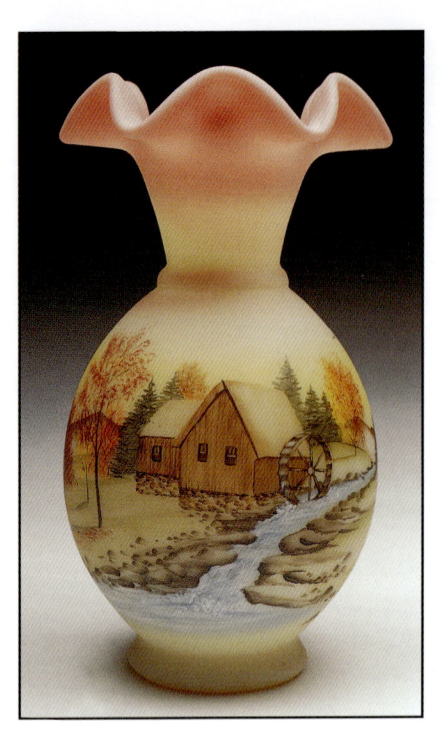

172   The New Century

Vase #6151, hand painted old mill by stream scene decoration, 9" tall, Mould designed by Jon Saffell, Special order made for John Gager 2001, **$325**

The Connoisseur Collection featured two Burmese items in new moulds. The flip style of vase was decorated with Hummingbirds. This vase was designed by Jon Saffell. The new style of lamp featured a melon shape that was hand painted with sparrows. This painting was created by Stacy Williams. The lamp is quite huge and is the largest lamp Fenton has ever hand painted.

Detail of hand painted hummingbird by fuchsia trellis "Hummingbird" decoration.

2002

For 2002, there was another egg collection offered in the Spring Supplement. All four of the eggs in the collection had designs from Stacy Williams and were limited to 3000. The Burmese egg is decorated with Mauve Floral.

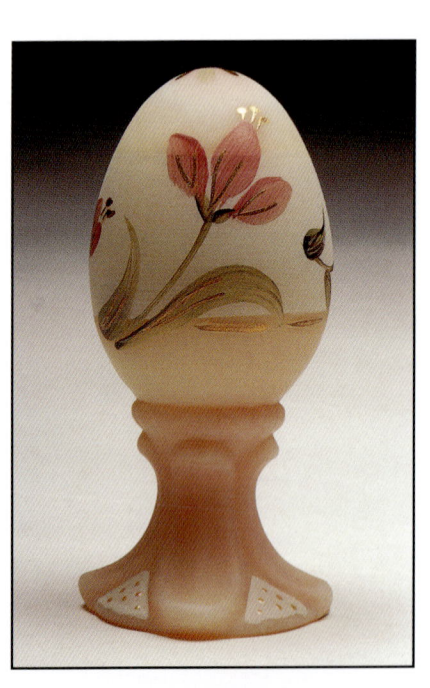

Egg on stand #5146KB, hand painted band of stylized "Mauve Floral & English Tulip Garden" decoration designed by Stacy Williams, 3.75" tall, Mould designed by Jon Saffell, Limited to 3000, from Limited Edition Collectible Eggs collection, General Catalog spring 2002, **$65**

Vase #2994QH, hand painted hummingbird by fuchsia trellis "Hummingbird" decoration designed by Kim Plauche, 8" tall, New mould designed by Jon Saffell, Limited to 2500, Connoisseur Collection 2002, **$160**

Melon Gone with the Wind lamp #5505ZP, hand painted birds & blackberries orchard scene "Song Sparrow" decoration designed by Stacy Williams, 27.5" tall, single crimp melon shade, oversized lamp, Limited to 950, Connoisseur Collection 2002, **$595**

The New Century 173

The mini-catalog featured three exclusive items. The matching sitting cat and vase were available to any customer. The cat was signed by Shelley Fenton and the vase was signed by Don Fenton. Each person who purchased the vase or cat was entered in a drawing to win the lamp. The Arabella design was from Kim Plauche.

Lamp #4209F5, hand painted white & purple flowers "Arabella" decoration designed by Kim Plauche, 23" tall, 10" single crimp shade, Limited to 250, Bill & Frank Fenton signatures, Catalog Exclusive 2002, **$450**

Vase #9867F5, hand painted white & purple flowers "Arabella" decoration designed by Kim Plauche, 6.75" tall, single crimp, Mould designed by Jon Saffell, Don Fenton signature, Catalog Exclusive 2002, **$65**

Sitting cat #5165F5, hand painted white & purple flowers "Arabella" decoration designed by Kim Plauche, 3.75" tall, 2.75" wide, Shelley Fenton-Ash signature, Catalog Exclusive 2002, **$45**

Some more differently painted items showed up in the Fenton gift shop. The clowns hadn't been made for several years and yet they showed up made in Burmese and decorated for a special treat for visitors.

Vase (flip vase style) #2994, hand painted red & blue pansies decoration, 8" tall, Mould designed by Jon Saffell, From Fenton Gift Shop 2002, **$95**

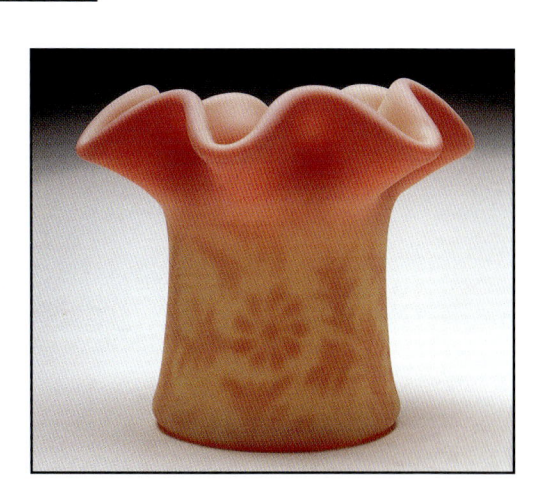

Hat vase #3191, 4.6" tall, 5.75" wide, "Daisy & Fern Optic" treatment satin finish, single crimp, From Fenton Gift Shop 2002, **$115**

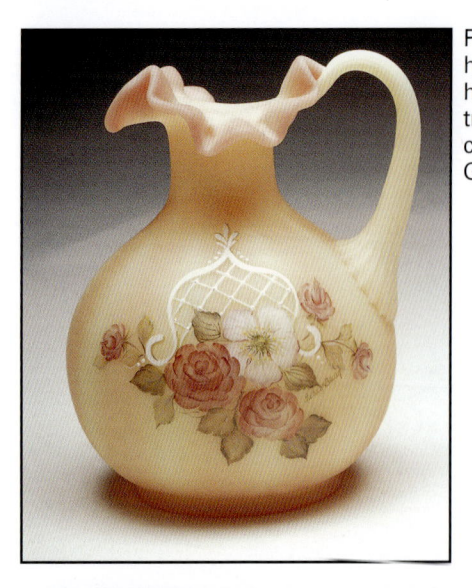

174 The New Century

Pitcher #3275BR, hand painted roses & hibiscus on white trellis, 6.5" tall, single crimp, From Fenton Gift Shop 2002, **$85**

Clown #5217, hand painted accents decoration on satin finish, decoration designed by Diane Gessel, 4" tall, Bill Fenton signature, From Fenton Gift Shop 2002, **Left:** Yellow flower & accents, **$85**; **Right:** Pink flower & accents, **$85**

Snail #5134BR, plain satin finish, 2.75" tall, 4.25" long, From Fenton Gift Shop 2002, **$35**

Turtle #5266BR, plain satin finish, 1.75" tall, 4" long, Mould designed by Jon Saffell, From Fenton Gift Shop 2002, **$40**

Egg on stand #5146, hand painted floral & butterfly decoration, 3.75" tall, Mould designed by Jon Saffell, From Fenton Gift Shop 2002, **$48** Shown front side showing Fenton label.

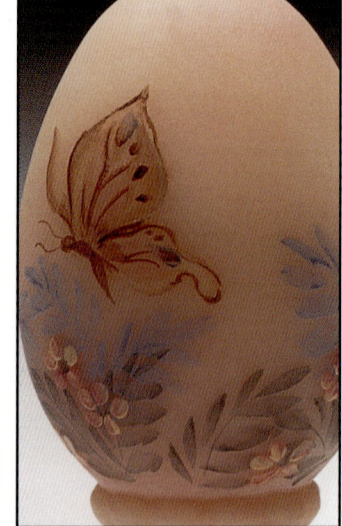

Detail of Egg back side showing butterfly.

The New Century 175

Frog #5274BR, plain satin finish, 2.4" tall, 3.25" long, From Fenton Gift Shop 2002, **$38**

Goldfish #5276, hand painted fish & seahorse, 3.75" tall, 5" long, Mould designed by Jon Saffell, From Fenton Gift Shop 2002, **$60**

Goldfish #5276, plain, 3.75" tall, 5" long, Mould designed by Jon Saffell, From Fenton Gift Shop 2002,
Top: Iridized (Carnival) finish #5276Bl, **$38**; **Bottom left:** Satin finish #5276BR, **$45**; **Bottom right:** Gloss finish #5276BE, **$40**

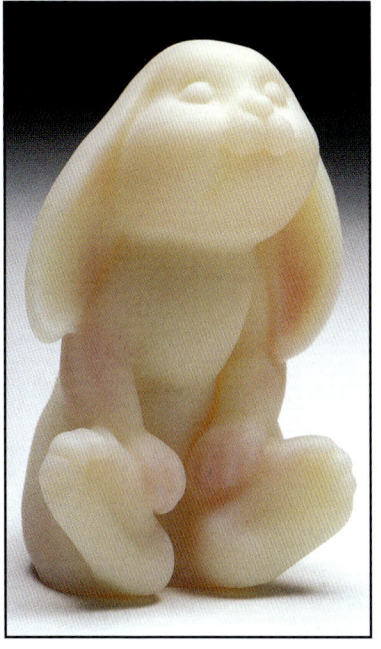

Flop ear bunny #5293BR, plain satin finish, 3.75" tall, 2.25" wide, Mould designed by Jon Saffell, From Fenton Gift Shop 2002, **$48**

Goldfish #5276, hand painted aquatic scene, 3.75" tall, 5" long, Mould designed by Jon Saffell, From Fenton Gift Shop 2002, **$60**

Ginger jar vase #5302, hand painted heart shaped floral wreath with bird's nest, decoration designed by Frances Burton, 7.25" tall, special decoration for Fenton Gift Shop 2002, **$145** Note, this vase has the ginger jar stand with it.

176 The New Century

Ginger jar vase #5302, hand painted butterfly & pink dogwood, decoration designed by Frances Burton, 6" tall, special decoration for Fenton Gift Shop 2002, **$98**

Melon Gone with the Wind lamp #5505, plain satin finish, 27.5" tall, single crimp melon shade, oversized lamp, From Fenton Gift Shop 2002, **$450**

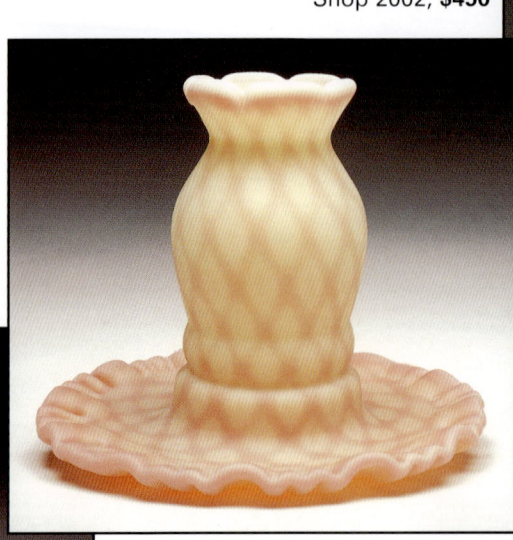

One piece fairy light #7392, "Diamond Optic" treatment satin finish, 6" tall, 6.25" wide, tight single crimp (at base), From Fenton Gift Shop 2002, **$150**

Atlantis bell #5364BR, plain satin finish, 6.5" tall, 5" wide, Mould designed by Jon Saffell, From Fenton Gift Shop 2002, **Left:** Single crimp, **$75**; **Right:** Smooth edge, **$65**

Atlantis bell #5364BE, plain gloss finish, 6.5" tall, 5" wide, Mould designed by Jon Saffell, From Fenton gift shop 2002, **$65**

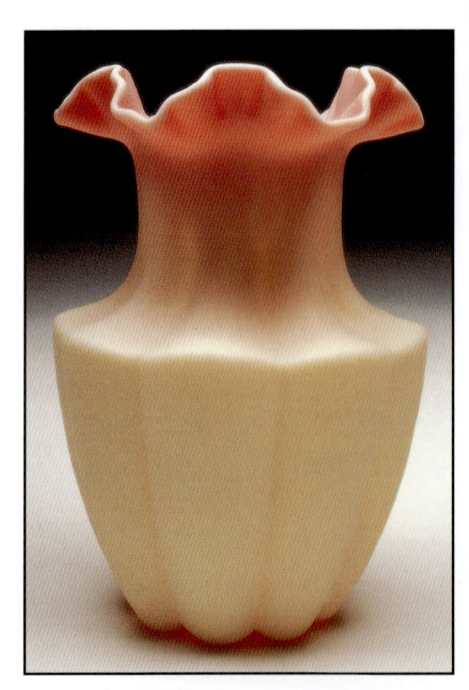

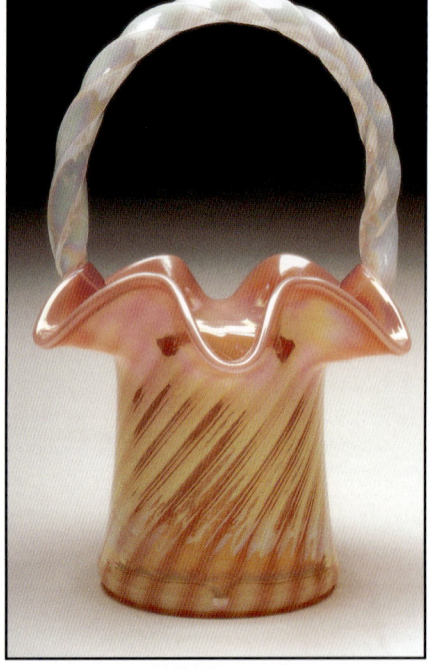

Basket #7733, iridized (Carnival) finish on "Spiral Optic" treatment, 8.5" tall, 5.75" wide, single crimp, From Fenton Gift Shop 2002, **$150 Note**, it looks more like Burmese in real life, than this photo shows.

Melon shoulder vase #7450BR, plain satin finish, 9.25" tall, double crimp, From Fenton Gift Shop 2002, **$125**

The New Century 177

Diamond Optic pieces made a reappearance in the QVC programs. A new Snowman fairy light by Jon Saffell was issued hand painted in Burmese. A one piece fairy light that hadn't made for several years was also offered as part of the Museum Collection.

Two piece fairy light #C1700WL, hand painted floral decoration on "Diamond Optic" treatment, 4.5" tall, 3.15" wide, Bill Fenton signature, Made for QVC Show January 2002, **$85**

Pitcher, progressive pieces showing development steps in making the pitcher, shown for comparison only, **Left:** piece after the first air is blown in; **Center:** piece after the rib optic is struck; **Right:** piece after blown into the mould
Note, when Burmese is photographed on black background it appears to be more yellow than it really is.

Pitcher, progressive pieces showing development steps in making the pitcher, shown for comparison only, **Left:** piece after the crimped edge treatment; **Center:** piece after the rib optic handle is added and the top is hand formed; **Right:** what the gather of glass that is used to form the handle looks like with the rib optic pattern
Note, when Burmese is photographed on black background it appears to be more yellow than it really is.

Pitcher #C3275VR, hand painted "Hibiscus" decoration designed by Kim Plauche on "Rib Optic" treatment, 6.5" tall, single crimp, Bill Fenton retirement piece, Made for QVC Show January 2002, **$110**

Bird #C5163VR, hand painted "Hibiscus" decoration designed by Kim Plauche, 2.75" tall, 4" long, Made for QVC Show May 2002, **$60**

Frog #C5274N2, hand painted "Hibiscus" decoration designed by Robin Spindler, 2.4" tall, 3.25" long, Made for QVC Show April 2002, **$60**

Melon shoulder vase #C7450VR, hand painted "Hibiscus" decoration designed by Kim Plauche, 9.25" tall, Shelley Fenton-Ash signature, double crimp, Made for QVC Show June 2002, **$135**

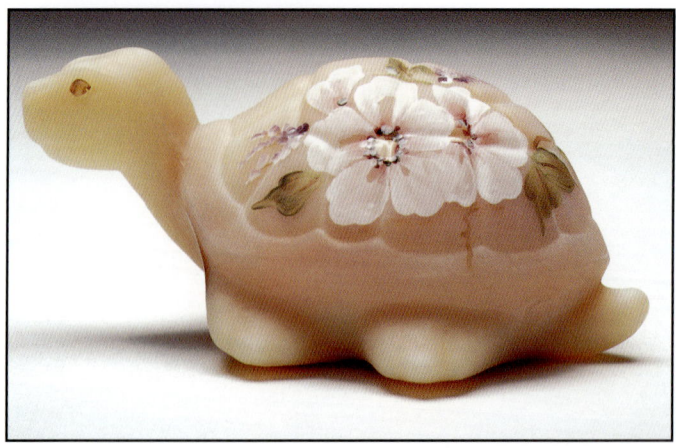

Turtle #C5266VR, hand painted "Hibiscus" decoration designed by Kim Barley, 1.75" tall, 4" long, Mould designed by Jon Saffell, Bill Fenton signature, Made for QVC Show December 2002, **$65**

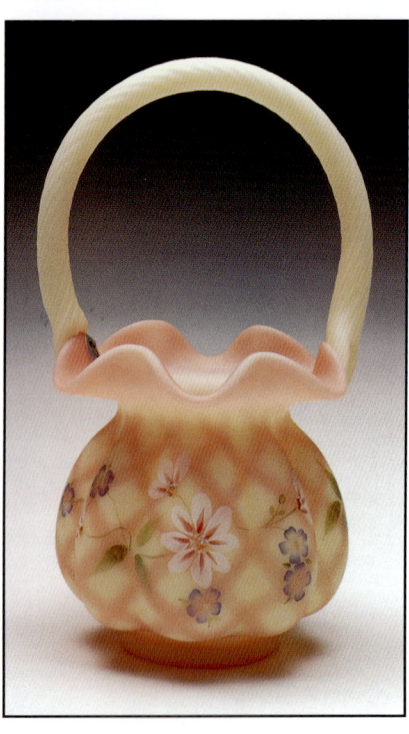

Melon Basket #CV433T7, hand painted white daisies & blue pansies decoration Designed by Kim Plauche on "Diamond Optic" treatment, 7.5" tall, 4.25" wide, single crimp, Made for QVC Show August 2002, **$98**

Snowman fairy light #C5940, hand painted rose buds decoration designed by Kim Barley, 7" tall, 4" wide, Mould designed by Jon Saffell, Made for QVC Show November 2002, **$98**

Fawn #C51602M, hand painted "Grapes" decoration designed by Stacy Williams, 3.75" tall, 3.75" long, Made for QVC Show October 2002, **$60**

One piece fairy Light #CV476N2, hand painted "Hibiscus" decoration designed by Robin Spindler on "Diamond Optic" treatment, 5.75" tall, 6.5" wide (at base), QVC Museum Collection, Made for QVC Show December 2002, **$135**

The New Century 179

Detail of one piece fairy light progressive pieces showing development steps in the making. Shown for comparison only.
Note, when Burmese is photographed on black background it appears to be more yellow than it really is.

Several special orders were made for 2002. The Fenton Art Glass Collectors of America (FAGCA) issued a hurricane lamp for their convention souvenir piece. It was hand painted with butterflies and flowers. The Basket Candle Lamp was made for the Kansas City Gala. There were two different versions: one painted with Violets and the other with Dogwoods.

Hurricane lamp #9252, hand painted with butterflies & flowers decoration, 10" tall, two piece lamp, double crimp shade, decorated by M. Young, Special order made exclusively for FAGCA (Fenton Art Glass Collectors of America) 2002, **$150**

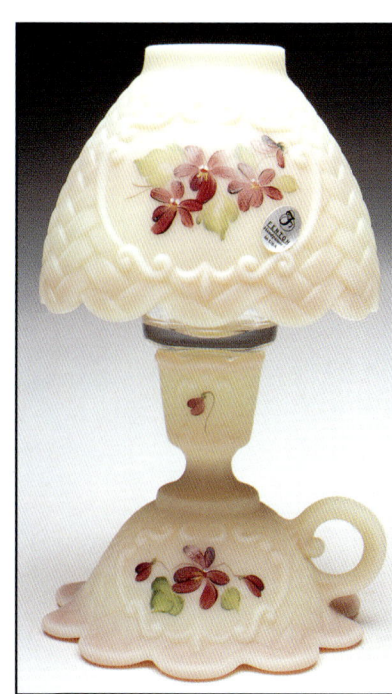

Basket weave candle lamp #9234, hand painted Violets decoration, 8.5" tall, three piece (finger candle holder, candle cup insert & shade), Decorated by Diane Gessel, Special order made exclusively for Kansas City Gala September 2002, **$145**
Note, the candle cup insert is clear glass.

Basket weave candle lamp #9234, hand painted Dogwood decoration, 8.5" tall, three piece (finger candle holder, candle cup insert & shade), Special order made exclusively for Kansas City Gala September 2002, **$145**
Note, the candle cup insert is clear glass.

Joyce Colella issued one item in Burmese as part of her continuing Circle of Love collection. This item was a Diamond Optic tumble up set made in both gloss and satin. In gloss there were only 51 made, while in satin were 116. Two different pictures were taken to show the painting on the front and back sides. The same tumble up was also made in green Burmese.

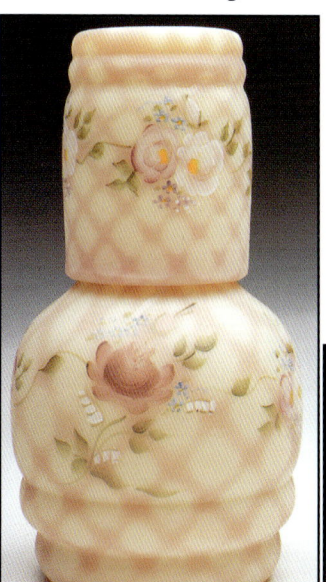

Guest set #5904, hand painted "Circle of Love Bouquet" decoration on "Diamond Optic" treatment, 6.8" tall, Limited to 116, Special order made exclusively for Joyce Colella 2002, **$225**
Note, front side show with pink rose. Also called a night set or tumble up set.

Detail of decoration back side on Guest set
Note, back side show with white flowers.

180   The New Century

Marian Thornton, owner of Collectors Showcase in Snohomish and Centralia, Washington had a mallard duck decorated to look like a natural drake.

Mallard #5147, hand painted accents like a Mallard drake, 2.25" tall, 5" long, Special order made for Collectors Showcase 2002, **$45**

John Gager had a ginger jar decorated for himself with a country house scene.

Ginger jar #5302, hand painted country house scene, 9.25" tall, three piece set (jar, cover & base), decorated by Bev Cumberledge, Special order made exclusively for John Gager 2002, **$375**

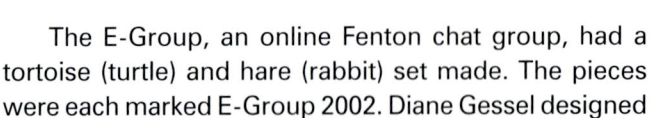

The E-Group, an online Fenton chat group, had a tortoise (turtle) and hare (rabbit) set made. The pieces were each marked E-Group 2002. Diane Gessel designed this decoration. For Christmas time, they issued a Mr. and Mrs. Santa decoration that were on the #5262 rabbit. Both the rabbit and turtle had been designed by Jon Saffell.

Special order exclusively made for E-Group, hand painted purple roses decoration, both of these moulds were designed by Jon Saffell, 2002, **Left:** Hare (Rabbit) #5262, 2.75" tall, 2.25" wide, **$45**; **Right:** Tortoise (Turtle) #5266, 1.75" tall, 4" long, **$45**

Special order exclusively made for E-Group #5262, hand painted Santa suits & accents, 2.75" tall, 2.25" wide, Mould designed by Jon Saffell, 2002, **Left:** Rabbit, Mrs. Santa, **$60**; **Right:** Rabbit, Santa, **$60**

2003

Nancy Fenton decided the time had come to have a line of Burmese back in their general catalog. The new line called Let's Bee Burmese was based on a design by Frances Burton. Bright orange poppies featured a yellow and black bee buzzing by them. The four items in this line were: basket, butterfly, rabbit, and vase. The rabbit and butterfly were both new moulds by Jon Saffell. These animals were both limited to 3500 pieces, while the vase and basket limited to 2500.

Detail of hand painted red poppies with a bee "Let's Bee Burmese" decoration.

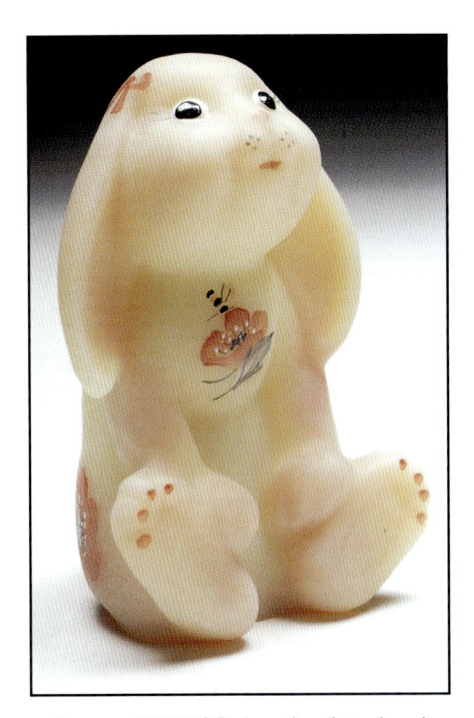

Bunny #5293QR, hand painted red poppies with a bee "Let's Bee Burmese" decoration designed by Frances Burton, 3.75" tall, 2.25" wide, Mould designed by Jon Saffell, Decorated by A. Deem, Limited to 3500, Spring Supplement 2003, **$39**

Vase #6853QR, hand painted red poppies with a bee "Let's Bee Burmese" decoration designed by Frances Burton, 8.75" tall, single crimp, Mould designed by Jon Saffell, decorated by S. Hart, Limited to 2500, Spring Supplement 2003, **$99**

Detail of basket bottom showing signature & number.

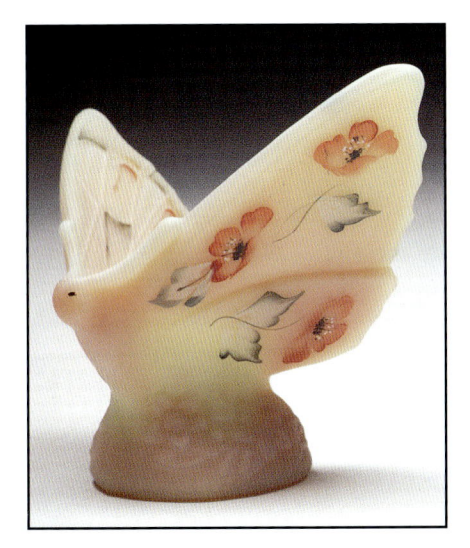

Butterfly #5296QR, hand painted red poppies with a bee "Let's Bee Burmese" decoration designed by Frances Burton, 3" tall, 2.75" long, Mould designed by Jon Saffell, Decorated by B. Razzon, Limited to 3500, Spring Supplement 2003, **$39**

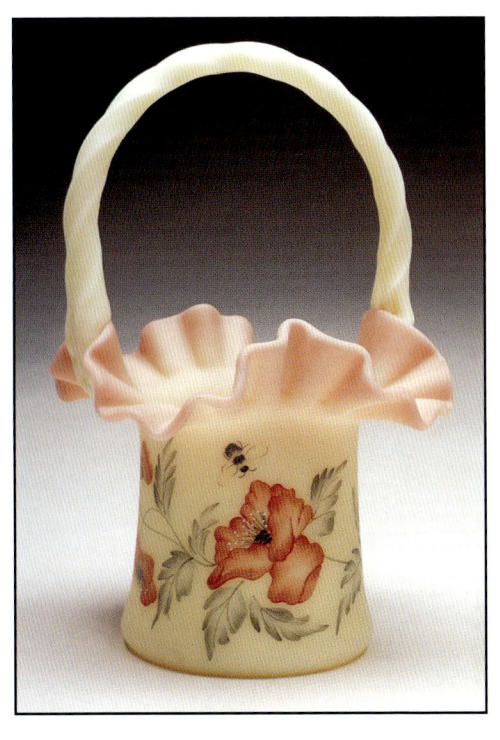

Basket #7733QR, hand painted red poppies with a bee "Let's Bee Burmese" decoration designed by Frances Burton, 8.25" tall, 5.75" wide, double crimp, decorated by CC Hardman. Limited to 2500, Spring Supplement 2003, **$110**

Detail of June Supplement 2003 (Reprinted with permission from the Fenton Art Glass Company); **Bottom right:** Basket #2735ZP, hand painted birds & blackberries orchard scene "Song Sparrow" decoration designed by Stacy Williams, 8" tall, Limited to 2450, Connoisseur Collection 2003, **$150** Note, this is a companion piece to the 2002 Connoisseur Melon GWTW lamp; **Center:** Vase #5957BD, hand painted "Adoration Rose" decoration designed by Stacy Williams, 9" tall, Limited to 2950, ten Fenton family member signatures, Bill Fenton memorial piece, Connoisseur Collection 2003, **$130**; **Lower left:** Vase #4254B2, hand painted grape motif "Neo-Classic" decoration designed by Robin Spindler, 8.5" tall, George Fenton signature, Limited to 1950, Showcase dealer exclusive 2003, **$120**

182   The New Century

So far the gift shop has only offered undecorated versions of the items from the catalog or QVC. A decorated ginger jar was also found there.

Ginger Jar #5302, hand painted with red roses & butterfly decoration, 8.5" tall, three piece set (jar, cover & base), From Fenton Gift Shop 2003, **$195**

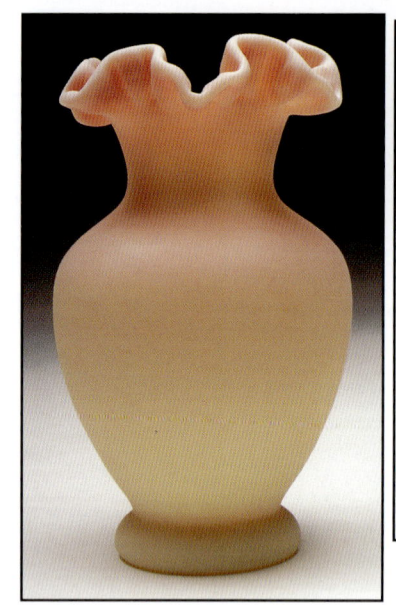

Vase #1573BR, plain satin finish, 6.5" tall, double crimp, From Fenton Gift Shop 2003, **$45**

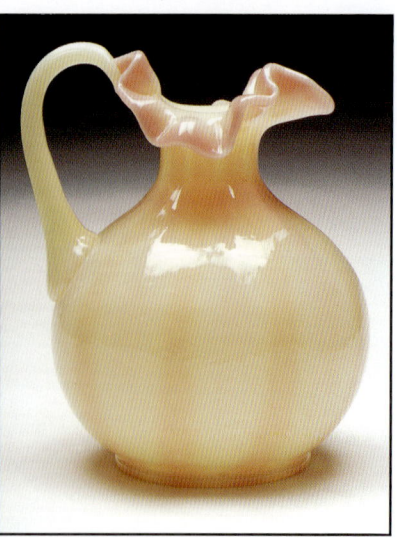

Pitcher #3275BE, plain gloss finish on "Rib Optic" treatment, 5.75" tall, From Fenton Gift Shop, 2003, **$110**

Turkey covered dish #6410BE, plain gloss finish, 4.25" tall, 5.25" long, From Fenton Gift Shop 2003, **$65**

Pitcher, "Diamond Optic" treatment satin finish, 8.25" tall, single crimp, From Fenton Gift Shop 2003, **Left:** Plain edge & plain handle, **$85**; **Right:** Crimped edge & ribbed handle, **$95**

Ballerina #5270BE, plain gloss finish, 6.25" tall, Mould designed by Jon Saffell, From Fenton Gift Shop 2003, **$60**

Butterfly #5296BE, plain gloss finish, 3.25" tall, 3.75" wide, Mould designed by Jon Saffell, From Fenton Gift Shop 2003, **$29**

Vase, "Diamond Optic" treatment plain, 8.5" tall, single crimp, From Fenton Gift Shop 2003, **Left:** Gloss finish, **$75**; **Right:** Satin finish, **$85**

The New Century 183

The Burmese offerings on QVC so far have proved to be hits among collectors. The new Atlantis bell created by Jon Saffell was an absolute hit with its hand painted decorations. A Diamond optic basket was part of the Heirloom Optics Collection. The basket had both Frank and George's signatures. The Rib Optic pitcher was featured as a part of the Victorian Collection.

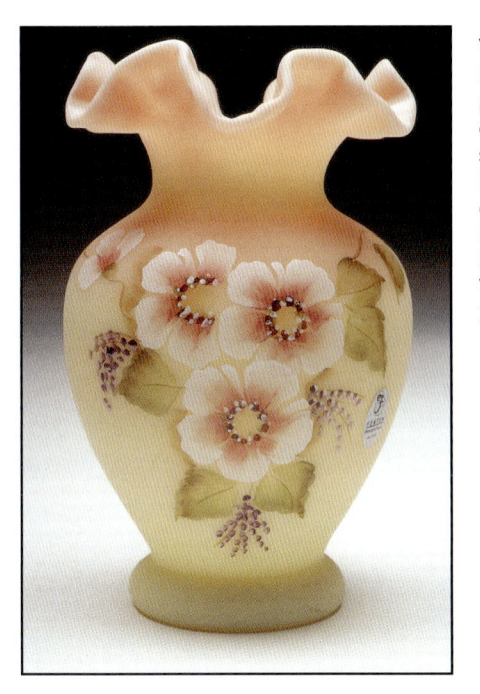

Vase #1573VR (C128609), hand painted "Hibiscus" decoration designed by Kim Barley, 6.5" tall, double crimp, Bill Fenton signature, Special for IQVC Web Site January 2003, **$82**

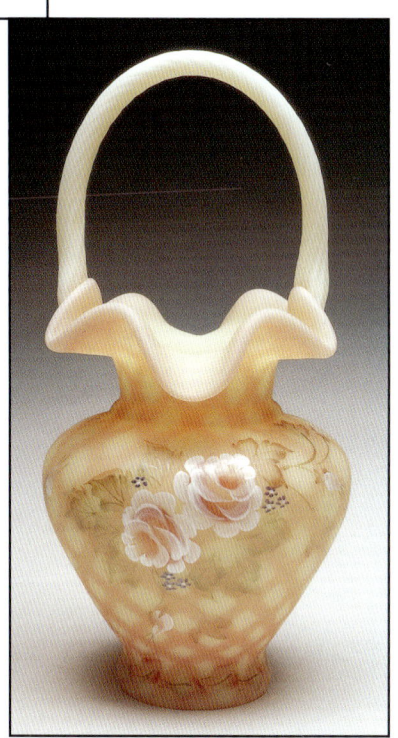

Melon bell, hand painted "Hibiscus" decoration designed by Kim Barley, 6" tall, George Fenton signature, Made for QVC Show February 2003, **$59**

Basket #V51468, hand painted floral decoration on "Diamond Optic" treatment, 10" tall, 5" wide, Heirloom Optics Collection, Designed by Francis Burton, Frank & George signatures, Made for QVC Show April 2003, **$89**

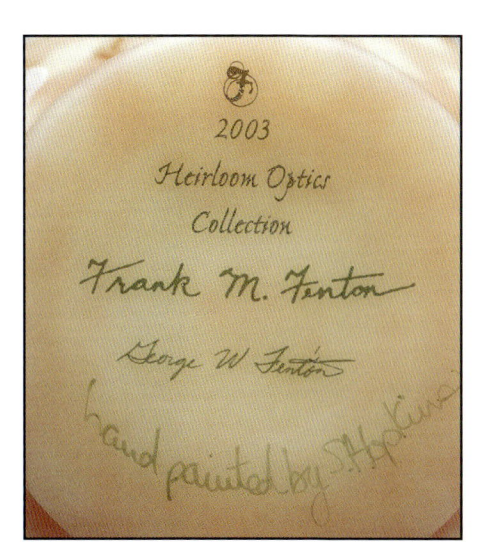

Detail of basket bottom showing signatures & number.

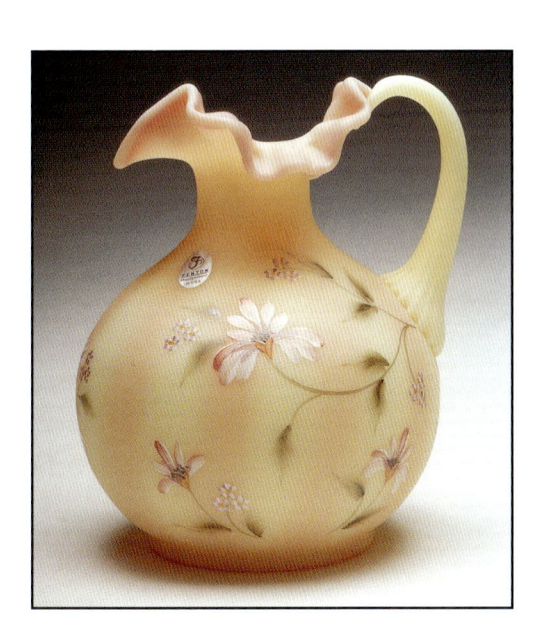

Pitcher #C327541 (#3275), hand painted wildflowers decoration designed by Stacy Williams on "Rib Optic" treatment, 6.25" tall, single crimp, Victorian Collection, Made for QVC Show January 2003, **$110**

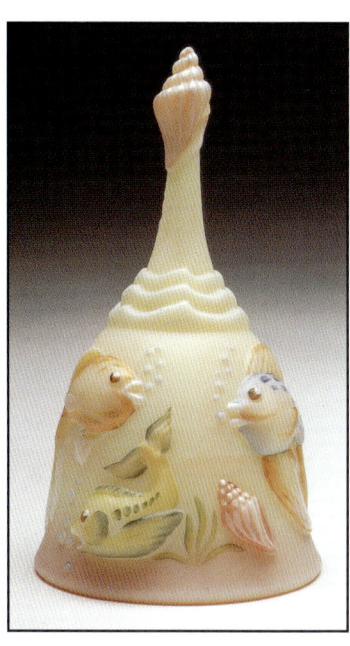

Atlantis bell #C536476, hand painted accents decoration designed by Francis Burton, 6.5" tall, 5" wide, Mould designed by Jon Saffell, decorated by D. Breesen, Made for QVC Show April 2003, **$65**

The New Century

Sitting cat #C516568, hand painted with roses, 3.6" tall, Designed by Francis Burton & decorated by D. Cline, Made for QVC Show April 2003, **$38**

Detail of hand painted "Faith Bouquet" decoration.

Frog #5274, hand painted "Faith Bouquet" decoration designed By Diane Gessel, 2.4" tall, 3" long, Limited to 222, Special order made exclusively for Mary Jachim 2003, **$75**

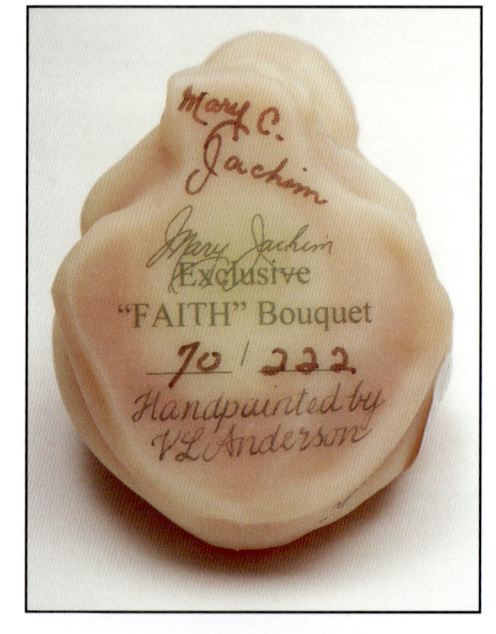

Detail of Frog bottom showing signature & number.

One of the special orders so far this year comes from Mary Jachim. Many changes had taken place for Mary Walrath in the last year. At age 86, the unexpected happened when she felt totally blessed to marry Stanley Jachim, by faith. The marriage meant many changes for her including a move from Michigan to New York and consolidating two households. So happily married, Mary once again felt the need to express her faith and joyously make known her new name. Diane Gessel worked very closely with Mary to come up with a new design, titled, My Faith Bouquet. Coming up with this artwork was a trying experience for several months until the Love Bouquet flashed into view. The centered white Rose proclaims Jesus is the Prince of Peace and the two white Rose buds signify two lives joined in holy matrimony. The pink Lilies of the Valley are a hymnal description of Jesus. The Forget-me-nots testify that without faith it is impossible to please Jesus. Yes, these are pink Lilies of the Valley. A huge circle of them accented the Walrath gardens. A special inscription will be put on all items, along with a decal saying Faith Bouquet Exclusive Mary C. Jachim. Mary also will personally sign each one. A Willow Green cat was the first Faith piece, limited to 222. As their first anniversary approached, a Rosalene feather vase was made and limited to 55. The third piece is a Burmese frog that is inscribed with "Leap with Faith" and limited to 222. This limited number of 222 has a special meaning to Mary. She was married on February 2, 2002. Each was decorated by Diane Gessel. Mary has said this will be the last of her exclusives. She is now devoting all her time to spiritual writings. With the encouragement she has received while attending the Christian Writers Conference in North Carolina and with Stan's total support, Mary is presently developing a line of stationary and bookmarks with all the profits going to the Salvation Army and Rescue Mission. God bless her in all future endeavors.

Other special orders are from Mary's daughters, Joyce and Carol. Joyce is continuing with her Circle of Love Bouquet. This new edition is a frog limited to 75 pieces. Carol has developed a new collection titled Spring Bouquet. These pieces will consist of a yellow Daffodil, a white Narcissus, a pink tulip and a bed of Violets. A Burmese frog will be the first item and limited to 70.

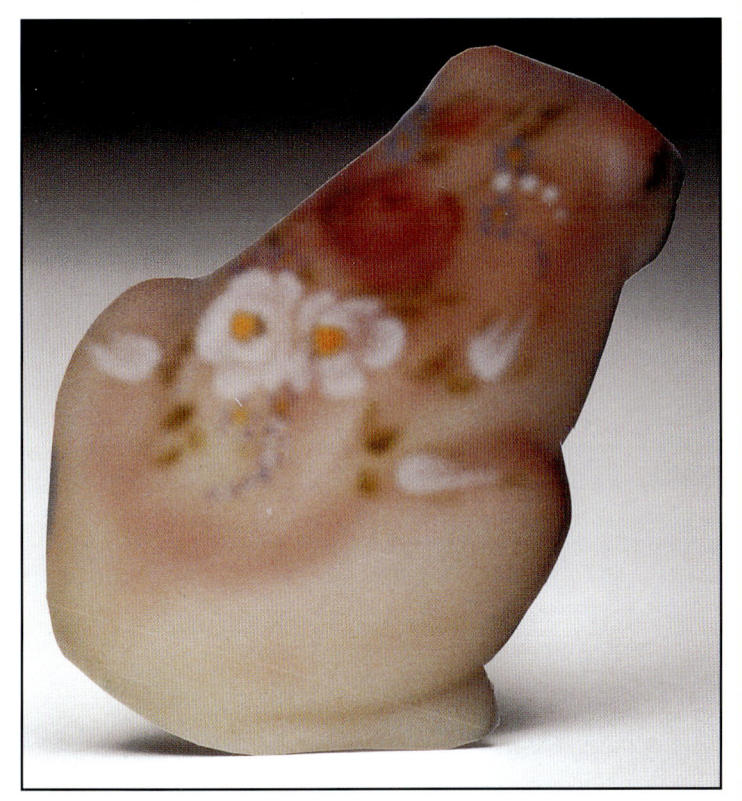

Frog #5274, hand painted "Circle of Love Bouquet" decoration, 2.4" tall, 3" long, Limited to 75, Special order made exclusively for Joyce Colella 2003, **$65**

The other special order is from Singleton Bailey. As part of his Poppy Show series for 2003, he is having a tulip vase made. This one has an iridized finish. For 2004 he plans to have some made with a satin finish.

Vase, embossed "Poppy Show" pattern with iridized (Carnival) finish, 14" tall, Limited to 170 first quality & 13 second quality, Special order made exclusively for Singleton Bailey 2003, **$120**
Note, this mould was an old Imperial Glass Company mould and these made by Fenton have the Fenton logo on the bottom of them.

The Future

Burmese glass will remain part of Fenton's future offerings in the Connoisseur and QVC collections. In 2005, for Fenton's 100th anniversary, plans are being made for an Old and New Century Collection with each of the special colors included and Burmese will be part of this collection

Blue Burmese

When Charlie Goe was experimenting to develop the Burmese color, one of the first variations was a bluish gray color. In order to perfect the Blue Burmese color, Wayne King decided against using notes from Charlie Goe and went back to the original Burmese formula to make his adjustments. Wayne removed the uranium oxide and added what he calls powder blue, also known as cobalt oxide. With the addition of this, the Burmese lost its yellow appearance and took on a beautiful bluish purple hue. Wayne King continued to work on the formula between 1983 and 1985, before finally perfecting the color. The gloss version of this color resembles the Peach Blow from Mt. Washington.

A sampling of the pieces that have been made are presented here.

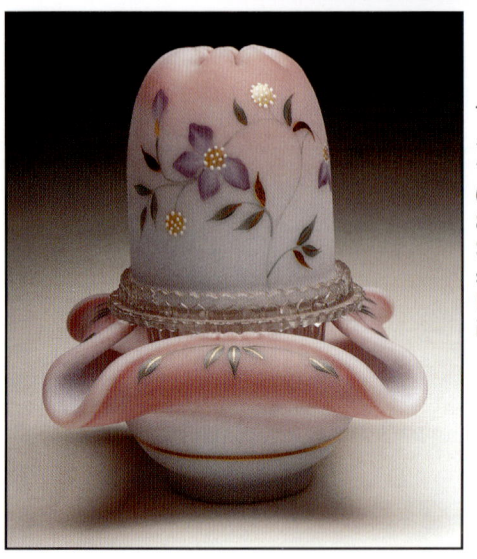

Hat vase #S3191, hand painted lavender pansies decoration, 4.5" tall, 5.75" wide, single crimp & two sides turned up, Special order made exclusively for FAGCA (Fenton Art Glass Collectors of America) 1996, **$95**

Three piece fairy light #7501TA, hand painted "Periwinkle" decoration, 6.75" tall, 5.5" wide, Frank & Bill Fenton signatures, Showcase dealer exclusive 1999, **$175** Note, the insert was done in clear.

Ribbed vase #9055, plain gloss finish, 4.75" tall, tight ribbon single crimp, General Catalog 1984, **$150**

Perfume Bottle #2906QZ, hand painted purple "Hibiscus" decoration designed by Kim Plauche, 5.75" tall, Limited to 2750, Spring Supplement 2000, **$95**

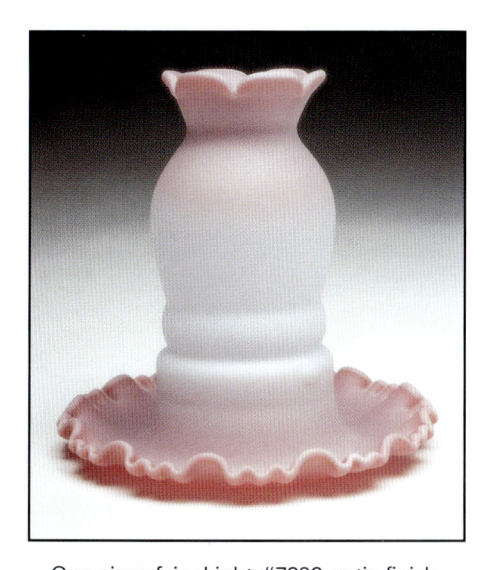

The Future & Blue Burmese   187

One piece fairy Light #7392, satin finish, 6" tall, 6.25" wide, tight single crimp (at base), Special order exclusively made for FAGCA (Fenton Art Glass Collectors of America) 1995, **$250**

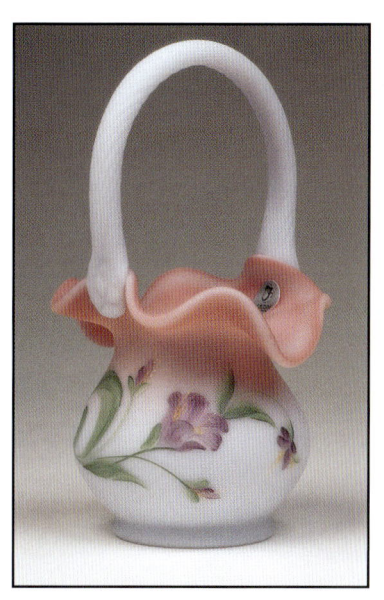

Basket #5934VG, hand painted lavender "Lily" decoration designed by Frances Burton, 7.5" tall, Limited to 2750, Spring Supplement 2002, **$99**

Vase #5975VG, hand painted lavender "Lily" decoration designed by Frances Burton, 10" tall, single crimp, Limited to 2750, Spring Supplement 2002, **$115**

Left: Flop ear bunny #F5293G5, hand painted "Jacobean Floral" decoration designed by Frances Burton, 3.5" tall, 2.5" wide, Mould designed by Jon Saffell, Glass Messenger Subscriber Exclusive 2003, **$39**

Right: Tumble up set #F5904G5 (#5904), hand painted "Jacobean Floral" decoration designed by Frances Burton, 6.8" tall, 3.5" wide, Glass Messenger Subscriber Exclusive 2003, **$99**
Also called a night set or guest set

Lotus Mist

George Fenton asked Wayne King if the Burmese formula could be adjusted to take on a green color. Once again Wayne went back to work on the original Burmese formula. A chromium compound was added to the formula to produce a green hue instead of the lemon yellow. The same salmon blush appears on these pieces. Since this new color imitated the Asian Lotus flower, it was named Lotus Mist. Once again Wayne has created a brand new color at Fenton. Lotus Mist Burmese made its debut in 2000.

A small variety of the pieces that have been made are presented here.

Right: Cruet #2985VF, hand painted "Berry & Butterfly" decoration designed by Martha Reynolds, 6.75" tall, rib stopper, Showcase dealer exclusive 2000, **$120**

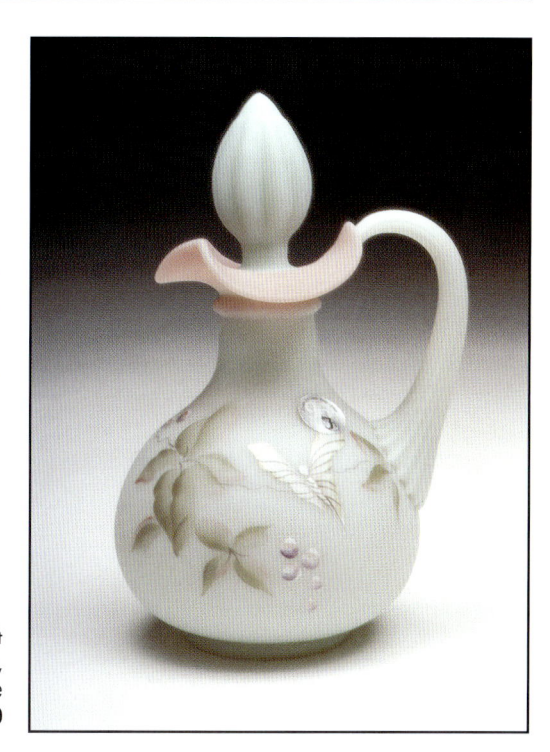

Left: Basket #2735VF, hand painted "Berry & Butterfly" decoration designed by Martha Reynolds, 8" tall, 5.1" wide, single crimp, Limited to 2950, General Catalog 2000, **$95**

One horn epergne #6509VF, hand painted "Berry & Butterfly" decoration designed by Martha Reynolds, 9.25" tall, single crimp, Limited to 2950, General Catalog 2000, **$150**

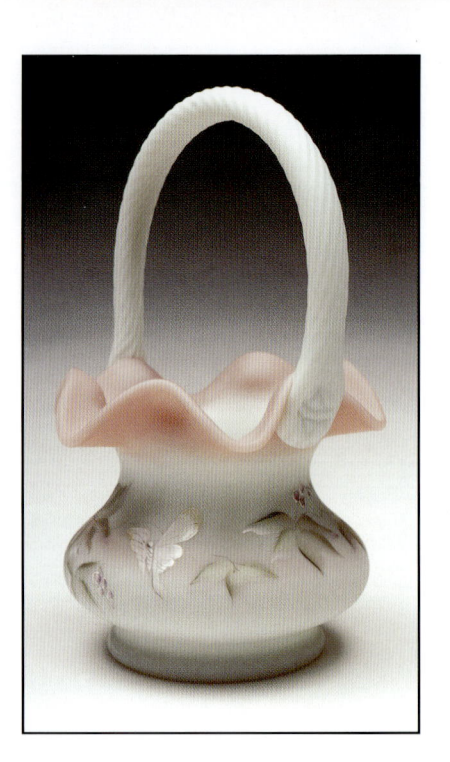

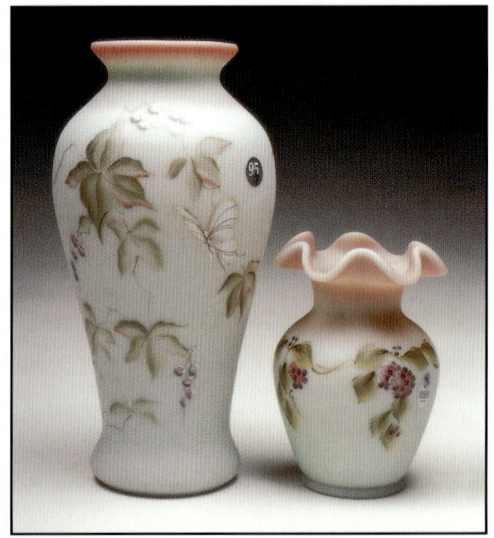

Lotus Mist group,
Left: Vase #2955VF, hand painted "Berry & Butterfly" decoration designed by Martha Reynolds, 9.5" tall, Limited to 2950, General Catalog 2000, **$95**; **Right:** Vase #9869V2, hand painted "Berry" decoration designed by Stacy Williams, 5.5" tall, Frank Fenton signature, Catalog Exclusive 2001, **$75**

Lotus Mist group, hand painted "Daisy & Butterfly" decoration designed by Kim Plauche, Spring Supplement 2001,
Left: Basket #6531ES, 10" tall, single crimp, Limited to 2750, **$115**; **Center:** Stylized cat #5065ES, 5.25" tall, 2.5" wide, Limited to 4750, **$48**; **Right:** Vase #6548ES, 10" tall, single crimp, Limited to 2750, **$105**

Lotus Mist special order exclusively made for E-Group, hand painted rose decoration, 2001,
Left: Mini bear #5051, 2.75" tall, 1.75" wide, depicted as asleep, **$35**; **Center:** Sitting bear #5151, 3.5" tall, 2.25" wide, **$48**; **Right:** Mini bear #5051, 2.75" tall, 1.75" wide, depicted as awake, **$35**

Other Companies

Gibson Glass Company

Gibson Glass Company is located in Milton, West Virginia. They are a smaller glass company that specializes in small novelty type items. Most of their items are mould blown. Frequently during the 1970s and 1980s, Gibson workers would go over to Fenton and buy the Burmese shards (broken pieces of glass that are discarded during production). By doing this, they didn't have to worry about mixing chemicals or the EPA regulations to make Burmese. The shards were taken back to Gibson, melted and poured into their moulds. The Burmese takes on an unique appearance when it is reheated this way. All of the Gibson glass is marked and dated which makes it easy to identify.

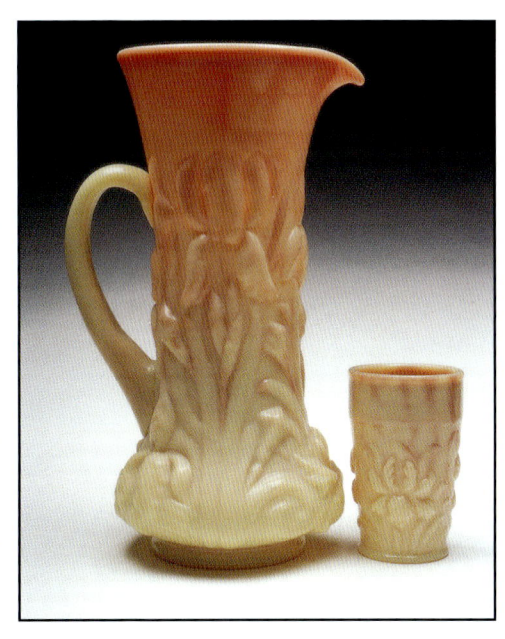

Pitcher set, embossed "Heavy Iris" pattern plain gloss finish, pitcher 12.5" tall, tumbler 4.5" tall, Made by Gibson from Fenton's shards 1990, **$350** seven piece set

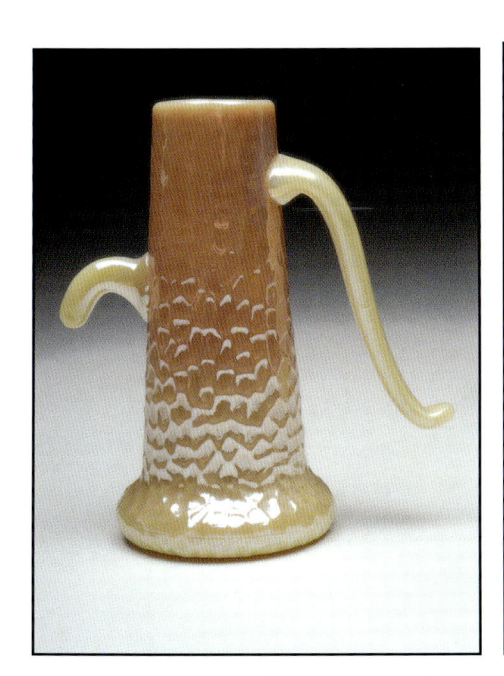

Town pump, 5.8" tall, plain Iridized (Carnival) gloss finish, Made by Gibson from Fenton's shards 1986, **$45**

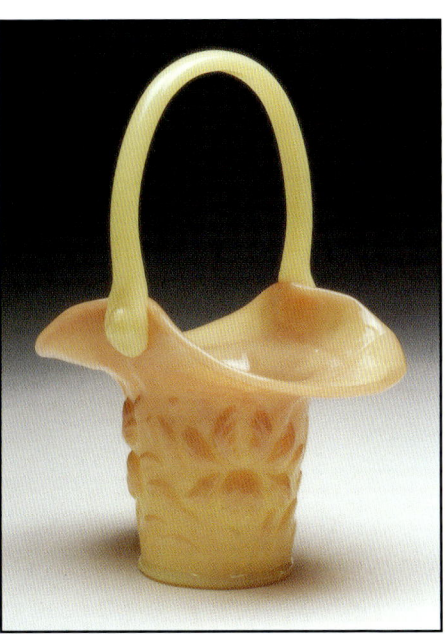

Basket, embossed "Heavy Iris" pattern plain gloss finish, 7.75 " tall, 5.75" wide, Made by Gibson from Fenton's shards 1987, **$48**

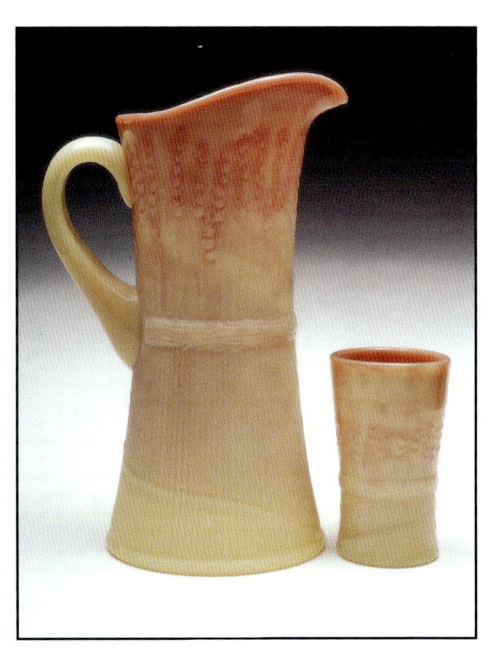

Pitcher set, embossed "Wheat" pattern plain gloss finish, pitcher 11.25" tall, tumbler 4.75" tall, Made by Gibson from Fenton's shards 1990, **$350** seven piece set

Other Companies

Free hand apple paperweight, 4.25" tall, 3" wide, Made by Gibson from Fenton's shards 1990, **Left:** Satin finish, **$40**; **Right:** Gloss finish, **$45**

Free hand pear paperweight, 5" tall, 3" wide, Made by Gibson from Fenton's shards 1990, **Left:** Satin finish, **$40**; **Right:** Gloss finish, **$45**

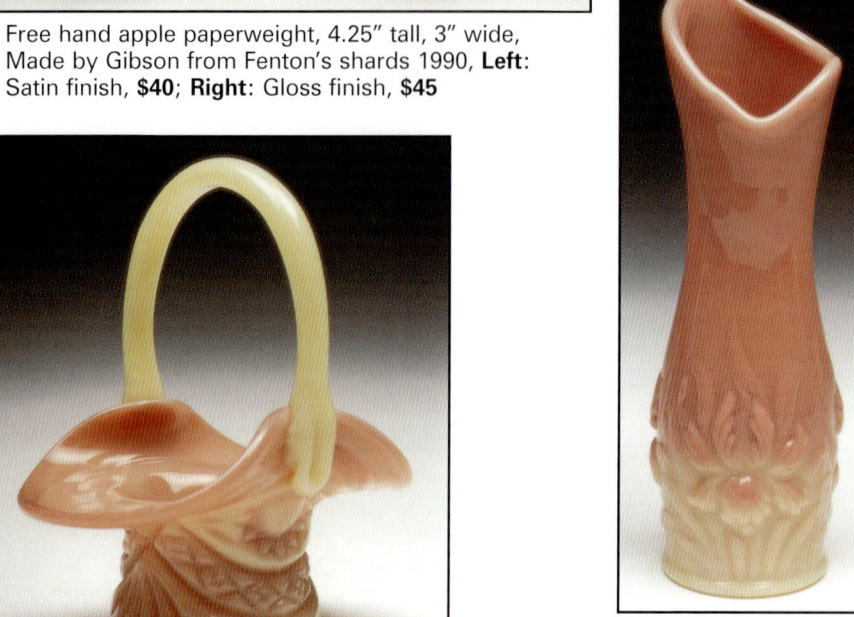

Swung vase, embossed "Heavy Iris" pattern plain gloss finish, 8.75" tall, Made by Gibson from Fenton's shards 1992, **$40**

Basket, embossed quilted pattern plain gloss finish, 4" tall, 3.75" wide, Made by Gibson from Fenton's shards 1992, **$38**

Toothpick, embossed pattern plain gloss finish, 2.5" tall, Made by Gibson from Fenton's shards 1993, **$24**

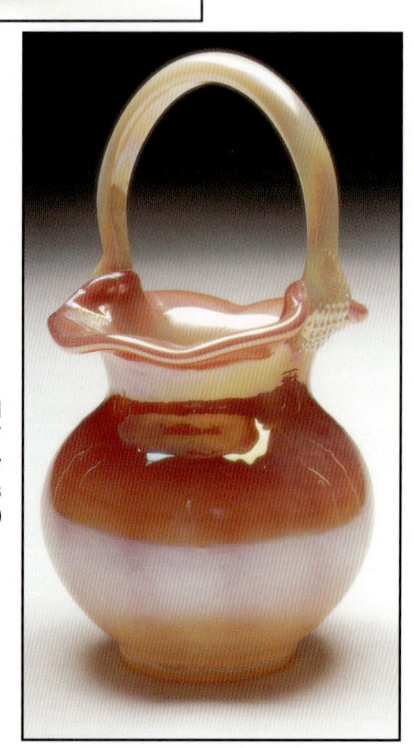

Basket, iridized (Carnival) finish, 7" tall, 4" wide, Made by Gibson from Fenton's shards 1995, **$60**

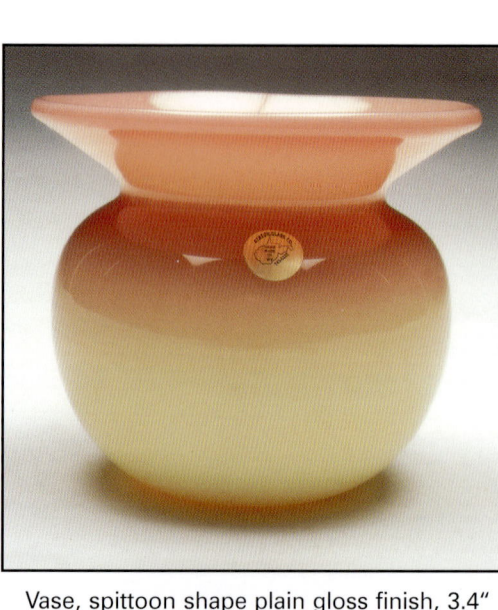

Vase, spittoon shape plain gloss finish, 3.4" tall, 4" wide, Made by Gibson from Fenton's shards 1999, **$35**

Crider Glass Company

Crider Glass Company of Ohio also purchased Fenton shards and re-melted the glass into their moulds. Like Gibson, all of Crider's pieces are marked with their name. Examples are not shown here.

Confusing Burmese

Making Burmese glass is expensive. The LG Wright Company tried to make items that looked like Burmese by having the Davis Lynch Company make milk glass and LG Wright workers decorated it. The blown milk glass lamp had paint air brushed over the top to simulate Burmese. At a distance, this lamp looks like Burmese, but upon close examination you realize it is not authentic. This piece was purchased on-line from E-bay and had been listed as Burmese. Unfortunately, there was no way to physically examine the lamp. Luckily, the price was reasonable for this type of lamp and the people decided to keep it as an example of Burmese-style painting.

Student lamp, **NOT FENTON**, hand painted rose decoration, 25" overall height, 10" single crimp shade, 1970-1980s, **$195**
Note, this lamp looks like Burmese, but it has the pink blush airbrushed onto the glass.

Resources

No matter what pattern you collect, we encourage you to belong to a non-profit organization that works to preserve the history of the American glassmaking industry. These organizations enable you to gather more information on a particular glass company. All of the national organizations listed below provide information by publishing an educational newsletter, doing study guides, reprinting of company catalogs, doing seminars, holding a convention, having a museum and presenting other educational activities.

Pacific NW Fenton Association
P. O. Box 881, Tillamook, OR 97141
Phone contact: 503-842-4815
$23/year. 4 newsletters *The Fenton Nor'Wester* and exclusive piece of Fenton glass
E-mail: jshirley@oregoncoast.com
Web site: www.glasscastle.com/pnwfa.htm
Info: They sponsor two glass shows (March & October) called "All American Glass Show & Sale" in Hillsboro, Oregon and a convention is held in June of each year in Springfield, Oregon

Fenton Art Glass Collectors of America
P. O. Box 384, Williamstown, WV 26187
Phone contact: 304-375-6196
$20/year 6 newsletters "Butterfly Net"
E-mail: kkenworthy@foth.com
Web site: www.collectoronline.com/club-FAGCA.html
Info: Convention in August

National Fenton Glass Society
P. O. Box 4008, Marietta, OH 45750
Phone contact: 740-374-3345
$35/year. 6 newsletters *Fenton Flyer*
Email: nfgs@ee.net
Web site: www.fentonglasssociety.org
Info: Convention in August

Glass Messenger
700 Elizabeth Ave., Williamstown, WV 26187
Phone contact: 1-800-249-4527
$12/year. 4 issues and a voucher for the purchase of an exclusive subscriber item

West Virginia Museum of American Glass
P. O. Box 574, Weston, WV 26452
$25/year 4 newsletters "All About Glass" formerly Glory Hole
Email: tbredehoft@nextek.net
Web site: http://members.aol.com/wvmuseumofglass
Info: Convention in October

Web Sites
Fenton Art Glass Company Web Page: www.fentonglass.com
Fenton Forum: www.forum.fentonartglass.com
Fenton Fanatics: www.fentonfan.com
Courtesy of John Gager, Webmaster.

Replacing Items
Many times in our collections we get items that get damaged or broken. The best way to try to find a replacement is to contact dealers in your area to assist you. Go to every glass show and related convention you can. Many dealers will put you on their mailing list for locating items. Belong to an organization that specializes in the glass you collect. Another way is to contact Replacements. They have a huge data base and a large staff geared towards matching up your requests.
Replacements P.O. Box 26029 or 1089 Knox Road, Greensboro, NC 27420 1-800-737-5223 Web Site: www.replacements.com

Bibliography

Books
Coe, Debbie & Randy. *Glass Animals & Figurines*. Atglen, Pennsylvania: Schiffer Publishing, 2003.
Coe-Hixson, Myra. *Glass Elephants*. Atglen, Pennsylvania: Schiffer Publishing, 2004.
Coe-McRitchie, Tara. *Fenton Glass Cats & Dogs*. Atglen, Pennsylvania: Schiffer Publishing, 2002.
Fenton Art Glass Company. *Company Catalogs*. Williamstown, West Virginia: Fenton Art Glass Company, 1970-2003.
Grover, Ray & Lee. *Art Glass Nouveau*. Rutland, Vermont: Charles & Tuttle Company, 1967.
Hammond, Dorothy. *Confusing Collectibles*. Leon, Iowa: Mid-America Book Company, 1969.
Heacock, Bill. *Fenton Glass The Third Twenty Five Years*. Marietta, Ohio: O-Val Advertising Corporation, 1989.
L. G. Wright Glass Company. *Company Catalogs*. New Martinsville, West Virginia: L. G. Wright Glass Company, 1960-70s.
Lechler, Doris Anderson. *Children's Glass Dishes, China & Furniture*. Paducah, Kentucky: Collector Books, 1991.
Lee, Ruth Webb. *Nineteenth Century Art Glass*. New York, New York: M Barrows & Company Inc., 1964.
Measell, James. *Fenton Glass The 1980s Decade*. Marietta, Ohio: The Glass Press, 1996.
_____. *Fenton Glass The 1990s Decade*. Marietta, Ohio: The Glass Press, 2000.
_____. *Fenton Glass Especially for QVC*. Williamstown, West Virginia: Richardson Printing, 2002.
Revi, Albert Christian. *Nineteenth Century Glass*. New York, New York: Thomas Nelson & Sons, 1964.
Rice, Ferill J.. *Caught in the Butterfly Net*. Williamstown, West Virginia: Fenton Art Glass Collectors of America, 1991.
Ruff, Bob and Pat. *Fairy Lamps, Elegance in Candle Lighting*. Atglen, Pennsylvania: Schiffer Publishing, 1996.
Shuman, John A. *Collectors Encyclopedia of American Art Glass*. Paducah, Kentucky: Collector Books, 2003.
Sisk, Betty. *Mt. Washington Art Glass*. Paducah, Kentucky: Collector Books, 2003.
Taylor, Dorothy. *Encore on Burmese*. Kansas City, Missouri: Dorothy Taylor, 1990.
Walk, John. *Fenton Glass Compendium 1970-1985*. Atglen, Pennsylvania: Schiffer Publishing, 2001.
_____. *Fenton Glass Compendium 1985-Present*. Atglen, Pennsylvania: Schiffer Publishing, 2003.
_____. *Fenton Rarities 1940-1985*. Atglen, Pennsylvania: Schiffer Publishing, 2002.
_____. *Fenton Special Orders 1940-1980*. Atglen, Pennsylvania: Schiffer Publishing, 2003.
_____. *Fenton Special Orders 1980-Present*. Atglen, Pennsylvania: Schiffer Publishing, 2003.

Periodicals
Butterfly Net: 1985-2003.
Depression Glass Daze: 1970-1997.
Fenton Flyer: 1995-2003.
Fenton Nor'Wester: 1995-2003.
Glass Collectors Digest: 1987-1997.
Glass Messenger: 1996-2003.
Glass Review: 1975-1987.
Glory Hole: 1990-2002.

Personal Correspondence
Burton, Frances. E-mail to author, Fenton Art Glass Company, 2003
Colella, Joyce. E-mail & telephone conversation to author, Joyce's Collectibles, 2003
Crail, Gerald. Telephone conversation to author, Crail & Son, 2003
Dick, Pam. Letter & telephone conversation to author, Fenton Art Glass Company, 2003
Fenton, Frank M. Letter & telephone conversation to author, Fenton Art Glass Company, 2003
Fenton, George & Nancy. Telephone conversation to author, Fenton Art Glass Company, 2003
Hill, Bob. E-mail to author, Fenton Art Glass Company, 2003
Jachim, Mary. Letter & telephone conversation to author, Love Bouquet Collection, 2003
King, Wayne. E-mail & telephone conversation to author, Fenton Art Glass Company, 2003
Levi, Gary. Telephone conversation to author, Levay Distributing, 2003
Maston, Jennifer. Telephone conversation to author, Fenton Art Glass Company, 2003
Saffell, Jon. E-mail & telephone conversation to author, Fenton Art Glass Company, 2003
Seufer, Howard. E-mail & telephone conversation to author, Fenton Art Glass Company, 2003
Walk, John. E-mail & telephone conversation to author, Fenton books author, 2003

Internet
Fenton Fanatics: www.fentonfan.com (John Gager, Webmaster).

Index

Acorns and Vine 166
Adoration Rose 181
Aladdin 148
Alley Cat 129, 134
Angel 129, 134
Apple 111, 190
Arabella 173
Atlantis 117, 170, 176, 183
Aurora 149, 164
Bailey, Singleton 109, 127, 185
Ballerina 16, 182
Barley, Kim 19, 178, 183
Baskets 16, 25, 27, 28, 36, 42, 44, 49, 50, 52, 54, 56, 59, 63, 66, 73-75, 79, 84, 88, 92, 94, 97, 100, 102, 103, 104, 110, 122, 125, 127, 128, 130, 132, 133, 135, 136, 139, 149, 151-153, 156-158, 160, 165, 176, 178, 181-183, 186-190
Bear 81, 86, 140, 143, 153, 160, 164, 188
Bee 128, 180
Bell 51, 70, 72, 73, 83, 87, 91, 93, 130, 131, 138, 142, 149, 160, 170, 171, 176, 183
Bird 102, 114, 153, 169, 170, 177
Blackberry 114, 149, 172, 181
Blackberry Bouquet 19, 149
Bleeding Hearts 149
Blue Burmese 15, 186
Bluebird 16, 114, 156
Boot 86, 89, 92, 93, 163, 165
Bountiful Harvest 149
Bowls 25, 27, 35, 39, 82, 109, 122, 124
Bridesmaid 125, 126
Buckeye Bash 110
Bulging Tear Drop 148
Bunny 16, 175, 180, 181, 187
Burton, Frances 18, 19, 80, 97, 98, 104, 119, 121-123, 126, 128, 138, 143, 150, 153, 159, 161, 162, 164, 165, 175, 176, 181, 183, 184, 186, 187
Butterfly 16, 19, 38. 40, 49, 70, 71, 77-79, 88, 94, 111, 114, 116, 122, 135, 138, 139, 148, 149, 150, 153, 158, 159, 163, 174, 176, 179, 181, 182
Butterfly and Berry 84, 132
Butterfly and Flowering Branch 73, 74
Butterflies and Roses 148
Cactus 108
Candle Lamp 179
Candy Dishes 42, 84, 85, 108, 153, 154
Cane 168
Caprice 119
Cats 16, 107, 112, 126, 129, 134-136, 157, 160, 163, 165, 167, 173, 184, 188
Centennial Collection 19, 22, 161, 162
Cherries 82
Cherry Blossom 122
Christmas Tree 144
Church 108
Circle of Love 144-147, 155, 160, 167, 179, 185
Clock 143
Clown 174
Collela, Joyce 144-147, 155, 160, 167, 179, 185
Collins, Tom 111
Connoisseur Collection 16, 19, 20, 22, 54, 93, 95, 104, 112, 128, 138, 139, 149, 156, 162, 168, 172, 181
Crail and Son 108
Creamer 25, 27, 37, 59, 61, 112, 113
Crider Glass 191
Cruet 41, 50, 97, 102, 132, 187
Daffodil 119
Daisy 107, 126, 153, 154, 159, 162, 164, 165
Daisy and Button 72, 80, 85, 86
Daisy and Fern 173
Daybreak 19, 123
Decorated Burmese 41
Diamond Lattice 81
Diamond Optic 14, 17, 119, 125, 126, 129, 129, 132-134, 142, 143, 152-154, 158-161, 163-165, 176-179, 182, 183
Dick, Pam 16, 17
Dogwood 54-59, 61, 87, 94, 111, 120, 176, 179
Dolphin 169
Donkey 108
Dragonfly 19, 128
Drapery Optic 124
Duck 164, 165
Egg 108, 154, 159, 161, 172, 174
Elephant 164, 169
Embossed Poppy 47, 140, 142
Embossed Roses 31, 47, 89, 127
Embossed Strawberry 116
Empress 46
Encore 110
Epergne 45, 70, 76, 81, 95, 96, 188
Ewer 14, 119, 120, 156, 162
Faith Bouquet 184
Fairy Lights 7,8, 16, 24, 26, 30, 32-34, 37, 40, 44, 50, 55, 62, 83, 121, 126, 134, 166, 170, 176-179, 186
Farewell Bouquet 136
Farmyard 109
Fawn 81, 86, 178
Fenced Garden 16, 19, 138, 139
Fenton, Bill 9-11, 13, 14, 19, 65, 73, 103, 104, 116, 128, 133, 142, 154, 157, 160-162, 173, 174, 177, 178, 181-183
Fenton, Frank 9-11, 14, 17, 65, 73, 100, 132, 161, 173, 182, 183,
Fenton, George 14, 133, 154, 164, 165, 182, 183, 188
Fenton, Nancy 14, 180
Fenton Art Glass Collectors of America 23, 70-72, 79, 116, 127, 135, 148, 167, 179, 186, 191
Fish 78, 117, 118, 128, 170, 176
Floral and Butterfly 138
Forest Cottage 138
Fox 118
Frederick and Nelson 18, 49
Frog 16, 52, 168, 175, 177, 184, 185
Gibson Glass 189
Ginger Jar 152, 154, 162, 175, 176, 180, 182,
Glass Messenger 18, 23, 95, 150, 187, 191
Goe, Charlie 10, 11, 13, 180
Gold Burmese 95-101
Gold Fish 20, 168, 175
Golden Gourds 156
Grape 159, 160, 178, 181
Grape and Cable 141
Griffith, Shirley 108
Guest Set 143, 166, 179
Gupta, Subodh 10, 15
Hallmark 149
Hand 120, 121, 171
Hanging Heart 108
Happy Cat 135
Hat 54, 60, 61, 70-72, 173, 186
Heacock, Bill 110
Heart 105-109, 111
Heat Sensitive 7, 11
Heisey Club of America 117
Hibiscus 156, 166, 170, 174, 177, 178, 182, 183
Hill, Bob 16
Hobnail 29, 105, 111, 120, 128, 163, 165, 166
Horse 117
Horseshoe 137
Hummingbird 16, 106, 122, 125, 172
Hurricane 179
Indiana Glass 137
Iris 189
Jachim, Mary 184
Jacobean Floral 149, 187
Jeweled Heart 109
King, Wayne 10, 15, 73, 186, 188
Kitten 107, 110, 140, 143, 170, 171
Lamps 19, 31, 35, 43, 47-49, 52, 55, 56, 58, 73, 85, 99, 100, 104, 121, 123, 125, 126, 128, 147-149, 152, 156, 158, 172, 173, 176
Lattice Rose 119
Leaf 112
Leaf Decorated 26
Lechler, Doris 64
Let's Bee Burmese 14, 180, 181
Levay 50, 52, 53
Lighthouse 161, 167
Lily of the Valley 121
Little Brown Church 108
Log Cabin 151
Logo 91
Lotus Mist 15, 187, 188
Love Bouquet 65-69, 91, 92, 136, 144
Mallard 169, 171, 180
Mandarin 46
Maple Leaf 17, 26, 27, 32, 33, 38, 40
Mariners 80, 85
Maston, Jennifer 17
Mauve Floral 172
McMillen and Husband 108
Memories 19, 156
Memories in Glass 137, 148
Mermaid 108
Morning Glories 122, 125, 149, 150
Mouse 112
Mt. Washington 7, 8, 10, 11, 122, 186
Mug 79
National Association of Limited Edition Dealers 149, 155
National Fenton Glass Society 127, 135, 167, 168, 191
Neo Classic 181
Nymph 144, 147
Ogee 154
Old Mill 172
Open Heart Arches 130, 133, 160
Orange Tree 82, 154
Ornament 137, 148
Pacific Northwest Fenton Association 100, 191
Pairpoint 8
Paisley 104, 121, 124, 126, 159
Palm Tree 106, 114
Paneled Daisy 83, 84
Pansy 84, 130, 131
Papillon 19, 150
Peacock 82, 87, 88
Pear 190
Perfume 138, 139, 151, 154, 160, 186
Persian Medallion 81, 83
Petite Floral 95-97
Pink Butterflies 18, 49
Pink Dogwood 54, 55-58, 111, 176
Piper, Louise 13, 18, 19, 26, 38, 41, 49, 50, 52, 71, 75, 76, 77, 94, 97, 103
Pitchers 25, 27, 37, 59, 61, 64, 100-103, 112, 113, 121, 122, 125, 128, 129, 133, 136, 146, 149, 155, 165, 169, 170, 174, 177, 182, 183, 189
Plauche, Kim 19, 121, 126, 143, 144, 149, 152, 159, 160, 161,, 165, 167, 171-173, 177, 178, 186
Plues, Louise 103, 104
Plug Horse 117
Poppy 156, 161, 180
Poppy Show 185
Portland Head Lighthouse 161
Powder Box 138, 141
Puppy 151, 153
Queen Victoria 8
Queen's Bird 20, 128
QVC 10, 14, 17, 23, 54, 93, 104, 116, 121, 126, 132-134, 142-144, 152-155, 159, 160, 165, 166, 170-172, 177, 178
Raspberry 100, 101, 104, 112
Ratcliff, Lois 79, 111
Reynolds, Martha 20, 112, 122, 125, 126, 128, 132-134, 142, 143, 149, 153-157, 159, 160, 164-166, 188
Rib Optic 166, 168-170, 177, 182, 183
Rosalene 144, 147
Rose 17, 18, 33-39, 41, 42, 45, 47, 48, 51, 64, 72, 76, 79, 80, 86, 98, 99, 103-107, 112, 116, 119, 121, 126, 130-134, 142, 143, 151, 152, 154, 159, 160, 162, 165, 166, 171, 174, 180, 182
Rose Bed 162
Rose Bowl 24, 27, 36, 39, 44, 49, 50, 53, 67, 89, 92, 121, 140, 142, 146, 147, 159
Rose Poppy 161, 162
Rosenthal, Jacob 9, 10
Rooster 16, 140, 159
Saffell, Jon 15, 16, 128, 132, 138-140, 143, 151, 154-158, 161, 163, 166, 168-175, 177, 178, 180, 181, 183, 187
Santa 16, 140, 143, 155, 166, 180
Scene 18, 42-45
Sea of Dreams 19, 123
Seahorse 75, 78, 85, 93
September Morn 147
Seufer, Howard 12, 65
Shakers 127, 148
Shell 73, 75, 85, 93
Shirley, Frederick 7, 8, 122
Slipper 80, 90, 93, 124, 126, 159
Snail 174
Snowflake 137
Snowman 16, 177, 178
Song Sparrow 20, 172, 181
Southern Belle 137, 140
Special Orders 13, 18, 23, 64-72, 79, 80, 85, 91-93, 108-111, 116, 117, 127, 135-137, 144-149, 155, 160, 161, 167, 168, 179, 183-185
Spindler, Robin 19, 128, 132, 137-139, 149, 155, 156, 162, 166, 170, 171, 177, 178, 181, 183, 184
Spiral Optic 128, 151, 153, 176
Spittoon 109, 190
Squirrel 164, 166
Swan 123, 126, 127
Taylor, Dorothy 110
Temple Jar 135
Thumbprint 75
Tobacco Jar 141
Toothpick 83, 90, 92, 110, 116, 190
Tree 144
Tree Scene 18, 42-45, 97, 98, 114, 132
Trillium 19, 115, 138
Trout 16, 128
Tulip Vase 47, 48, 53, 55, 57, 60, 66, 67, 76, 79, 94, 106, 112-114, 149, 150, 155, 185
Tumble Up 187
Tumbler 64, 100-102, 189
Turkey 182
Turtle 174, 178, 180
Unicorn 152, 154
United States Glass 13, 117
Vanity 137, 138
Vases 24, 26, 28-34, 36-61, 63, 64, 66-71, 75-80, 82, 85, 87-89, 91, 94, 98, 99, 103-106, 108, 113-117, 119-126, 128, 132, 134, 138, 139, 142, 143, 146, 147, 149, 153, 156-160, 163-165, 167, 168, 171-173, 176, 178, 181-183, 186, 188, 190
Veil Tail 16, 20, 168
Verlys 13, 46, 108, 117
Vintage 122
Violet 18, 50, 61, 62, 85, 90, 102, 107, 111, 113, 115, 179
Walrath, Mary 65-69, 85, 91-93, 136, 144, 160, 167, 184
Water Lily 128
Wavecrest 75, 76, 79, 80
Webb 7, 8
Wheat 121, 122
Whitton 83, 142
Wild Rose and Bowknot 52, 53
Willard, Isaac 10, 15
Williams, Stacy 20, 168, 170-172, 178, 181, 183